Language Development

Understanding Language Diversity in the Classroom

Sandra Levey
Lehman College–CUNY

Susan Polirstok
Kean University

$SAGE

Los Angeles | London | New Delhi
Singapore | Washington DC

For information:

SAGE Publications, Inc.
2455 Teller Road
Thousand Oaks, California 91320
E-mail: order@sagepub.com

SAGE Publications Ltd.
1 Oliver's Yard
55 City Road
London EC1Y 1SP
United Kingdom

SAGE Publications India Pvt. Ltd.
B 1/I 1 Mohan Cooperative Industrial Area
Mathura Road, New Delhi 110 044
India

SAGE Publications Asia-Pacific Pte. Ltd.
33 Pekin Street #02-01
Far East Square
Singapore 048763

Printed in the United States of America

Library of Congress Cataloging-in-Publication Data

Language development: Understanding language diversity in the classroom / editors: Sandra Levey, Susan Polirstok.
    p. cm.
Includes bibliographical references and index.
ISBN 978-1-4129-7407-3 (pbk.)
    1. Children—Language. I. Levey, Sandra. II. Polirstok, Susan.

LB1139.L3L326 2011
372.6—dc22   2010031671

This book is printed on acid-free paper.

10   11   12   13   14   10   9   8   7   6   5   4   3   2   1

Acquisitions Editor:	Diane McDaniel
Editorial Assistant:	Ashley Conlon
Production Editor:	Eric Garner
Copy Editor:	Megan Speer
Typesetter:	C&M Digitals (P) Ltd.
Proofreader:	Joyce Li
Indexer:	Judy Hunt
Cover Designer:	Bryan Fishman
Marketing Manager:	Eric DeLuca

Brief Contents

Detailed Contents

4 Hearing and Listening Skills   59

5 The Production of Speech Sounds   79

6 The Role of the Brain in Speech and Language   101

7 Language Development From Birth to Age 3   115

9 Language Development From Age 6 Through Adolescence   161

10 Supporting the Development of Literacy Skills From Infancy Through School Age   185

11 Educational Implications of Narrative Discourse 209

12 African American English in the Classroom 227

13 Bilingual Language Acquisition and Learning

14 Bilingual Speech Sound Development and Disorders   263

Preface

The vision for writing a language-development textbook began when Sandra Levey was a graduate student. She began her graduate studies in the late 1970s, at a time when the education system in Ann Arbor, Michigan, was under fire over the large number of African American children who were being referred for speech-language pathology services or placed in special education classrooms. The courts at the time found that schools were unfamiliar with the characteristics of African American English and instead perceived these characteristics to indicate language disorders. As a graduate student in speech-language pathology, she studied with professors who provided expert testimony in the Ann Arbor case, and was able to learn firsthand the importance of distinguishing cultural language differences from actual language disorders. This experience motivated her to obtain a degree in linguistics to develop a deeper and better understanding of the structure and meaning of language, along with her study of the origin of language differences. Over the past decade, she has been engaged in research to understand the difficulties children face in acquiring language, particularly when they are learning English as a second language.

Susan Polirstok joined this project as an experienced special educator with a background in providing professional development for teachers on classroom-based interventions for diverse learners. She worked collaboratively with Sandra Levey to bring perspectives from two different academic disciplines together. Our collaboration resulted in this unique textbook on language development, which offers strategies that teachers will find helpful when working with both typical and atypical students including English language learners and those with special needs. Together with contributors from various fields, we have compiled a book that we hope provides you with all the necessary information from our research and teaching experience to help you understand the language development process, distinguish language differences from disorders, and facilitate learning in the classroom.

This book is written for classroom teachers and preservice teacher candidates who want to understand how language development can affect learning and who want to learn strategies for working with students with language differences and disorders. We have incorporated classroom examples and case studies throughout the book to illustrate some of the most common speech and language behaviors found in classrooms.

THE GOALS OF THIS BOOK

Language Development: Understanding Language Diversity in the Classroom is intended to prepare K–12 teachers to appreciate and understand the role of language development in learning. There are two main reasons why we as teachers need to understand the role of language development in the classroom. First, kindergarten teachers report that language deficiencies commonly affect children's school readiness and are becoming an acute problem in today's schools. Intact language skills provide an important foundation for reading and writing skills and social interactions with teachers and peers. Consequently, one goal of this book is to enhance teachers' knowledge of typical and atypical language development and demonstrate the vital connection between language and learning in the classroom so that teachers are prepared to address language differences and disorders in their classrooms. To enhance teachers' understanding of how language development can impact classroom learning, we provide examples of typical and atypical language development throughout the lifespan, case studies of students with language development difficulties, and classroom strategies that teachers can implement.

Second, the population of second-language learners in the K–12 classroom continues to increase, and teachers need to be able to distinguish between language *differences* and language *disorders*. Thus, another goal of this book is to help teachers become more aware of cultural and language differences. To help teachers distinguish between differences and disorders, we have included three chapters in this book that are specifically designed to illustrate this distinction. These chapters include case studies that distinguish the most common characteristics of disorders and differences found in the K–12 classroom. Armed with this book, teachers will feel more confident in the classroom as they gain a deeper understanding of cultural language differences and how they may affect second-language learners.

As teachers learn more about the role of language development in learning through this book, they will be better prepared to address the challenges they may face as they encounter students with various language differences and disorders in their classrooms.

To help us achieve the goals we set out when writing this book, we drew on the knowledge of specialists in the fields of early childhood education, special education, speech-language pathology, and audiology. Through their chapter contributions, these specialists provide our book with a unique perspective on language differences across various disciplines. Each of these chapters has been carefully organized to focus on the important ideas and issues that teachers need to be aware of as they learn about language development.

THE ORGANIZATION

This book consists of 15 chapters, each of which is presented in an uncomplicated manner that focuses on the main components of language development (morphology, phonology, semantics, syntax, and pragmatics), along with other essential aspects of learning. Each chapter combines significant facts and insights with case studies and classroom examples to form a narrative that is refreshing and thoughtful. The book walks teachers through typical language development (and signs of disorders and differences) in infancy, preschool, and late childhood and adolescence. In addition, because of the significance of literacy skills in academic progress, the book also provides a strong focus on pre-academic skills, such as emergent literacy. As mentioned earlier, the book includes three important chapters on second-language learners and cultural language differences. The book concludes with a chapter on the role of the family in supporting language development. A more detailed description of what you will find in each chapter follows.

Chapter 1: An Introduction to Language and Learning provides teachers with an introduction to the role of language in the classroom. Although language development is a complex process, the goal of this book is to make this process accessible to teachers. This chapter introduces the basic concepts and definitions that you will need to know as you discuss language, speech, and communication and familiarize yourself with the role of the classroom teacher in supporting language development.

Chapter 2: Theories and Explanations of Language Development presents the theories of language development and focuses on how language development is closely associated with learning. The chapter also includes strategies associated with these theories to assist in language development and to provide a connection between theory and practice.

Chapter 3: Typical and Atypical Language Development describes the components of language development (form, content, and use) along with the disorders that may affect these components. This chapter also provides a brief overview of disorders versus differences, focusing on differences that are due to dialect or second-language learning, which is discussed in more detail later in the book.

Chapter 4: Hearing and Listening Skills explains the importance of hearing and listening skills in language and academic development. The chapter also describes the effects of mild hearing loss and provides information on how hearing loss and auditory processing disorders can affect speech and academic skills and how classroom teachers can assist students with hearing loss and impairments.

Chapter 5: The Production of Speech Sounds provides a general overview of the three physiologic components of speech production: the respiratory system, the laryngeal mechanism, and the supralaryngeal mechanism (oral, nasal, and pharyngeal cavities). The chapter introduces the basic anatomy of speech production and a detailed discussion of American English sound production.

Chapter 6: The Role of the Brain in Speech and Language reviews the major components of the brain, including those landmarks of the cerebral cortex and brain stem involved in cognition language comprehension and production, reading, and writing. This chapter provides teachers with some insight into children's executive functioning and gives them suggested classroom strategies to help their students achieve academic success.

Chapter 7: Language Development From Birth to Age 3 describes the development of language and communication in infants and young children. This chapter focuses on the characteristics and development of typical infants and toddlers but also includes information on communication delays and disorders and provides some general strategies for supporting and fostering early language development.

Chapter 8: Language Development From Ages 3 to 5 focuses on the language development and communication milestones in preschool-age children. This chapter focuses on the characteristics of typical children but also includes information on communication delays and disorders and provides some general strategies for supporting and fostering language development.

Chapter 9: Language Development From Age 6 Through Adolescence explores the nature and scope of language development in older school-age children, ages 6 through adolescence. This chapter describes cognitive, semantic, syntactic, pragmatic, and phonological development, which are necessary to provide the foundation for success in academic and interactive contexts.

Chapter 10: Supporting the Development of Literacy Skills From Infancy Through School Age explores typical literacy development from birth through adolescence, emphasizing the connections between language and literacy. This chapter explores the relationship between oral language, reading, and writing in normal literacy development and provides strategies for teachers in connecting reading, writing, listening, and expressive language skills. The chapter also discusses the varied spelling patterns encountered in various contexts across the life span and incorporates a discussion of phonology, morphology, and orthography.

Chapter 11: Educational Implications of Narrative Discourse highlights the importance of narrative discourse for literacy, socialization, and communication. This chapter also compares different narrative genres (personal narrative and fiction) by focusing on their structure and content and looks at cultural variations in narratives for African American, Spanish, and Asian communities. The chapter concludes by introducing some signs of impaired narration for different cultures and provides suggestions for fostering narrative coherence.

Chapter 12: African American English in the Classroom describes the role that language plays in the performance of African American children in the classroom. In addition, this chapter presents the language variations that African American children often bring to school, the potential impact of this variation on learning, and strategies and implications for the classroom teacher.

Chapter 13: Bilingual Language Acquisition and Learning contains a review of some of the main theories and components of the second-language acquisition process, such as the attitude of the community, teaching methodology, and personal characteristics and experiences. The main purpose of this chapter is to enable teachers to differentiate a language disorder from a language difference when working with children who are learning a second language by providing concrete examples and foundational information about second-language acquisition. The chapter also discusses cross-linguistic phenomena, such as code switching and transfer errors, that are common in this process.

Chapter 14: Bilingual Speech Sound Development and Disorders describes speech sound production in typically developing bilingual children and in bilingual children with speech sound disorders. The purpose of this chapter is to provide teachers with knowledge about how to identify bilingual children with speech disorders and refer them to speech-language pathologists for additional speech assessment and diagnosis.

Chapter 15: Fostering Teacher and Family Partnerships in the Development of Language and Literacy focuses on the role of the classroom teacher as a resource for parents as they learn to support the language and literacy development of their children. The chapter provides teachers and other intervention personnel with strategies to support children's language development and helps teachers understand how families can contribute to the success of students in the classroom.

KEY FEATURES OF THE TEXT

This textbook incorporates several important pedagogical features into each chapter to aid in your understanding of the material and to help you relate it to your individual needs.

Case Studies included at the beginning of each chapter illustrate key chapter concepts and present various scenarios of language production and social interaction in the classroom. These vignettes are designed to help you understand the chapter information by providing you with examples often found in classrooms.

Strategies for the Classroom sections, included in most chapters, provide specific suggestions for how you can address various language differences and disorders in the classroom.

Case Study Revisited sections, included at the end of each chapter, revisit the vignettes presented at the start of each chapter. These sections illustrate the classroom teacher's response to the scenarios illustrated in the vignettes and provide general classroom strategies that you can implement if you encounter similar scenarios in your own classroom.

Study Questions included at the end of each chapter focus on helping you understand and retain key concepts from the chapters.

Suggested Projects at the end of each chapter provide opportunities for you to take your understanding of the chapter content to a new level through practical application.

Key Terms listed at the end of each chapter are defined in the Glossary to support your better understanding of the meaning of these terms.

Suggestions for Further Reading at the end of each chapter enable you to expand your knowledge of key topics discussed in that chapter. We hope that these key features will make this text even more useful to you as you develop a deeper understanding of the connection between language and learning.

ANCILLARIES FOR INSTRUCTORS AND STUDENTS

Additional ancillary materials further support and enhance the learning goals of *Language Development: Understanding Language Diversity in the Classroom*. These ancillary materials include:

Password-Protected Instructor Teaching Site

www.sagepub.com/levey

This password-protected site offers instructors a variety of resources that supplement the book material, including:

- A **test bank** in Microsoft Word offers a diverse set of test questions and answers for each chapter of the book. Multiple choice, true/false and essay questions are included for every chapter to aid instructors in assessing students' progress and understanding.

- **PowerPoint presentations** are designed to assist with lecture and review, highlighting essential content, features, and artwork from the book.

- Carefully selected, web-based **video resources** feature relevant content for use in independent and classroom-based exploration of key topics.

- **Lecture outlines** summarize key concepts on a chapter-by-chapter basis to assist in preparing for lecture and class discussion.

- Links to relevant **web resources** direct instructors to additional tools for further research on important chapter topics.

- Chapter-specific **discussion questions** help launch discussion by prompting students to engage with the material, and by reinforcing important content.

- **Sample syllabi** for quarter, semester, and online courses.

Open-Access Student Study Site

www.sagepub.com/levey

This web-based student study site provides a variety of additional resources to enhance students' understanding of the book content and take their learning one step further. The site includes:

- **Self quizzes** allow students to independently assess their progress in learning course material.

- **E-flashcards** are study tools to reinforce student understanding and learning of key terms and concepts that are outlined in the chapters.

- Carefully selected, web-based **video resources** feature relevant content for use in independent and classroom-based exploration of key topics.

- Links to relevant **web resources** direct students to additional tools for further research on important chapter topics.

- Interesting and relevant **recommended readings** provide a jumping-off point for course assignments, papers, research, group work, and class discussion.

- **Sample forms and assessment tools** are also provided for easy access to students.

—Sandra Levey
Lehman College, City University of New York

—Susan Polirstok
Kean University

Acknowledgments

We are tremendously grateful for everyone who worked so hard to make this book possible. Writing this textbook was an extensive process, and all the chapter contributors worked tirelessly to create a unique and outstanding book. We'd also like to thank Diane McDaniel, executive editor at SAGE, who understood the importance of this book and shepherded it through the editorial process with the help of her editorial assistant, Ashley Conlon. Thanks also go to Elise Caffee, developmental editor, who offered invaluable suggestions for preparing this book for publication and made it more readable and comprehensible. Thanks also go to Megan Speer for her copyediting work. Finally, thanks go to Marlene Moore for her contribution to the Glossary section of this book.

We would also like to acknowledge the many reviewers who provided feedback on the manuscript throughout the development process:

Angela Baum, *University of South Carolina, Columbia*

Amanda Branscombe, *Athens State University*

Anita Choice, *University of Florida*

Gail Choice, *University of Florida*

Jeanne Clidas, *Roberts Wesleyan College*

David Coker, *University of Delaware*

Roberta Dorr, *Trinity College*

Rosalind Raymond Gann, *East Tennessee State University*

Laura Boynton Hauerwas, *Providence College*

Lisa Hyde, *Athens State University*

Tywanda Jiles, *Governor's State University*

Mary Blake Jones, *College of Charleston*

Mary Love, *University of Massachusetts, Boston*

Judy Lysaker, *Butler University*

Diana K. Nabors, *Sam Houston State University*

Sandy Putnam-Franklin, *University of Massachusetts, Boston*

Kimberly M. Ray, *Morrisville State College*

Alan L. Seitel, *Texas A&M International University*

Susan M. Schultz, *St. John Fisher College*

Renarta Hutchinson Tompkins, *Mississippi State University*

Carolyn Wilson, *Virginia State University*

Last, we'd like to thank the parents who supplied us with examples of children's typical language development. Thanks go to Joanne Mathieson, Marissa Levey, and Robyn Heiberger for providing interesting examples of their children's language development.

—Sandra Levey
Lehman College, City University of New York

—Susan Polirstok
Kean University

C H A P T E R   1

An Introduction to Language and Learning

Sandra Levey

CASE STUDY: The role of language in the classroom

Kimberly, a first-grader in her first few weeks of school, was unable to answer questions about stories read aloud to the class. She appeared distracted during story time, and she fidgeted and played with her hands. Ms. Benjamin, the classroom teacher, decided that she had to make careful observations to informally assess the nature of Kimberly's inability to answer questions about a story read aloud to the class. The goal was to determine if Kimberly's behavior suggested developmental immaturity, inattention, impulsivity, or distractibility suggestive of an attention disorder or if she seemed to have problems understanding words, sentences, or stories read to the class, which would be suggestive of a language disorder. The teacher knew that Kimberly was a native English speaker and eliminated learning a new language as a factor in her inability to answer questions about stories. Consequently, the teacher planned to use her observations of Kimberly to create a more descriptive profile of how this child was performing. Such data can be very useful in making recommendations to the Child Study Team should a formal request for evaluation need to be made.

What might the classroom teacher do to help Kimberly respond to questions about stories read to the class? On what information and experience did you base your answer?

INTRODUCTION

Several factors play a role in children's academic success. Among them are good health, emotional well-being, and intact learning abilities (Hadley, Simmerman, Long, & Luna, 2000). In

1

spite of the importance of all these factors, kindergarten teachers overwhelmingly report that language deficiencies are the most acute problems affecting children's school readiness (Boyer, 1991). Correspondingly, one of the major health problems reported for preschool-age children is language delay (Rescorla, 1989). The case described at the beginning of this chapter illustrates the importance of understanding how spoken language capability is vital for the development of literacy skills. For example, children must be able to attend to and understand spoken language in order to develop the skills needed in all academic areas.

New Language Rules

Within the classroom, children are exposed to new rules for using language. They must now understand the social rules for interacting with teachers and peers and must also learn to listen carefully to directions and information that relate to learning. Understanding the components of language and their impact on the academic and social functioning of students is key for classroom teachers.

Within the classroom, children are exposed to new vocabulary and rules for using language, along with learning to listen carefully to directions and information.

Observation and Intervention

Not only is spoken language the primary means of communication in the classroom, but teachers are in an optimal position to observe students' language development and level of function. In the modern classroom, a teacher must determine whether observed problems are a function of learning English as a second language; a function of a learning/behavioral challenge requiring other professionals trained to deal in these areas; or a symptom of a language disorder that requires referral, evaluation, and intervention by a speech-language pathologist. The first step for the classroom teacher is to make careful observations of the child's language or behavioral issues to understand the nature of the problem but not to affix a label to it. Once such an analysis takes place, the teacher can determine what she or he can do to address the performance or behavioral concerns and monitor how the child responds to these interventions. This process of observation and classroom-based intervention provides important data for the Child Study Team should a more formal evaluation need to be conducted relative to a child's communication development.

Chapter Concepts

To help the classroom teacher begin to understand what she or he should be monitoring regarding communication and language, the following concepts are discussed in this chapter:

- *Communication:* the exchange of information, ideas, and concepts

- *Speech:* a mechanical process involving a coordinated effort involving breathing and movement of the tongue, lips, and jaw to produce sounds

- *Language:* conveying meaning through words, signs, or written forms

- *Reading:* the process of understanding the meaning of characters/letters and words in written material

- *Writing:* the mechanical act of forming characters/letters to create meaning

- *Executive functions:* the cognitive functions that involve planning, organization, memory, and monitoring work for accuracy

- *Critical thinking:* the cognitive function that allows determining the meaning and significance of something that has been observed or read

THE COMPONENTS OF COMMUNICATION: SPEECH AND LANGUAGE

Communication is the process of exchanging information, ideas, needs, and desires (Owens, 2008). The speaker sends information (**encodes**), which the receiver of this information comprehends (**decodes**). We are able to communicate using various modalities: verbal, written, gesture, pantomime, drawing, or sign language. For verbal (spoken) communication, a speaker can convey intent (meaning) through words, sentences, or longer utterances, such as conversation or narrative (storytelling). Communication depends on speech and language.

Speech

Speech is the verbal production of meaningful sounds. The speech process involves movements of the articulators (e.g., lips, tongue, and jaw) and coordination of the muscles that move these articulators to produce sounds. (A complete description of speech skills is provided in Chapter 5.) The most important aspect of speech is that movement of the articulators results in the production of sounds that compose the language we hear—speech is the movement and language is the concepts or ideas that are expressed.

Language

Language consists of a socially shared code or conventions (set of rules) for representing **concepts** (beliefs, thoughts, and ideas) through the use of arbitrary symbols (words) as well as rule-governed combinations of those symbols in sentences (syntax). For every language in the world, there is a socially shared code that a speaker uses to represent meaning through beliefs (e.g., "I think she is coming soon"); thoughts (e.g., "I think that's a great plan"); ideas (e.g., "Let's try to find a new way to get there"); space and time (e.g., *in front of* and *later*); and a description of things, people, and events in the environment (e.g., *objects, parties,* and *parades*). We would be unable to understand one another if this code were not shared.

As noted earlier, language involves the combination of words to form sentences (syntax). English syntax rules allow for the word order subject + verb + object (e.g., *Jane drank milk*). Other languages may use other orders, such as subject + object + verb (SOV), verb + subject + object (VSO), verb + object + subject (VOS), object + subject + verb (OSV), and object + verb + subject (OVS). This is one of the most interesting aspects of language: different rules for different language.

The importance of language in the classroom is described in the following section of this chapter and the chapters that follow in this book.

LANGUAGE AND THE CLASSROOM

The following language components are essential in children's academic development (Secord, 2002; Sotto & Prendeville, 2007): receptive language (understanding), spoken language (expression), literacy (reading and writing), social communication, and speech and phonological skills. Descriptions of these language components follow, along with examples of a child's performance in each of these components. Other essential factors for classroom success are the cognitive components, which include executive functioning and critical thinking. We begin with a discussion of receptive language, defined as the ability to understand spoken language.

Receptive Language

Receptive language consists of a child's listening skills. In the classroom, these skills involve understanding a classroom teacher's directions, instructions, and explanations. In addition, good receptive language skills allow a child to understand words, sentences, stories, and directions. Intact language requires that children understand directions that are short (e.g., "Open your books and read the first page") or long (e.g., "Get your coats, pack up your backpacks, line up at the door, and report to the gym teacher"). In the first case, children must remember two pieces of information and in the second, four. Children with receptive language difficulties frequently forget the earlier portion of directions, especially when lengthy or containing multiple steps.

Receptive language skills allow a child to understand words, sentences, stories, and directions.

Receptive language also allows a child to remember details from stories read in class by the teacher, especially in preschool and in earlier grades. These details may contain events or vocabulary items that contribute to language development and literacy. Children´s inability to respond to questions about these stories in the earlier grades allows early identification of potential language difficulties. The following vignette illustrates difficulty with lengthy directions.

> Jonas was able to remember certain spoken directions (e.g., "Open your blue notebooks and find last week´s vocabulary words") but had difficulty with others (e.g., "Open your blue notebooks, find last week´s vocabulary words, and underline the words that were in the story we just read"). Note that the second example contains three pieces of information that must be remembered and understood in a particular sequence. His teacher noticed the problem and decided to express directions in shorter chunks of information. Each direction was given and followed by a pause (e.g., "Open your notebooks . . . pause . . .").

Sounds in words last only briefly after being spoken. It is in this brief time that the listener must make sense of the spoken message, analyze it, and figure out the speaker's meaning. Some children are unable to accomplish this rapid processing of the spoken signal and require additional support for their receptive language problems.

Receptive Language Problems and Solutions

Two behaviors may alert the classroom teacher to the presence of receptive language difficulties: missing longer directions and frequently asking for repetition. Children's receptive language abilities are supported when directions are shorter and repeated or when they are asked to repeat the directions to make sure they are understood. Good teaching practices should incorporate repetition of directions or asking students to recap directions to help teach listening skills. Both strategies are essential to academic success for all learners. For older children, tape recording and writing directions for homework assignments may be effective. Additional supports within the classroom are pictures on the wall to illustrate the topic at hand. These supports benefit all children within the class, not just those with receptive language difficulties.

There are also cases when children do not respond to questions because of expressive language difficulties. They understand the question but may not have the vocabulary or the knowledge to structure sentences to respond. To understand this component of language, we next examine expressive language.

Expressive Language

Expressive language consists of the ability to express ideas and needs in a meaningful manner that is understood by listeners. An essential factor in expression is the ability to convey meaning (semantics) in a manner that is understood by listeners. Another factor is the ability to sequence words in the correct order to produce sentences (syntax) and longer utterances (conversations and stories about events). Communicative interaction with others requires that a speaker express language according to certain rules (pragmatics) such as maintaining a topic or taking turns as a speaker or a listener.

Expressive Language Problems

Expressive language problems may be revealed when children cannot find the word they want to say (e.g., "It's that thing, you know") or genuinely have difficulty learning new vocabulary items. In essence, expressive language skills are illustrated by the fluent flow of ideas or concepts in a manner that is easily understood. The following vignette illustrates difficulty with this component of language. In this example, the child has difficulty expressing her ideas in a clear manner, often using fillers or empty words when responding to questions or retelling events.

> It was difficult to understand what Erin wanted to say. Fillers interrupted her fluency (e.g., "and then," "uh...uh...uh..."), and empty words (e.g., "that thing") lacked meaningful reference. Her sentences were shorter and less complex than those of her classmates. Her classroom teacher noticed this problem and decided to provide props in the classroom to help her retrieve certain words. For example, pictures were placed around the room to illustrate the topic under discussion. She also asked children to draw a picture illustrating aspects of the topic at hand, thinking that this would provide rehearsal for vocabulary elements to be discussed in class. In this case, children were given the opportunity to talk about the picture they had drawn. The classroom teacher also sent home vocabulary word lists for all children to give them additional practice for

words in current use in the class. The teacher made sure that vocabulary words were taught in context and not in isolation. Teaching words in context helps students remember these vocabulary items.

Expressive Language Solutions

Children with expressive language difficulties are helped when given the type of supports described above. Additional support can be supplied through intervention by a speech-language pathologist, working closely with the teacher to support academic activities in the classroom. A caution here is that teachers need to be aware of various cultural practices involving student interaction with adults. Expressive language skills are frequently a means of identifying children with language difficulties. However, some children who are learning English as a second language go through a period of silence because they are not comfortable or willing to take risks producing words or sentences in learning a new language. (This behavior is discussed in detail in Chapter 13, and additional information on second-language learning is provided in Chapter 14.)

One of the ways that expressive or oral language skills can be stimulated and taught in the classroom is through modeling. For example, the classroom teacher can talk about his or her actions when completing a task, and students can be asked to verbalize their actions. In this way, expressive language begins with a simple description of current activities. Another activity is to have students ask questions. These questions can be about an upcoming event or just something hidden in a box (e.g., "Is it round?" "Can you eat it?" "Is it alive?").

Another expressive language activity focuses on asking how things are different or what characteristics distinguish one thing from another when children are presented with two similar objects that differ in size, shape, or color. Other tasks consist of asking children to describe the scene of a story or object function (e.g., "How do we use a . . . ?"). More advanced tasks elicit expressive language by asking children questions like "What might happen next?" and "What would happen if . . . ?" It may be important to introduce the vocabulary needed to engage in the expressive language task before beginning. In summary, children talk more when they feel comfortable and when they are engaged and interested. Children who appear to have more significant difficulties may benefit from referral for additional help.

READING

Another component of language in the classroom is reading, an essential factor in academic success. The classroom teacher must keep in mind that reading depends on the earlier development of receptive and expressive language skills and that reading requires more than mere exposure to books. This exposure is essential but does not fulfill all the requirements for reading development, which begin well before children enter school.

The Foundations of Reading Skills

Emergent literacy skills are the early prereading abilities that support later literacy skills: holding a book and "pretending to read" at 2 to 3 years of age, understanding that words on the page have meaning, and understanding the connection between letters on the page and sounds that are heard. Later literacy skills consist of the ability to identify words and comprehend (understand) written materials appropriate to age and academic grade.

One of the skills essential to succeeding in reading is the ability to decode (to interpret print), especially when faced with new words. For example, in later grades, children may encounter a novel word. In this case, they use context or try to sound out the word, depending on their earlier acquisition of the correspondence of sounds with letters.

Reading Problems and Solutions

One of the signs of potential reading difficulties materializes when children avoid reading tasks.

> Rory didn't seem to enjoy reading time as much as his peers during independent reading time or when stories were read to the first-grade class. He preferred looking at books with pictures instead of books with words. He also chose the same books for reading each time, and even when a new book was added to his desk, he never opened it. The teacher noticed his lack of interest in reading materials. She decided to send books home and asked his family to engage in nightly story reading. Her goal was to familiarize Rory with the story that would be introduced to the class the following day. She thought that this might contribute to his engagement in reading tasks and his degree of comfort when asked questions about the reading materials.

In the classroom, before a book is read (to the class in younger grades or by the class in older grades), vocabulary items from the story can be placed on the board (pictures and words for younger children and words for older children). These words can be discussed even before the book is read. During the reading task, the teacher can ask questions that require responses (e.g., "Why do you think . . . ?"). After the story has been read, the teacher can ask students questions that target the children's ideas about the story (e.g., "What did you like/not like about . . . ?"). Children's interest in reading may also be developed when books are sent home to be read with family members and later read in class. Familiarity with the stories encourages children's participation when the teacher reads books or asks questions about the material. Asking children to "act out" stories is another way to encourage interest in reading. If a genuine reading problem is suspected, referral is essential to provide the early supports that will allow a child to develop good reading skills. In the case of genuine reading problems, it is appropriate to refer for specialized instruction.

WRITING

Another important language component in the classroom is writing, and reading and writing are two language skills that are closely connected. In fact, children need to learn that written text is simply someone's verbalization that was written down, and linking oral speech to written text is an important understanding. In addition, both reading and writing skills emerge from children's receptive and expressive language abilities. (See Chapters 7 and 8 for a deeper discussion of the precursors of reading skills.)

The Foundations of Writing Skills

Similar to the development of reading, emergent literacy skills later reinforce intact writing abilities. These emergent skills begin with toddlers' drawing and scribbling as they pretend to write. A broader discussion of these emergent skills can be found in Chapter 8. The language skills essential for good writing are semantics, the ability to express ideas and needs in written form; syntax, the ability to create well-formed sentences in written texts; and mechanics and organization, the ability to follow rules for letter formation, information organization, and structure. It is in grades one through three that literacy is introduced. Within the first-grade class, children will have varying levels of writing (and reading) skills. Some will need special guidance, while others can be helped with classroom strategies that enhance their skills. The following vignette describes good writing skills in the first grade.

Emily's writing was similar to that of other children in the first-grade class. Her sentences were short, and she sometimes used a combination of writing and drawing. She was able to write at least three sentences when asked to describe something that happened to her over the weekend. Her teacher noticed that other children had more difficulty expressing themselves through writing. She decided to initiate a strategy to engage children's interest in writing. She gave children an assignment to write/draw a story about a recent trip the class made to the science museum. She knew that, in the first grade, children should be given plentiful practice in using writing and drawing to express their ideas and concepts about the world. She also knew that some children would need additional tutoring to develop good writing skills.

SPEECH AND PHONOLOGICAL SKILLS

We next discuss speech and phonological skills: the vehicles for verbally expressing ideas and concepts derived from language. Both speech and phonological skills allow a child to be intelligible (understandable). Speech is the ability to produce sounds with accuracy, while phonology involves the ability to sequence sounds to produce words and longer utterances. Children with speech difficulties frequently have difficulty with certain sounds—generally *s*, *l*, or *r* sounds. Those with phonological difficulties have problems combining sounds or syllables in words. In this case, productions may consist of "wed" for *red* or "teep" for *keep*.

Sabrina has problems with speech, such as correctly producing some consonant sounds— for example, /s/ (see), /r/ (red), and /l/ (low). She also has some problems with phonology rules, producing "nana" for *banana* and "raef" for *giraffe*. At times, the kindergarten classroom teacher and Sabrina's peers cannot understand her speech.

Speech sound difficulties and phonological difficulties are typical for younger children but should be resolved by about 4 years of age. It is appropriate to refer children for speech-language pathology intervention if problems persist.

SOCIAL COMMUNICATION

The ability to follow social interaction rules for conversation and interaction allows children to interact with peers and with adults in conversation. These rules consist of eye contact, taking turns as speaker and listener, and maintaining the topic at hand. Children with social interaction difficulties often require support and training to improve the frequency and quality of their social interactions.

> Otis joined other children while they were engaged in a game. He enjoyed playing with the other children and had a number of friends in the classroom. On the other hand, Danny hung back, watching other children but seeming unsure how to enter an existing playgroup.

The Supports for Social Communication

Children with social communication difficulties can improve their interactions through observing appropriate models interacting with other children. The classroom teacher can ask children to role-play "wanting to play with another child" or "asking another child to play with you." The classroom can also be organized to encourage more interaction (a model for this goal is described in Chapter 3). Some of the strategies that target social communication include grouping children with more and less advanced social skills to provide models. Another method is to have children explain something to each other, again pairing children of unequal skill levels. Social communication difficulties can also be addressed through reading stories about children with these same difficulties and examining with the class how these difficulties are resolved in the story. Having students discuss these kinds of social problems can be a good way of increasing student awareness, especially for those students who do not experience these problems, and thereby sensitizing them to what they can do to help another student.

COGNITIVE COMPONENTS: EXECUTIVE FUNCTIONS AND CRITICAL THINKING

We follow the discussion of social communication with a discussion of the cognitive components that play a role in the classroom. These components involve the ability to understand, plan, organize, and process information. It is clear that these are essential factors in academic success. Executive functions and critical thinking are based on children's cognitive abilities. Cognitive abilities provide the ability to acquire knowledge and understand and process incoming and outgoing information.

Executive Functions

Executive functions consist of organization, initiation, planning, organization, problem solving, making changes when necessary, and/or implementing a task. Functions also consist of attention, the ability to attend to the task at hand; memory, the ability to remember spoken information; and self-regulation, the ability to stay focused on the task at hand and monitor output for accuracy. The following vignette presents an example of an executive function disorder.

> The teacher asked children in the class to complete three worksheets that involved cutting and pasting pictures and then matching them to words. The children promptly began working, first cutting out all the pictures. One of the children began a few minutes later, cutting only one picture out without pasting it or drawing a line to match it to a word. This child seemed to have no plan about how to proceed and was not able to self-monitor or know that he or she wasn't doing what the other children were doing. The teacher needed to intervene, focusing the child on the steps of the task and helping develop a plan for how to complete the assignment.

The question the teacher needs to consider is whether this behavior indicates planning problem or whether the student has difficulty recalling the directions. Determining which possibility is actually impacting the behavior can provide important insight into follow-up activities and supports. Frequently, children with executive function difficulties show poor organization, losing books and other classroom tools, and lack the ability to recognize or correct errors in work. (Additional examples of executive difficulties are presented in Chapter 6, along with classroom strategies.)

Critical Thinking

Critical thinking involves the ability to identify and gather important information, evaluate output to determine if the work is accurate, and problem-solve. The following vignette presents an example of a child who hasn't learned how to think critically about a problem.

> After reading a story to the class, the teacher asked each student to offer a solution to a problem faced by one of the characters in the story. One of the children could not come up with a solution and seemed surprised by some of the answers the other students in the class offered.

This child cannot identify the information necessary to solve a problem or propose a solution and evaluate the quality of that solution, even though he or she may have intact basic language abilities. It may be necessary to model various solutions to problems to develop critical thinking skills. In this case, all children can be involved in the process, but some time should be devoted to working with a child alone.

STRATEGIES FOR THE CLASSROOM

Language Development Across Grades

The role of the classroom teacher is to provide children with supports for their language development when needed and provide a nurturing environment for learning. Language supports for younger children are more readily available, given that early grades have pictures on the wall that portray classroom themes along with a number of other environmental supports that provide children with language cues (Bernstein & Levey, 2009). Pictures frequently act to remind children of words that they may not otherwise be able to produce from memory.

Later grades lack these environmental cues or supports, with children required to rely more on their internal language skills. In addition, classroom tasks become more complex as children encounter expository reading materials that require intact and age-appropriate language skills along with developed schemas, attention, and memory. Students also need to learn how to derive meaning from new words embedded in sentences, using context (the surrounding words) to provide the meaning of the unknown word. For students in later grades, "learning to read" is not the focus; the focus becomes "reading to learn," as concepts in science and history are presented in texts. Consequently, it is essential that classroom teachers become aware of the role that they can play in language development, in early as well as later grades.

Reading Skills

Frequently, young children are introduced to books for the first time in the classroom. Many classroom teachers are aware of the importance of print recognition as an early precursor to reading development. Children must also learn to associate the sounds they hear with the alphabet letters on the page to help them decode (interpret) words. Later reading skills require that children use their early knowledge of sound-letter association to identify unknown words in texts. Language also plays a role in mathematics, with children acquiring knowledge of the vocabulary associated with math problems (e.g., *more than, less than, dividend, multiplier*), along with the spatial terms associated with later mathematics tasks (e.g., *above, below, perpendicular, adjacent*). In addition, using words such as *because* helps them understand the connection between concepts (e.g., "He was mad because the dog stole his catcher's mitt").

Listening Skills

Teachers across all grades must continuously work to develop and maintain listening skills with respect to the teacher and peers. To ensure that listening skills are functioning optimally, students can be encouraged to repeat information. They can also be asked to elaborate on another child's productions, adding information of their own. The following strategies can help promote language learning in the classroom and support children's learning in the presence of potential language difficulties (Quale, Peters, & Matkins, 2010).

- Seat children so that all can see the classroom teacher's face.
- Monitor children's attention and pause until attention is focused on the task at hand.
- Pause to highlight important information and to capture children's attention.
- Allow children to express ideas versus lecturing or only asking them questions.
- Encourage children to ask questions and explain what is not clearly understood.
- Monitor background noise, such as noise from computers and other distractions, to enhance listening.
- Ask questions and ask children to repeat information to ensure that materials or information have been understood.

Connecting Language to Environment

Finally, the most important aspect of language and the classroom is that *language* needs to be related to the environment. Visual supports are necessary to relate spoken language to concrete examples for younger children. For both younger and older students, classroom language strategies can include reading, writing, drawing pictures, role play, and discussion to enhance learning concepts. Communication through language is the means by which the classroom teacher can identify children who may have language difficulties (Peets, 2009).

Visual supports help children associate spoken language with classroom tasks.

Additional classroom strategies in the following chapters provide teachers with methods for developing children´s language skills in the classroom.

We now return to the case study presented at the beginning of the chapter to determine the outcome of the classroom teacher's observations of Kimberly's difficulties in responding to questions about stories read in class.

CASE STUDY REVISITED

The vignette presented earlier in this chapter provided an example of a child experiencing difficulty answering questions when the teacher read books aloud to the class. The teacher planned to observe this child to determine why she could not answer such questions.

Observation of this child in different contexts was essential to determine if her language skills were better in certain situations than others. As you can see, this approach was successful in determining the basis of Kimberly's difficulties when books were read to the class.

Case Study Revisited: The role of language in the classroom

To determine if there was a problem with attention or focus, the teacher read a story to Kimberly in a one-to-one situation. The goal was to determine if being in a larger group setting with other children led to distraction. In the smaller group setting, she found that Kimberly was able to answer more questions about the story but still had problems providing details from the reading task. However, given leading questions (e.g., "But what happened after the little girl met the old woman on the path?"), she was able to retrieve this information. Consequently, her teacher determined that Kimberly understood the story but required help to retrieve certain details.

To improve her performance in the classroom, the teacher sent books to the child's parents each night, choosing books that she planned to read in class the next day. Kimberly's parents were encouraged to read the stories to her and discuss the events in the story. The goal was to provide Kimberly with familiarity with the story to enhance her success answering questions in the group-reading context, along with potentially improving her self-esteem. Over the next few weeks, Kimberly's performance became more consistent with that of her peers, even when the teacher introduced new books not read at home. Subsequently, she showed more engagement, less fidgeting, and provided more appropriate responses to questions. She also showed more interest in reading new books and less interest in picture books.

SUMMARY

This chapter introduced the basic components of language that are discussed in depth in the following chapters. Given that kindergarten teachers have reported that language difficulties are the main obstacle affecting children's school readiness, language is the focus of this chapter and this text. Language is the vehicle for communication within the classroom, and knowledge of its components allows the classroom teacher to identify children who may have language difficulties that may impact their learning. The basic components discussed in this chapter were:

- Communication as the means for exchanging information;

- Speech as the means for producing the sounds that comprise words;

- Language as the means for representing beliefs, thoughts, and ideas through spoken language;

- Social communication as the means for using language in interaction;

- Executive functions as the means for successful planning and monitoring work in the classroom;

- Critical thinking as the means for grasping important information.

To begin our journey into understanding language development and learning, Chapter 2 provides knowledge of the theories that underlie language development: the environmental theories of Vygotsky, Piaget, and Bates; the innateness theory of Chomsky; the emergentism theory of Bates and MacWhinney; and the Theory of Mind of Baron-Cohen and others. Chapter 2 also offers strategies to enhance language development related to these theories. As you prepare to move forward in this text, pay close attention to the role of the classroom teacher in facilitating language development.

KEY WORDS

Communication

Concepts

Decode

Encode

Expressive language

Language

Receptive language

Speech

STUDY QUESTIONS

1. Explain the importance of decoding in the development of literacy.

2. Describe executive functions. Explain the importance of executive function difficulties in the classroom.

3. Explain the reason why the classroom teacher in the case study needed to observe Kimberly's responses to questions in other contexts.

4. Explain why empty words indicate a language disorder.

5. Describe the language disorders that would be associated with receptive language and with expressive language. How do these disorders differ?

PROJECTS

1. Observe a classroom. Make notes on how the classroom teacher interacts with the children in the class. Are there any children with speech or language difficulties? If so, make notes on how the classroom interacts with these children versus children with typical speech and language abilities.

2. Observe the interactions of children at play. Are there any children with speech difficulties? How do the other children interact with this child? Make notes on any differences between their interactions with this child and their interactions among themselves.

3. Choose five journal articles from this chapter's references. After reading your choices, write an article that compares these articles in the following manner: the main research project, the number and age of the participants, and results. In your article, describe how you would use the information you gained in your classroom.

STUDENT STUDY SITE

Visit the Student Study Site at **www.sagepub.com/levey** for these additional learning tools:

- Video Links
- Self Quizzes
- E-Flashcards

- Sample Forms and Assessment Tools
- Recommended Readings
- Web Resources

SUGGESTIONS FOR FURTHER READING

Fromkin, V., Rodman, R., & Hyams, N. (2006). *An introduction to language.* Florence, KY: Cengage.

Hall, B. J., Oyer, H. J., & Haas, W. H. (2000). *Speech, language, and hearing disorders: A guide for the teacher* (3rd ed.). Boston: Pearson.

Haynes, W. O., Moran, M. J., & Pindzola, R. H. (2005). *Communication disorders in the class.* Sudbury, MA: Jones & Bartlett.

McLaughlin, C. (2006). *Introduction to language development* (2nd ed.). Florence, KY: Cengage.

Power, B. M., & Hubbard, R. S. (2001). *Language development: A reader for teachers.* Boston: Prentice Hall.

C H A P T E R   2

Theories and Explanations of Language Development

Sandra Levey

CASE STUDY: How children learn the names of things in the world

Billy's preschool teacher noted that the 2-year-old looked at a picture of a cow and called it "doggy." Billy's teacher also noted that he called all four-legged animals "doggy." She also noticed that he looked at her when naming these new animals, seeming to say, "I know that's not a doggy!" She complied with the implied request for help and said, "That's a cow." Billy's language skills, in all other aspects, were similar to those of his peers. His social interaction was also within typical limits. There were no concerns about his communication skills, and his hearing skills were intact. His teacher wondered if calling a cow by the name "doggy" was part of typical language development or not.

What is the basis of this child's labeling a cow as "doggy?" On what information or experiences did you base your answer?

INTRODUCTION

Billy's use of the word *dog* in place of the word *cow* is an example of children learning language through two paths. The first path consists of an **innate**(inborn) ability to learn about the world and create ideas about entities (objects and things) and actions in that world. The second path consists of input from the world, with children's interpretations of the world initially based on the appearance and function of these entities and actions. Evidence for the role of both paths appears in children's **overextensions**, when children extend the label from one entity (dog) to another animal with similar features (cow). This is an example of the innate early ability to form hypotheses or ideas about categories in the world. The second path provides children with the language to describe this world. We are interested in how children learn language for one primary reason: Knowledge of their learning processes gives us insight into methods of enhancing their language development.

17

Children learn the names of things and often extend the label from one entity to another if they share similar features or descriptions.

Theories of Language Acquisition

This chapter presents three dominant explanations of language acquisition and development: the **environmental** theory (sometimes termed the pragmatic view); the **innateness theory** (based on children's innate language skills); and **emergentism** and the **guided distributional learning** theory, which ascribe language development to both foundations (i.e., innate skills and the environment).

This chapter ends with an explanation of the theory of mind, essential in understanding children's language learning. Theory of mind describes the ability to understand someone else's mind, which is an essential factor in understanding why characters in stories act in certain manners (de Villiers & de Villiers, 2003). It is important for classroom teachers to understand that there is an association between theory and practice, as these theories have led to strategies for supporting children's language development, especially for children who may not be able to take advantage of environmental cues.

Environmental Theory

Proponents of environmental theories argue that the milieu (surrounding context) plays a major role by providing children with information that supports their language development (Bates & MacWhinney, 1982; Skinner, 1957). Environmental experiences consist of interactions with individuals, objects, and events that provide children the opportunity to learn language and symbols (words or labels) associated with objects and events.

Vygotsky (1935) and Piaget (1923/2007) viewed the impact of the environment in somewhat different ways. In Vygotsky's view, adults and children with greater knowledge should provide guidance to support children's language development and learning. Piaget placed greater emphasis on children solving problems on their own, with less emphasis on environmental input for guidance.

Bates (1976) introduced the term *pragmatics* to describe the connection between language development and the environment. In this view, social interaction is an important factor in children's early language acquisition.

Innateness Theory

Proponents of the innateness theory (sometimes termed the nativist or psycholinguistic theory) argue that children possess innate (inborn/native) abilities that provide the basis for language development (Chomsky, 1964; Pinker, 1994). These natural or inherent abilities allow children to process and establish grammatical information from spoken language, such as the rules for combining words into sentences. Thus, the role of the environment is only to provide information for the language learner. In Chomsky's (1957) view, children use the environmental context to develop their syntactic abilities for combining words to produce sentences.

Emergentism and Guided Distributional Learning Theories

Proponents of the emergentism and related guided distributional learning theories argue that innate skills and the environment, together, are essential factors for language development (Hirsh-Pasek, Golinkoff, & Hollich, 1999; Karmiloff-Smith, 1992). In this view, language may develop through one of two sources: (a) the effect of the environment on children's innate language-learning abilities or (b) the effect of interaction with the environment on the structure of the brain (Karmiloff-Smith, 1992). In both explanations, there is an interaction between a child's innate skills and the environment.

Theory of Mind Concept

The concept of theory of mind explains children's learning about others' mental states. Theory of mind develops through exposure to mental state verbs that describe these mental states (e.g., *thinks*, *knows*, and *believes*). It is this ability that marks the difference between typical language development and atypical language development, with typical development characterized by understanding others' mental states.

   The following is a discussion of the advocates of these theories, along with strategies to address children's language development drawn from these explanations of language and learning development. We begin this discussion with the environmental theory of language acquisition, the idea that experiences and events in the external environment are essential in language learning.

THE ENVIRONMENTAL THEORIES OF LANGUAGE ACQUISITION

We begin with the theories that assign the environment with the most crucial role in language learning. The term **environment** refers to external events such as people (e.g., adults and children), entities or things (e.g., animals or objects), actions (e.g., running, eating, and drinking), and events (e.g., birthday parties, weddings, and parades).

   Three proponents of the environmental theory are Vygotsky (1935), Piaget (1954), and Bates (1976). These authors define the environment as language and experiential input from adults and other children, along with input from contact with animals, objects, activities, and challenging events that require problem solving. Children's early problem-solving skills are stimulated when toddlers face a problem, such as reaching a desired item that is out of reach. Pushing and standing on a box to reach the desired item is an example of early problem-solving skills. The importance of the environment is that it provides children with

The classroom environment should provide children with activities that require problem solving.

a variety of events and experiences that challenge their problem-solving skills, along with providing the labels or names for these events and experiences (e.g., "fix" a broken toy).

Vygotsky and the Zone of Proximal Development

Vygotsky's (1935) theory of the **zone of proximal development** describes the distance between two levels of the development of children's problem-solving abilities: (a) a child's actual developmental level, determined by independent problem solving and (b) the child's level of potential development, determined through problem solving under adult guidance or in collaboration with more advanced peers. The zone of proximal development is the distance between *what children can do by themselves* (retrospective mental development) and the concepts or skills that *they need to learn with assistance* (prospective mental development). The types of skills that require guidance are those that have not yet matured.

Retrospective or Prospective Mental Development

Retrospective mental development is a child's actual developmental level at a current point in time (defined by independent problem solving). **Prospective mental development** is the zone of proximal development (defined by guided problem solving). When children are engaged in social interaction with adults or peers with greater knowledge, they are able to achieve developmental goals. These individuals provide the child with the knowledge needed to bridge the distance between the child's current development level and his or her potential level of development. Tasks that demand conscious reflection or problem solving lead to progress in children's developmental skills (Vygotsky, 1962/1988). Social interaction is the vehicle that facilitates development of the skills that have not yet matured.

Social Interaction

The major premise of Vygotsky's (1935) theory is that **social interaction** is the primary factor in development. Vygotsky argued that language begins with communication between children and individuals in the environment. The process of learning a particular skill, such as communication, activates children's internal developmental processes. These processes are operational when children are interacting with individuals in the environment or engaged in the imitation of more advanced skills, such as those that children observe older or more advanced peers performing.

Egocentric Speech or Private Speech

Language skills are initially based on **egocentric speech**(Vygotsky, 1986), frequently called **private speech**. At this point of development, children focus on themselves, their own experience with objects and events, and their own needs and wants. Thus, their language efforts do not focus on communication with others. Egocentric/private speech appears in situations when children are talking themselves through the steps of a difficult task (Berk, 1992). Children will talk aloud about what they are doing or the steps involved in accomplishing a task (e.g., "First . . . , and then . . .").

As cognitive skills increase, egocentrism recedes. Children become aware that activities and objects have properties separate from their own direct perception, and they are able to put themselves into the place of another person. Now, language becomes inner speech, an internal mental function responsible for organizing thoughts in terms of mental orientation and conscious understanding of objects and events. This is the main instrument for verbal thought used to guide children's actions. Now, children are able to work through a problem using mental operations, as opposed to private speech or verbal strategies (i.e., talking themselves through a solution).

Piaget and Cognitive Development

Piaget (1954) developed a theory of children's cognitive development. **Cognition** is the mental ability to adapt to the environment, to draw abstractions, to generalize experiences, to think about objects and events at various times, to compare and contrast objects and events, to infer conclusions, to use symbols (words) to represent objects and events, to learn language, and to store information for later retrieval (Gentner, 2003). Cognition presupposes two essential factors: attention and working memory. Attention consists of the ability to focus on the essential factors in a particular context or a task, along with the ability to ignore distractions and irrelevant information. Working memory, also sometimes termed short-term memory, provides the ability to store information, such as when one must remember a series of spoken directions.

Schema

Piagetian theory has contributed to a better understanding of children's language learning skills. According to Piaget, children have psychological structures (**schema**or schemata) that allow the processing of information and events. Early cognitive development involves a process by which children construct a representation of the verbal and nonverbal events around them (Witt, 1998), akin to literally connecting new ideas and images to add to those that already exist within children's minds. Schemata change with exposure to new information or events in the environment (adaptation).

Returning to the case study at the beginning of this chapter, let's examine Billy's interpretation of *cow* in light of schemas.

- Billy viewed a dog as the first animal seen in his environment.

- He used the visual and movement characteristics of this animal to establish the identity of *dog*.

- Having created a schema for *dog*, he used the existing schema to label *cow* as *dog* because of the perceptual similarities between these two animals.

When exposed to some new information or event that fits into a preexisting schema, the child can add this data into that existing schema (**assimilation**). When exposed to some new information or event that does not easily fit into a preexisting schema, the schema must undergo change (**accommodation**). Accommodation occurs when children change their understanding of objects or events based on new information. **Equilibrium** (cognitive balance) is the goal of assimilation and accommodation. Schemas for nonlinguistic events differ from those for language (Tomasello, 1999). For example, visual and movement characteristics act to establish animals and objects, while auditory and various nonlinguistic factors (e.g., eye gaze and gesture) act to establish language. According to Piaget, children create their own understanding of objects and events, without the intervention of adult or peers. However, children may be provided with guidance, taking the form of scaffolds.

Scaffolds

Piaget and Vygotsky share the view that **scaffolds** support learning and language development. Consequently, scaffolds (supports) are appropriate for developing children's language skills, as shown in the following examples. Classroom teachers can use scaffolds for **expansions**, **recasts**, and **models** when children require guidance in their responses. Figure 2.1 provides a list of strategies for language development for younger children.

Cognitive Prerequisites

According to Piaget (1954), children's cognitive development passes through stages that begin at birth and continue until maturity, with similar developmental stages for children from various backgrounds. (Chapter 7 provides a detailed discussion of these stages of cognitive development.) The primary aspect of Piaget's theory is that language depends on cognitive prerequisites—such as **object permanence**, when a child searches for an object that has been hidden out of sight (Harris, 1971; Piaget, 1967). For example, the ability to combine words to form sentences (e.g., "doggy go") frequently depends on the ability to produce words for entities or events that are "out of sight."

Bates and the Pragmatic Theory

Bates (1976) contributed to the theory of language acquisition through a comprehensive examination of environmental factors that played a role in children's developmental skills. Bates introduced the term **pragmatics** to define the connection between language development and the environment or context in which communication occurs.

Figure 2.1	Strategies for Language Development for Younger Children

Expansion: When a child's production is corrected but lacks elaboration or is missing elements, a teacher can provide a model of the missing elements to address the language factors that are missing from the child's production.

Child: "He is walking."

Teacher: "That's right. The boy is walking to school because the bus broke down."

Recast: When a child's production is repeated, but the errors in this production are corrected—without telling the child that there was an error.

Child: "They *is* walking."

Teacher: "They *are* walking."

Cloze procedure (sentence completion): When a child is given a cue to give support for a specific target, a teacher can use an open-ended phrase that stimulates a child's language skills.

Teacher: "You could say, 'I want to . . .'" (e.g., "play with you")

Model: When a child requires a model of an appropriate response, the adult can provide an example. This may be helpful when a child lacks the sentence-forming skills to produce a specific utterance.

Teacher: "You could say, 'I want to play with you.'"

Context

All pragmatic theorists share the belief that children first use expressions in a social manner, with more advanced language use related to more advanced cognitive development occurring later (Dore, 1978; Gopnik & Meltzoff, 1988). All pragmatic theorists use the term *context*. This term has at least four subcategories (Prutting, 1982, p. 125). The first is the cognitive and social context (e.g., knowledge of physical setting, communicative partner, and communicative rules such as eye contact and turn taking). The second is the physical context (e.g., perceptual properties of people, places, and objects). The third is the linguistic context (e.g., information associated with composing and interpreting communication), while the fourth is the nonlinguistic context (e.g., nonverbal information associated with generating and interpreting meaning). All subcategories are important for learning and language skills. Contextual factors are responsible for providing children with the information that allows them to develop language.

As discussed earlier, scaffolds provide children with cues and supports that allow them to establish grammar (Proctor-Williams, Fey, & Loeb, 2001). Scaffolds consist of *models* that teach a word or a grammatical form, *expansions* to extend the length of an utterance, and *recasts* to correct a grammatical error. In this way, environmental cues provide children with the information to increase their understanding of language, while playing a significant role in learning grammatical structure (Proctor-Williams et al., 2001).

Communication

The vehicle for social interaction is **communication** (Prutting, 1982), consisting of both verbal acts (e.g., words, sentences, narratives, and conversations) and nonverbal acts (e.g., eye gaze, gesture, turn taking in conversation, and facial expressions). The ability to read nonverbal cues, such as facial expressions, is an important characteristic of communication that can distinguish typical from atypical behaviors. According to Coleman (1995), the ability to determine a speaker's attitude is a key component of emotional intelligence. Environmental or contextual cues provide the means for a child's acquisition of symbols (labels) that refer to objects and actions. Bates (1976) attributes language development to the perception of association between language and events. Over time, a child learns that seeing his or her mother putting on a coat is an indicator that she is leaving. Consequently, an association is drawn between coat and leaving. Seeing his or her mother putting on a coat is an index (predictor) of a mother's leaving, while the word *coat* is a symbol for this object.

Continuity

Bates (1976) argued for **continuity** between children's preverbal behaviors and early language development, given that preverbal behaviors (e.g., gestures, eye contact, and prelinguistic vocalizations) demonstrate that children are expressing the intention to communicate (Bates, Camaioni, & Volterra, 1976). Typically, developing children focus on a speaker's eye region as early as 2 months of age, because a speaker's eyes convey the social information connected with verbal and nonverbal communication (Carter, Ornstein, Davis, Klin, & Volkmar, 2005; Hainline, 1978; Haith, Bergman, & Moore, 1977). In contrast, children who tend to focus on a speaker's mouth region may be at risk for difficulties in typical language acquisition (Jones, Carr, & Klin, 2008). These findings, derived from research in autism, bring new meaning to the concept of early intervention, as the ability to eliminate eye gaze aversion could optimize outcomes in children's language development.

Early Grammar

Examples of toddlers' early communication consist of (a) the *instrumental* function, used to obtain a goal; (b) the *regulatory* function, used to control others' behaviors; (c) the *interaction* function, used to obtain joint attention; and (d) the *personal* function, used to express feelings or attitudes (Halliday, 1975). These preverbal behaviors provide the precursors for the emergence of words (Ninio & Snow, 1996). (See Chapter 7 for a full discussion of children's early language abilities.)

Dore (1978) described the communicative intentions produced by infants and toddlers at the prelinguistic and one-word utterance stage as primitive speech acts. Young preschoolers use language to direct themselves, to instruct others, and to report experiences from the past or present (Hulit & Howard, 1997). Imitation constitutes an early example of *labeling* (Bates & Snyder, 1987). Later communicative development involves the use of language in more complex tasks, such as reasoning.

The Competition Model

Bates's (1976) pragmatic theory of the emergence of language led to the later development of the **competition model** to explain language acquisition (Bates & MacWhinney, 1982). In this model, children have the innate ability to perceive connections between symbols (words) and objects and events. Rather than learning the grammar of a language, language learners are able to store linguistic and nonlinguistic information in the form of codes available for later processing for meaning. The competition model includes a theory of **parallel distributed processing** In this theory, words, language, and phonological patterns frequently repeated are able to activate and strengthen connections in children's processing of language (Hulit & Howard, 1997). Thus, children may produce words such as "eated" due to the higher frequency of regular past morpheme forms (i.e., add -*ed*). Over time, as language and cognitive abilities develop, children are able to establish the correct form (e.g., *ate*).

THE ENVIRONMENTAL THEORIES: STRATEGIES FOR LANGUAGE DEVELOPMENT

We will now examine the strategies drawn from the environmental theories. Scaffolds (verbal supports) are the supports provided to guide children's language learning. These scaffolds are frequently used with younger children to increase their language and problem-solving skills (Fey, Long, & Finestack, 2003). (Examples of four scaffolds can be found in Figure 2.1 on page 23.) Scaffolding is the best form of guidance to preserve children's self-esteem during language learning tasks. This approach acts to enhance a child's language skills without directly focusing on language errors.

Scaffolds provide the minimal support necessary for a child to succeed in learning. This requires an optimal balance between scaffolding and allowing children to rely on their own initiative. If supports are above (or below) a child's level of development, learning will not occur. To provide the correct level of scaffolding, classroom teachers may follow this hierarchy (Garhart Mooney, 2000): First, a model for a target skill is provided, allowing the child to imitate the model; next, the child is encouraged to model the target for other children.

A good test of a child's learning of a particular skill is his or her ability to teach the imitated skill to other children. The transfer to other children demonstrates that the child has learned the skill. Scaffolds can also be used by adults or peers with more advanced skills. In the classroom, scaffolding processes can be established by observation, planning, and encouragement (Garhart Mooney, 2000). Classroom teachers should observe children carefully to determine if they experience difficulties with certain tasks and encourage children to work in groups to enhance the transfer of skills from children with more advanced skills to those who require support.

Play

Piaget emphasized the important of authentic play events as an essential part of learning language (Garhart Mooney, 2000). Consequently, a trip to a farm is an effective learning task, while reading about farms is not. Play skills represent imitation of activities in the environment along with the language used in these activities. For example, play schemes frequently involve activities and language above those of a child's independent skills (e.g., taking care of a baby, shopping, cooking, going to school, or going to the doctor). Play involves the use of language to reconstruct these observed events and interactions, and adults can elicit (draw out) children's language during play (e.g., "What is happening?" "What could she or he say?" "What would happen if . . . ?" "Which one is it/is it not . . . ?") (Westby, 2007).

Pragmatics

There are also strategies associated with pragmatics (de Villiers & de Villiers, 2003). These strategies focus on the use of language in social interaction. For example, present a child with a picture that the adult or another child cannot see. She or he has to describe an event that is happening in part of the picture. The goal is to provide enough information so that the adult/other child can pick out the person or object involved in the event from a set of similar people or objects.

In this way, children can engage in tasks that are more complex over time (e.g., a group of square shapes that differ only by color, requiring that the child use adjectives, such as *red*, to label the target object). Linguistic forms can increase in complexity from adjectives to prepositional phrases (e.g., "the red square *in the circle*") and, finally, to relative clauses (e.g., "the red square, *next to the house*, in the circle").

According to this pragmatic model, language skills develop because children desire to interact in a social manner. Thus, children who lack the motivation to engage in communication must be encouraged. Younger children have been found to learn new linguistic rules through imitative modeling (Zimmerman & Rosenthal, 1974). Thus, group work and collaboration to foster generalization are successful means of developing this interaction (Garhart Mooney, 2000). Pragmatic strategies that target **narrative** and **speech acts** (doing things with words and sentences; e.g., dramatizing stories, collaborative class projects, and guessing games) are also effective in developing language. Additional strategies consist of personal narratives, anecdotes, and puppet shows (de Villiers & de Villiers, 2003).

We have reviewed the environmental theories of language acquisition as advocated by Vygotsky, Piaget, and Bates. The environmental theories stress the importance of interaction, experiences, and play for language development. We next examine the innateness theory. Here, the child's innate or inborn mechanism explains language acquisition and development.

THE INNATENESS THEORY

Language Acquisition Device

Chomsky (1957, 1959, 1965) proposed an innate (inborn) mechanism to account for language acquisition and development. This innate mechanism was termed the **language acquisition device (LAD)**, a device that allows children to process the language spoken in the environment. The LAD also contains universal information (applicable to all languages) that allows children to form hypotheses regarding language output and form rules.

The LAD allows children to analyze heard sentences and use this analysis to produce grammatical sentences. Children's innate abilities allow them to derive grammatical rules or principles from limited language input or information. In spite of limited data or information, children produce sentences (never heard before) that reflect the creativity of the human mind (e.g., "I'm crackering my soup" produced by a child putting crackers in his soup).

Sentence Production

Sentence production is the basis of Chomsky's (1965) theory of language development. Thus, syntax (combining words according to rules) is the focus of this theory. Chomsky argued for an interaction between two factors (McLeish & Martin, 1975):

1. The child's innate linguistic competence (i.e., the language-learning device) that equips the child with knowledge of the principles of universal grammar (i.e., rules for producing sentences in any and all languages of the world)

2. Linguistic data (information) that children use to develop the language that is consistent with the language of their home environment

There are two sets of rules that allow children to produce sentences. The first rules are the **phrase structure rules** that use the basic sentence structure (N + V = "Dogs bark") to develop more complex sentences. The rule can be read as the following: A sentence (S) must contain ($\rightarrow$) a noun (N) and a verb (V):

$$S \rightarrow N + V$$

This basic sentence can be further rewritten to state the rule that a sentence must contain a noun phrase (NP) and a verb phrase (VP):

$$S \rightarrow NP + VP$$

In this case, the NP can contain a determiner (Det), such as *the,* and an adjective (Adj), such as *big.* The VP can contain a verb, such as *eats,* and another noun, such as *cookies,* to read "The big boy eats cookies."

The second set of rules is made of **transformational rules.** The transformational rules provide a connection between **deep structure** (a structure in the brain that determines the meaning of the sentence) and **surface structure** (the spoken sentence). The transformational rules allow a basic structure (S $\rightarrow$ N + V) to be transformed into a question (e.g., "Does mommy eat cookies?"), a negative (e.g., "Mommy doesn't eat cookies"), a passive (e.g., "The cookies were eaten by mommy"), an imperative (e.g., "Eat cookies"), and more complex structures (e.g., "Mommy eats cookies, and she also drinks milk").

THE INNATENESS THEORY: STRATEGIES FOR LANGUAGE DEVELOPMENT

Children possess the innate skill and form ideas about language based on input. To fulfill this goal, children require abundant language input to allow them to form hypotheses or ideas about structure. To this end, the classroom teacher should provide clear and complete examples of grammar in short, complete sentences. Lessons within the classroom can demonstrate a variety of sentence types (e.g., questions, negative forms, and passive structure) and grammatical forms (e.g., present, past, and future tense) in books and storytelling to provide abundant examples of the adult language.

The Classroom

A psycholinguistic approach in the classroom is focused on children's underlying mental processes for speaking, comprehending auditorily presented language (i.e., perception and understanding), writing, and reading. A child with difficulties following directions in the classroom may have auditory working memory problems (Gathercole & Baddeley, 1990). These are essential skills for a child to store, internalize, and establish information in a language and retrieve information. A psycholinguistic approach focuses on the processing (i.e., language production and comprehension) and memory. Using this approach, a teacher can ask children questions about current and previously learned lessons to assess their understanding and memory. Additional strategies consist of highlighting important information and overlearning through repetition of difficult concepts or ideas (Huitt, 2000).

Input

Input consists of information presented to the child. This input must be delivered in a manner that allows children to derive full benefit from this information (Abbeduto & Boudreau, 2004). To this end, the classroom teacher should consider the child's level of comprehension or understanding and use complete sentences when explaining a topic or concept. The teacher can also prominently introduce key words associated with the lesson or topic or use a variety of sentence forms when teaching a lesson or concept.

For older children, there are specific tasks that can be used in the classroom that combine learning science and new vocabulary terms that are essential to developing sentence production. Conezio and French (2002) describe one example of a task that fulfills this goal.

> Back in February, Mrs. O'Shea's preschool children had explored the concept of light and shadows. They collected many types of materials to see which ones would create a shadow in the bright light and which ones the light would just pass through. After several days of experimentation, they realized that while opaque materials create shadows and transparent materials allow light to pass through easily, there are some things that don't fit either category. These materials allow some light to pass through (although not as much as window glass) and they cause very light shadows.
>
> Later in the school year, a visitor to the classroom was present during snack time when the children were trying new clear strawberry-flavored Jell-O with stars and moon shapes in it. The visitor overheard the following conversation among the 4-year-olds: "It's transparent!" remarked one little girl with surprise. "No, it's translucent," countered another girl. "Why do you say it's translucent?" asked Mrs. O'Shea. "Because you can only see through it a little," the girl responded. (p. 12)

This strategy presented children with two concepts (ideas and perceptions of entities or things in the world). Teaching the concept of *transparency* consisted of varied experiences with a variety of materials that illustrated different degrees of transparency. New concepts are more effectively learned if vocabulary is associated with experiences that are being described.

We have reviewed two theories of language acquisition, the environmental and innate theories. In the first, language acquisition emerges from experience and interaction with the environment. In the second, innate skills provide the foundation for language acquisition and learning. Next, we examine emergentism, according to which the environment and innate skills are essential for language acquisition and development.

EMERGENTISM: INNATE SKILLS AND ENVIRONMENTAL FACTORS

Many investigators argue that it is only reasonable to conclude that genes (innate skills) and the environment interact to determine outcomes in children's language and cognitive development (Bates et al., 1998). These investigators reject the theory that innate skills and context interaction alone are responsible for language development. Instead, cognitive skills (e.g., attention preference and working memory) are essential for processing environmental activities and language input (Bates & Elman, 1996; Seidenberg & Elman, 1999). In summary, emergentists argue that language develops from an interaction between a child's cognitive structures and the environment.

Emergent Effects

Emergentism ascribes language learning to the "emergent" effect of cognitive, social-pragmatic, and attentional factors. The cognitive basis for language learning consists of the child's innate learning skills. The social-pragmatic factors consist of sensitivity to pointing and eye gaze, which also play a significant role in early word learning. Attentional factors consist of the child's ability to connect sight and sound, leading to the ability to connect words with objects. Language input plays the most essential role in language learning, with cues to learning based on the rhythm, stress, and intonational patterns of spoken language. In the guided distributional learning theory, children's language learning is "guided" by their bias to attend to certain environmental cues.

Children attend to particular environmental inputs or information at different stages of development (Hirsh-Pasek & Golinkoff, 1997). For example, infants are sensitive to the prosodic aspects of language (e.g., intonation, rhythm, and the duration of sounds). **Intonation** is produced by pitch changes in a speaker's voice, associated with moving upward or downward. **Rhythm** refers to the tendency for certain syllables to be given more emphasis in words, along with equal interval in speakers' utterances (e.g., "I *know* you *love* cookies") (Borden, Harris, & Raphael, 2003). **Duration** refers to length, with greater length of syllables in words that are given more emphasis (e.g., baNANa). Children's sensitivity to these prosodic cues in speech allows them to notice repeated sequences of sounds, such as the sounds in their name.

Children are also able to distinguish sounds in their own language from sounds in another language as early as 9 months (Jusczyk, Friederici, Wessels, Svenkerud, & Jusczyk, 1993). This early bias or sensitivity represents the beginning of children's awareness of spoken language. For example, children become sensitive to syntax (sentence structure) by 2 years of age. These environmental cues may contribute to language development in two different ways: (a) as a trigger to children's innate skills or (b) as an influence on the structure of the brain to support language development (Karmiloff-Smith, 1992). In fact, listening to lengthy speech utterances from adults in the environment is an important factor in school readiness and in later school success.

EMERGENTISM: STRATEGIES FOR LANGUAGE DEVELOPMENT

The strategies connected with both the environmental and nativist theories of language development are appropriate for supporting children's language development, given that both innate skills and environmental factors play a role in their development. Emergentism is a theory that posits that the mind functions in a similar manner to neural networks in the brain (Abbeduto & Boudreau, 2004). According to this theory, language develops through associations among nodes. A node represents input (i.e., information established by the language learner). Each node has a link to output (i.e., expressive production or auditory comprehension). The more frequent occurrence of a particular feature of spoken language results in greater strength of a node and the association among nodes.

One example of this is young children's productions of past-tense irregular verbs (e.g., *eat/ate, throw/threw, blow/blew,* and *go/went*). Instead of the irregular form (e.g., *ate*), children produce these verbs as though they are past-tense regular verbs (e.g., *talk/talked, walk/walked, date/dated,* and *bait/baited*) in sentences like "I *eated* the cookie." Consistent with predictions of the emergentism theory, children (incorrectly) produce the past-tense form heard more frequently in spoken language—the regular past-tense form (e.g., *walked*). In other words, children have better learned the regular past-tense form rule (e.g., add *-ed*) because of the greater strength of these forms when compared to the less frequent experience with the irregular past tense. Thus, the use of words such as *eated* and *throwed* reflects learning features that occur more frequently in the environment.

Within the classroom, there are certain strategies that can enhance a child's language development: repetition and practice for better learning and meaningful exchanges involving topics of interest to the child (Abbeduto & Boudreau, 2004, p. 187).

Children need to develop the ability to understand the actions, feelings, thoughts, and motivations of people or characters in stories. This ability is called a theory of mind. In the next section, we discuss the importance of theory of mind for all aspects of communication.

THE THEORY OF MIND

Research on communicative disorders has led to an understanding that pragmatic skills are associated with social cognition (Turkstra, 2007), such as a theory of mind. **Theory of mind** describes the ability to understand someone else's mind in terms of mental states, such as desires, beliefs, and knowledge (Miller, 2006). Theory of mind also describes the ability to predict how someone will act, to explain why this person acted in a certain manner, and to describe the action in psychological terms with mental state verbs (de Villiers & de Villiers, 2003). Examples of mental state verbs consist of *think, know, believe,* and other terms that refer to someone's mind.

Children's theory of mind understanding develops through exposure to social discourse about these mental state concepts (Astington, 1990). A failure to develop a theory of mind is a factor in certain disorders, such as autism (Baron-Cohen, 1996). Wimmer and Perner (1983) began experiments that examined young children's ability to understand false beliefs, as shown in the following task described by Lantz (2002).

> A character named Maxi places a chocolate candy in a kitchen cabinet and leaves the room to play. While he is playing, his mother enters the room and moves his candy into a drawer, without Maxi witnessing this switch. Next, the investigator asks the child participants where Maxi will search for his candy, in the cabinet or the drawer. (p. 20)

When asked what Maxi would "think," children with autism answered that Maxi would search for the candy in the drawer. This is because at least 80% of children with autism are unable to understand Maxi's perspective (Baron-Cohen, 1993). In other words, children with autism answer that Maxi will look for the candy in the drawer, where his mother, without Maxi's knowledge, has placed the candy. Presented with false belief tasks, 4-year-olds are able to accurately perform well above chance (Wellman, Cross, & Watson, 2001), while autistic children face difficulties with reading other people's minds in terms of beliefs and emotions throughout their lifetime.

Language

Language plays an essential role in the development of theory of mind. The role of theory of mind is essential for understanding and performance in narratives (Guajardo & Watson, 2002) and conversations (Astington, 1990). Narratives allow children to develop knowledge about feelings, beliefs, and thoughts while providing them with the language to discuss these concepts. Narrative skills are necessary for understanding characters, prediction, and motivations. The ability to go beyond the actions inherent in a narrative involves understanding the main point of a story, not the scope of action (Bruner, 1986). Conversation plays a role in theory of mind, given that adults frequently converse about beliefs and mental states while using mental state terms such as *think, know,* and *believe.* Competent communicative skills also require awareness of others' thoughts, feelings, and knowledge for successful interaction (Miller, 2006).

Social Cognition

The beginnings of social cognition emerge prior to language acquisition (Lohmann & Tomasello, 2003), with shared eye gaze and attempts to gain attention by pointing. These early skills provide the foundation for developing a theory of mind. Toddlers first begin to use mental state terms in pretend play (Miller, 2006), with terms such as *know, think, mean, forget,* and *guess* appearing between the ages of 28 and 32 months (Shatz, Wellman, & Silber, 1983). While children may produce these mental verbs, they do not truly represent mental state terms at this age. The true use of the mental state terms *think* and *know* does not appear until around 31 months (Bartsch & Wellman, 1995). There is general agreement that the ability to understand someone else's mind may not emerge until 4 years of age (Feinfeld, Lee, Flavell, Green, & Flavell, 1999; Hale & Tager-Flusberg, 2003; Miller, 2006; Schult, 2002; Wellman, 1990).

The Development of Theory of Mind

One view on the development of theory of mind derives from Piaget's (1929) theory of schemas. According to this theory, children develop theory of mind through reasoning, with their psychological structures (schema or schemata) providing the ability to process information and develop theories based on their observations. Children use data from the world, in the form of behaviors and events, and form hypotheses about these actions. They are able to develop and change their theories rapidly within the space of a few months (Gopnik & Meltzoff, 1998).

For example, when an object shown to a child is hidden under a cover, the child looks for it where it was hidden. If the object is moved from this spot and hidden under another cover, very young children continue to search under the first cover. At 8 to 10 months, children no longer search for an object that was in the first cover. Instead, they search under the correct cover. Gopnik and Meltzoff (1998) argue that children now have a new sophisticated object theory of actions and consequences (p. 138).

In addition, they also understand that they must have contact with objects to make them move (rather than just waving their arms to make the object move). Children must construct new theories in response to observed behaviors in social/communicative interactions (Gopnik & Wellman, 1992). When children understand that contact with the object makes it move, they develop a new theory that explains this action.

Another explanation of the development of theory of mind derives from a **socio-interactional** explanation (Bruner, 1990). In this theory, children's development of concepts takes place when the environment interacts with internal factors to foster cognitive development. This occurs because social and communicative interaction provides experience with others' mental states. Participation in communicative interaction provides children with exposure to mental states (e.g., sadness, anger, happiness, and other types of mental states) and mental terms (e.g., "He is *sad* because he fell down"), while providing examples of the behaviors that correlate with these terms (e.g., seeing someone fall). Thus, communicative interaction is a factor in both explanations of theory of mind development—Piaget's schemas and social interaction.

THEORY OF MIND: STRATEGIES FOR LANGUAGE DEVELOPMENT

The strategies associated with theory of mind are those that challenge children's independent thought-processing and problem-solving skills. Children need to develop the independent ability to use their problem-solving skills when faced with issues or problems that are new to them. Children's problem-solving abilities are enhanced when given the opportunity to experiment with problems in free play contexts (Thompson & Hixson, 1984, p. 175). The play context also allows a child to experiment with solutions to problems in less risky situations (Bruner, 1972).

For example, a child may have trouble putting a puzzle piece in place. If an adult helps by putting the piece in place, he or she will prevent independent problem solving. Giving the child time to experiment allows learning. If difficulties persist, a gentle nudge to the puzzle piece remains the best way to encourage independent problem solving. Presenting older children with new vocabulary items (e.g., *marsupial*) can develop their independent problem-solving skills by asking them to search the web for definitions and examples, list characteristics of this term, and make a picture/find dictionary illustrations of marsupials.

Pushing and standing on something to reach a desired item is an example of early problem-solving skills.

Epstein (2003, pp. 4–7) also provides classroom strategies for developing children's independent thinking and problem-solving skills. These strategies consist of asking open-ended WH questions (e.g., *who, what, where, when, why,* and *how*), encouraging elaboration (e.g., "Tell me more"), and asking children to write/draw to express their ideas. Strategies that classroom teachers can use to integrate theory of mind into lessons consist of presenting children with stories that portray a variety of emotions to help children understand a character's state of mind (e.g., happy, sad, scared), examples of false beliefs (e.g., that something in an egg basket is not necessarily an egg), and using an abundance of mental terms.

An example of a false beliefs task is found in the study of 3- to 5-year-old children's theory of mind skills (Jenkins & Astington, 1996). First, children were shown a box labeled "bandages" and asked what was in the box. All children answered, "Bandages." To their surprise, when the box was opened, it contained pencils. Next, children were asked, "What would children who had never seen the box think was in the box?" Children at age 3 answered, "Pencils," while 4- to 5-year-olds answered, with a grin, "Bandages." Thus, by 4 to 5 years of age, children have developed a theory of mind that allows them to understand another person's beliefs or thoughts.

The mental state terms that classroom teachers can incorporate into lessons consist of *know, remember, bet/reckon, wish, think, guess, hope, mean, pretend, believe, forget, dream, wonder,* and *understand* (Shatz, Wellman, & Silber, 1983). These are terms that help children understand the state of mind of characters in stories. Consequently, they are better able to understand their actions and motivations.

CASE STUDY REVISITED

The case study presented at the start of the chapter gives us insight into children's early language development for learning labels for entities and events in the environment. This example shows the role of the environment in providing input for learning through experience with entities (things) in that environment in addition to the child's innate skills to develop a hypothesis or a theory for labeling this animal. Looking at his teacher while producing the label "dog" is also an example of very early problem-solving skills for obtaining the label for new entities.

Case Study Revisited: How children learn the names of things in the world

Billy's first experience with animals consisted of seeing a neighbor's dog, along with learning that this entity was linked with the label "dog." A subsequent encounter with a cow, viewed while visiting the children's zoo with his class, presented him with another entity that possessed similar characteristics. The production of "dog" for the cow shows that he had internalized or stored a representation (image) of an animal that shared visual characteristics for a similar entity. Thus, he had created a schema of the animal dog. This showed that he had perceived a similarity between dogs and other animals with similar features. This example shows that

- Billy is learning about the world through exposure to a wide set of experiences,

- he is equipped with the ability to draw on his stored representations of known entities or things to identify new entities, and

- looking at his teacher to signal a request for help—just in case the label is incorrect— reflects an early problem-solving strategy.

SUMMARY

The goal of this chapter was to provide classroom teachers with an understanding of the theories that explain language acquisition. These theories help us better understand both typical development and atypical development, along with providing strategies to help children who may need more focused and specific guidance. It was concluded that both innate skills and environmental input play a role in the development of language given that innate abilities are reflected in children's rapid learning of language and the necessary materials (e.g., people, entities, and events) for language development are found in the external environment.

It is also important that children possess the ability to understand other individuals' meanings and feelings, along with the motivations associated with their behaviors. Theory of mind describes the ability to step into another person's shoes or to understand another person's mind. Theory of mind is also essential for understanding the motivations that explain the behaviors of other individuals or characters in stories.

Now that you have learned the theories that underlie typical language development, you will explore the components of language and associated disorders in Chapter 3. The next chapter highlights key terms used in educational evaluations from learning-disabilities evaluators and speech-language pathologists, while also providing strategies for identifying children with communication disorders.

KEY WORDS

Accommodation

Assimilation

Cognition

Communication

Competition model

Continuity

Deep structure

Duration

Egocentric speech

Emergentism

Environment

Environmental

Equilibrium

Expansions

Guided distributional learning

Innate

Innateness theory

Input

Intonation

Language acquisition device (LAD)

Models

Narrative

Object permanence

Overextensions

Parallel distributed processing

Phrase structure rules

Pragmatics

Private speech

Prospective mental development

Recasts

Retrospective mental development

Rhythm

Scaffolds

Schema

Social interaction

Socio-interactional

Speech acts

Surface structure

Theory of mind

Transformational rules

Zone of proximal development

STUDY QUESTIONS

1. Explain the role of mental state verbs in language development. Describe how you would include mental state verbs in a story of your choice.

2. How would you apply Vygotsky's theory of language development to help a child independently solve a problem in the classroom? At what point might you provide support?

3. How would you explain why a child is using the wrong word to label an animal (e.g., *dog* for *horse*)? What theory best explains this error? How would you correct this error?

4. Explain the importance of environmental factors on a child's language development. What factors are most important? How would you incorporate these factors in the classroom?

5. Explain how you would use scaffolds to help a child express his or her needs to interact with other children in the classroom.

PROJECTS

1. Observe children playing. Focus on describing their sentence productions to determine if there are any examples of unique productions that show the creativity of children's innate language skills. In your observation, determine to what extent age, gender, and cultural diversity impact children's play.

2. Create a series of pictures that illustrate behaviors that require a description of an individual's intention or meaning to investigate the theory of mind (e.g., a picture that shows someone hiding a present). Present these pictures to children of various ages to determine the age that mental terms (e.g., *thinks, wants, believes*) emerge.

3. Engage young children of various ages in conversation and observe the conversation rules (e.g., turn taking, initiation, topic maintenance, and topic elaboration) that are present at different ages. In turn, engage your peers in conversation and note if there are any violations of these rules, along with explaining why violations may occur.

STUDENT STUDY SITE

Visit the Student Study Site at **www.sagepub.com/levey** for these additional learning tools:

- Video Links
- Self Quizzes
- E-Flashcards
- Sample Forms and Assessment Tools
- Recommended Readings
- Web Resources

SUGGESTIONS FOR FURTHER READING

Crystal, D. (2003). *A dictionary of linguistics and phonetics*. Hoboken, NJ: Wiley.

Fromkin, V. A. (2001). *Linguistics: An introduction to linguistic theory*. London: Blackwell.

Ohio State University Department of Linguistics. (2007). *Language files: Materials for an introduction to language and linguistics*. Columbus: Ohio State University Press.

Parker, F., & Riley, K. (2009). *Linguistics for non-linguists: A primer with exercises* (5th ed.). Boston: Allyn & Bacon.

Pinker, S. (1995). *The language instinct: How the mind creates language*. New York: HarperCollins.

C H A P T E R   3

Typical and Atypical Language Development

Sandra Levey

CASE STUDY: The use of language in social interaction

Tommy, a 3-year-old native English speaker, has just entered preschool. Ms. Benjamin, his teacher, noted that he seems to have poor social skills, shown in problems initiating interaction with the other children in the class. Ms. Benjamin decides to spend some time observing and taking notes during play periods and table time. Her observations show that Tommy has difficulty entering playgroups, sometimes standing alone and watching the other children play. Tommy's language skills are consistent with those of his peers, but he does not seem to use his language skills to interact with the other children or to ask them to let him enter a playgroup.

What are the main strategies that you might use to support Tommy's interaction with other children? On what information and experiences did you base your answer?

INTRODUCTION

This chapter provides examples of the language factors that play a role in classrooms. The purpose is to provide definitions and examples of linguistic/language factors so that the classroom teacher has a solid grasp of the components that underlie language use and understanding. The goal is also to introduce key terms identified as components of language and explain their meanings as a foundation for material presented in other chapters in this textbook.

This chapter also presents a brief discussion of *disorders* versus *differences,* differences being associated with speakers who are learning English as a second language, children from culturally and linguistically different backgrounds, and factors that may be connected to gender. The following section addresses form, content, and use—the basic components of language skills.

THE COMPONENTS OF LANGUAGE

Language development components can be divided into three main categories: form, content, and use. Each category describes an essential factor in development.

Form: Phonology, Morphology, and Syntax

The form category of language development contains the concepts of phonology, morphology, and syntax. Phonology describes the rules that govern the sequencing of speech sounds, such as the rules for combining sounds to form words (e.g., *m + a + t = mat*). Morphology involves the rules that govern the structure of words, such as adding plurals, possessives, and past-tense endings (e.g., *cat + s = cats*; *Dad + 's = Dad's*; *run + ning = running*). Syntax defines the rules that govern the structure of sentences (e.g., subject + verb + object = *I + eat + candy*).

Content (Semantics)

The content, or semantics, category involves rules for meaning in words, sentences, narratives, and conversation.

Use (Pragmatics)

The use, or pragmatics, category involves rules for conversation, such as eye contact and turn taking as sender and receiver.

Now that you have been given a brief description of the three components of language (form, content, and use), the next section further explains the role these factors play in learning. We begin with a more detailed discussion of **form**, which comprises phonology, morphology, and syntax.

FORM

Phonology

Phonology is an important component of language development, given that children's understanding of the sounds in words provides the support for learning words and, over time, the ability to combine words to form sentences and longer utterances. The term *phonology* describes the rules that govern the sequencing of speech sounds, such as the rules for combining sounds to form words (e.g., *d + o + g = dog*).

Articulation is the ability to form these words. **Articulation** describes the motor movements of the tongue, lip, soft palate, and jaw (articulators) used to produce these speech sounds. Thus, movement of the articulators results in the production of sounds, while phonology involves the rules for combining these sounds to form words. (See Chapter 5 for a complete discussion of articulation.)

Phonemes are the abstract representation of speech sounds (phones), with phonemes of a language indicated by slashes (e.g., /b/), as found in the word *bat* /bᵃt/. See Table 3.1 (page 40) for examples of consonant phonemes and Table 3.2 (page 41) for examples of vowel phonemes.

The classroom teacher can improve children's language skills by organizing the classroom to develop increased social interaction.

Orthography

Orthography describes the symbols (alphabet letters termed *graphemes*) of a written language. Children must learn the alphabetic codes so that, later, they can concentrate on meaning when reading (Owens, 2008). There is not a strict one-to-one correlation between orthography and the phonemes or sounds of a language. For example, the phoneme /f/ is the first sound in the words *fast* and *physician* and the last sound in the word *laugh*.

There is also a lack of correspondence between symbol and sound for vowels. For example, the grapheme *a* is produced as the phoneme /æ/ in the word *cat,* the phoneme /ɔ/ in the word *paw,* and the phoneme /e/ in the word *date.* Difficulty in phoneme-grapheme correlation may also result from the similarity of certain sounds. For example, the vowels found in the words *pawed (/ɔ/)* and *pod (/ɑ/)* have been found to present discrimination difficulty for native English-speaking children (Levey & Schwartz, 2002) and, frequently, for speakers of other languages in which these phonemes are absent (Levey, 2004).

Phonological Awareness

Phonological awareness is the knowledge that words are composed of sounds (phonemes). There are several expressions used interchangeably to refer to phonological awareness, such as **phonological processing**, phonemic awareness, phonological sensitivity, and phonetic awareness (Justice & Schuele, 2004). There are, however, meaningful differences between the phenomena described by these terms. There is a close relationship between the definitions of the terms *phonological awareness* and *phonological sensitivity*: Both terms describe the ability to break down words into basic units—syllable,

(Text continued on page 41)

Table 3.1	Consonant Phonemes: Examples of Sounds in Words With Phonemes in Initial, Medial, and Final Position

		Word	
Phoneme	Initial	Medial	Final
/p/	pea	apple	tap
/b/	be	table	tab
/t/	tea	attic	pat
/d/	date	ladder	pad
/k/	cat	actor	pack
/g/	game	tiger	leg
/m/	map	drummer	sum
/n/	no	tunnel	pan
/ŋ/		hanger	rang
/f/	fat	taffy	half
/v/	vine	silver	leave
/s/	see	passive	bus
/z/	zoo	buzzard	buzz
/θ/	thumb	bathtub	bath
/ð/	them	father	bathe
/ʃ/	shoe	pressure	push
/ʒ/		treasure	beige
/l/	lip	balloon	tall
/r/	red	farmer	far
/j/	you	tri(_)al	
/w/	wheel		
/ʧ/	chair	teacher	peach
/dʒ/	jar	badger	ledge

NOTE: The consonant phoneme /ʒ/ occurs only in medial and final position in words, while the phoneme /w/ occurs only in initial position in words.

Table 3.2	Vowel Phonemes: Examples of Sounds in Words
Phoneme	
/i/	sk<u>i</u>, h<u>e</u>, b<u>ea</u>t
/ɪ/	s<u>i</u>t, b<u>i</u>t, m<u>i</u>ddle
/e/	s<u>ay</u>, d<u>ay</u>
/ɛ/	l<u>e</u>t, f<u>ea</u>ther
/æ/	h<u>a</u>t, l<u>a</u>dder
/u/	y<u>ou</u>, tw<u>o</u>, br<u>ew</u>, S<u>ue</u>
/o/	g<u>o</u>, s<u>ew</u>, h<u>o</u>se
/ʊ/	b<u>oo</u>k, p<u>u</u>sh
/ɔ/	l<u>aw</u>, p<u>aw</u>
/ɑ/	f<u>a</u>ther, b<u>o</u>ther, b<u>o</u>ttle
/ʌ/	c<u>u</u>p, d<u>u</u>ck, ab<u>o</u>ve
/ə/	<u>a</u>lone, <u>a</u>bove
/ɝ/	b<u>ir</u>d, f<u>ur</u>, f<u>ur</u>ther
/ɚ/	broth<u>er</u>, farm<u>er</u>, furth<u>er</u>
/aɚ/	f<u>ar</u>, c<u>ar</u>
/eɚ/	b<u>ear</u>, f<u>air</u>
/ɔɚ/	<u>or</u>, c<u>ore</u>
/ɔɪ/	b<u>oy</u>, t<u>oy</u>
/aɪ/	sk<u>y</u>, p<u>ie</u>
/aʊ/	c<u>ow</u>, b<u>ough</u>

NOTE: The vowels /ɝ/ and /ʌ/ occur in stressed syllables (those with higher frequency, intensity, and duration), while their counterparts (/ɚ/ and /ə/) occur in unstressed syllables.

onset-rime, and phonemes. But **phoneme awareness,** or **phonemic awareness,** has a more specific meaning, referring to the awareness of phonemes—that words are composed of individual sounds and that individual sounds combine to form words (Torgesen, Al Otaiba, & Grek, 2005).

Syllables

The ability to break words down into units requires the awareness of syllables, **onset-rime**, and phonemes. Each **syllable** contains a vowel sound, but keep in mind that certain written consonant symbols are actually produced as vowels (e.g., *baby* [/bebi/], with *y* produced as the vowel sound "ee" and the phoneme /i/) (Treiman, 1993).

Word Meaning

Phonemes act to distinguish word meaning. An example is the word *dog,* composed of the alphabet letters *d, o,* and *g*. Each alphabet letter is associated with a sound, with sounds combined to form the word *dog*. Replacing the initial sound /d/ with /l/ results in the word *log*. The process that describes a child's ability to form an association between alphabet letters and spoken sounds is the phoneme-grapheme (sound-letter) correlation, also frequently termed the **alphabetic principle**. The ability to recognize the correlation between phonemes and graphemes allows a child to develop basic reading skills, while also providing the ability to "sound out" new words in more complex reading tasks.

Phonological Processing

Phonological processing refers to the awareness of phonological information in spoken and written language (Wagner & Torgesen, 1987). Phonological processing is a cognitive process that involves the recognition, comprehension, storage, retrieval, and production of linguistic codes, along with the ability to manipulate the sounds in words (Troia, 2004, p. 271). Gillon (2004) presents the following tasks that characterize phonological manipulation:

- Alliteration: recognition of the same (or different) sounds in words; for example, "Which word does not belong: *ball, bat, dog*?"

- Phoneme matching: recognition of the sound that is the same in other words; for example, "Which word doesn't begin with the same sound as *bat*: *ball, bag, kite*?"

- Phoneme isolation: for example, "What is the first sound in the word *bat*?"

- Phoneme completion: for example, "Finish the word that matches this picture (of a cat): *ca_*"

- Phoneme deletion: for example, "Say the word *stop* without the /s/"

- Phoneme segmentation with words (or novel words): for example, "How many sounds are there in the word *cat* (or *gub*)?"

- Phoneme reversal: for example, "Can you say *bus* backward (*sub*)?"

- Phoneme manipulation: for example, "How would you say the word *top* if we changed the /ɑ/ to /ɪ/ (*top* to *tip*)?"

Phonological awareness is one of the primary factors that predict and support reading skills. Perception involves the ability to perceive and discriminate between sounds, especially sounds similar to one another (e.g., /f/ versus /v/ [*fan* vs. *van*] and *ah* /ɑ/ versus *aw* /ɔ/ [*pod* vs. *pawed*]). The discrimination of sounds provides children with the ability to distinguish visual differences between written letters (Catts & Kamhi, 2005; Levey & Schwartz, 2002), along with the ability to represent the different sounds. Roth and Troia (2006) propose a hierarchy of difficulty in the development of phonological abilities, shown in Table 3.3.

Table 3.3   The Development of Phonological Awareness

Phonological Skill	Recognition Abilities	Example
Rhyming	Sameness or difference in sound contrasts	*bat-mat*
Alliteration	Words beginning with the same onset	*big bad bears*
		eight apes ate
Blending	Synthesize sounds, syllables, and words	*f - i - s - h = fish*
Segmentation	Breaking sounds into smaller units	*fish = f - i - s - h*
Manipulation	Adding sounds to form a word	*at + b = bat*
	Deleting sounds to form new words	*smile – s = mile*
	Substituting syllables or sounds	*bug → bun*

Phonological Processes

A child's early production of words shows the presence of **phonological processes**, which are variations in the production of sounds, syllables, and words (see Table 3.4).

One example of a phonological process is unstressed syllable deletion, or the omission of unstressed syllables (e.g., "baNAna" produced as "Nana"). Stress plays an important role in learning new words (Levey & Schwartz, 2002). For example, unstressed syllables contain vowels produced with lower intensity (loudness), duration (length), and frequency (higher pitch) than vowels in stressed syllables, produced with higher intensity, greater length, and higher frequency. An example of stressed and unstressed syllables exists in the word *banana:* ba- (unstressed) -na (stressed) -na (unstressed), with young children producing this word as "nana."

A second example of a young child's production of words is consonant cluster reduction. This process involves the production of only one consonant in words that contain two consonants, such as *stop, stay,* and *school.* These words may be produced as "top," "tay," and "cool." The phonological process that leads to substitution of one sound for another includes fronting, the production of a sound that should be produced in a more posterior position in the oral cavity (e.g., /k/) with a target sound produced in a more anterior position in the oral cavity (e.g., /t/). This process occurs in the production of the word *tea* rather than the target word *key.* Most of these processes disappear by 3 years of age or earlier.

The ability to associate spoken sounds and alphabet letters depends on the ability to perceive differences between sounds (auditory discrimination). Children must be able to internalize and store the difference in sounds so that they may later use this information to identify words. The persistence of phonological processes may affect reading skills, especially the ability to associate sounds and alphabet letters.

If a child is an English language learner, this auditory discrimination process may become even more complicated if the target sound or sounds are absent from the child's native language. For example, there are English vowels that are not found in the Spanish language (e.g., *pot*, *law*, *pet*, *pat*, *put*, *book*, and *pit*). Consequently, second-language learners who have none of these vowels in their first language must learn these new sounds, along with differentiating them from their first language.

Table 3.4 Phonological Processes

Phonological Skill	Adult Target	Child's Production
Unstressed syllable deletion	banana	"nanuh"
Consonant cluster reduction	stop	"top"
Final consonant deletion	bus	"bu"
Syllable repetition	daddy	"dada"
Fronting	top	"cop"
Backing	cop	"top"
Assimilation	dog	"gog"
	cat	"cac"

NOTE: Most phonological processes disappear by age 3, except for consonant cluster reduction, which generally disappears later.

Morphology

Morphology involves the rules that govern the structure of words, such as adding plurals (e.g., *dog* + *s* = *dogs*). A morpheme is a minimal element that is associated with meaning in words. For example, the word *dogs* can be broken down into two morphemes: a root form (*dog*) and a plural morpheme (*-s*). If the word *dog* were broken down any more, meaning would be lost. Morphological development consists of a child's awareness of the structure of words and the acquisition of morphemes over time (described further in Chapter 8).

There is also a sequence in a child's awareness of the components of words. Children first become aware of whole words (*banana*), then syllables in words (ba-na-na), and then the segments of the words (b-a-n-a-n-a). It is necessary to identify these skills to determine if a child may need assistance in acquiring language more broadly, along with acquiring the awareness of individual words, sounds, and structures.

Bernstein and Levey (2009) explain that the morphemes in words take the form of articles (e.g., *a, the*), prepositions (e.g., *in, on*), pronouns (e.g., *I, he*), and auxiliary verbs (e.g., *is, are*). Inflectional morphemes take the form of the plural (*-s*) attached to nouns to indicate plurality, the possessive (*'s*) to indicate possession, the present progressive (*-ing*) attached to verb stems to indicate present and ongoing action, and the past-tense marker (*-ed*) to indicate prior activity. The inclusion of these forms acts to expand young children's utterances, making utterances more adultlike and less telegramatic. They progress from producing utterances such as "More milk" at 12 to 18 months to utterances such as "I want more chocolate milk" at 24 to 36 months.

Syntax

Syntax defines the rules that govern the structure of sentences (e.g., subject + verb + object = "baby eat cookie"). Basic sentences are composed of subject + verb + object noun (e.g., "Baby drinks milk"). Nouns label a person, place, or thing (e.g., *mother, dog, home, book*), and verbs label an action (e.g., *run, cry, eat*). More complex sentences can contain a prepositional phrase, which acts to label a place, location, or the position of an object in space (e.g., *in, on, under, between*). An adverb acts to specify a verb's action (e.g., *quickly*), while an adjective identifies the attributes or characteristics of nouns (e.g., *red*). Finally, a pronoun can substitute for a noun (e.g., *he, she,* and *himself*).

Two-word utterances, produced at 18 months of age, emerge from children's early words, produced at about 12 months of age. At this point, syntactic development begins. Examples of sentences at this stage consist of "More cookie" and "No bed." Syntactic development occurs with an increase in the length and complexity of sentences over time, based on the inclusion of grammatical morphemes and the development of vocabulary skills, as seen in Table 3.5. Initially, children develop an understanding of sentences that follow the word order subject-verb-object (SVO), such as "Daddy (S) is eating (V) cookies (O)." Typical development is based on the understanding of more complex sentence structures over time, such as passive sentence structure (OVS; e.g., "The cookies (O) were eaten (V) by Daddy (N)").

Children's syntactic abilities begin with combining two words, with later abilities characterized by the ability to understand and construct complex sentences that contain embedded clauses (e.g., "The man, who drives our bus, is a friend of my dad"). Written language requires more complex syntactic skills, and by 12 to 13 years of age, children's written syntax surpasses their syntax in spoken language (Gillam & Johnston, 1992). (Chapter 8 provides a complete discussion of syntactic development for preschool children, and Chapter 9 addresses development for older children.)

The following section describes the component of language that conveys meaning. In this case, meaning is developed through interaction and experience as the child is exposed to spoken language that labels or describes people, things, and events in the world.

CONTENT/SEMANTICS

Semantic (**content**) rules govern the meanings of words and how these words relate to people, places, and things in the environment (e.g., the word *dog* labels the entity *dog*). Semantic development consists of the awareness of word meaning, while children later become aware of broader definitions of words. For example, the word *block* is first learned

Table 3.5 Semantic Relations

Semantic Relation	Example	Environmental Case
Agent + Action	Daddy throw	Daddy is throwing the ball
Entity + Attribute	Doggy bad	The dog is chewing a shoe
Action + Affected	Throw ball	Throwing a ball
Possessor + Possession	Mommy shoe	Pointing to his/her mother's shoe
Entity + Location	Doggy bed	Pointing to the dog's bed
Recurrence	More cookie	Asking for another cookie
Negation	No bed	Rejecting going to bed

as the label for a toy (e.g., toy block), later as a place (e.g., going around the block), a verb (e.g., blocking the hall), and later as a metaphor (e.g., mental block). Word production gives way to word combinations, which are termed semantic relations (meaning relations). See Table 3.5 for examples of these relations.

Semantic knowledge involves knowledge of words and knowledge of the world (Owens, 2008). Word knowledge, as described above, is the knowledge of the labels for entities (e.g., people and animals), actions (e.g., *run* and *eat*), and concepts (e.g., feelings, space, time). Word knowledge involves information learned from the environment. Thus, it develops from interaction with the environment (such as a child's learning the word *dog*).

Children initially learn the identity of entities through their visual (seeing) and auditory (hearing) perception. This is why young children call all four-legged animals "doggie." We call this **overgeneralization**, described in detail in Chapter 7. A child's experiences with the world contribute to his or her semantic language abilities, such as exposure to spoken language and literacy artifacts (e.g., books, pictures, and television). This exposure is essential to children's language development.

Beginning at birth, children perceive things, people, and actions in the environment. Thus, they begin to develop inferences (assumptions) about these entities at a very early age. For example, overgeneralization disappears when children learn that things, such as dogs, differ from other things, such as cows, based on differences in their features. School-aged children develop an understanding of **figurative language**, when words are used in an abstract (conceptual) rather than literal (factual) sense (e.g., *mental block* vs. *alphabet block*). This knowledge is essential when children enter higher grades that use more abstract reading materials.

Children's semantic abilities begin with words associated with meaning. Over time, semantic abilities develop for more abstract tasks, such as learning that words can have multiple meanings (e.g., *block*) and that language can be used to create imaginative meanings, as in figurative language (e.g., "Eyes like a hawk"). Children's semantic development receives a rich discussion in Chapter 7.

The previous sections described the first two components of language, referred to as form and content. The following section introduces the language component that describes the use of language in interaction, known as pragmatics.

USE/PRAGMATICS

Pragmatic (use) rules are those that involve the use of language in interaction (e.g., eye contact, turn taking, and maintaining the topic under discussion). These skills develop over time, with an increase in a child's awareness of appropriate means of interaction and the development of language skills. Young children ask for a cookie by saying "Gimme cookie" or "Wanna cookie." An older child requests a cookie in a more polite manner, asking, "Can I have a cookie?" This type of utterance depends on learning a set of words called **modal auxiliaries**, used to create polite forms (e.g., "*Can* I have a cookie?" "*Could* I have a cookie?" or "*Should* I take a cookie?"). In the middle school years, children employ more indirect methods to obtain goals, producing sentences such as "Those cookies sure smell good." Pragmatics in the classroom involve children using language to interact with peers and adults. For example, they may use requests to engage in play with other children or enter a playgroup already in session (e.g., "Can I play, too?").

Pragmatics also pertains to learning the rules of conversation: eye contact, turn taking, repairing errors or misperceptions, and maintaining a topic. These skills are refined over time. A 3-year-old may be able to sustain a topic about 20% of the time but will be able to contribute more information to a conversation if he or she introduces the topic. Experience and models are the vehicles for learning the rules of conversation. Consequently, young children are initially unaware of these principles. This is why early requests (e.g., "Gimme a cookie") evolve into more rule-governed requests produced by older children (e.g., "Can I have a cookie?"). Pragmatic abilities develop over time and through interaction with adults and more advanced (and pragmatically appropriate) peers.

We have reviewed the three components of language: form, content, and use. The next section describes *cognition,* defined as the ability to develop concepts about events and entities that the child encounters.

COGNITION

Cognition also plays an essential role in the development of language abilities, based on thought processing, memory, attention, and discrimination. Cognition involves the ability to form concepts (ideas) about objects and events in the world, while language involves the ability to describe these objects and events.

Thought processing involves the ability to cope with information in terms of solving complex tasks without the need for physical trial and error manipulation. Memory involves the ability to store information. Attention involves the ability to focus on a certain feature of the environment or task while not being distracted by irrelevant or less important features in the environment. Discrimination is the recognition of differences between or among items.

Cognition consists of the underlying thought processes that support learning. There is a connection between cognition and language that provides support for children's learning skills in the classroom. Consequently, cognition plays an important role in classroom learning.

Working memory helps children understand, remember, and complete assignments.

Thought Processing

Thought processing is also termed *language of thought,* defined as the ability to solve problems, plan, organize, predict, speculate, and hypothesize (Tommy, 2007). Formal operational thought provides a child with the ability to determine if thought processing (such as problem solving) was correct and successful. Good academic skills require that children are able to process, perform, and reflect on their accurate performance.

Verbal reasoning is one of the areas that reflect thought processing. Verbal reasoning allows a child to use language to provide solutions to problems. In early grades, verbal reasoning is reflected in the ability to process opposites (e.g., hot/cold; up/down), categorize items (e.g., animals vs. toys), and use one object to represent another (e.g., a block for a telephone). Children should also be able to discuss events and items that are beyond the here-and-now, such as past or future events. Later grades require that children draw inferences, determine the main idea in written text, and understand more complex written text.

Memory

Memory involves two main processes: **working memory** and long-term memory, with the concept of working memory replacing the earlier concept of short-term memory (Baddeley, 1986).

Working Memory

Working memory (auditory or visual) has limited capacity, while long-term memory (auditory or visual) holds a large amount of information over time. Working memory allows a child to understand and remember a series of directions and provides temporary storage for unfamiliar sounds (Baddeley, Gathercole, & Papagno, 1998). Both abilities are essential skills in academic success. Working memory problems might occur in tasks that require remembering a lengthy and/or complex series of instructions. While some children with working memory problems are aware that they have to ask speakers to repeat directions, other children (and teachers) may be unaware of their working memory problems. Consequently, these children may not complete their assignments or may make errors when completing the assignment. The following example shows the connection between working memory and classroom tasks.

> A teacher gave her third-grade class the following directions: "When you complete your spelling assignment, open your math book, and answer the first 10 questions on page 38."
>
> While most of the children were able to understand, remember, and complete this assignment, one of the children had difficulty remembering the series of directions. In this case, the child sat in his chair, hesitant to raise his hand and ask for repetition of the assignment. For children with working memory problems, seeing other children promptly begin their work may lead to reluctance to ask for help.

Attention

Attention allows a child to focus on a task, such as listening to directions. This ability also allows a child to filter out sounds or activities that are not relevant to the task at hand. Attention difficulties are frequently associated with language disorders, such as learning disabilities. The ability to maintain attention allows a child to focus on storytelling at an earlier age and supports overall learning skills at earlier and later ages. There are three components of attention:

1. Coming to attention: initial awareness of change (e.g., a new sound, a person entering a room, or changing tasks in the classroom)

> Mary was sitting in class when the teacher announced that she was going to introduce the class to a new set of vocabulary words related to their trip to a farm. Mary sat up straight and looked at the teacher.

2. Focusing attention: focusing on the task at hand (e.g., the person entering the room or the change in the classroom task)

> Mary opened her notebook, found a new page, and waited to write the words that the teacher was about to introduce to the class.

3. Sustaining attention: exploration of the task at hand for a required duration of time in order to satisfy task demands (e.g., attempts to solve a problem or to attain a goal)

> Mary continued to listen carefully as the teacher spoke. She ignored sounds in other parts of the room, where some of the kids were giggling. Suddenly, her pencil broke. She couldn't find another pencil in her desk or pencil case. She raised her hand to ask the teacher for help.

For children with learning disabilities or with attention-deficit hyperactivity disorder, the first two components of attention improve with maturation, while the last component (sustaining attention) continues to be discrepant in comparison with typical peers into adulthood.

Discrimination

Discrimination is a skill that allows a child to distinguish the salient characteristics between two pictures (visual discrimination) or between two words or sounds in words (auditory discrimination). For example, given several objects that are round and others that are square, a child should be able to distinguish the different objects when given directions (e.g., "Show me all the blocks that are round"). The discrimination of sounds is essential to the ability to distinguish differences in words, such as *bee* and *pea*. Discrimination allows individuals to identify the sound structures in words (Apel, Masterson, & Niessen, 2004; Torgesen, 1999). The awareness of sounds is a strong predictor of reading abilities (Gillon, 2004; Gottardo, 2002; Juel, Griffith, & Gough, 1986; Kamhi & Catts, 1991; Siegel, 1993; Stanovich, 1994; Stanovich, Cunningham, & Cramer, 1984; Stanovich & Siegel, 1994; Tunmer & Nesdale, 1985; Vellutino & Scanlon, 1987).

Second-Language Learners and Discrimination of Sounds

At this point, teachers and other practitioners may have difficulty identifying learning problems because of the increased number of second-language learners in schools in the United States (Wong-Fillmore & Snow, 2002). The knowledge of differences among languages is essential, given a history of incorrect judgments of reading deficits in children who are second-language learners (Cummins, 1984). The increased understanding of differences among languages and difficulties in learning a new language has also led to caution in the diagnosis of disabilities in second-language learners, often resulting in delayed assessment of academic difficulties (Limbos & Geva, 2001).

Limbos and Geva (2001) found a need for screening measures to determine if second-language learners have reading difficulties, as teachers frequently focus on oral language proficiency as a basis for academic abilities. Oral production, as opposed to discrimination, is also the focus of most practitioners who provide services to second-language learners (Rochet, 1995). This emphasis on language production shifts the focus away from the discrimination of sounds and language patterns.

We now turn to differences in language that are found in spoken, written, and nonverbal (e.g., gestures or signing) language. The American Speech-Language-Hearing Association (2005) describes language differences that can occur in verbal and nonverbal communication, discourse and narrative style, greetings, conversation, and learning styles.

LANGUAGE DIFFERENCES

It is essential that classroom teachers be able to distinguish between speech and/or language disorders and linguistic or cultural differences so that they may determine if a communicative disorder actually exists. To this end, Chapters 12, 13, and 14 present an in-depth discussion of factors that will contribute to understanding differences due to learning English as a second language.

Investigators have also found language differences between females and males in terms of earlier female language acquisition for vocabulary (Bornstein, Han, & Haynes, 2004), word learning (Huttenlocher, Haight, Bryk, Seltzer, & Lyons, 1991), written narratives (Nelson &

Van Meter, 2007), literacy (Moore, Yin, Weaver, Lydell, & Logan, 2007), phonological processing (Shaywitz et al., 1995), and sentence complexity (Bornstein et al., 2004). These differences generally disappear by around 6 years of age (Bornstein et al., 2004).

Gender differences may result from both biological and/or environmental factors. In terms of biological factors, a study of phonological processing tasks found that brain activation appeared in the left frontal gyrus region in males and in the left and right inferior frontal gyrus in females (Shaywitz et al., 1995). In addition, females may show earlier neurological development than males (Geschwind & Galaburda, 1985), given that estrogen is one of the elements that play a role in neurological development. That is because this hormone facilitates the development of myelin, an insulator of many fibers in the nervous system. (See Chapter 6 for a deeper discussion of the brain's role in language development.)

In terms of environmental factors, parents have been found to emit animated sounds more frequently when engaged in play routines with more masculine-type toys, such as trucks, while they emit verbal expressions, comments, and questions when playing with more feminine-type toys, such as dolls (Caldera, Huston, & O'Brien, 1989).

Verbal input may also play a role in female children's earlier language development. In general, play activities may, in fact, socialize children by gender accompanied by key differences in the use of language. Differences play a role in children's language development, not only for second-language learners but also for children who develop skills at different ages as part of typical developmental patterns. Differences in language exist because of the process of acquiring a new language, gender variations in language, or children's styles of learning. These differences make the classroom a rich environment for learning.

CLASSROOM STRATEGIES TO SUPPORT LANGUAGE DEVELOPMENT

For children who have language difficulties, it is important to provide supports within the classroom. Chapter 2 provided strategies based on the theories of language development. Within the classroom, there are certain basic strategies to support children's academic abilities (Brown & Ford, 2007):

- Speak slowly and clearly.
- Reduce background noise.
- Avoid idioms (e.g., "off the top of your head"), especially for second-language English learners.
- Allow children time to respond to questions, as some children may need more time to compose an answer.
- Provide supports, such as pictures, videos, or objects, for learning new concepts and words.
- Repeat instructions and ask children with listening or attention difficulties to repeat instructions back to you.
- Alert students when information is important or new (e.g., "Here is something important").

For older children, these additional classroom strategies may be useful:

- Allow tape recording.
- Provide written outlines of tasks.
- Use computer-assisted programs.
- Suggest organizers such as notebooks and journal writing.

The following chapters provide a significant number of strategies for both native English speakers and English learners. For example, Chapter 10 provides strategies for children with literacy or reading difficulties. We now examine communication disorders to better understand the difference between typical language development and language difficulties.

A SURVEY OF COMMUNICATION DISORDERS

The American Speech-Language-Hearing Association (1993) defines a communication disorder as an impairment in the ability to receive, send, process, and comprehend concepts present in verbal, nonverbal, and graphic symbol systems. A language disorder is the impaired comprehension and/or use of spoken, written, and/or other symbol systems. The disorder may involve (a) the *form* of language (phonology, morphology, and syntax), (b) the *content* of language (semantics), and/or (c) the *function* of language in communication (pragmatics) in any combination.

Disorders may also be associated with cognitive abilities, such as the ability to maintain attention and understand signals and concepts communicated by a speaker. Listeners must be able to comprehend or understand concepts, along with being able to understand nonverbal and graphic symbols (e.g., gestures and written language). Communication disorders may have a developmental or acquired origin that affects any of the factors that are required for communicative skills.

The American Speech-Language-Hearing Association (1993) provides a definition of disorders that encompass language, articulation, fluency, voice, hearing, and processing (see Figure 3.1). See Figure 3.2 for strategies to identify children with communication disorders.

| Figure 3.1 | Speech and Language Disorders |

Articulation: An articulation disorder is the impaired production of speech sounds characterized by substitutions, omissions, additions, or distortions that may interfere with intelligibility.

Fluency: A fluency disorder is an interruption in the flow of speaking characterized by deficits in rate, rhythm, and repetitions in sounds, syllables, words, and phrases. Frequently, excessive tension, struggle behavior, and secondary mannerisms are characteristics of fluency disorders.

Voice: The abnormal production and/or absence of vocal quality, pitch, loudness, resonance, and/or duration, which is inappropriate for an individual's age and/or sex are characteristic of a voice disorder.

Hearing: A hearing impairment is the result of impaired auditory sensitivity of the physiological auditory system that limits the development, comprehension, production, and/or maintenance of speech and/or language.

Deafness: A hearing disorder that limits an individual's aural/oral communication performance to the extent that the primary sensory input for communication may be other than the auditory channel. Reduced hearing acuity, whether fluctuating or permanent, adversely affects an individual's ability to communicate using the auditory channel as the primary sensory input for communication.

Central auditory processing disorders (CAPD): These are deficits in the information processing of audible signals (signals heard and understood) not credited to impaired peripheral hearing sensitivity or intellectual impairment (ASHA, 1993). According to ASHA, information processing involves perceptual, cognitive, and linguistic functions that allow effective receptive communication of auditorily presented stimuli. CAPD refers to limitations in the ongoing transmission, analysis, organization, transformation, elaboration, storage, retrieval, and use of information contained in audible signals. CAPD may involve the listener's active and passive (e.g., conscious and unconscious, mediated and unmediated, controlled and automatic) abilities (ASHA, 1993).

Figure 3.2   Strategies to Identify Children With Communication Disorders

Expressive Language

- Rarely initiates verbal interactions or activities with peers or family members
- Does not respond verbally to questions or comments from peers or family members
- Language observed to be lower than the level used by peers
- Smaller vocabulary than expected for age, in first language or second (if second-language learner)
- Shorter, less complex sentences than expected for age
- Difficulty communicating verbally with peers or family members
- Relies heavily on gestures and nonverbal means to communicate
- Peers rarely initiate verbal exchanges
- Does not attempt to repair communication failures
- Does not verbally request help or clarification when needed
- Makes frequent use of empty, meaningless words (e.g., *it, thing, this,* or *that*)

Receptive Language

- Repeat instructions so that children understand and remember
- Slow in responding to questions or instructions
- Peers have difficulty understanding the child's speech or language efforts
- Does not learn new concepts or vocabulary
- Forgets material

(Continued)

(Continued)

Pragmatics

- Does not take turns or maintain conversations with peers
- Eye contact may be absent or inconsistent
- Does not engage peers in an appropriate manner (e.g., "Can I play with your truck please?")

CASE STUDY REVISITED

The case study presented at the beginning of this chapter described a child displaying difficulty interacting with his peers, in spite of the presence of intact language skills. His classroom teacher observed his behaviors over a period of time and decided to develop a plan to support his interactional skills while also developing a classroom context that allowed greater interaction for all the children.

Case Study Revisited: The use of language in social interaction

Ms. Benjamin noted Tommy's difficulty interacting with the other children, which indicated that he needed help with his social skills or his pragmatics. She began planning to organize the classroom in a way that provided contexts for learning these skills. First, she noticed that certain activities in the classroom discouraged group interaction: computers, puzzles, and painting at an easel. In addition, the preschool classroom contained at least six play or interest centers (e.g., building materials, kitchen, books, transportation, music, and sand tray). In a class of 15 children, this meant that as few as 2 to 3 children might be in a group at any one time. In contrast, there were other tasks that encouraged group interaction: painting on long pieces of paper and role-playing familiar stories and stories read in class. She also noticed that the introduction of novel toys and objects in the classroom led to more conversational interaction between the teacher and the children and among other children. With classroom aides, she began planning to organize the classroom to encourage more social interaction.

The classroom teacher first reduced the number of interest groups to four. This led to a greater number of children in each group at any one time. Next, she planned for the position of children in circle time, seating Tommy next to a child with good social and pragmatic skills. She knew that this child would provide a good model for communicating requests, comments, and needs. Positioning children with good social skills across from those with less advanced or poor social skills allows them to observe the social interactions of these children.

Ms. Benjamin also decided to work with Tommy in a one-to-one context when the other children were engaged in other tasks. She began to play a game that required at least two players. The teacher asked him, "Would you like to play with me?" Tommy said, "Yes." The teacher then said, "You could say, 'Can I . . . ?'" providing an open sentence to encourage

Tommy to complete this sentence by saying, " . . . play with you?" Ms. Benjamin provided Tommy with these first few words, and not the whole sentence, because she wanted him to use his inherent language knowledge and thinking skills to provide the phrase to complete this sentence. Ms. Benjamin repeated this sentence and said, "That is a good way to let the other children know that you want to play with them."

Over a short period of time, observations showed that Tommy had mastered the skill to communicate his desire to play with the other children and began to use language in social interaction during play with peers. The classroom teacher can improve children's social and pragmatic skills through modeling and organization of the classroom environment.

While thinking about the problems children might have in the classroom, it is also important to observe and note a child's strengths. These strengths may consist of good social communication, knowing sound and letter correspondences, or enjoying reading during story time. This assessment of strengths and weaknesses will give a full picture of the child's skills, along with the revealing the skills that need extra attention to help the child achieve academic success.

Pragmatic rules involve the appropriate use of language in interaction through eye contact, turn taking, and maintaining the topic under discussion.

SUMMARY

This chapter presented an overview of the components of language development. The chapter also presented a case study that described a child who needed help with social and pragmatic skills. One method for addressing these areas is organizing the classroom to promote social interaction (Odom et al., 1997; Sandall, McLean, & Smith, 2000). The chapter also presented a brief discussion of differences associated with different dialects or second-language learning, although differences are covered in greater depth in the chapters that trace children's development from infancy through adolescence (Chapters 7, 8, and 9) and the chapters that directly address differences due to dialect or learning English as a second language (Chapters 12, 13, and 14). The main points of this chapter follow:

- Knowledge of the components of language is necessary so that we are able to identify the areas that may require attention. Children's difficulties in various language factors often first appear as difficulties in the classroom.

- Language difficulties frequently affect more than one modality. For example, a child who has difficulty with expressive language (e.g., producing good sentences) most likely has difficulty with auditory comprehension (e.g., understanding spoken language).

- Collaboration between classroom teacher, parents, and specialists in assessment and intervention is essential to address any language factors that may influence a child's academic progress.

The next chapter stresses the importance of collaboration between classroom teacher, parent, and specialists in assessment and intervention when trying to determine whether a child has hearing loss, given the impact of hearing loss on language development. The key issues addressed in Chapter 4 include types and common causes of hearing loss in children and speech, language, and literacy problems associated with childhood hearing loss. Specialized instructional approaches that can serve as excellent resources for classroom teachers are also presented.

KEY WORDS

Alphabetic principle	Morphology	Phonological processing
Articulation	Onset-rime	Phonology
Attention	Orthography	Pragmatics
Cognition	Overgeneralization	Semantics
Content	Phoneme awareness	Syllable
Discrimination	Phonemes	Syntax
Figurative language	Phonemic awareness	Thought processing
Form	Phonological	Use
Memory	awareness	Verbal reasoning
Modal auxiliaries	Phonological processes	Working memory

STUDY QUESTIONS

1. What approaches would you use to support a child with expressive language difficulties? Describe at least three.

2. Describe the role of phonological awareness in academic development. How might a child's difficulties with phonological awareness affect his or her learning of new words?

3. Describe the behaviors that would indicate a problem in social interaction with peers. Along with those used by Tommy's teacher in the case study, what strategies would you use in the classroom to help a child with problems in social interaction?

4. Explain why a second-language learner of English may have difficulty with certain English vowels.

5. Describe the behaviors associated with attention problems. Explain how these problems would appear in the classroom. How would you address these problems? Describe at least three ways you would help a child sustain his or her attention while you are teaching a lesson.

PROJECTS

1. To understand the factors associated with language, collect a language sample from a child who produces sentences that contain at least three words or more. In this sample, you will categorize the child's productions under articulation (sounds produced correctly or incorrectly), semantics (vocabulary and sentences), syntax (the structure of sentences that are produced), and pragmatics (analysis of the child's interaction with peers and adults). Place your analysis into these categories, using this chapter as a guide.

2. Interview at least three children along with a person unknown to them. Ask the children to find out all the information they can about this person, such as the person's name, where he or she lives, and what he or she likes to eat. Do not give the children any directions. Note any differences in their questions. Next, note any of the factors that may have affected their questions, such as gender or age.

3. Show children of different ages a series of pictures cut from a magazine or newspaper or downloaded from the web. Ask the children to make up a story about what the individuals might be saying or doing. Note the language abilities of children at different ages based on their vocabulary or sentence length and complexity.

STUDENT STUDY SITE

Visit the Student Study Site at **www.sagepub.com/levey** for these additional learning tools:

- Video Links
- Self Quizzes
- E-Flashcards

- Sample Forms and Assessment Tools
- Recommended Readings
- Web Resources

SUGGESTIONS FOR FURTHER READING

Bernstein, D. K., & Levey, S. (2009). Language development: A review. In D. K. Bernstein & E. Tiegerman-Farber (Eds.), *Language and communication disorders in children* (6th ed., pp. 28–100). Boston: Allyn & Bacon.

Bernthal, J. E., & Bankson, N. W. (2004). *Articulation and phonological disorders* (6th ed.). Boston: Allyn & Bacon.

Fromkin, V. A. (2006). *Language* (8th ed.). Orlando, FL: Harcourt Brace.

Goldstein, B. (2000). *Cultural and linguistic diversity resource guide for speech-language pathologists.* San Diego, CA: Singular.

Owens, R. E. (2007). *Language development: An introduction.* Boston: Allyn & Bacon.

Hearing and Listening Skills

Rochelle Cherry

CASE STUDY: The effect of undiagnosed hearing loss on language abilities

Sally is a 9-year-old native-English-speaking child in Mr. Smith's fourth-grade class. Mr. Smith has noted that Sally occasionally seems to exhibit behavior problems, such as getting upset when he asks her questions about a story read in class. She frequently responds with answers that are ambiguous and do not really answer the question at hand. Her academic work is generally good, but her vocabulary skills are below average. Her reading skills are average, but she demonstrates difficulty in identifying new words. Her written work is characterized by problems with certain morphological markers: plural -s (e.g., *cats*), possessive's (e.g., Matt's hat), past-tense marker -ed (e.g., He walked), and the third-person singular -s (e.g., She hits). Her spoken language is characterized by the substitution of sounds, especially with the sounds *s, z, sh, ch*, and *th*. She also appears more tired at the end of the day than other children in the class. Her IQ falls within the normal range. Sally is a child with an undiagnosed hearing loss, and because of this, she is missing important auditory cues.

What are the main problems that would affect Sally's academic skills? On what information or experiences did you base your answer?

INTRODUCTION

The importance of hearing and listening with respect to the development of speech and language cannot be overstated. Hearing primarily involves the ear's ability to provide acoustic access to the brain, whereas listening involves focusing and attending to the available acoustic events that occur in the brain. Hearing must occur before listening can be taught (Cole & Flexer, 2007), although good hearing does not guarantee good listening.

Since most children acquire speech and language abilities through hearing and listening, a hearing problem can cause communication, educational, and social difficulties. To understand the differences between the language development of a child with hearing loss and a child with typical hearing, review the chapters that describe typical children's language development (Chapter 7 for infants and toddlers, Chapter 8 for preschool-age children, and Chapter 9 for school-age children and adolescents). The main differences found between children with typical and atypical hearing abilities are found in vocabulary, grammar, conversation, literacy, and speech or the production of sounds in words.

Hearing loss ranges from minimal to profound. Some types of hearing loss are easily detectible through observation, whereas others may be difficult to identify without testing (Kuder, 2003). Some losses are equal at all frequencies (pitches); for some, hearing may be poorer in the low frequencies, whereas for others, it may be poorer in the high frequencies. The loss can be stable, fluctuate, or get progressively worse and can affect either one ear (unilateral hearing loss) or both ears (bilateral hearing loss). Even minimal hearing loss can affect language and literacy skills (Bess, Dodd-Murphy, & Parker, 1998), and problems of hearing loss are exacerbated by delay in treatment. Children with unilateral losses may also have social and academic problems, especially if left untreated (Bess et al., 1998).

Children with hearing loss increasingly are being included (mainstreamed) in general education classes for all or a portion of the school day. This is the case even for those children with more severe losses who are currently benefiting from new and more

Children learn speech and language abilities through hearing and listening.

successful **habilitation technologies** and protocols. Teachers are frequently required to address the academic needs of these children. Consequently, knowledge of children's special needs is required. They must also develop strategies to optimize each child's performance and potential for success. This chapter discusses hearing problems in children from preschool through high school and the challenges they pose for educators, along with recommendations to assist these students in the classroom.

PREVALENCE

Hearing impairment is among the most common disabilities found in children (English, 1995). According to the National Institute of Deafness and Other Communication Disorders (2008), there are approximately 17,000 infants and toddlers identified with hearing loss each year, making it the most common birth defect (Flexer & Madell, 2008). Looking at several studies, Ross, Brackett, and Maxon (1991) estimated that among school-age children, approximately 16 to 30 students per 1,000 had significant hearing loss. More recently, Niskar and associates (1998) estimated that almost 15% of U.S. school-age children have either low- or high-frequency hearing loss in one or both ears. Based on this more recent data, it is expected that "131 of every 1,000 school-age children have some degree of hearing loss that can potentially affect communication, learning, psychosocial development, and academic achievement" (American Speech-Language-Hearing Association [ASHA], 2002, p. 4).

The U.S. Department of Education (2002) reported that about 70,000 students age 6 to 21 receive services for hearing loss, representing 1.3% of all students with disabilities. The prevalence of a relatively new classification of hearing problems, auditory processing disorder, estimated to affect between 2% and 5% of school-age children, may affect a larger number of children in schools (Chermak & Musiek, 1997). In addition, about 30% of children with hearing loss have at least one additional handicapping condition (Joint Committee on Infant Hearing, 2007).

THE CLASSIFICATION OF HEARING LOSS IN CHILDREN

Traditionally, there are two categories of children's hearing impairment, based on severity of hearing loss: **hard-of-hearing** or **deaf**. The degree (severity) of hearing loss is determined using a graph, called an **audiogram**, with which the audiologist plots a child's hearing thresholds (lowest response levels) by frequency (pitch) and intensity (loudness). The identification of a hearing loss occurs when an individual's threshold is above that considered "normal."

Children are classified as minimally hearing impaired if the hearing level is between 20 and 25 decibels (dB) hearing level (HL); mild if 30 to 40 dB HL; moderate if 45 to 55 dB HL; severe if 60 to 90 dB HL; and profound if 95 dB HL or greater. Most of these children have hearing losses in both ears. When classifying children based on the degree of hearing loss, the following guidelines are used based on hearing level in the better ear:

- Children with losses up to 90 dB HL in the better ear: hard-of-hearing

- Children with greater hearing loss: deaf

It should be noted that the hard-of-hearing/deaf classifications based on degree of loss were established before the advent of early identification of hearing loss (e.g., via more effective newborn hearing screenings) and improved technology (e.g., cochlear implants), which offer children with profound hearing loss earlier and significantly greater access to auditory information. As a result, a functional definition has become increasingly more appropriate when classifying children with hearing problems. Children with reduced hearing sensitivity are classified as hard-of-hearing if they acquire oral language primarily through hearing with or without the use of vision and hearing aids or other devices. By contrast, children who are classified as deaf primarily develop communication skills through vision, using signs or speech reading. Thus, with early identification and more effective treatment of hearing loss (including use of new technologies), some children with the most severe hearing problems function more like children who are hard-of-hearing.

Hearing screenings to identify children with hearing loss.

TYPES AND COMMON CAUSES OF HEARING LOSS IN CHILDREN

Audiologists also classify hearing loss in terms of the location or site of the pathology within the auditory system. The cause of a **conductive hearing loss (CHL)** is a problem with the transmission of sound in the outer and/or middle ear. The result of CHL is generally a loss of sensitivity (loudness) without distortion. CHL may occur at birth (**congenital**) or afterward (acquired) and often can be medically or surgically treated.

Conductive Hearing Loss

The leading cause of CHL in children is **otitis media (OM),** which is an inflammation of the middle ear, usually secondary to an upper respiratory infection or cold. This inflammation often begins before the age of 6. Between 85 % and 90 % of children in the United States have at least one bout of OM (Northern & Downs, 2002). OM is common in children for several reasons:

- Their immune system is still developing;

- their eustachian tube (a small passageway that connects the throat to the middle ear) is shorter and straighter than an adult's, allowing pathogens to invade the middle ear more easily;

- they may have enlarged adenoids blocking the opening of the eustachian tube; and

- they may have a variety of allergies that can contribute to the problem.

The eustachian tube is normally closed but opens to ventilate the middle ear, equalizing air pressure between the middle ear and the environment. If the eustachian tube cannot open, negative pressure builds up and fluid from the lining of the middle ear can accumulate, resulting in OM with effusion (fluid), or OME. OME may cause pain or be without symptoms. It can also cause a CHL that is usually mild (30 dB HL) but may be moderate (up to 50 dB HL), and it may affect one or both ears. The hearing loss is usually temporary but if untreated may cause speech, language, and learning problems (Gravel & Nozza, 1997). Since the hearing loss may fluctuate, a child may have normal hearing one day and a CHL on another day.

Treatment of OME includes periodic monitoring, since for 80 % to 90 % of the children, this condition will resolve within 3 months (Rosenfeld, Culpepper, & Doyle, 2004). While antibiotics have been widely used, their use is questionable as an effective method for long-term treatment. If fluid persists for longer than 3 months and is associated with hearing loss, there may be a recommendation to surgically insert "tubes" (myringotomy) to ventilate the middle ear and equalize pressure. Some children require more than one surgery. A new device, the EarPopper, is a nonsurgical treatment for OME. It is a handheld, battery-operated device that, when placed in the child's nasal cavity, ventilates the middle ear. This approach has resolved hearing loss after 2 months of use in 74 % of children age 4 years and older (Arick & Silman, 2005).

Sensorineural Hearing Loss

Sensorineural hearing loss (SNHL) occurs when there is damage to the cochlea (inner ear) and or the auditory nerve. SNHL is usually irreversible. The characteristics of this type of hearing loss are reduced sensitivity to sound as well as distortions that affect the clarity of speech sounds. Severity can range from mild to total loss of hearing, can be congenital or acquired, can be caused by genetic or environmental factors, and can affect one or both ears. There are some SNHLs confined to specific frequencies, while others affect the entire hearing range.

The most common environmental causes in children include **cytomegalovirus**, **ototoxic drugs**—especially those in the mycin family—**meningitis**, and **noise-induced hearing loss (NIHL).** Many babies born prematurely can have hearing loss resulting from the side effects of drugs (ototoxic) used to treat them during the critical neonate period.

Noise-Induced Hearing Loss

NIHL is generally caused by exposure to loud sounds over a period of time but may also be the result of one exposure to a very loud sound (e.g., a firecracker). The loss may be temporary, but with continued exposure, it will become permanent. The loss generally occurs in both ears and affects high frequencies first. Most children are not aware of their hearing loss until they sustain permanent damage. Estimates are that approximately 5.2 million school-age children have NIHL in at least one ear. Boys have a higher prevalence of NIHL than girls, and the prevalence increases with age (Hidedecker, 2008).

Increases of NIHL in school-age children result from greater exposure to louder recreational activities, including noisy toys, personal CD/MP3 players, and the use of firearms and motorbikes for older children. In addition, school activities, such as band and shop classes, may be hazardous. It is not possible to reverse NIHL when it becomes permanent. However, it is possible to prevent it.

To see more Web Resources, go to **www.sagepub .com/levey.**

In response to this increasing hazard, school-based hearing conservation programs have formed, including WISE EAR, Dangerous Decibels, and Crank It Down (Folmer, 2008). In 2008, the National Institute on Deafness and Other Communication Disorders launched a website aimed at children 8 to 12 years old and their parents, named "It's a Noisy Planet, Protect Their Hearing" (www.noisyplanet.nidcd.nih.gov). Other websites also provide information on hearing problems.

Appropriate materials are available for improving the prevention of NIHL, but they are not widely used. A hearing conservation program should

- include education about the hazards of noise,
- identify high noise areas in school and post warning signs,
- periodically check the hearing of children, especially those who are exposed to loud sounds, and
- implement mandatory noise safety instructions and use of ear protection (DeConde Johnson & Meinke, 2008).

School personnel should be aware of hearing loss warning signs, such as when a child reports ringing in the ears or trouble hearing after a noisy activity, to minimize further exposure. There should be discussions of hearing conservation at Parents Association meetings, helping parents understand what they should be doing at home to prevent NIHL.

Mixed Hearing Loss

Mixed hearing loss occurs when there is a problem in both the transmission of sound in the outer and/or middle ear and damage to the inner ear and/or auditory nerve. Causes of mixed hearing loss include a combination of those that cause CHL and SNHL. CHL and SNHL are peripheral hearing problems. If a child with a permanent SNHL develops OME, his or her degree of hearing loss can be significantly increased, affecting the child's ability to function.

Auditory Processing Disorder

Another type of hearing problem, **auditory processing disorder (APD),** occurs when there is a problem in the brainstem and/or the auditory centers of the brain. Therefore, it is a problem with the central nervous system. Children with APD generally have normal audiograms (i.e., normal peripheral hearing) but have difficulty understanding speech, especially under adverse (noisy) listening conditions. Children with APD have problems with one or more of the following auditory skills: localization, auditory pattern recognition, temporal aspects, auditory performance in competing acoustic signals, and degraded signals (ASHA, 2005).

These children have problems with following oral instructions, especially when given rapid or distorted speech input (Cherry & Rubinstein, 2006; Jerger & Musiek, 2000). Some of these children have additional problems, such as attention-deficit disorder (Chermak, Tucker, & Seikel, 2002). Many exhibit behaviors similar to those found in children with a peripheral hearing loss (CHL and/or SNHL), especially in poor acoustic environments, such as most classrooms. If a child appears to have difficulty responding to speech but does not have a peripheral hearing loss, then the recommendation for an APD evaluation is necessary for the initiation of appropriate treatment.

SPEECH, LANGUAGE, AND LITERACY PROBLEMS ASSOCIATED WITH CHILDHOOD HEARING LOSS

There is a great deal of variability in the effects of hearing loss on speech, language, and literacy development. Delays in vocabulary development, grammatical and conversational skills, literacy, and speech production activities of children with hearing loss have been documented (Carney & Moeller, 1998). Examples of some of these difficulties appear in our case study subject, Sally. In general, there is less effect on children with milder hearing problems than on children with more severe hearing losses. Common problems found in children with hearing impairments include **vocabulary**, **grammar** (**syntax** or sentence structure), **conversational skills** (**pragmatics** or following the rules that govern interaction), literacy, and speech production.

Vocabulary

Some children with hearing impairment tend to have reduced receptive and expressive vocabulary, difficulty with multiple meanings (e.g., write/right) and problems with figurative language (Culbertson, 2007; Tye-Murray, 2009). In contrast, another study conducted over the same time period found that many children with mild-to-moderate hearing loss performed as well as their normal-hearing peers (Moeller, Tomblin, Yoshinaga-Itano, McDonald, & Jerger, 2007).

Grammar (Syntax)

Some children with hearing impairment tend to use shorter and simpler sentences; overuse specific sentence patterns (e.g., subject-verb-object), even when inappropriate; infrequently use adverbs and conjunctions; and incorrectly use irregular verb tense (Culbertson, 2007). Elfenbein, Hardin-Jones, and Davis (1994) found that there is an overall delay in grammatical patterns of these children but that they are similar to younger, normal-hearing children.

Conversational Skills (Pragmatics)

Some children with hearing impairment demonstrate a lack of knowledge concerning conversational conventions (e.g., changing the topic or closing a conversation). In addition, they have a limited use of communication repair strategies (e.g., "Please say that another way"), which affects their understanding of what someone else has said (Tye-Murray, 2009).

Literacy

While some children with hearing impairment have difficulty with reading comprehension and phonological processing, many children with hearing impairment are normal readers (Moeller et al., 2007).

Speech Production

Children with mild-to-moderate hearing loss tend to make fewer errors and have more intelligible speech than children with more severe hearing problems (Carney & Moeller, 1998), with most errors occurring in the production of high-frequency consonants (e.g., *s, sh, ch*) and blends (Culbertson, 2007). Some children with more severe hearing loss have historically demonstrated poor intelligibility, unpleasant voice quality, and problems correctly producing vowels, as well as consonants. This pattern shows "deaf speech" (Hedge & Maul, 2006).

The recent widespread use of cochlear implants for this population seems to have dramatically reduced these problems. For example, Peng, Spencer, and Tomblin (2004) found that half of the 24 deaf children they studied achieved an intelligibility score of 85% or better, and their intelligibility showed steady improvement over time. In addition, several studies have shown that children using cochlear implants acquire speech in the same pattern as normal-hearing children and with a greater proficiency than children with the same degree of hearing loss who use hearing aids (Blamey, Barry, & Jacq, 2001; Tye-Murray & Kirk, 1993).

Despite this finding, cochlear implants remain a controversial subject. This is because some individuals who are profoundly deaf maintain that use of sign language should be regarded as its own culture and that attempts to use implants should be viewed as politically incorrect.

FACTORS THAT AFFECT LANGUAGE LEARNING IN CHILDREN WITH HEARING LOSS

Most children with hearing loss are classified as hard-of-hearing and have varying degrees of language problems. As previously noted, they have more difficulty learning vocabulary, grammar, and idiomatic expressions than their normal-hearing peers (English, 1995). The severity of the language disorders found in these children is variable and depends on several factors. In general, the greater the degree of hearing loss, the greater the severity of the language disorder. A congenital (acquired at birth) or **prelinguistic** (occurring before the age of 3) hearing loss would have a greater effect than one acquired after language is learned. In terms of site of lesion, SNHL causes both sensitivity and clarity problems, whereas a CHL causes mainly sensitivity problems that are easier to overcome. Given all conditions, a child's language skills and subsequent academic achievement are better when a hearing loss is detected and treated early (Yoshinaga-Itano, 2003).

Detection without treatment will not benefit a child's language. The method of language learning may consist of oral language, sign language, and total communication, but programs that emphasize oral communication generally result in better oral language skills (Hedge & Maul, 2006; Reed, 2005). Family involvement and demographics, including the presence of other family members with hearing loss, is essential.

Although the speech and language problems of a specific child with a hearing loss are impossible to predict, Anderson and Matkin (2007) developed a chart that describes the possible impact of different degrees of hearing loss on the understanding of speech and language, social skills, and projected necessary educational accommodations. For example, a child with a mild hearing loss (35 dB HL) may miss between 25% to 40% of the speech signal without appropriate accommodations. This chart allows educators to make recommendations until assessment of the child's specific skills is conducted. Projected accommodations and services may include the use of a frequency modulation system in the classroom; favorable seating; and attention to auditory skills, speech, language development, and speech-reading training.

To see more information on the Relationship of Hearing Loss to Listening and Learning Needs, go to **www .sagepub.com/ levey.**

Children with hearing loss, especially when more severe, may have very different speech and language problems. Therefore, assessment must determine each child's specific strengths and weaknesses. This is also important for children with APD, because there are several subtypes that require different modifications (Bellis, 2002).

STRATEGIES TO IDENTIFY CHILDREN WITH HEARING IMPAIRMENTS

It is necessary to identify a hearing loss before treatment, but identification does not ensure a successful outcome without timely intervention. Methods for identification of children with hearing impairments include infant testing, parent education, hearing screening programs, and classroom monitoring.

Infant Testing

At the time of this writing, about 95% of all infants receive screenings for hearing loss (National Center for Hearing Assessment and Management, 2007) as part of an early hearing detection and intervention program. The screening procedures advocated by the Joint Committee on Infant Hearing (2007) do not require infant cooperation.

These tests are based on otoacoustic emissions and/or auditory brainstem response. They can identify children with a mild or greater hearing loss and evaluate each ear individually. These procedures have significantly lowered the average age at which hearing loss is identified. If a child fails or is considered at risk for hearing loss, he or she is referred for further evaluation by a trained specialist (audiologist).

Parent Education

Infant testing procedures can miss some mild hearing losses as well as progressive and later-onset hearing loss. Therefore, it is important to distribute information on the detection of hearing problems to parents, even if their child passed the screening. In addition, some parents do not bring their infants back after failing the initial screening, resulting in a delay of treatment (Kochkin, Luxford, Northern, Mason, & Tharpe, 2007).

Hearing Screening Programs

Hearing screening programs for children in kindergarten through high school are fairly routine. The screening procedure usually consists of listening to pure tones at various frequencies and at predetermined intensity levels in each ear under headphones (ASHA, 1997). The American Speech-Language-Hearing Association (ASHA) recommends screening for all children on entry to school and annually from kindergarten through third grade, and in seventh through eleventh grade. In addition, children at risk for hearing loss, such as those with OM or those who failed a grade, among others, should also be evaluated.

Screening tympanometry checks the integrity of the middle ear to identify the presence of OM, but this testing is infrequently included in screening programs. These procedures can be adapted to use with children as young as 3 years old. If children do not pass either of these tests, a follow-up evaluation with an audiologist should be scheduled (Hall, Oyer, & Haas, 2001).

Screening programs for APD are less routine, though they are available, and include the Screening Test for Auditory Processing Disorders in Children (Keith, 1986), the Selective Auditory Attention Test (Cherry, 1980, 1992; Cherry & Rubinstein, 2006), and several questionnaires such as the Children's Auditory Processing Performance Scale (Smoski, Brunt, & Tannahill, 1992, 1998). A recommendation for referral to an audiologist for evaluation is appropriate if the classroom teacher suspects APD.

Signs of Hearing Loss in the Classroom

Teachers may suspect a hearing problem if a student

- routinely asks for repetition,

- frequently misunderstands what is said,

- appears to be inattentive,

- has speech problems,

- watches others to see what they are doing,

- has fatigue at the end of the day, and/or

- withdraws from situations that require careful listening (Hall et al., 2001).

Teachers should be especially concerned about students with a history of OM since they have greater risk for both CHL and APD. If a classroom teacher suspects a hearing problem, referral for screening or a complete audiological evaluation should occur in a timely fashion. If assessment confirms normal hearing, then it is important that there be further specialized testing for APD. In addition, the teacher may want to fill out one of several available questionnaires that evaluate how the child functions auditorily in the classroom. For example, the Screening Inventory for Targeting Educational Risk is designed to target academic areas in which children with hearing problems may be at risk (Anderson, 1989).

A TEAM APPROACH TO MANAGEMENT

Management of a child with hearing problems requires a collaborative team approach. Many different professionals should be involved in providing services to these children and their families. The composition of the team may be different for different children but should include an audiologist.

According to ASHA (2002), an **educational audiologist (EA)** is the preferred service delivery provider for school-age children with hearing problems. The EA should provide comprehensive audiological services, including

- identification of hearing problems;

- audiologic assessments;

- determination of the need for and appropriateness of hearing technology;

- audiologic (re)habilitation;

- assistance in educational management;

- provision of information and training to teachers, administrators, children, and parents;

- provision of counseling, follow-up, and monitoring of services;

- provision of an accessible acoustic environment; and

- management of hearing conservation programs.

If an EA is not available, the school should contract a certified clinical audiologist to ensure appropriate service to children with hearing problems. Many of these services, such as hearing screening and hearing conservation programs, benefit all the children in the school.

The team should also include a speech-language pathologist, to assess speech and language skills and provide instructional services to the child as needed, and a psychologist who performs educational assessments and counseling. A teacher of the deaf is generally included for school-age children; he or she may be the primary provider of educational services if the child is in a self-contained class or may function as support personnel for mainstreamed children, assessing classroom materials and monitoring amplification. Classroom teachers should also be included if the child is mainstreamed, along with parents and siblings, who can provide effective at-home support.

If available, a school-based EA should function as the case manager, and when that's not possible, the school-based speech-language pathologist should assume this role (ASHA, 2002; Hall et al., 2001; Sorkin, 2008). The team manager must provide team consistency and continuity.

EDUCATIONAL CONSIDERATIONS

A hearing loss and APD are educationally significant disabilities because academic success depends on the ability to use language effectively. The Individuals With Disabilities Act

(IDEA) mandates that children with hearing impairment are entitled to a free and appropriate public education in the least restrictive environment (LRE). IDEA focuses on school-based programs for children 3 to 21 years old. Early intervention services provide support for younger children with hearing impairment (birth to age 3) and their families.

Each child with a hearing impairment should have an Individual Educational Plan (IEP), which is an annually updated legal contract written by the team (see above), specifying the provision of special education and related services. The IEP should include the child's current performance, educational and behavioral goals for the academic year, an explanation of how the team members will meet these goals, classroom placement, and criteria for evaluating progress (Sorkin, 2008). These goals must be reasonable, attainable, and measurable.

The LRE does not necessarily mean 100% inclusion of all children with hearing impairments. Evaluation determines each child's optimal placement. Some children are best served in a full-time regular classroom, whereas others may do better when also placed part-time in a resource room with a teacher of the deaf or when placed full-time in a special education class, which is usually small and relies heavily on visually based instruction. There are several factors to consider when determining the appropriate LRE, including the child's communication needs; proficiency in spoken and written English; the preferred mode of communication; academic level; and social, behavioral, and emotional issues (English, 1995; Kuder, 2003).

Children with hearing impairment placed in inclusion classes have higher academic achievement and better speech than their nonincluded peers (Nevins & Chute, 1996). A child being evaluated for general education placement, however, should have at or near age-appropriate speech, language, academic, conversational, and social skills (Thibodeau & DeConde Johnson, 2005). Children who are included are entitled to special accommodations such as interpreters, preferential seating, captioned films/videos, use of a personal frequency modulation system, and note takers, as well as special services including speech, language, reading, and auditory training. Most children with hearing impairments will require some of these additional services to reach their maximum potential. It is necessary that the IEP contain all the child's needs, with success over time being monitored.

LANGUAGE INSTRUCTION FOR CHILDREN WITH HEARING IMPAIRMENTS: COMMUNICATION APPROACHES

Children who are functionally hard-of-hearing learn language much like normal-hearing children, primarily through hearing. This includes some children with more severe losses because advances in technology, along with earlier identification and treatment, have resulted in better speech and language skills for this population. The most common auditory-based approaches to communication for children with hearing loss are the auditory-oral and auditory-verbal techniques. Auditory-visual techniques are also common.

Auditory-Oral Approach

The **auditory-oral approach** relies on residual hearing through hearing aids and other devices, accompanied by **speech reading** (lip reading) to receive language and use speech as the child's mode of expression.

Auditory-Verbal Approach

The **auditory-verbal approach** stresses the use of active listening through technology. In this approach, children learn all speech and language through hearing, much like normal-hearing children, putting less emphasis on visual cues.

Auditory-Visual Approach

Visually based communication techniques rely on manual communication (sign language). These include American Sign Language (ASL) and Manually Coded English (MCE). ASL is a language that has its own set of rules and uses signs that represent concepts and finger spelling rather than speech. Total Communication combines the auditory-oral approach with MCE.

AUDITORY TECHNOLOGIES

Hearing Aids

Once a hearing loss is identified and the degree and type of loss is known, intervention can begin. Children as young as a few months old can be fitted with hearing aids by a pediatric audiologist. **Hearing aids** have a tiny microphone that picks up sound and converts it to electrical energy, an amplifier that makes the signal louder, and a receiver that converts the electrical signal back into sound waves. A battery supplies power. Most children with hearing loss wear behind-the-ear hearing aids, but some older children may wear smaller in-the-ear aids.

Cochlear Implants

A **cochlear implant** may be recommended for children with the most severe hearing problems. A cochlear implant does not work like a hearing aid but instead bypasses the damaged parts of the ear and directly stimulates the auditory nerve. An electronic device, which includes a receiver and an electrode array to stimulate the auditory nerve, is implanted in the child's inner ear (cochlea). In addition, there are external components that are attached to the implanted device: a microphone to pick up the sound, sending it to a signal processor that manipulates the signal so that it will be more easily understood, and a wireless transmitter that sends this information to the implanted device.

Distance from the classroom teacher, along with background noise, may make it difficult for children to hear what is being said.

Assistive Listening Devices

Assistive listening devices (ALDs), or hearing assistive technology systems, are a group of products designed to address specific listening needs. There are many types of ALDs, but in school the most commonly used is the **frequency modulation (FM)** radio-wave system. A personal FM is a wireless system in which the speaker (teacher) wears a wireless microphone close to her mouth (3 to 6 inches) and a transmitter. The child with a hearing impairment wears a receiver tuned to the same frequency that can be attached to his or her hearing aid or cochlear implant or sent to a dedicated set of earphones. The child will receive the signal as if he or she is within close proximity to the speaker but can be as far away as 50 feet.

THE LISTENING ENVIRONMENT

For optimal learning, all children need good access to communication in the classroom. Approximately 75% of the average school day is spent in listening activities (Eberhard, 2008). The child's listening environment can affect how much the child understands, yet most classrooms fall short because of poor room acoustics. The effects of distance, background noise, and **reverberation** make it more difficult for children to learn and require them to exert extra effort. There is a link between poor classroom acoustics and poorer academic achievement, decreased literacy, and increased behavior problems for all children

(Blumsack & Anderson, 2004). In addition, poor room acoustics can have a deleterious effect on teachers, resulting in a higher incidence of vocal problems than the general population experiences (Crandell, Smaldino, & Flexer, 2005). These and other research findings have led the American National Standards Institute (2002) to issue a guideline for classrooms recommending that background noise be no greater than 35 dB(A) SPL (Sound Pressure Level), a sound level comparable to quiet conversation.

STRATEGIES FOR THE CLASSROOM

The classroom teacher plays an important role in providing support for students with hearing loss in the classroom. Being able to provide the needed level of support requires that substantial time be committed to professional development and hands-on training devoted to classroom accommodations and developing attitudes necessary for teachers to be effective with students who have hearing losses. The classroom teacher must understand that even children with minimum or unilateral hearing losses may need assistance and support for their specific needs. Training, attitude, **accommodation**, and class participation are the factors that will address these children's needs.

Training

The school system should provide each teacher with in-service training. The EA is the best person to do this, but if one is not available, the classroom teacher may contact the school-based speech-language pathologist to address the effects of hearing loss on learning, hearing technologies and how they work, classroom acoustics, teaching strategies for students with hearing loss, and developing listening skills (English, 1995).

Attitude

The teacher should promote an atmosphere of acceptance and encouragement. This positive attitude will set the tone for the entire class.

Accommodation

It is critical to ensure that the sound reaching the student is optimal. The teacher should confirm that the child is using hearing aids and other hearing technology as recommended and that all devices are in good working condition.

Visual cues reinforce communication, and access to visual cues supplements what the child hears. The teacher should avoid walking while talking, placing hands or papers in front of his or her face, or talking with his or her back to the class (when writing on the blackboard). Writing key words, new vocabulary words, and new topics and assignments on the blackboard is also helpful, as well as using closed captions when watching videos. Before talking to the class, the teacher should wait until the students have settled down.

The teacher also should incorporate certain specialized communication strategies before and during the interaction to maximize understanding, such as gaining the student's attention by using his or her name before communicating with the child and facing the student and waiting for eye contact before speaking. To assist the student in anticipating and predicting the communication, it may also be necessary for some teachers to introduce (preteach) new vocabulary and concepts through parents and support personnel or clue students in to topic changes. Classroom teachers should give older children an outline of the lesson prior to each class for the same purpose. They should also check the child's fatigue level during the day, because listening with a hearing loss can be tiring; the child may require periodic breaks to continue to sustain attention.

The teacher must have realistic expectations; children with hearing problems should not be expected to understand every word. Strategies to assist during potential communication breakdowns are also necessary. The classroom teacher can establish a "secret signal" so the student can alert the teacher when information was not understood. The teacher can periodically monitor comprehension by asking the child specific questions to confirm understanding, rather than simply asking whether the children heard. Sometimes children with hearing loss are unaware that they misunderstood. Therefore, nodding does not ensure correct understanding. If the child has not understood something, rephrase using simpler vocabulary or syntax.

Class Participation

Participation in classroom discussions, including interactions with classmates, and involvement in extracurricular activities should be encouraged. One good practice that teachers can adopt to check for understanding is to have students keep a journal in which they report what they understood well and what they still need more clarification on. This can be made into a regular assignment, to be completed either daily or weekly.

CASE STUDY REVISITED

The case study presented at the beginning of this chapter is not an unusual example of a classroom situation. Sally has an undiagnosed mild hearing loss in both ears. Children with even a mild hearing loss are at risk for academic, social, and behavioral difficulties when the underlying hearing problem has not been treated (Irwin, 2009). Children with mild hearing losses frequently underestimate the problems encountered in different listening situations (Kopun & Stelmachowicz, 1998).

Because they have not developed a full awareness of their listening problems, these children may become frustrated when they realize that they have not fully grasped the transmitted information. Communication problems occur because children with a hearing loss may not have heard a speaker's entire message (Elfenbein et al., 1994). Because they are unaware of the need to develop compensatory strategies, they do not use repair strategies such as asking speakers to repeat or rephrase their utterances. Consequently, their answers to questions or requests for information may reveal ambiguity and lack of focus. Reduced vocabulary skills are also associated with even a very mild hearing impairment (Blair, Peterson, & Viehweg, 1985), most likely due to their difficulty hearing all the information transmitted.

The listening problems children with a hearing loss encounter are aggravated in the presence of noise both inside and outside the classroom. Specific listening problems are associated with the high-pitched sounds, such as *f, v, th, s, z, sh, ch,* and *h* (Elfenbein et al., 1994), even with a mild hearing loss. Consequently, these children may have difficulty producing sounds that they cannot hear. Their listening problems also affect their ability to perceive, store, and associate sounds with written letters in words, an essential factor in good reading skills.

Reading skills for children with a mild hearing loss are not as poor as those found in children with more significant hearing difficulties. However, these children may have problems when faced with the task of identifying new words in written text (Halliday & Bishop, 2005). In this case, the ability to associate sounds with written letters is absent, a skill that allows children to interpret new vocabulary items by sounding them out. The impact of a mild hearing loss on writing is found in problems with grammatical morphemes—for example, *-ed* used to mark past tense (e.g., *walk + -ed*) and the third-person singular morpheme *-s* used to mark third-person singular (she *hit + s*). Finally, fatigue results from the extra effort required to listen throughout the entire school day (Hicks & Tharpe, 2002).

CASE STUDY REVISITED: The effect of undiagnosed hearing loss on language abilities

Sally's teacher consulted with the school speech-language pathologist and with an audiologist. They developed classroom strategies to help Sally in her communication and learning skills. Sally's teacher followed the strategies suggested in this chapter. First, Sally received a full audiological examination. Sally was placed in the front row of the class so that she could see and hear the teacher at all times. The audiologist recommended an assistive listening device to maximize Sally's ability to hear information in the classroom. Sally's teacher became more aware of background noise and ceased speaking when planes flew overhead. She also scheduled important listening events when no other activities occurred (e.g., games or computer time). The teacher asked Sally to repeat instructions and important information to make sure that she understood. The speech-language pathologist taught Sally's teacher to write instructions and homework assignments to support Sally's understanding.

The audiologist and speech-language pathologist met with Sally's parents and explained the importance of facing Sally when speaking. They also suggested that they read with her to help her understand written tasks. Sally's parents were encouraged to ask her to repeat information and instructions to make sure that she understood. The audiologist gave her parents a list of tips to assist them. These tips included getting Sally's attention before speaking to her and checking her understanding by asking specific questions.

The speech-language pathologist worked with Sally's ability to associate sounds with letters in words to support her reading development. There was also a concentration on words that may be more difficult for her to hear: auxiliary verbs (e.g., *am, is, are, was, were, be, been, have, has, had, shall, should, will, would, do, did*) and inflectional morphemes in words (e.g., *-ed*, plural *-s*, and *-ing*). The school's reading specialist worked on Sally's reading skills. The speech-language pathologist and reading specialists made use of materials used in the classroom to provide a functional approach to intervention.

SUMMARY

In this chapter, we discussed the importance of hearing and listening in the development of speech, language, and literacy skills. We also reported that hearing problems are common in children, with most classified as hard-of-hearing rather than deaf and with less effect on children with milder hearing problems than on children with more severe hearing losses. You were introduced to the specific speech, language, and literacy problems associated with hearing impairment and the role of the classroom teacher in working with children with a hearing loss. The most important information conveyed in this chapter is that any degree of hearing impairment can put a child at risk for language learning and academic achievement impairment, but earlier detection and treatment can minimize this risk. In addition, you were introduced to the fact that earlier detection and technological supports have resulted in an increasing number of children with hearing problems being taught in regular classrooms. This chapter also advocated for these guidelines:

- All children with hearing loss should have an IEP team that will develop an individualized program to meet each child's specific needs, including the use of hearing technology, environmental modifications, and support services.

- Classroom teachers must be integral members of the child's IEP team and be willing to meet the challenges of a child with a hearing problem in their classroom.

This chapter explored the various types of hearing loss and associated language disorders. Chapter 5 focuses on the mechanical aspects of speech production through a discussion of the structure and function of key components of the speech mechanism with respect to their contributions to speech sounds. By the end of the next chapter, you will understand that speech is a very complex neuromuscular process.

KEY WORDS

Accommodation

Assistive listening devices (ALDs)

Audiogram

Auditory processing disorder (APD)

Auditory-oral approach

Auditory-verbal approach

Auditory-visual approach

Cochlear implant

Conductive hearing loss (CHL)

Congenital

Conversational skills

Cytomegalovirus

Deaf

Educational audiologist (EA)

Frequency modulation (FM)

Grammar

Habilitation technologies

Hard-of-hearing

Hearing aids

Literacy

Meningitis

Mixed hearing loss

Noise-induced hearing loss (NIHL)

Otitis media (OM)

Ototoxic drugs

Pragmatics

Prelinguistic

Reverberation

Sensorineural hearing loss (SNHL)

Speech reading

Syntax

Vocabulary

STUDY QUESTIONS

1. List six reasons why a classroom teacher might suspect a hearing problem and the steps that the classroom teacher should take to deal with this suspected problem.

2. List the possible members of an IEP team for a child with a hearing loss and their potential roles. When should a family with a child with a hearing loss request inclusion? What are their rights under IDEA?

3. Why are most classrooms categorized as poor listening environments? List three groups who are at greatest risk of missing information in adverse listening conditions and why they are at increased risk.

4. Describe five modifications that the classroom teacher can make to help children with hearing and listening problems reach their maximum potential.

PROJECTS

1. While watching a video, turn off the sound for 10 minutes. Write down what you think the characters are saying to one another. Next, rewind and replay the video with sound and check the accuracy of your responses. Write a paragraph describing the impact of not hearing on understanding.

2. Visit a classroom with a child wearing a cochlear implant. Note if the classroom teacher developed any accommodations for this child. Write down any additional accommodations that you read about in this chapter.

3. Develop a hearing conservation program for your class using the resources found in this chapter.

4. View the information found on Project REAL's website. After viewing this material, institute at least five ways to improve the auditory environment of your classroom.

STUDENT STUDY SITE

Visit the Student Study Site at **www.sagepub.com/levey** for these additional learning tools:

- Video Links
- Self Quizzes
- E-Flashcards

- Sample Forms and Assessment Tools
- Recommended Readings
- Web Resources

SUGGESTIONS FOR FURTHER READING

Berg, F. S. (1987). *Facilitating classroom listening: A handbook for teachers of normal and hard-of-hearing students.* Boston: College-Hill Press/Little, Brown.

Kuder, J. (2007). *Teaching students with language and communication disabilities* (3rd ed.). Boston: Allyn & Bacon.

Maxon, A., & Brackett, D. (1992). *The hearing impaired child: Infancy through high-school years.* Boston: Andover Medical.

Paul, P. V. (2009). *Language and deafness* (4th ed.). Boston: Jones & Bartlett.

Stewart, D. A. (2001). *Teaching deaf and hard-of-hearing students: Content, strategies, and curriculum.* Boston: Allyn & Bacon.

CHAPTER 5

The Production of Speech Sounds

Stephen A. Cavallo

CASE STUDY: **The impact of speech skills on communication and social interaction**

Daniel is a 5-year-old child in Ms. Lawton's kindergarten class. Ms. Lawton is concerned about Daniel's speech intelligibility—that is, his ability to produce clear, easily understood words and sentences. She has noted that the children in her class frequently have difficulty understanding Daniel's speech and that he is beginning to show signs of frustration when not understood. Daniel's speech is characterized by typical developmental sound production errors known as **phonological processes** (described in detail in Chapter 7).

For example, Daniel has difficulty producing consonant clusters (two-to-three consonant combinations, such as pl-, st-, and str- found at the beginning of words such as *play*, *stop*, and *street*). At this stage in his speech development, he is unable to execute the speech movements necessary to produce consonant blends. Consequently, he produces these words as "p_ay," "_top," and "__reet," respectively. In addition, Daniel consistently omits the final sounds of words (e.g., he says "bu_" for *bus* and "ca_" for *car*). Although Daniel can produce the /s/ and /r/ sounds in the beginning and middle of words (e.g., *see*, *horsie*, and *rabbit*), he does not produce these sounds at the end of words. His omission of these sounds at only the end of words is characteristic of a rule-based phonologic problem, rather than an articulation problem.

Due to the presence of multiple phonological errors, Daniel's speech is difficult to understand. His teacher, Ms. Lawton, is usually able to understand Daniel after several repetitions, and she uses the strategy of recasting (repeating the child´s error production using a correct model), as described in Chapter 2. Ms. Lawton has noticed that the other children often avoid playing with Daniel, particularly in situations that require conversation. She has come to realize that his speech problems not only interfere with his ability to communicate, but they also negatively impact his social interaction with peers.

Ms. Lawton made some astute observations about Daniel's communication and socialization skills in the classroom. What actions do you think she should take to address her concerns? On what information or experiences did you base your answer?

INTRODUCTION

Clear and understandable speech is necessary for successful communication.

The primary goal of this chapter is to provide classroom teachers with an overview of the process of speech production through a review of basic anatomy and physiology of the speech mechanism and definitions of specialized terminology. An educator who possesses such knowledge will have a greater appreciation of the challenges faced by children with communication difficulties.

Another objective of this chapter is to offer classroom teachers strategies that will support their students' speech attempts. The classroom teacher can play a pivotal role in facilitating the development of a child's communication skills by identifying and referring to the school speech-language pathologist (SLP) any child suspected of having a speech problem. Once a speech problem has been identified, the teacher can employ strategies that will minimize penalties a child might experience as a consequence of his or her speech problem. It is very important for the SLP and classroom teacher to communicate with each other. Through collaboration, the classroom teacher can adopt approaches that will facilitate improved speech production, and the SLP can be made aware of and address specific teacher concerns regarding a child's communication skills in the classroom.

THE INTERNATIONAL PHONETIC ALPHABET

The disparity between spoken and written English was noted by George Bernard Shaw, who suggested that one might as well spell *fish* as *ghoti*: *gh* for the /f/ sound in *enough,* *o* for the /ɪ/ sound in *women*, and *ti* for the /ʃ/ sound in *nation*.

Because there is often a significant difference between the sound a speaker produces and the way that sound is represented in the word (e.g., the /g/ sound in the word *ghost* is represented by the letters *gh*), symbols of the International Phonetic Alphabet (IPA) will be used throughout this chapter to represent speech sounds. The IPA is a system that uses symbols to represent sounds (**phonemes).** The reader can readily identify IPA symbols since they are always placed between virgules (slashes). For example, the phoneme /æ/ is the sound represented by the letter *a* in the word *hat*.

Because spoken sounds and written alphabet letters (**orthography**) do not always have a one-to-one correspondence, IPA symbols serve to identify the sounds that make up words and sentences. Consider the word *box*, which has four sounds but is represented by only three letters. If you say the word *box* aloud and listen carefully to your production of this word, you will discover that it consists of four sounds. The IPA symbols /b/, /a/, /k/, and /s/ represent the four sounds that make up the word *box* (/baks/).

The differences between spoken and written language pose a significant challenge to early readers, who must learn to associate spoken sounds with the written representations of those sounds in words. Phonological awareness is the ability to associate sounds with words. (See Chapter 8 for a detailed explanation of this process.) Children who lack strong phonological awareness skills often experience difficulty learning to read.

SPEECH AS THE BASIS OF COMMUNICATION

The following sections explore the process of speech production and its importance to **communication**. R. H. Stetson described speech as "movements made audible" (Kelso & Munhall, 1988). The term *audible* means capable of *being heard*. Kent (1997) refined Stetson's definition of speech, describing it as a pattern of sounds created by movements of a set of structures "for the purpose of communication." Kent's description highlights the importance of speech to human communication.

In order to produce intelligible speech (speech that is readily understood), a speaker needs to exercise control over the movements of his or her **articulators** (the structures used to produce speech sounds). The lips and tongue are examples of articulators.

Speech production begins with neural impulses in the brain. In the case of normal speech, these neural impulses result in well-timed muscle contractions that move structures (the articulators) with great precision. In addition to the motor act of speaking, sensory feedback is essential to normal speech production. For example, **auditory feedback** (a speaker's ability to hear his or her own speech) is important to regulate speech production. A hearing-impaired speaker has reduced auditory feedback and, as a consequence, may have difficulty coordinating the articulators to produce certain speech sounds.

The process of speech production is extremely complex. In order to assist your understanding of how speech is produced, the following section describes the structure and function of the speech mechanism.

STRUCTURE AND FUNCTION OF THE SPEECH MECHANISM

There are three systems that support the production of speech sounds:

- the **ventilatory system,** which provides the breath support for speech;
- the **larynx** or voice box, where voice is generated; and
- the vocal tract, within which speech sounds are produced and modified (resonated).

The following section explores these systems and mechanisms in greater detail in order to provide you with a basic understanding of how speech is produced and an appreciation of the challenges facing young children learning to speak.

The Ventilatory System: The Breathing Mechanism

The ventilatory system (breathing mechanism) consists of a complex set of structures that are responsible for the exchange of air into and out of the lungs. The ventilatory system serves as the **power source** for speech. For speech to occur, the speaker must draw air into the lungs. The term for this process is **inspiration (inhalation)**. During inspiration, the **diaphragm**, a muscle separating the abdomen and the **thorax** (chest cavity), flattens while the **rib cage** (thorax) expands. Consequently, the lungs, which are attached to both the diaphragm and rib cage, expand as well (see Figure 5.1).

Figure 5.1 Pleural Linkage: The Connection of the Lungs to the Rib Cage and Diaphragm

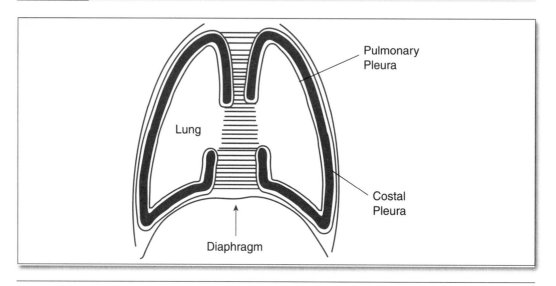

SOURCE: Levey and Osterberg (2009).

After the expanded lungs fill with air, the speaker closes the **vocal folds** (also known as **vocal cords**). As the chest wall moves inward against the closed vocal folds, air within the lungs is pressurized. Like a pressure-cooker, the pressure below the vocal folds (**subglottal pressure**) increases. It is this increase in subglottal pressure that supports and drives speech and phonation. **Phonation,** by definition, is the sound that results from setting the vocal folds into rapid vibration. The following section describes how "voice" is generated and its importance to speech production.

The Larynx: The Voice Box

Located at the upper end of the **trachea** (windpipe) is the larynx, commonly referred to as the Adam's apple. Housed within the larynx are two tiny folds of tissue, the vocal folds (see Figure 5.2). The vocal folds are capable of opening and closing. During at-rest breathing, they open to allow air to enter the lungs (inspiration) and they close slightly while air is being expelled from the lungs (**expiration**). The vocal folds close completely and with great force when someone coughs or clears his or her throat.

The vocal folds are the source of our "voice." When the vocal folds are approximated (closed or nearly closed) and pressure is built up below them (increased subglottal pressure), they can be set into rapid vibration to produce voice (phonation).

As the vocal folds vibrate (open and close rapidly), they "chop" the airstream from the lungs into puffs of air, which are released into the **vocal tract** (see Figure 5.3). These puffs

Figure 5.2   Vocal Folds in the Closed and Open Positions

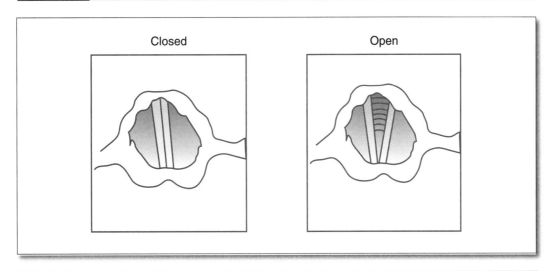

SOURCE: Levey and Osterberg (2009).

Figure 5.3   The Air-Filled Cavities of the Vocal Tract

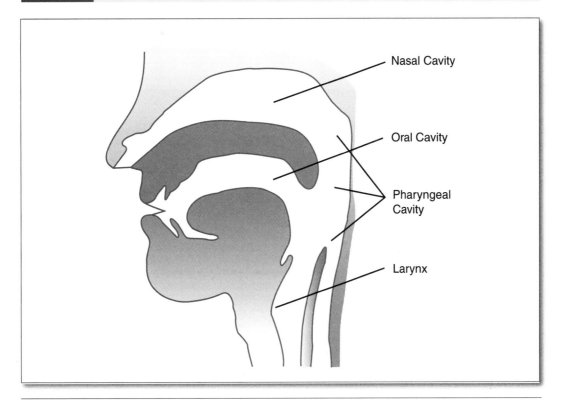

SOURCE: Levey and Osterberg (2009).

of air serve as the sound energy for all vowel sounds and as you will soon discover, for many other speech sounds as well.

The following section introduces the vocal tract, a series of interconnecting cavities where speech sounds are formed and modified.

The Vocal Tract: Cavities of the Upper Airway

The vocal tract consists of the oral cavity (mouth), nasal cavity (nose), and pharyngeal cavity (**pharynx**). Throughout the vocal tract, there are a number of structures known as articulators. There are two types of articulators: **dynamic** (movable) **articulators** and **static** (nonmovable) **articulators**. The dynamic articulators include the

- lips,
- tongue,
- mandible (lower jaw), and
- velum (soft palate).

You can view the dynamic or movable articulators (shown in Figure 5.4) as a series of adjustable valves (Netsell & Daniel, 1979). These articulators can be moved so that they completely obstruct (close off) the airstream to produce speech sounds. Consider the /t/ sound in _top_. Speakers produce this sound by placing the tongue against the **alveolar ridge** (a series of ridges found on the hard palate just behind the upper teeth). After pressure is built up in the mouth (**intraoral pressure**), the closure is suddenly released to produce a burst of noise (the /t/ sound). A speaker can also adjust the articulators to form a **constriction** (near closure) through which the air from the lungs is forced. When producing the /s/ sound in _sit_, for example, the speaker forces the air stream through a narrow opening created by placing the tongue very close to the alveolar ridge of the **hard palate** (roof of the mouth).

The teeth and hard palate are static (nonmovable) articulators. The dynamic articulators make contact with the static articulators to produce speech sounds. For example, when a person produces the /t/ sound in _top_, he or she places the tongue (a movable articulator) against the alveolar ridge of the hard palate (a static articulator). In the following section, you will discover how individual speech sounds are formed, keeping in mind that speech sounds are the basic components of words (e.g., /b/ + /o/ + /t/ = _boat_).

THE PRODUCTION OF SPEECH SOUNDS

This section introduces how a speaker adjusts the articulators to produce speech sounds, the fundamental units of words and sentences.

Vocal Fold Vibration: A Major Speech Sound Source

Vocal fold vibration is an important sound source for many of the sounds of English. As noted earlier, phonation is the term for the sound produced in the larynx when the vocal folds are closed and are set into rapid vibration by the pressurized airstream from the lungs.

Figure 5.4	Speech Articulators

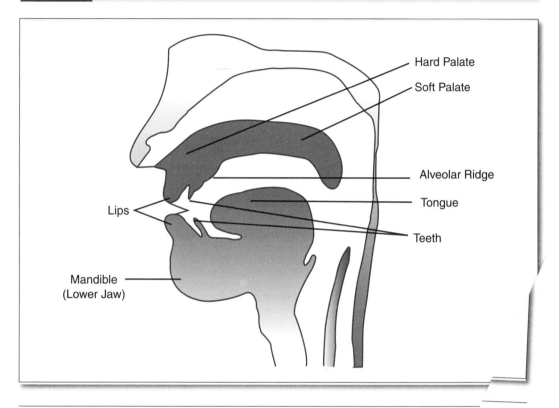

SOURCE: Levey and Osterberg (2009).

Unvoiced and Voiced Sounds

Some speech sounds are voiced (produced with vocal fold vibration), iile others are unvoiced (produced without vocal fold vibration). In the case of unvoice ounds, the vocal folds are open and are not vibrating. You can listen to and feel the differ e between voiced and unvoiced speech sounds by placing your fingers lightly on your nx (Adam's apple) while producing the following two words: *bus* (ending in the unvo consonant /s/) and *buzz* (ending in the voiced consonant /z/). As you produce both wo prolong the final /s/ and /z/ sounds. You should feel vibration during /z/ production be ie it is a voiced sound (the vocal folds are vibrating to produce that sound). You sho not feel any vibration during /s/ production since that sound is a "noise" sound luced by adjusting the articulators to form a narrow constriction in the oral cavity. n. The classes of sounds

Vocal fold vibration is essential for normal speech prod **diphthongs**, **nasals**, and produced exclusively by vocal fold vibration include vo his chapter introduces these **approximants (liquids** and **glides)**. The following sectio Chapter 3 (Tables 3.1 and 3.2) speech sounds and how they are produced. You may also r for a review of these phonemes.

SPEECH SOUNDS PRODUCED IN THE LARYNX: VOICED "PERIODIC" SOUNDS

Vowels

Vocal fold vibration is the source of sound energy for all vowel sounds. Vowel production begins in the larynx, where the vocal folds are set into vibration by the pressurized air stream from the lungs. The tongue assumes a slightly different position for each vowel sound. In addition, the production of vowels occurs, to varying degrees, with the lips either unrounded (for the /i/ sound in the word _tea_) or rounded (for the /u/ sound in the word _to_). The effect of these different vocal tract shapes on vowel quality is known as **resonance**. It is the resonance characteristics of the vocal tract that are responsible for transforming vocal fold vibration into the unique vowel sounds that emerge from a speaker's mouth.

The Vowel Quadrilateral

The traditional vowel quadrilateral is shown in Figure 5.5. The vowel quadrilateral is a graph depicting the unique tongue position of the American English vowels. Note that vowels are classified as Front and Back, Low and High.

Figure 5.5 The Vowel Quadrilateral

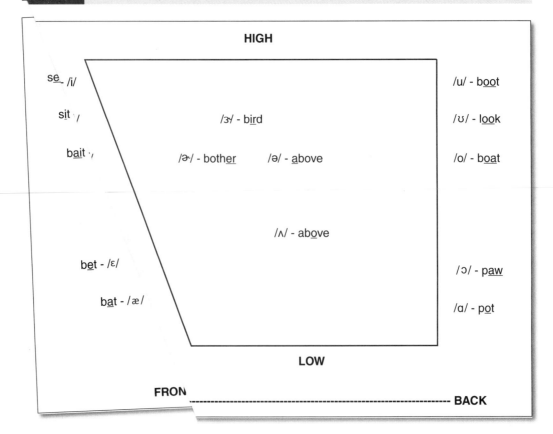

Front Vowels

The American English vowels /i/ as in *beat*, /ɪ/ as in *bit*, /e/ as in *cake*, /ɛ/ as in *pet*, and /æ/ as in *cat* are all produced with the tongue positioned in the front portion of the oral cavity. Consequently, these vowels are all classified as Front vowels.

The Front vowels are produced with varying degrees of tongue height. For example, the vowel /i/ is classified as a High Front vowel and the vowel /æ/ as a Low Front vowel. This is because the tongue is higher when producing the speech sound /i/ in *he* (a High vowel) than when producing /æ/ in *at* (a Low vowel). The tongue is highest for /i/ (a High Front vowel), mid-high for /e/ (a Mid Front vowel), and lowest for /ae/ (a Low Front vowel). All Front vowels are produced with retracted (unrounded) lips.

Back Vowels

The Back vowels consist of the vowels /u/ as in *boot*, /ʊ/ as in *put*, /o/ as in *boat*, /ɔ/ as in *taught*, and /ɑ/ as in *hot*. These vowels are produced with the tongue positioned in the back portion of the oral cavity. The vowel /u/ is a High Back vowel, /o/ is a Mid Back vowel, and /ɑ/ is a Low Back vowel. Speakers produce the vowels /u/, /ʊ/, and /o/ with varying degrees of lip rounding. Contrast your own production of /i/ (a Front vowel) and /u/ (a Back vowel) and you will note that your lips are pursed (rounded) for /u/ and spread (retracted) for /i/.

Diphthongs

Diphthongs are vowel-like sounds produced with a gradually changing articulation (Shriberg & Kent, 2003). Like vowels, diphthongs are sounds that result from vocal fold vibration. Unlike vowels, the articulators change gradually during diphthong production. Note the gliding movement of your articulators and the shift from a relatively open mouth posture to a nearly closed mouth with rounded lips when you produce the diphthong /aʊ/ (as in the word *cow*). The sounds following the /t/ in *toy, tie,* and *toe,* and the sounds following the /b/ in *bough* and *bay* are examples of diphthongs.

Nasal Sounds

We refer to certain sounds as "nasals" because the sound created in the larynx (vocal fold vibration) passes through the nose, also known as the **nasal cavity.** All other American English speech sounds pass through the mouth or the **oral cavity.** As is the case for vowels and diphthongs, vocal fold vibration is also the source of sound energy for the nasal sounds (/m/ as in *mom,* /n/ as in *nun,* and /ŋ/ as in *ring*). During nasal production, the speaker must close the oral cavity and lower the **velum (soft palate)** so that sound energy passes through the nasal cavity and out the nose. Consider the /m/ sound, for example. The speaker closes the mouth at the lips and lowers the soft palate. Because the soft palate is lowered, the sound passes through the nasal cavity, giving it a unique nasal sound quality. Figure 5.6 contrasts the velum (soft palate) in its raised and lowered positions.

Approximants

There is a group of consonant sounds formed by "approximating" the articulators (positioning the articulators relatively close to one another without forming a major

Figure 5.6	The Velopharyngeal "Valve" in the Open and Closed Positions

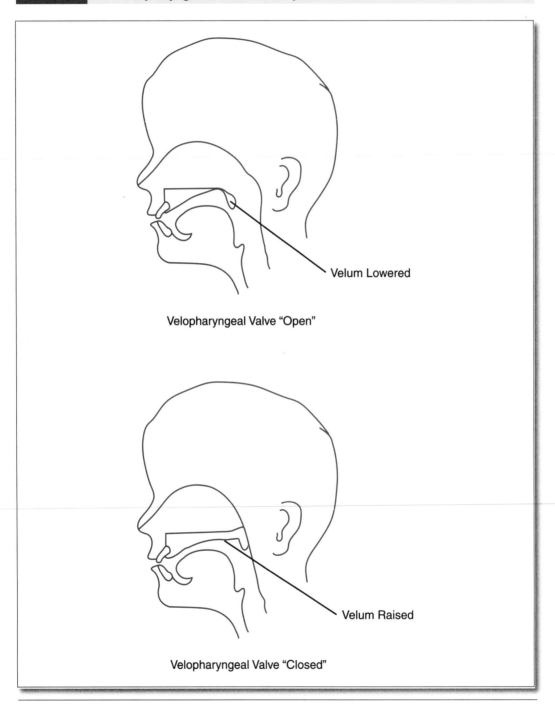

Velum Lowered

Velopharyngeal Valve "Open"

Velum Raised

Velopharyngeal Valve "Closed"

SOURCE: Levey and Osterberg (2009).

constriction or complete closure (Mackay, 1987). These sounds are called approximants. There are two classes of approximants: glides and liquids.

Glides

The glides /w/ (as in _wake_) and /j/ (as in _yellow_) are vowel-like sounds. Both sounds are produced in the larynx as a result of vocal fold vibration. The production of /w/ and /j/ involves a gliding movement from a more constricted (narrower) vocal tract to a more open (wider) vocal tract for the vowel that follows (Shriberg & Kent, 2003). Hence, the term _glide_, which captures the gliding movement of the articulators as they change the vocal tract from a constricted to relatively unconstructed state.

Liquids

The liquids /l/ (as in _lake_) and /r/ (as in _rake_) are also vowel-like sounds produced by vocal fold vibration. Liquids are similar to glides, but a major difference is that production of the liquids /l/ and /r/ does not require movement (Shriberg & Kent, 2003).

Recall that Daniel, the child described in the case study, had difficulty producing the liquid sound /r/ in certain contexts. He omitted this and other sounds in the final position of words (e.g., _car_). It is important to recognize that, although Daniel could not produce /r/ at the end of words (final position), he was able to produce the /r/ sound in other contexts (e.g., in the beginning of words, as in _red_, and middle of words, as in _mermaid_).

Daniel's omission of the /r/ sound in only the final position of words indicates a rule-governed error sound pattern, rather than simply a problem producing the /r/ sound. If Daniel presented an articulation error, it is likely that he would be unable to produce the /r/ sound in any word positions: initial position (as in _red_), medial or middle position (as in _parrot_), and final position (as in _car_). In Daniel's case, he was able to produce /r/ in other word positions but consistently omitted this and other sounds in the final position of words. He was able to produce an /r/ sound but had not mastered the "rule" of producing /r/, and other sounds, in the final position of words. Consequently, when Daniel was seen by the SLP for intervention, sessions focused not on any particular sound or sounds but on the rule of producing final sounds in words.

SPEECH SOUNDS PRODUCED IN THE VOCAL TRACT: UNVOICED "NOISE" SOUNDS

There are three classes of "noise" sounds in English: **stops**, **fricatives**, and **affricates**.

Stop Sounds

To produce stop sounds, sometimes referred to as **stop-plosives**, the speaker must

- form a complete closure in the oral cavity,

- build up pressure behind the point of closure, and then

- suddenly release the closure.

The result is a brief "burst" of noise. In order to build up adequate pressure behind the point of closure to produce a noise burst, the velum (soft palate) must be elevated, closing off the nasal cavity. **Velopharyngeal closure** is the term for this valve-like raising of the velum to seal off the nasal cavity (see Figure 5.6). The velopharyngeal mechanism (a dynamic articulator) needs to be closed (velum raised) for all American English sounds, with the exception of the three nasal sounds: /m/, /n/, and /ŋ/. Recall that the nasal sounds pass through the nasal cavity. This occurs by keeping the velopharyngeal valve open and the oral cavity closed. The velopharyngeal valve must be closed to produce the stop sounds, which require a buildup of pressure in the oral cavity.

Places of Articulation for Stops

Place of articulation refers to the location in the vocal tract where a sound is produced. In the case of stops, place of articulation refers to the point of closure. For example, to produce a /b/ sound, such as the first sound in the word _bee,_ closure occurs at the lips, which are brought together by the speaker.

There are three places of articulation for the American English stop sounds: the lips, alveolar ridge, and soft palate (velum).

- The /p/ and /b/ sounds are produced with closure at the lips (bilabial stops).

- The point of closure for the /t/ and /d/ sounds is the tongue tip pressed against the alveolar ridge (lingua-alveolar stops).

Clear and intelligibile speech is important for success in the classroom and interaction with peers.

- The /k/ and /g/ sounds are produced with the tongue bunched against the velum or soft palate (velar stops).

The /p/, /t/, and /k/ sounds are considered **voiceless stops** (produced with no vocal fold vibration), and the /b/, /d/, and /g/ sounds are classified as **voiced stops** (produced with vocal fold vibration).

Sometimes a child's speech is difficult to understand because he or she produces sounds using an incorrect tongue position. For example, the stop sound /k/ (as in _key_) should be formed with the tongue stopping the airstream in the back of the mouth. It is not unusual for a young child to attempt to produce the /k/ sound by forming the tongue closure in the front of the mouth. In this case, the word _key_ is produced as _tea_. This is a common rule-based developmental error seen in young children called _fronting_. If a child presents with fronting and other phonological processes, his or her speech may be unintelligible or very difficult to understand. Unintelligible speech can interfere with a child's ability to perform and succeed in the classroom.

Fricative Sounds

Fricative sounds are "noise" sounds that can be prolonged by the speaker. To produce a fricative sound, the speaker must

- form a significant constriction in the vocal tract,
- build up pressure behind the constriction, and then
- force air through the constriction.

Speakers produce fricatives by creating a narrow constriction (near closure) and forcing air through the constriction. Unlike stops (e.g., /p/ and /b/), this closure is not complete. The American English fricative sounds are /f/ as in _fish_, /v/ as in _vase_, /θ/ as in _thumb_, /ð/ as in _them_, /s/ as in _sun_, /z/ as in _zoo_, /ʃ/ as in _shoe_, /ʒ/ as in _beige,_ and /h/ as in _hot_.

The constriction for /f/ and /v/ is formed by the upper teeth and lower lip (labio-dental). The constriction for /θ/ and /ð/ is formed by the tongue and teeth (lingua-dental). The /s/, /z/, /ʃ/, and /ʒ/ are produced by forming a constriction between the tongue and various points along the palate (lingua-alveolar and lingua-palatal). In the case of /h/, the constriction is formed between the vocal folds. The space between the vocal folds is called the **glottis**. Consequently, /h/ is referred to as a glottal fricative. The /f/, /θ/, /s/, /ʃ/, and /h/ sounds are voiceless fricatives, and the /v/, /ð/, /z/, and /ʒ/ sounds are voiced fricatives. The voiceless fricatives are produced exclusively by creating noise in the vocal tract (without vocal fold vibration). The voiced fricatives have two simultaneous sound sources: noise created in the oral cavity and vocal fold vibration.

Recall that Daniel, the child in the case study, was unable to produce the /s/ sound in words such as _stop_ (which he produced as _top_). Daniel had mastered production of the /s/ sound when the sound occurred alone (e.g., in _sun_), but when the /s/ sound occurred in a sequence of two consonants (e.g., /s/ + /t/), he omitted it. It is not uncommon during early stages of speech development for young children to master production of a sound when it occurs alone (e.g., _sit_) but not when it occurs with another consonant sound (as in _stop_).

Affricate Sounds

The affricate sounds are best viewed as combination sounds involving a stop closure (as in the production of the /t/ sound in _top_) followed by a fricative release (Shriberg & Kent, 2003). The affricate sounds are /ʧ/ as in _church_ and /ʤ/ as in _judge_. The /ʧ/ sound is a voiceless affricate (noise only) and the /ʤ/ sound is a voiced affricate (noise combined with vocal fold vibration).

The stop, fricative, and affricate sounds all require velopharyngeal closure in order to build up adequate intraoral pressure to produce a "noise" sound.

The following section considers the connection between the voice and language and how the voice is used to convey meaning.

THE CONTRIBUTION OF THE VOICE TO LANGUAGE

Thus far, we have considered only the contribution of the voice to speech sound production. The voice (vocal fold vibration) is an important source of energy for many speech sounds, but it also contributes to **language content** (meaning). For example, the voice is responsible for **stress** (emphasis) and **intonation,** variations of pitch that mark differences between a statement and a question: a statement that "John _is_ coming" versus a question asking "John is com**ing**?" (with bold and underline indicating a higher or rising pitch or intonation).

Both stress and intonation influence language content (Atkinson, 1978). A speaker can alter the intensity of phonation. A change in intensity corresponds to a change in loudness. The speaker can also alter the **fundamental frequency** (f_o) of vocal fold vibration (the rate of vocal fold vibration). A change in f_o corresponds to a change in pitch. By changing the f_o of vocal fold vibration (intonation), the speaker can alter meaning. A rising intonation denotes a question, and a rising-falling intonation signals a statement (e.g., "John is coming?" said with a rising intonation asks the question "Is John is coming?" whereas "John is coming" said with a falling (lowering) intonation means that John is definitely coming).

Word stress is created by producing a syllable within a word in a manner that is louder, longer, and higher in pitch than other syllables in that word. Consider the following example (Cavallo, 1999): An identical sentence is repeated three times with varying stress (the underlined and bolded word in each sentence receives primary stress).

Ben loves Jerry.

Ben **loves** Jerry.

Ben loves **Je**rry.

If the reader produces this phrase aloud, each time altering word stress, the effect of the voice on language content (meaning) will become apparent. In the first example, in which stress is placed on the word _Ben_, the speaker conveys that it is Ben who loves Jerry, not Steve or Edy. In the second case (stress on the word _loves_), it is apparent that Ben doesn't merely like

Jerry, he loves him. In the third example (stress on the first syllable in the word *Jerry*), the speaker is commenting on the fact that Ben loves Jerry, not someone else (Edy or Steve, for example). Thus, the voice is not only important for the production of speech sounds; the voice also contributes to language content. By varying the pitch, loudness, and duration of the voice, the speaker can alter stress and intonation, which influence the meaning of an utterance.

The following section describes the complex neuromuscular activity that underlies speech production. While reading this section, recall the challenges confronting Daniel, the child discussed in the case study at the beginning of this chapter, and consider the following question: Is there a connection between Daniel's speech production difficulties and his neuromuscular motor abilities? Consider, for example, Daniel's inability to execute the speech movements necessary to correctly produce words that contain consonant clusters (as in *play* and *stop*).

SPEECH PRODUCTION: A COMPLEX NEUROMUSCULAR MOTOR ACTIVITY

During speech production, the speaker must carefully coordinate the contraction of hundreds of muscles throughout the speech mechanism (i.e., the ventilatory system, larynx, and vocal tract).

Consider, for example, a young child producing the simple consonant-vowel combination /ma/ ("ma"). The child must contract the inspiratory muscles of the ventilatory system (muscles of inhalation) while opening the vocal folds (vocal cords) to draw air into the lungs. He or she then must coordinate the expiratory muscles of the ventilatory system (muscles of exhalation) with the muscles of the larynx to close the vocal folds in order to generate adequate subglottal pressure to set the vocal folds into rapid vibration to produce the initial consonant sound (/m/). At the same time, numerous muscles in the vocal tract need to contract in order to move structures (close the lips and lower the velum or soft palate) so that the sound produced in the larynx (vocal fold vibration) is directed through the pharyngeal and nasal cavities to produce the /m/ sound.

In order to produce the second sound, /a/, the child must simultaneously coordinate the movement of several speech articulators: the mouth must open, the tongue must assume a specific position in the mouth, and the soft palate must close, sealing off the nasal cavity. Once these articulatory adjustments are accomplished, sound (produced by vocal fold vibration) will pass through the oral cavity and an intelligible /a/ sound will result.

If the movements of the articulators are incomplete or mistimed, even by only a few milliseconds, abnormal airflow and air pressures will result and speech intelligibility will be compromised. Given the complex articulatory adjustments required to produce a simple consonant-vowel combination such as /ma/, one can imagine the neuromuscular challenges more complex speech targets would pose for a child who has difficulty coordinating movements of the articulators.

Returning to the case of Daniel, the production of two consonants in sequence (e.g., /p/ followed by /l/ in the production of the word *play*) was too complex given his current level of neuromotor development. Daniel's error pattern is typical of young children who are just beginning to produce words. With time, as his motor skills improve, Daniel will be able to move his articulators (e.g., lips and tongue) with greater precision and control and he will be able to produce consonant clusters in words such as *sky, tree, skip,* and *play.*

STUDENTS WITH SPEECH PROBLEMS: COMMON SIGNS

This section provides brief descriptions of speech disorders that the teacher might observe in the classroom. A classroom teacher is in a unique position to identify and refer children who present with speech problems. A child who presents with aberrant speech patterns should be referred to the SLP.

Stuttering

It is not uncommon for young children to occasionally repeat one or two syllables. Research has demonstrated, however, that children who stutter repeat more than 10 words, syllables, or sounds per 100 words (Guitar, 1998). A stutterer may repeat the first syllable of a word (as in *ra-ra-rabbit*), prolong a sound in a word (as in *s-s-s-sing*), or find it difficult to initiate speech.

Cluttering

Clutterers tend to talk too quickly and slur or omit syllables in longer words (St. Louis, Raphael, Myers, & Bakker, 2003). A child who clutters may speak in bursts of speech and introduce pauses in the middle of an utterance. Speech will sound jerky rather than smooth.

Articulation Disorders

A child with an articulation disorder has difficulty producing sounds in words. The child may substitute sounds such as /ə/ for /s/ (*thoup* for *soup*), omit sounds (e.g., *top* for *stop*), or add sounds to words (e.g., *cupuh* for *cup*).

Apraxia

Apraxia is a disorder of motor planning. A child with apraxia has difficulty sequencing sounds in words and will exhibit more difficulty with multisyllabic words. He or she might produce the word *banana* as *nabana*.

STRATEGIES FOR CLASSROOM TEACHERS

The classroom teacher may observe signs of a speech disorder that have the potential to interfere with a child's ability to communicate effectively. Several basic strategies that the classroom teacher can use with children who have speech problems are listed below (Fujiki & Brinton, 1984).

It is important to pay attention to children's attempts to communicate, as this provides a good model of listening for other children.

- *Create a climate of emotional acceptance in the classroom.* By accepting all children's attempts to communicate, the teacher fosters communication and encourages children to express ideas and contribute to class discussions without the fear of penalty.

- *Be an attentive listener.* By paying attention to children's attempts to communicate, the teacher provides a good model for other children and communicates that he or she is interested in what the children are saying.

- *Use a slower speaking rate when talking.* By adopting a moderate rate of speech (not too fast and not too slow), the teacher facilitates children's understanding of spoken information (language comprehension) and provides a good model for his or her students' speech.

Additional strategies to foster good communication in the classroom follow:

- *Reduce classroom noise.* Ambient noise is a factor that will adversely affect communication in the classroom. A classroom in which background noise is minimized provides an ideal environment for communication.

- *Avoid correcting a child's speech errors*, which can damage a child's self-esteem. Instead, use recasting (see the case study at the beginning of the chapter)— repeat the child's production using correct sounds at an appropriate speech rate.

- *Collaborate with the SLP* to make sure that you are using appropriate and effective strategies in the classroom to support students' speech attempts.

- *Emphasize children's strengths* as much as possible to encourage communication. This will also help children maintain good self-esteem.

It should be noted that these general strategies are appropriate to use with all children, not only those who present with speech and language difficulties.

CASE STUDY REVISITED

Throughout this chapter, we have made references to Daniel, a kindergarten-age child with unclear speech. His teacher and peers were experiencing difficulty understanding his speech, and Daniel was showing signs of frustration when not understood.

CASE STUDY REVISITED: The impact of speech skills on communication and social interaction

Ms. Lawton met with Daniel's parents to determine their perspective on Daniel's speech production abilities. Daniel's mother reported that, although she was able to understand about 75% of Daniel's speech, other members of the family had more difficulty understanding him. Ms. Lawton recommended referring Daniel to the Committee on Special Education (CSE) in order to evaluate the nature and severity of his speech difficulties and determine his eligibility for speech services. His parents readily agreed. At the conclusion of their conference, Ms. Lawton introduced Daniel's parents to the school SLP.

As part of a CSE team evaluation, the school SLP assessed Daniel's speech skills using a formal test of articulation, observing his spontaneous speech in the classroom and on the playground and obtaining relevant background information from his family. The SLP recommended a hearing screening to rule out the possibility that a hearing problem could be contributing to Daniel's speech difficulties. Results of the speech evaluation confirmed Ms. Lawton's observation that Daniel had difficulty producing consonant clusters (e.g., *pl-* and *st-*) and that he omitted final sounds in words (e.g., "bu_" for *bus*). The SLP found no evidence of any neuromuscular problems (problems with the strength or control of the articulators), since Daniel was able to move his speech articulators with adequate precision and range of motion. Based on the presence of these normal developmental speech sound production errors and the resulting negative effects on Daniel's performance in the classroom, intervention was recommended and approved by the CSE.

The SLP initiated an intervention program designed to strengthen Daniel's ability to discriminate between sound contrasts. For example, to address his difficulty producing *pl-*, she presented him with picture pairs (with words below each picture). One picture illustrated *pay,* and the other illustrated *play.* The SLP and Daniel took turns asking each other to point to the picture that showed *pay* versus *play.* She also developed a similar discrimination game for use at home. To address Daniel's lack of final sound production in words, the SLP presented Daniel with sound contrasts, consisting of two pictures (with words) that illustrated contrasts such as *boo* versus *boot* and *bee* versus *beet.* Note that these word pairs (called minimal contrast pairs) differ only by the presence (*boot*) or absence (*boo*) of the final sound. This approach taught Daniel that the production of the final sound is important to language content (meaning).

After several months of intervention, Daniel's speech intelligibility improved considerably. Daniel's teacher reported that his speech was easier to understand and that his play interactions with peers had improved. Daniel's mother reported that she and other family members were better able to understand his speech. Intervention continued throughout the school year. During therapy sessions, the SLP introduced pictures of words that promoted sound-letter awareness to support Daniel's reading development. In consultation with Ms. Lawton, she also used materials from the classroom to facilitate generalization (the carryover of skills learned in the classroom to other contexts). To maximize generalization, all work conducted in the therapy setting was incorporated into speech games that were developed for use at home.

SUMMARY

This chapter provided an overview of the structure and function of the mechanisms underlying speech production. It stressed the complexity of speech production as a neuromotor activity. The classroom teacher who has a basic understanding of the processes underlying speech production is likely to be sensitive to and able to identify typical problems that occur during a child's early speech development.

Key points discussed in this chapter include

- a very basic discussion of the structure and function of the speech mechanism,

- how the breathing mechanism supports the production of speech sounds,

- a description of the various sounds of speech (vowels and consonants) and how they are produced, and

- the contribution of the voice to language content (meaning).

In the case study presented in this chapter, a child's speech problem interfered with his ability to communicate with peers and adults. The child's poor speech intelligibility resulted in rejection by his peers and social isolation in the classroom. His teacher's ability to identify the child's speech problem and refer him to the school SLP had a positive impact not only on the child's speech production abilities but also on his overall performance in the classroom. As was evident in this case study, early identification and treatment of a speech delay can have a positive effect not only on a child's ability to communicate but on his or her social and emotional development as well.

This chapter introduced the mechanics underlying speech production. In Chapter 6, you will learn about the role of the brain in speech and language development. We will consider the complexity of the brain's structures, the skills associated with various regions of the brain, and the functions of the brain that relate to language and academic performance. Knowledge of how the brain works is essential to understanding how children learn and develop language.

The classroom teacher plays an important role in identifying a variety of developmental problems that often first become apparent in the classroom. The teacher, through collaboration with other professionals, plays a critical role in the development and implementation of strategies to address these problems.

KEY WORDS

Affricates	Inspiration	Rib cage
Alveolar ridge	Intonation	Soft palate
Approximants	Intraoral pressure	Static articulators
Articulators	Language content	Stops
Auditory feedback	Larynx	Stop-plosives
Communication	Liquids	Stress
Constriction	Nasal cavity	Subglottal pressure
Diaphragm	Nasals	Thorax
Diphthongs	Oral cavity	Trachea
Dynamic articulators	Orthography	Velopharyngeal closure
Expiration	Pharynx	Velum
Fricatives	Phonation	Ventilatory system
Fundamental frequency	Phonemes	Vocal cords
Glides	Phonological processes	Vocal folds
Glottis	Place of articulation	Vocal tract
Hard palate	Power source	Voiced sounds
Inhalation	Resonance	Voiceless sounds

STUDY QUESTIONS

1. Identify the three components of the speech mechanism and describe their respective functions. Daniel, the child in the case study, presented with specific speech sound production difficulties. Given his speech problems, what components of the speech mechanism were most likely involved?

2. Describe at least two strategies you would use in the classroom to help Daniel, the child in the case study. Are there specific questions you would pose to the SLP?

3. List the sounds that presented Daniel, the child in the case study, with difficulty. Describe the mechanisms that are involved in the production of these sounds.

4. Frequently, children who have difficulty controlling the air that supports speech production have shorter sentences than their peers. Can you explain why this might occur? In other words, what is the connection between respiratory support for speech and sentence production?

PROJECTS

1. Video or tape record a variety of different speakers: children, adult females, and adult males. Note the differences in their voices in terms of pitch and intonation patterns. Chart the differences in how they produce different sentences in terms of rising or falling intonation.

2. Observe the movement of several speakers' dynamic articulators. Ask them to open their mouths and say /a/ ("ah"). Note the movement of the soft palate or velum. Ask them to produce the fricative sound /ʃ/ ("sh") and listen to the noisy quality of this sound and then the affricate sound /tʃ/ ("ch"). Compare the difference in the movement of the articulators and duration of these sounds. Which of these sounds could the speakers prolong?

3. Listen to a speaker who has learned English as a second language. Note any differences in his or her stress and intonation patterns during speech. Did you discover any unusual stress patterns? Next, research the stress patterns associated with the person's first language.

STUDENT STUDY SITE

Visit the Student Study Site at **www.sagepub.com/levey** for these additional learning tools:

- Video Links
- Self Quizzes
- E-Flashcards

- Sample Forms and Assessment Tools
- Recommended Readings
- Web Resources

SUGGESTIONS FOR FURTHER READING

Bernthal, J. E., Bankson, N. W., & Flipsen, P. (2008). *Articulation and phonological disorders*. Boston: Allyn & Bacon.

Hall, B. J., Oyer, H. J., & Haas, W. H. (2001). *Speech, language, and hearing disorders: A guide for the teacher*. Upper Saddle River, NJ: Pearson.

Haynes, W. O., Moran, M. J., & Pindzola, R. H. (2005). *Communication disorders in the class*. Sudbury, MA: Jones & Bartlett.

McLean, S. (2002). *The basics of speech communication*. Boston: Allyn & Bacon.

Williams, A. L. (2003). *Speech disorders resource guide for preschool children*. Clifton Park, NY: Thomson/Delmar.

The Role of the Brain in Speech and Language

Sandra Levey and Joyce F. West

CASE STUDY: **The role of the brain in language processing**

Mary is a student in Mr. Wald's fourth-grade class. She has been diagnosed with a learning disability. He noticed that she had forgotten to do her homework again. She reported that she forgot about the homework that required a book report. She also could not find the template provided by Mr. Wald to guide her in writing this report. Her classroom teacher was also concerned about other difficulties that he observed in the classroom. For example, Mary had difficulty drawing conclusions or inferences from written texts (e.g., what events caused a character to behave in a certain manner). Consequently, Mr. Wald concluded that strategies for homework assignments and drawing inferences from reading tasks were the primary areas that required attention.

What do you think Mr. Wald should suggest to Mary to help her remember homework assignments? On what information and experiences did you base your answer?

INTRODUCTION

This chapter introduces the role of the brain in children's learning and language development. Research from neuroscience (the study of the brain and nervous system) and cognitive science (the study of the mind and intelligence) has contributed to our knowledge of the role of the brain in children's development, providing the classroom teacher with approaches that enhance learning.

The brain is the most creative and inventive organ in the body. All mental life occurs within the brain, allowing us to think, remember people and events, acquire information, and express our feelings through music, art, and dance. The brain allows an individual to plan, organize, and learn. The brain also controls all the organs and movement in the body, along with providing the ability to process and understand **sensory information** (information heard, seen, touched, tasted, and smelled). Much of the information on the brain comes from early studies that have examined the functional abilities of this organ (Penfield & Roberts,1959; Springer & Deutsch, 1985), along with more recent studies of anatomy and function (Binder et al., 2000; Carpenter, Just, Keller, Eddy, & Thulborn, 1999; Embick, Marantz, Miyashita, O'Neil, & Sakai, 2000; Friederici, Opitz, & von Cramon, 2000; Hirano et al., 1997; Horwitz, Rumsey, & Donohue, 1998; Laine, Rinne, Krause, Teras, & Sipila, 1999; Poldrack et al., 1999; Rumsey et al., 1999; Simos, Breier, Fletcher, Bergman, & Papanicolaou, 2000). The brain has the ability to make continued learning possible, an ongoing process that lasts a lifetime. The brain plays a role in all aspects of learning, including the development of language.

The brain provides the ability to express our ideas and feelings through words, art, music, and dance.

THE BRAIN AND LANGUAGE DEVELOPMENT

Language learning depends on two factors: innate abilities and input from the environment, as described in Chapter 2. Although we know that the brain is equipped, or "prewired," to develop language (Chomsky, 2002), it is people, things, and events in the environment that stimulate the brain to develop and learn. In fact, language and other learning skills will not develop without the stimulation that comes from interaction with language and events in a child's environment.

We are born with about 100 billion neurons. The infant's brain discards (**prunes**) the neurons not used or stimulated. At the same time, connections (**synapses**) develop between those neurons that have survived the pruning process. By 5 years of age, a child's brain structure is similar to that of an adult (Mildner, 2008), while learning and life experiences continue to affect the brain throughout the life span.

The Brain at Birth

At birth, the brain has the potential to take advantage of its **genetic inheritance**. It is at this point that language begins to develop. Heredity plays a role in language development, as does learning (Shulman, 1998). Learning requires experience, enriched and enhanced by sensory events and input from the environment, such as interactions with individuals and activities.

The brain is not fully developed at birth and soon begins a rapid acceleration of growth. Given learning experiences, the infant's brain changes according to the stimulation received. The brain's ability to make connections to new information based on experience is termed **cerebral plasticity**, and there are stages when the brain is more sensitive to experiences and learning new information (Kleim & Jones, 2008). If a particular pathway is damaged, cerebral plasticity makes it possible for the brain to adapt and for new pathways to be created.

Language begins at birth and requires a stimulating environment with opportunities for learning (Shulman, 1998). For example, expressive language begins with an infant's making sounds. The response to these sounds from adults and other children in the environment helps shape these early efforts into real words. Typical language development emerges from interaction with adults and other children; a stimulating environment with opportunities for learning is a prerequisite.

The Brain at 3 to 4 Months

As early as the first 3 to 4 months of age, children are able to discriminate one person from another based on the perception of facial expressions and vocal characteristics (Shulman, 1998). During the first 2 years of life, children become aware of the world around them and use words to refer to entities (things), properties (characteristics), and actions or events (Bernstein & Levey, 2009).

Children develop concepts that govern their understanding of the world around them: the concepts of space, time, and quantity (2 to 7 years of age), logical thinking (7 to 11 years of age), and logical abstract thought (11 to 15 years of age and all the way into young adulthood). Logical thinking (e.g., "What will happen if . . . ?") and logical abstract thought involve children thinking about possible outcomes or consequences, along with planning for these outcomes.

Innate Abilities

One of the most interesting abilities of the brain is that this organ possesses the **innate** (inborn) capability to develop any language that exists in the world. For example, infants are able to react to differences between sounds (e.g., *s* and *z*) and among sounds (e.g., *s*, *z*, and *sh*) in all languages, including languages that are vastly different from the language spoken in the infant's environment. They lose the ability to respond to these differences at about 10 to 12 months of age (Werker & Tees, 1984). At this point in development, toddlers' brains become more selective to sounds, responding only to differences in sounds in their native language. Thus, children possess the early ability to learn any language, while exposure to their native language leads to the loss of sensitivity to nonnative languages. This ability is not completely lost, as most individuals are able to learn new languages during their lifetime (although this process may be more laborious than learning at an earlier age).

THE BRAIN AND THE CLASSROOM

The case study presented at the beginning of this chapter describes a problem often seen when children are identified as having a learning disability in the classroom. The classroom teacher first notes difficulty with a child's organization and completion of work in a timely manner. It would be incorrect to consider children with a learning disability as willfully lazy or disinterested. Children with this type of disorder have intact intelligence, as the cause of this disorder is a neurological dysfunction that affects attention, working memory, and/or executive functions (Zera & Lucian, 2001). These are the factors mediated by the frontal lobe of the brain (Barkley, 1997; Denckla, 1996).

The **brain** is the organ that governs **executive functions**, an essential factor in academic success (Singer & Bashir, 1999). In the classroom, executive functions appear in a child's ability to use language, taking the form of inner speech to talk themselves through difficult tasks (Berk, 1992). There is a detailed description of inner speech in Chapter 2.

There is a strong connection between language and executive control (Denckla, 1996). Through language and **metacognition** (a child's self-knowledge of his or her own language and thought processes), children learn to self-monitor to determine (a) what they need to do and (b) how well they are doing. Another way that language connects with executive functions is when children learn to talk with other students and teachers to obtain information and engage in the classroom experience. Children learn to "make plans, discuss, evaluate ideas, participate in groups, reflect on their work, change their minds, and rewrite their papers" (Singer & Bashir, 1999, p. 267). They also use language (verbal or inner speech) to remind themselves to plan for and finish academic work on time, especially in the early school years.

Self-Regulation

An important executive function of the brain is **self-regulation**, defined by a child's ability to guide, monitor, and direct his or her performance in a task (Singer & Bashir, 1999, p. 266). In this way, a child can perceive her or his abilities, level of motivation, the task demands, and most likely performance outcomes. Self-regulation skills provide the child with the ability to self-monitor and self-evaluate his or her work (Zimmerman, 1989). Self-regulation is also key to helping children better modulate their behavior in relation to environmental demands, which can be problematic for students with learning disabilities because they often miss key cues in the environment.

Additional Executive Skills Required for Success in Academic Contexts

Children must possess the ability to maintain attention, control impulses, be flexible if there is a need to modify or make a change, manage time, be organized, use mental planning, apply problem solving, establish priorities, and execute a task (Geffner, 2007). Many of the disorders that affect academic abilities and learning skills may be associated with the role of the frontal cortex in executive functions. Geffner states that individuals frequently describe a child who lacks these executive functions as lazy, unmotivated, confused, and disorganized. Thus, without good executive function, these children may not be able to get work done. Children who lack some or all of the executive functions frequently lack self-awareness and are unaware of the need to monitor their behaviors because they incorrectly believe that they are already doing this monitoring.

The role of executive functions in the classroom in terms of attention, memory, organization, and study skills is discussed in Chapter 3. Executive functions are also involved in **abstract thought** and self-monitoring, characterized by the following abilities:

- Drawing conclusions from written materials

- Changing and modifying plans (to review academic work and to correct errors)

- Initiating action (to prepare for exams and to complete home assignments)

- Rejecting inappropriate actions (such as inappropriate interaction with peers)

- Learning from past mistakes or prior errors

Certainly, poor executive functioning can lead to academic difficulties, such as those associated with learning disabilities and attention-deficit hyperactivity disorders. Thus, the child discussed in the case study may not be avoiding work. Instead, she may require guidance in developing the executive functions that will help her successfully achieve academic goals. Understanding how the brain functions and how to activate the brain can help the classroom teacher stimulate children's brains to achieve these goals. Given the appropriate supports in the classroom, children with a learning disability can perform better with academic skills for planning, organization, and learning.

Stimulating Children's Brains

Research shows that classroom teachers can stimulate children's brains through tasks that involve processing information. For example, there is increased activity and blood flow to the front regions of the brain when children are asked to think about someone else's state of mind (Baron-Cohen et al., 1994). This frequently occurs in the classroom, when the teacher asks children what a story character *thinks, feels, wants,* or *believes.* To understand how the brain learns, it is important to understand the basic structure of the brain: the brain cell.

BRAIN CELLS

All the body's organs consist of **cells**. In the brain, these cells are called neurons. Neurons are the functioning foundations of the brain. Neurons make connections with other neurons through synapses (connections) and transmit information in two directions: (a) from the brain to the body and (b) from structures and organs in the body back to the brain. Each neuron may communicate directly with as many as 2,000 other neurons (Seikel, King, & Drumright, 2008). Neurons form **white matter** and **grey matter**. Grey cell bodies form the

The brain provides children with the ability to solve problems and review their work to determine errors.

cerebral cortex, the surface of the brain. The white inner mass of the brain is called the **cerebrum,** and it consists of myelinated (white) axons that interconnect different regions.

Neurons

A neuron often consists of a **cell body** and a single long fiber called the **axon** (see Figure 6.1). Some axons are **myelinated**, consisting of a white sheath that serves to insulate the axon and speed the transmission of impulses. **Dendrites** attached to the cell body receive impulses from other neurons. They then transmit these impulses along the axon, which transmits this information across a synapse. There are up to 100 billion neurons in the human brain. These neurons allow the brain to process information and to store memories, experiences, information, and learning.

To understand the brain, it is also necessary to understand that different areas of the brain are responsible for different functions. For example, the functions associated with the left brain hemisphere are different than those associated with the right. The next section presents these differences.

AREAS OF THE BRAIN

The brain is the body's largest organ (see Figure 6.2 on page 108). It is encased in a bony structure (the skull) that is remarkably resilient and flexible during the first year of life, providing protection to the fragile brain within. It is part of the **central nervous system**. The cerebral

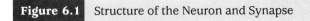

Figure 6.1   Structure of the Neuron and Synapse

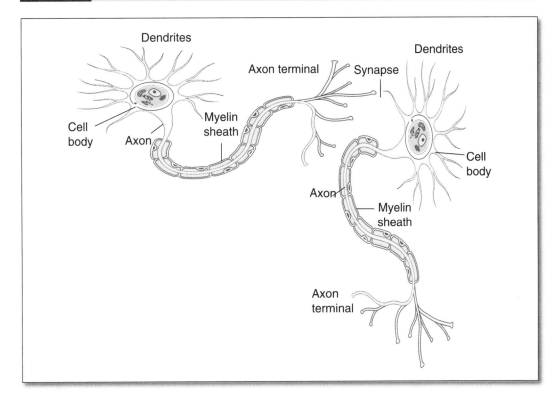

SOURCE: Otto, *Language Development Early Childhood,* Figure 2.2 p. 40 and Figure 2.3 p. 41, © 2010. Reproduced by permission of Pearson Education, Inc.

cortex is the outer surface of the brain. Cognitive functions such as awareness, attention, thought, language, and consciousness emanate from the cerebral cortex. It is only 2 to 3 millimeters thick, but it contains the cell bodies of billions of neurons that interconnect with one another. The brain sits on the **brainstem**, which in turn sits on the **spinal column**. The **cerebellum,** which lies at the base of the brain, is an important structure for balance, posture, and kinesthetic awareness (awareness of the position of the body in space, along with movement of the muscles, tendons, and joints).

The Two Halves of the Brain

The brain is divided into two halves: the **right brain** and the **left brain**. For the most part, the right side of the brain communicates with the left side of the body and the left side of the brain with the right side of the body. The left hemisphere of the brain is specialized for language and verbal reasoning, while the right hemisphere engages in processing emotional nuances and visuospatial tasks (tasks that require the visual perception of spatial relationships among objects).

The two halves of the brain work together for almost every task we undertake. For example, reading this page requires the use of the left brain to understand the words on the page and use of the right brain to provide images for the words you read. The **corpus callosum** is the primary connection between the left and right hemispheres of the brain and acts to convey neural information from one hemisphere to the other.

| **Figure 6.2** | Structure of the Outer Layer of the Left Hemisphere |

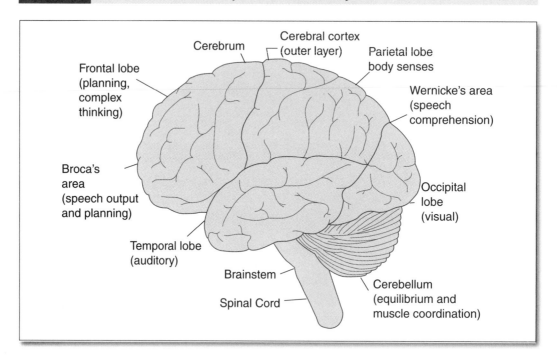

SOURCE: Otto, *Language Development Early Childhood,* Figure 2.2 p. 40 and Figure 2.3 p. 41, © 2010. Reproduced by permission of Pearson Education, Inc.

THE PARTS OF THE BRAIN

Frontal Lobe

The **frontal lobe** is the largest lobe in the brain. It contains the area called the **motor cortex**, which is responsible for planning and carrying out voluntary gross motor functions such as walking, running, or scratching your head and fine motor functions such as handwriting. Motor pathways originate in the cerebral cortex, travel through the center of the brain, and cross the middle of the brainstem to the spinal cord. At this point, the motor pathways innervate the opposite side of the body.

Broca's Area

Broca's area lies within the frontal lobe. Broca's area is involved in the motor (movement) planning necessary for speech. Broca's area is credited with language production, which was discovered when patients with lesions or injuries in this area lost the ability to speak.

Prefrontal Cortex

The **prefrontal cortex** is the anterior part of the frontal lobes of the brain. Most internal and external information travels to the prefrontal cortex. It is here in the frontal lobe that all information about the external environment and internal states are correlated (Hécaen & Albert, 1975). The prefrontal cortex is responsible for **cognitive functions** (working memory and decision making) and intelligent behavior. The prefrontal cortex is important in guiding or inhibiting an individual's responses to events (Constantinidis, Williams, & Goldman-Rakic, 2002). This area governs sensitivity to rewards and punishments.

Senses and the Brain

Information travels to the brain from the senses (sight, hearing, touch, smell, and taste). In the classroom, sight and hearing are the primary vehicles for learning. When children are learning, information first travels to the brain and is stored as immediate or **working memory.** There, this information is held for about 30 seconds in order to screen what one should be attending to in the environment. It is then coded to link the new information to information already known about this topic (Baddeley, 1986). Important information is then moved and stored in long-term memory. Findings show that the greatest amount of activity associated with working memory occurs in the frontal lobe of the brain (Sousa, 2006).

Prefrontal Lobe

The prefrontal lobe is the center of executive functions, functions that are important in academic skills (Singer & Bashir, 1999). These functions involve control processes that affect making and initiating plans for action, modifying these plans based on outcomes, and reconsidering options. Executive functions also involve being able to think abstractly, change and modify plans when necessary, initiate action, hold plans in working memory, and reject inappropriate actions. Another feature of executive functions is the ability to learn from past mistakes. Certainly, being impaired in executive functioning can have a negative impact on academic success, especially when assignments have multiple components and require planning and organization.

Parietal Lobe

Behind the frontal lobe lies the **parietal lobe**. This lobe serves to bring together sensory information from different senses. An example is the integration of sound (music) and vision that occurs when we listen to a piece of music. Centers in the parietal lobe are particularly good at sensing where the body is in space and helping navigate one's body through the world. The parietal lobe is involved with visuospatial processing, the manipulation of objects, and knowledge of numbers and their relations. Copying from the blackboard, basic numerical concepts, and navigating through space without banging into things are examples of skills controlled by the parietal lobe. Bodily sensations such as vision and hearing, touch, pressure, pain, and temperature are associated with the parietal lobe as well, which serves to integrate the senses to experience touch, pressure, or pain. Thus, if the motor strip sends signals to alert you to use your arm to scratch your head, then information about how it feels as you scratch and where you arm is in space are fed back to the sensory strip in the parietal lobe.

Temporal Lobe

The **temporal lobe** lies on the side of the brain. Auditory processing is a key function of this lobe of the brain. The **primary auditory cortex** is located here within **Heschl's gyrus**. Speech sounds activate the primary auditory cortex (Hirano et al., 1997), and sounds are interpreted by an adjoining region in the temporal lobe called **Wernicke's area**, where the understanding of spoken language occurs. The area that includes Heschl's gyrus differentiates linguistic from nonlinguistic information, with linguistic information, such as spoken language, sent to the left temporal lobe for processing (Owens, 2008). Sentences and longer spoken utterances are stored in working memory (sometimes called short-term memory) for processing.

Occipital Lobe

The **occipital lobe** sits at the back of the head. It is the location of the **primary visual cortex**. It receives and interprets visual information that is sent to this area from the eyes and is responsible for interpreting written material and associating this information with graphic representations. This lobe is also involved in visuospatial processing, discrimination of movement, and color discrimination (Westmoreland, 1994).

Cerebellum and Brainstem

The cerebellum coordinates movement, balance, and fine motor movement, also combining sensory information from the eyes, ears, and muscles. The brainstem sits on the spinal cord. The functions of the brainstem include breathing, swallowing, heart rate, and regulation of blood pressure.

We have reviewed the areas of the brain and their roles associated with learning, language, and basic functions. Next, we will examine strategies for supporting learning in the classroom.

STRATEGIES FOR THE CLASSROOM

The case study presented at the beginning of this chapter reported that this child had difficulty with inference, one of the hardest skills to teach. This is because the process of inference depends on understanding that there are things in a story that are implied while not actually presented. For example, the following scenario never directly states that it is raining outside:

■ I got up today and looked out the window. I put on my boots and took my umbrella.

The question that targets inference is "What is the weather like outside?" The listener or reader must infer the weather conditions from information in the sentence. The classroom teacher may ask children to play "detective," to find clues in the paragraph that could answer a question without an actual answer present in the paragraph (e.g., "Why do I need boots and an umbrella?").

A teacher may also work to address children's executive function challenges in the classroom, using strategies that support their learning (Sava, 2000).

- Providing clear directions for lessons

- Giving only one direction at a time to allow the child to repeat or record the instruction

- Planning for frequent breaks and decreasing the length of tasks to allow time for processing

- Using interactive teaching styles and techniques by asking questions about content and meaning (p. 157)

These strategies are illustrative of good teaching practices for a child who has difficulty in learning. However, these strategies can also be very helpful to a significant number of other students in the classroom.

CASE STUDY REVISITED

We first met Mary, a student in Mr. Wald's fourth-grade class who has been diagnosed with a learning disability, at the beginning of this chapter. Her teacher noted that she was having difficulty remembering tasks and items, along with experiencing difficulty with more abstract classroom requirements.

CASE STUDY REVISITED: The role of the brain in language processing

Mary's difficulties in Mr. Wald's classroom consisted of forgetting to complete the book report assignment, losing homework objects such as the report template, and experiencing difficulty in drawing inferences from written texts. Some of these difficulties began to emerge in the third grade, but Mary's parents were reluctant to have her evaluated then as there was no significant impact on her academic performance at that time. As the curriculum has become more demanding and the reading tasks much less literal (containing language that is more figurative), her difficulties have become more apparent in comparison with her peers.

We know that the first step is for the classroom teacher to talk to the child's parents to discuss these problems, along with suggesting some strategies for Mary to use at home. Since Mary was an identified student, Mr. Wald checked her IEP to see if there were specific strategies that could be helpful to him. Her IEP did in fact have some useful suggestions, but Mr. Wald felt that a consultation with Mary's parents and the Child Study Team would be helpful.

Mr. Wald scheduled a meeting with Mary's parents and the Child Study Team to discuss her program and appropriate follow-up. Her parents agreed that this was a good idea. The Child Study Team provided Mr. Wald with some suggestions to help Mary solve some of her study problems. For example, before leaving school each day, Mr. Wald would help Mary make sure that she had all the materials she would need to complete her homework. The team also suggested the following strategies for the home:

- Set a regular time for homework and begin homework at this time each day.

- Remove distractions as much as possible when doing homework.

- Check that the homework is complete and accurate (parents should initial).

- Make sure that homework and other materials needed for the next day are put into the backpack.

There is increased activity and blood flow to the front regions of the brain when children are asked to think about someone else's state of mind.

SUMMARY

This chapter introduced the reader to the structure of the brain, along with the role of the brain in children's learning in the classroom. The case study in this chapter showed that some children cope with an array of learning challenges that require a multitiered program of interventions both at school and at home. Consequently, it is important that the classroom teacher be able to identify children who have academic problems and meet with the Child Study Team and the child's parents to gain insight into how best to address the child's needs. To this end, this chapter provided useful classroom strategies for teachers. Chapter 15 presents additional strategies and methods for working with children's families. Chapter 15 also presents strategies for working with families whose language is not English.

This chapter is designed to provide understanding of the functions of the brain. This knowledge is critical to provide insight into some of the academic problems that may be encountered in the classroom. Teachers made aware of the basis of children's executive function difficulties are able to provide the kind of classroom strategies that are necessary to help them achieve academic success. These teachers are also able to understand the need for referral for assessment and intervention for certain language difficulties and use of school clinical professionals as resources. Finally, teachers are able to provide families with better understanding of children's academic difficulties, along with strategies for use in the home.

The important point here is that children should internalize these strategies and make them their own. In this way, they can apply them in a variety of classroom and social settings and can monitor their own progress over time. The strategies suggested in this chapter are associated with the executive functions important in academic skills:

- Making and initiating plans for action
- Revising or modifying plans based on outcomes
- Abstract thought
- Learning from errors
- Planning

These executive functions allow a child to succeed in the classroom, because weaknesses in executive functioning can have a negative impact on academic success.

The next few chapters examine speech and language from a developmental perspective. Chapter 7 examines the development of language and communication skills in infants and toddlers, including the impact of language and cultural differences on language development. This chapter also provides classroom and home strategies for infants and toddlers at risk for language delays.

KEY WORDS

Abstract thought	Corpus callosum	Prefrontal cortex
Axon	Dendrites	Primary auditory cortex
Brain	Executive functions	Primary visual cortex
Brainstem	Frontal lobe	Prune
Broca's area	Genetic inheritance	Right brain
Cell body	Grey matter	Self-regulation
Cells	Heschl's gyrus	Sensory information
Central nervous system	Innate	Spinal column
Cerebellum	Left brain	Synapses
Cerebral cortex	Metacognition	Temporal lobe
Cerebral plasticity	Myelinated	Wernicke's area
Cerebrum	Occipital lobe	White matter
Cognitive functions	Parietal lobe	Working memory

STUDY QUESTIONS

1. Define and provide examples of *executive functions*. Explain the role of each of these functions in developing good academic skills.

2. Define *cerebral plasticity.* Provide an explanation of cerebral plasticity in learning.

3. Describe the role of inference in the development of reading comprehension.

4. Explain why a child with executive function difficulties may be misunderstood as avoiding work. How would you explain the difference between these two behaviors?

5. Explain why tasks that involve describing a person's mind, feelings, or thoughts best stimulate children's brains.

PROJECTS

1. Examine the poetry of a famous poet. Compare the writing of this person over time, from young adulthood to later ages. What changes do you notice over time?

2. Interview a medical professional. Ask this professional to describe the different neurological conditions they have treated and the behaviors associated with each disorder.

3. Interview a friend who has a relative who has sustained brain damage due to a stroke or some other injury. Ask them to tell you about the communication problems they face when interacting with this individual. Next, can you tell what specific area of the brain is affected?

STUDENT STUDY SITE

Visit the Student Study Site at **www.sagepub.com/levey** for these additional learning tools:

- Video Links
- Self Quizzes
- E-Flashcards

- Sample Forms and Assessment Tools
- Recommended Readings
- Web Resources

SUGGESTIONS FOR FURTHER READING

Bear, M. F., Connors, B. W., & Paradiso, M. A. (2006). *Neuroscience: Exploring the brain.* Philadelphia: Lippincott Williams & Wilkins.

Jensen, E. (2005). *Teaching with the brain in mind.* Alexandria, VA: Association for Supervision & Curriculum Development.

Kolb, B., & Whishaw, I. Q. (2005). *Introduction to brain and behavior.* New York: Worth.

Nolte, J. (2008). *The human brain: An introduction to its functional anatomy.* Maryland Heights, MO: Elsevier Science.

O'Shea, M. (2006). *Brain: A very short introduction.* Oxford, UK: Oxford University Press.

Pinker, S. (2007). *Language instinct: How the mind creates language.* New York: HarperCollins.

C H A P T E R   7

Language Development From Birth to Age 3

Sandra Levey

Case Study: Delay in the development of expressive language

Mary was 2 years old, but she was much quieter than other children her age. Some of the time, she inconsistently produced single words (e.g., labels for toys, food, family members, the family dog, and requests of various kinds) but did not produce longer utterances when prompted or otherwise. Her hearing was fine—confirmed by testing—and her play, physical, and social skills were all similar to those of the other children her age. She also listened to and understood verbal directions and followed those directions, both at school and at home. The main concerns were that her expressive language skills were not consistent with other children her age. Specifically, this 2-year-old was not consistently producing single words and two-word (or longer) utterances, either spontaneously or in response to prompts. Because of the delay in her expressive language skills, her preschool teacher and parents were concerned about her speech and language development.

Do you think that Mary's preschool teacher and parents should be concerned about her language development? On what information and experiences did you base your answer?

INTRODUCTION

Children possess **innate** (inborn) skills that foster language acquisition from the verbal input in their environment (Hirsh-Pasek & Golinkoff, 1997; Karmiloff-Smith, 1995; Sokolov & Snow, 1994). Their innate learning skills enable them to take advantage of this environmental input during social interaction, conversation, and play. This input is essential to provide the language learner with information about sounds, words, actions, or events (e.g., falling) and labels for entities in the environment (e.g., people, animals, and objects).

The goal of this chapter is to introduce you to infants' and toddlers' speech language development (0 to 36 months). This description includes the factors associated with language development (Hirsh-Pasek, Golinkoff, & Eyer, 2003), along with a description of two paths of learning. A full discussion of these paths or theories of learning appears in Chapter 2.

- The first path consists of innate (inborn) skills with which we are born, such as the ability to learn.

- The second path consists of experience-dependent skills that are not innate and that require environmental input and guidance for learning, such as reading.

Children's innate learning skills enable them to take advantage of information and objects in the environment, especially when engaged in social interaction, conversation, and play.

We are born with visual abilities present. Thus, the capability to see is innate, and we do not need instruction or guidance to develop our visual aptitudes. In contrast, we are not born with reading abilities. Thus, the ability to read is not innate and requires instruction and guidance to develop. Experience-dependent skills, such as reading and writing, must be learned because children are not born with these skills (i.e., they are not innate).

Reading skills and vocabulary develop with environmental exposure to reading materials (e.g., books, letters, shopping lists, magazines) and exposure to language input. Vocabulary skills are an important factor in reading development, with labels for people and things acquired through social interaction, play, pointing and labeling, and a rich and varied amount of verbal input.

Children's language development begins when the infant and caretaker share social experiences, such as **joint focus** on events or objects in the child's environment (Watt,

Wetherby, & Shumway, 2006). Joint focus occurs when an infant and adult look at the same object or event, arising from the infant's interest, and the adult provides the label or name for that object or event. Joint focus is a significant factor in enhancing children's early language acquisition and language development (Tomasello & Farrar, 1986). As the infant's language develops over time, it is her or his language that becomes the primary method for further language learning (Tomasello, 2001). When language skills develop, the child can look at an object or event and ask, "What's that?"

INFANT AND TODDLER DEVELOPMENT: AN OVERVIEW

Language development begins in infancy, when children begin to learn about the world. Language plays an important role in all stages of learning about the world. Children learn that objects and events have labels (e.g., *apple* and *play*). Children also learn that language functions to attain needs and desires. The precursors for language begin in contexts that provide experience and stimulation for learning vocabulary labels, sentence construction, storytelling, conversation, and the appropriate language for interaction with others. The following examples of language development illustrate the changes in language that occur over time, as children at different ages request a cookie:

A 6-month-old: "Waaah" (reaching for the cookie)

A 2-year-old: "Wanna cookie!"

A 4-year-old: "Can I have a cookie?"

A 7-year-old: "Wow. Those cookies smell good!"

Notice that the request for a cookie becomes more subtle and socially appropriate over time through the use of the indirect request (it takes the form of a question by using *can*). This is because of two factors: Children begin to learn indirect forms (beginning at about 4 years of age) and possess the language skills to express their requests through more complex forms (e.g., "Can I go?" vs. the earlier form, "I can go?"). Although children are born with the innate skills to develop language, it is environmental input that gives them information provided by adults, peers, or events.

INFANT PERCEPTION

Children's language learning begins with **speech perception**, the awareness of sounds spoken in the surrounding language. Consequently, by 5 months of age, many children respond to their own names (Mandel, Jusczyk, & Pisoni, 1995), while often confusing their names with words that possess the same number of syllables and **intonation** patterns (e.g., *Mary* vs. *Carry*). Over time, children learn that entities and events have labels (e.g., *mommy*, *doggy*, *ball*, and *rain*).

Response to human language is found in infants as young as 4 weeks of age. At this early age, infants are sensitive to (and are able to **perceive)** differences between very similar sounds, such as "pah" and "bah" (Eimas, Siqueland, Jusczyk, & Vigorito, 1971). Most interesting is that infants from any language background (e.g., English, Swahili, or Greek) are able to distinguish sounds such as "pah" and "bah" even if these sounds are absent from the infant's native language and have never been heard before by the infant (Werker & Tees, 1984). Sensitivity to nonnative sounds disappears by 8 to 10 months of age when infants lose their early sensitivity to sounds absent from those spoken in their environment (Jusczyk, 1992).

The loss of sensitivity to nonnative sounds corresponds with a new developmental stage in which infants begin to produce sounds consistent with those in their native language. The loss of sensitivity to foreign sounds is based, most likely, on the need for infants to focus on their native language. This focus allows them to acquire the sounds for communication in their home environment. Thus, this loss of sensitivity to foreign sounds is not a total loss of perception of sound differences. On the contrary, to completely lose the ability to perceive sound differences in another language would make it impossible to learn a second language.

INFANT PRODUCTION AND EXPRESSION

Newborn productions consist of **reflexive** sounds (e.g., burping and crying). Sounds produced with the quality of vowels and very brief consonants are termed **quasiresonant nuclei** (Owens, 2008). At 1 month, the infant will gaze at his or her caretaker's face and produce reflexive sounds, such as vowel-like utterances (Stark, 1986). At 2 months, laughter and cooing appear, with partially correct productions of consonants and vowels. At 3 months, turn taking with an adult appears, with the production of syllables that contain more accurate representations of consonant and vowel sounds (e.g., "gah" and "bah"). The 4-month-old infant is now able to use her or his tongue with greater strength and control (Owens, 2008). At 5 months, the infant begins to imitate vowel sounds (e.g., "ah" and "oh"), including intonation (e.g., raising and lowering pitch).

At about 6 to 7 months of age, infants begin to produce consonant-vowel (CV) sequences such as "babababa," called **reduplicated babbling** (because syllables are duplicated). About 2 months later, infants begin to produce varied syllable sequences (e.g., "babigaguda"), called **variegated babbling** (because the syllable sequences are varied). Babbling is an important stage in language development, given that children store the patterns established during babbling (the associations between oral-motor movements and sounds) and draw on these patterns to produce meaningful speech at later ages.

> When Micah was 6 months old, he began to experiment with sounds. He produced a variety of CV sounds (e.g., "da") and CVCV sounds (e.g., "dagah") and began to produce sound combinations such as "bababa" and "dagada."

At 8 to 12 months of age, children begin to imitate what they hear (McLaughlin, 1998), such as words, phrases, and intonational patterns. At 9 to 12 months of age, children begin to produce sequences of syllables that sound a great deal like real words. Termed **jargon**, these productions are generally quite unintelligible. Early productions also consist of sounds called **phonetically consistent forms**, **vocables**, or **performatives** (James, 1990), productions that attempt to approximate real words. In this case, a child consistently produces a sound that identifies a thing or action, such as "ah" to ask the adult to pick him or her up and "uh" for food. This illustrates the connection between the development of cognition and language over time.

LANGUAGE DEVELOPMENT AT 18 TO 36 MONTHS OF AGE

The following set of descriptions shows that language develops rapidly from 18 to 36 months of age. These examples demonstrate that this child is able to use language in a creative manner as early as 24 months, indicating the innate ability to create utterances never heard in the environment. Children at 30 months and 36 months use language in social interaction, with these abilities developed from their observation of interactions within the environment.

> Mack's mother has an allergy. When her throat itches, she clears her throat. While clearing her throat, she puts her fist to her ear. At 18 months, before he began to talk, Mack saw her doing this and held his little fist to his ear, mimicking her and laughing the whole time.

In this example, Mack is imitating his mother's gestures prior to producing words. In this way, his prelinguistic communication shows that he is enjoying her motions and noises.

> When he was 24 months, Mack was having some gas. He had also just learned about burps, and his mother had taught him to excuse himself when he burped. One afternoon, he passed gas. Then he looked at his mother and said, "Excuse me, mommy, my bottom was burping."

Note that Mack's language changed significantly in the 6 months between 18 and 24 months. He now was able to produce a highly creative and original utterance never heard before (e.g., "my bottom was burping"). Thus, language does not develop only from environmental observations of language use. The use of a novel utterance reflects the innate skills that allow children to use language in a creative manner.

> Mack's daddy would often bring home flowers for his mommy. At 30 months, Mack noticed how much she appreciated them. On Mother's Day, Mack's daddy came home with a huge bouquet and asked Mack to give them to his mommy. Mack ran up to his mommy with the biggest smile on his face, carrying a bouquet that was half the size of his body. He handed them to his mommy and said, "Happy Mother's Day, mommy." She gave him the biggest hug and smile right back. From then on, whenever Mack's mommy scolded him, he ran into the guest room, picked up a fake bouquet of flowers, and ran into her room yelling, "Mommy, here's some flowers for you!"

The example above indicates that Mack is able to observe the interaction between his mother and father and develop an utterance (e.g., "Mommy, here's some flowers for you!") directed at distracting her from reprimanding him. The next example illustrates how Mack has learned the most common social communication utterance used by cell phone users.

> At 36 months, Mack started to keep his toy cell phone in his pocket, just like his dad. In the middle of a conversation with his parents, he'll say, "Hold on, my phone is ringing," and then will proceed to have a "conversation," pretending his friend Nate is on the other end of the call.

Progress in Mack's language development has taken place over a short period of time, between 18 and 36 months, without direct teaching. In other words, no one sat down and trained Mack to produce the utterances in these vignettes. Thus, we see an example of the role of children's innate skills in creativity, along with the role of the environment in learning socially appropriate communication skills and vocabulary to support creativity and interactions with others.

COGNITION AND LANGUAGE

Language development and cognitive development go hand in hand over time, with language development facilitating learning. **Organization** is a cognitive process based on the natural tendency to organize information into related, interconnected structures to aid understanding.

According to Piaget (1954), a **schema** is the basic psychological structure for organizing information. A schema provides a child with the ability to **process** (understand, interpret, make sense of) information. A good example of the development of schemas is in a child's schema development for *bird*.

> A child establishes the schema for *bird* when she sees a pigeon in the park. She sees the pigeon after her mother points and says, "Look at the bird." The child has established a schema for bird, based on her perception of the pigeon and learning that the word *bird* is associated with the pigeon.

Next, the little girl is walking down the street with her mother and sees a sparrow.

> The child points and says, "Bird." Thus, the child has assimilated the new entity (sparrow) into the schema for *bird*, which already contains pigeon.

The little girl has successfully assimilated the new example of a bird into her existing schema for *bird*. Next, on a trip to the zoo, the child encounters a penguin. Her mother points and says, "Look at the bird." A problem appears when the child cannot fit *penguin* into the schema for *bird*, given that she is unable to perceive any similar characteristics among *penguin, pigeon,* and *sparrow.* For example, the shape and size of the penguin does not match those of the other birds, along with the fact that the penguin is walking and not flying. Consequently, assimilation cannot take place and **cognitive dissonance** (a problem fitting an entity into an existing schema) occurs.

Given this difficulty, it is important to introduce another process involved with developing schema: **adaptation**. Adaptation describes the tendency of the organism to change in response to the environment. There are two means for adaptation:

- **Assimilation**: The new entity can be fit into a schema that already exists when there is a good fit between the new thing and the preexisting schema (e.g., *sparrow* and *pigeon*).

- **Accommodation**: The new entity does not fit into a schema that already exists; there is a change in an existing schema to meet the characteristics of information, objects, events, etc. (e.g., *penguin*).

The goal of fitting new information or input into a schema is **equilibrium** (cognitive balance). We are able to achieve equilibrium through accommodation. In this case, this child changes the existing schema to meet the demands of the new situation. Now, *penguin* joins *pigeon* and *sparrow* in the schema for *bird*. In summary, a child is able to achieve cognitive equilibrium through assimilation or accommodation, with equilibrium being the goal. It is important that children are able to form schemas, cognitive organizers that will provide a structure for new concepts that support ongoing language development. How the schema develops in stages is highlighted in the next section.

STAGES OF COGNITIVE DEVELOPMENT

According to Piaget (1954), there are six stages of cognitive development. These stages begin at birth and continue until maturity (Bernstein & Levey, 2009).

- Stage 1 (birth to 1 month): Children demonstrate accommodation or modification of a schema in response to environmental stimuli. For example, children become more efficient at locating the nipple on the bottle in response to environmental experience.

- Stage 2 (1 to 4 months): Eye-hand coordination, visual tracking of moving objects, and localization to sound improve.

- Stage 3 (4 to 8 months): Imitation appears and children anticipate the path of a moving object. They also begin to reach for and manipulate objects.

- Stage 4 (8 to 12 months): Children anticipate events, use means-end behavior (when a child establishes a goal and the means to achieve this goal), increase imitation (as a child is able to establish an observed behavior and imitate it), and remember that an object exists even when removed from sight (object permanence). Means-end behaviors appear in this stage (e.g., getting a toy out of reach).

- Stage 5 (12 to18 months): Children experiment, explore, and use earlier established schemes or patterns of behaviors to solve new problems.

- Stage 6 (18 to 24 months): Children solve problems through thought rather than through physical means, produce labels for objects or actions, observe an action, store it in memory, and reproduce this action later (**deferred imitation**). (pp. 31–32)

Play

Children's play behaviors are an essential component in cognitive and language development. Children's play begins with adults in charge of the play routine. For example, one study shows that the most popular early social-action activities between adults and infants consist of patty-cake, wave bye-bye, peek-a-boo, "so big," and "give kisses" (Platt & Coggins, 1990). Typically, an adult will clap to demonstrate patty-cake, providing a scaffold (model for learning) for the child to learn this game. By Age 1, a child is able to comply with requests to "wave bye-bye." These early games, coupled with the linguistic label (e.g., *bye-bye* and *patty-cake*), contribute to children's early language comprehension skills.

Symbolic Functions

Children's first words show that they have achieved the **symbolic function**, defined as using a word to represent an entity or activity through language (e.g., *ball* to represent the thing that is round, bounces, and rolls). The child may produce this word when the ball is present in his or her view (referent present) but achieves true symbolic knowledge when an entity is not within view (referent absent). Symbolic functions occur when children use one object (e.g., a block) to represent another (e.g., a car or train). According to Piaget (1954), these symbolic functions appear in the preoperational stage of cognitive development when a child is able to internalize action into thought. Stambak and Sinclair (1990/1993) argued that the enactment of play schemas (e.g., keeping house) also had an effect on cognitive development. For example, 3-year-olds begin to function symbolically through the use of language, and they can use their imagination or a box to represent another real object in their play. Thus, play allows children to symbolize objects, events, and activities through the use of language.

There is a strong relationship between play and language development (Patterson & Westby, 1998). Pretend (symbolic) play is the beginning of the ability to **decontextualize**, to separate an object from an immediate context (Bernstein & Levey, 2009). This occurs when a child uses a word to represent an object or action that is absent from the child's view. Patterson and Westby provide a description of symbolic or pretend play development that occurs during this period.

- At 12 months, play frequently includes banging, putting one thing in another, and some activities with dolls and stuffed toys that mimic the child's own experiences.

- At 18 months, play consists of familiar activities, such as things that the child actually does (e.g., sleeping or drinking from a cup).

- At 24 months, children's play consists of more complex sequences, again of familiar activities (e.g., making a cookie out of clay).

- At 24 to 30 months, children include props, such as stuffed toys or dolls, in their play. These toys are given a role in play, with needs such as thirst or fatigue (e.g., "Doggy tired").

- At 30 months, play widens to include familiar but less frequently occurring activities, such as going to the doctor.

- At 3 years of age, play becomes more complex, with activities consisting of multiple sequences, such as going to the doctor, getting medicine at the drug store, and medicating and comforting the baby; children also begin to use language in their play.

The Relationship Between Cognition and Language

There are two points of view on the relationship between cognition and language: the strong cognitive position and the weak cognitive position. Advocates of the strong position argue that cognitive developments parallel (match) language development (Piaget, 1962). In this view, a child's language development depends on achieving certain cognitive stages. For example, symbolic play reflects the ability to use an object to represent another (e.g., a train represented with blocks) or to symbolize an event through play (e.g., feeding a baby). The second is the weak cognitive position. Advocates of this position argue that factors other than cognition can influence language development (Kamhi & Masterson, 1989; Thelen & Bates, 2003), such as social interaction and developments in language itself.

Roth and Clark (1987) explored both hypotheses by examining the symbolic play and social skills of two groups of children, matched for language skills by mean length of utterance (the number of morphemes in their average utterances). Children who were language impaired (average age 6.7 years) matched with non-language-impaired children (average age 2.9 years). Findings were that language-impaired children demonstrated significant weaknesses in symbolic and play behaviors in comparison with the non-language-impaired children. For example, the children with impairments played more like the younger children (e.g., banging a toy bench on the floor, banging other toys, throwing toys, running about the room, lack of exploration, and no play schemes, such as "going to the store" or "playing house"). These findings show that the cognitive skills of the children with language impairment, as reflected in play behaviors, were significantly less complex and age-appropriate than those of the children matched for language skills, suggesting a connection between language and play. These findings also show that the observation of very young children's play skills may alert us to the possibility of difficulties in language development. Thus, early supports may facilitate their language development.

Along with play skills, it is also important that teachers understand speech and phonological development so that they may identify children who require supports. The following section describes this phonological development.

PHONOLOGICAL DEVELOPMENT

Toddlers' word productions are sometimes difficult to understand because toddlers don't always produce the adult target word or words with accuracy. This is because certain sounds do not appear in children's speech until 3 years of age or later, with tremendous variability in children's acquisition of sounds. (See Chapter 8 for more on normative sound development.) Children also show an early preference for a consonant-vowel shape (e.g., "ba"), resulting in words produced without a final consonant (e.g., "bu_" [consonant + vowel] for the word *bus* [consonant + vowel + consonant]). They do prefer a stress pattern consistent with their native language, such as the strong-weak syllable pattern associated with most English words (e.g., *BA-by* and *DO-ggy*).

To investigate English-speaking children's learning of new words, Levey and Schwartz (2002) presented 2-year-old children with novel (made-up) word pairs that were composed of strong-weak (e.g., "BI-guhduh") versus weak-strong (e.g., "guhbi-DUH") stress patterns.

Novel words provide a better test of children's word learning, given that they may have already established a representation of more familiar words. Findings were that children learned novel words with strong-weak stress patterns better than those with weak-strong stress patterns, showing a strong preference for the strong-weak stress patterns found in English (e.g., *BA-by*, *MO-mmy*, *DA-ddy*, and *JE-lly*).

Phonological Processes

These preferences appear in children's early attempts to produce words. The difference between children's productions and the adult target are termed **phonological processes.** Some of these processes involve omitting a weak syllable in a word, such as the first weak syllable in the word *banana* (e.g., "nana"). Other examples of toddlers' productions follow. These early processes generally disappear by 3 years of age.

- Unstressed syllable deletion: "nana" for *banana*

- Reduplication: "dada" for *daddy*

- Final syllable deletion: "bu_" for *bus*

- Consonant cluster reduction: "_top" for *stop*

Early childhood teachers need to have a good understanding of normative morphosyntactic development, or what typical infants and toddlers should be able to do with respect to combining morphemes and words to produce sentences at particular ages of development. For example, morphosyntactic skills show that children are able to form words (e.g., *coo* + *kie*) by 12 to 26 months and form lengthy sentences (e.g., "I" + "want" + "a" + "cookie") by 35 to 40 months. The following section describes early morphosyntactic development.

MORPHOSYNTACTIC DEVELOPMENT

Syntax is the language component that describes the rules for combining words to form sentences. Brown (1975) provided a means for describing children's syntactic development with stages that include the mean (average) number of morphemes that children produce in an utterance. For example, the utterance "my doggy" consists of two morphemes ("my" and "doggy"). A morpheme is the smallest linguistic unit that has meaning. For example, the word *dog* cannot be broken down into smaller units, or the meaning would be lost (e.g., "do" or "og" do not mean the same thing as *dog*). Therefore, the word *dog* consists of one morpheme. If we add the inflectional plural morpheme *-s* to *dog*, it changes the meaning to *dogs,* which consists of two morphemes (e.g., *dog* + *s*).

Children's mean number of morphemes begins with one to two morpheme productions in Stage I (e.g., "Daddy go") and ends with children's production of multiple morphemes in complex sentences at Stage IV (e.g., "My dad is going to work today, and he said that he would take me to football practice when he got home"). The stages of developmental expectancies for sentence development follow (Bernstein & Levey, 2009).

- Stage I (12 to 26 months): Single-word utterances and early multiword combinations that follow semantic rules emerge, such as "more," "eat cookie," "more juice," and "go car."

- Stage II (27 to 30 months): Grammatical morphemes appear, such as *-ing* (e.g., *going*), the plural *-s* (e.g., *cookies*), and the prepositions *in* and *on* (e.g., *shoe on*).

- Stage III (24 to 30 months): Children begin to produce negatives (e.g., "No go bed"), imperatives (e.g., "Gimme ball"), and interrogatives (e.g., "Where daddy?").

- Stage IV (35 to 40 months): Complex structures emerge, such as coordination (e.g., "I like cookies and candy") and relativization (e.g., "The boy who hit me is bad"). (pp. 42–45)

These stages have been normed on native English-speaking children, while other languages differ in morphological structure. Consequently, children from different language backgrounds vary in their acquisition patterns. Research has found that there is also great variability in morphological development for English-speaking children until they reach about 35 months of age (Lahey, Liebergott, Chesnick, Menyuk, & Adams, 1992), as shown in the following example.

> Dylan and Sara are both 18 months old. Sara is putting two words together (e.g., "More cookie") while Dylan produces only single words (e.g., "More"). In all other ways, the children show similar typical development.

The parents of each of these children need to understand that children develop at different rates. In addition, girls may achieve language targets earlier than boys. A professional with the ability to detect actual problems may be consulted to assess a child's overall language skills. In all cases, children's hearing skills should be assessed to determine that they are able to take advantage of the language spoken in the classroom and home.

An important task for teachers is to support children's semantic development through vocabulary, their awareness that entities (e.g., people and things) and activities (e.g., parties, running, and throwing) have labels or meaning. Most children understand the connection that labels represent things, but the classroom teacher can play an important role in expanding a child's vocabulary through increasing the number of labels they use. This vocabulary expansion helps develop student expression, understanding, and eventually reading abilities. The following section describes children's early semantic development.

SEMANTIC DEVELOPMENT

Semantics is the component of language that refers to meaning and rules that govern the assignment of meaning to entities (e.g., people, animals, and things), along with activities or events. Semantic development appears when children are aware that things have labels or names (e.g., *dogs* and *apples*). Over time, they are able to label more abstract entities, such as emotions (e.g., *happy*) or states (e.g., *boredom*). Children learn labels for entities and actions they encounter in the world, along with the meaning found in words (e.g., *cat*), sentences (e.g., "Let's feed the cat"), conversations (e.g., "When I got home, I had to feed the cat. Did you see him?"), and narratives (e.g., "Let me tell you a story about a cat. Once upon a time . . .").

Vocabulary development begins in infancy and continues to build through adulthood. First words appear at about 12 months of age, with children's early words generally based on things in the child's environment (e.g., *open, eat, go, down, up, bye, hi, hot, no,* and *more*). It is important to understand that a consistent connection between word and thing (e.g., only

Vocabulary skills are learned through social interaction, play, and pointing and labeling.

saying "mommy" when the child sees *mommy* and not using this word for other things, such as the family dog) is the definition of *real words.*

An interesting aspect of children's early word production is the lack of correlation between children's meanings and adults' use of these words. Peccei (1999) provides some examples of this difference in 1- to 2-year-old children's understanding of the common words *duck, white,* and *ball.*

- First child: says *duck* when seeing a duck swimming in a pond. Later, the word *duck* is used to refer to ducks in and out of water as well as water with or without ducks.
  - The first child learned the word *duck* when looking at a duck in water. This child has not yet learned that the word *duck* can be used in a context separate from the water in the pond.

- Second child: uses *white* only to describe snow. This child is puzzled when the word *white* is used by her father to refer to a white piece of paper.
  - The second child learned the word *white* when used to label *snow.* This child has a very restricted idea of the meaning of *white* but will learn over time that this word can apply to a number of things that share this color.

- Third child: uses the word *ball* to refer to balls, marbles, wheels, and cement mixers.
  - The third child has an expanded idea of the meaning of *ball* (contrast this behavior with the second child's restricted meaning). In this case, the child uses the word *ball* to label other objects that share certain characteristics, such as roundness and the ability to roll or turn. (p. 7)

These examples show us that children form a hypothesis or idea about meaning when they produce words. For example, they frequently label a number of other animals (e.g., sheep, cows, horses) as *dog* because of the perceptual similarity of shape or movement. This **overextension** or **overgeneralization** (extending a word meaning beyond a category) frequently occurs because a child does not know the correct word and chooses the best name for a known entity that matches the perceptual characteristics of this unknown entity. Children may also demonstrate a restricted set of meanings for a word, as shown in the following example.

> When Nikki was 2 years old, she was in the store with her mother. Nikki was playing with a mannequin and said, "Mommy, isn't she pretty?" and her mother said, "Yes, Nikki, the dummy is very pretty." Nikki said, "Mommy, dummy is not a nice word!"

Children develop and expand their understanding of meaning with more experience and knowledge of the world over time (Bernstein & Levey, 2009): one or more words at 12 months, four to six words at 15 months, twenty words at 18 months, and as many as two hundred to three hundred words at 24 months.

One important factor in children's vocabulary development is that their receptive vocabulary (words they understand) exceeds their expressive vocabulary (words they express). For example, children with a receptive vocabulary of 50 words generally have an expressive vocabulary of 10. This difference is most likely due to the difference in difficulty between receptive and expressive language; receptive language involves understanding words, while expressive language involves thinking of a word, along with its meaning, and producing the word. Consequently, there is less complexity involved in receptive language skills.

In addition to acquiring words that label objects and actions, children also begin to produce words that correspond to **semantic roles** (Bernstein & Levey, 2009). Semantic roles refer to a word (e.g., *daddy*) that has a relationship with another word in a sentence, such as a verb (e.g., *go*). Definitions and examples of some semantic roles can be found in Table 7.1.

Table 7.1   Semantic Roles

Semantic Role	Example
• Agent: doer of an action	daddy, mommy, doggy
• Action: event	kick, kiss, cry, bark
• Affected: entity influenced by the action	ball, baby
• Location: place	bed, car, chair
• Possessor: owner	mommy, daddy, baby, dog
• Possession: entity owned	purse, shoe, toy, bone
• Attribute: characteristic	big, little, pretty, hot
• Recurrence: repetition	more
• Negation: rejection	no

When children begin to produce two-word utterances, at about 18 months or when they acquire at least 20 words, they combine these semantic roles (e.g., "Daddy go") to create **semantic relations**: agent (*daddy*) + action (*go*). In this case, these utterances express a semantic relation between two things (e.g., *daddy* and *go*), with additional examples shown in Table 7.2.

Table 7.2 Semantic Relations

Semantic Relation	Example
• Agent + action	mommy kiss
• Action + affected	kick ball
• Action + location	sleep bed
• Entity + location	baby bed
• Possessor + possession	mommy shoe
• Entity + attribute	doggy big
• Nomination	that car
• Recurrence	more juice
• Negation	no bed

In this case, a semantic relationship has been created (e.g., "Daddy go") that leads to a new meaning (e.g., "Daddy is going" or "Daddy has gone"). The real meaning of this semantic relation can be found in the environment (e.g., what actually happened). In summary, once toddlers have a sense about semantic relations, they can then put some two- and three-word utterances together that can make their wants known.

Classroom teachers should also understand pragmatic development, as *pragmatics* is defined as rules for interacting with others. If children are not clearly aware of these rules, it may interfere with their interaction with other children. For example, a 2-year-old who wants to join a playgroup with other children must learn to communicate his wishes in the form of a *request* to play with them, rather than just sitting down in the middle of the group or grabbing other children's toys. The following section describes early pragmatic development or the ability to use language to appropriately interact with others.

PRAGMATIC DEVELOPMENT

Infants are capable of producing **intentional** communication. This means that they are able to use communication to indicate their specific wants and needs. In infancy, intentionality is signaled by the use of gesture and/or vocalization, coupled with eye contact, and by persistent attempts to communicate a request (James, 1990), frequently with the use of phonetically consistent forms (e.g., "uh").

Early gestures provide a picture of toddlers' mental representations or ideas about the world, even before they begin to produce words. Although children frequently combine a gesture (e.g., pointing) with verbalization (e.g., "doggy"), toddlers produce more gestures in isolation than older children (Capone, 2007). Capone points out that gesture and language originate in the same neural regions of the brain. Thus, the use of gestures is an indication of children's prelinguistic language skills.

Children's early attempts to communicate their intentions are called *functions* (Halliday, 1975) and are produced to satisfy a need or goal. The instrumental function is used to obtain a goal or satisfy needs (e.g., a child may lift his or her arms and say "up"). The regulatory function is used to control another's behavior (e.g., a child holds out a ball and says "play" or "throw"). The interaction function is used to obtain **joint attention**. In this case, the child may call "mama." Finally, the personal function is used to express feelings or attitudes (e.g., a child may say "yum" while eating a cookie).

Between the first and second year, communicative intents (meanings) appear (McShane, 1980). The regulation intent is based on gaining attention, requests, and calling. The statement intent is expressed by naming, description, and giving information that is beyond the here and now (past experiences). The exchange intent is defined by using descriptions of activities, intent to carry out an action, refusal, and protest. Finally, the conversational intent is conveyed through imitation, answer, conversational responses, and questions.

Language development begins when the infant and adult share social experiences, such as joint focus on objects in the environment.

Speech Acts

A speaker's intent or meaning can be categorized into different types of **speech acts** (Searle, 1983). These utterances are called speech *acts* because they sometimes result in another person's action.

There are two types of speech acts: speech acts that take a direct form (e.g., "Close the window") and speech acts that take an indirect form (e.g., "Can you close the window?"). The more indirect method of requesting an action is a polite type of speech act that requests action in a more subtle or roundabout manner. In fact, this type of speech act takes the form of a question. Over time, children learn to couch their requests in even more subtle forms (e.g., "It sure is cold in here"). This change depends on more advanced language learning and the observation of more polite forms used in their environment. The following examples consist of toddlers' speech acts.

- **Greeting:** "Hi."
- **Promise:** "I promise I eat my peas."
- **Request:** "Gimme cookie."
- **Indirect request:** "Can I have a cookie?"
- **Complaint:** "Why I can't play?"
- **Invitation:** "Come play with me?"
- **Refusal:** "No wanna go to bed."

While sentence structure rules (syntax) have not yet been completely acquired (e.g., "Why I can't play?" vs. "Why can't I play?"), these examples show that children are able to convey their intentions at a very early age.

Narratives

Narratives are a series of connected sentences that tell a story. Children first begin to talk about past events at about 22 months, given assistance from adults (Eisenberg, 1985). At 24 months, their narratives tend to focus on negative past events, such as injuries that they have sustained (Miller & Sperry, 1988). It is not until 42 months of age that children generally combine two events, even in their longest narratives (McCabe & Rosenthal Rollins, 1994).

There is a relationship between children's ability to understand and produce narratives and the development of literacy skills. For example, the ability to tell a complete version of *The Three Bears* has been found to predict later reading success (de Hirsch, Jansky, & Langford, 1966). Children benefit from joint storybook reading between child and adult. When children simply listen to a narrative read to them, they are being exposed to narrative structures (e.g., the beginning, middle, and end of stories) as well as new vocabulary words. The sequence of toddlers' narrative development is shown below (Bernstein & Levey, 2009):

- Scripts: narratives produced by 2-year-olds that involve everyday routines and events that they have experienced

- Chaining: At 3 years of age, talking about events that relate to a central topic with no particular order of occurrence

The ability to produce more cohesive (well-connected) narratives depends on the development of more advanced vocabulary, given that narrative organization is provided by connectives such as *and then, therefore, however,* and *nevertheless.* The narrative skills of preschoolers are presented in Chapter 8, with a comprehensive discussion of the development of narrative skills presented in Chapter 11.

LANGUAGE DIFFERENCES

There are cultural differences in the adult-child interactions found for gender and in various cultures. Owens (2008) reports that these differences may appear in play and social interaction. For example, gender differences appeared in mothers' interaction with 2-year-old girls. In these contexts, mothers produced longer sentences, more repetition, more acknowledgment of the child's answers, and more turn taking than when they interacted with 2-year-old boys.

There are also differences associated with socioeconomic status (SES), with middle-class Northern American mothers asking more questions, while mothers from lower SES classes use more imperatives or directives. Horton-Ikard and Weismer (2007) found that toddlers from low-SES homes performed significantly poorer than those from middle-SES homes on standardized receptive and expressive vocabulary tests and on the number of different words used in spontaneous speech. However, there were no significant SES group differences in their ability to learn novel word meanings. The Horton-Ikard and Weismer finding is one that gives us insight into the term *educational disadvantage.*

These differences in receptive and expressive vocabulary based on SES mean that children from low-SES homes must work harder in preschool and in the primary grades to extend their receptive and expressive vocabularies so that they can perform at similar levels to their comparable middle-SES peers. This is the very argument that launched the Head Start programs in the United States in the 1960s.

Beyond SES factors, there are different approaches to children's language learning across cultures. For example, Johnston and Wong (2002) found that Chinese mothers reported using picture books and flash cards to teach new words to a greater degree than did Western mothers, reporting their opinion that children learn best with direct instruction, rather than through play.

These differences must be recognized and understood as *differences* in acquiring and using language, and such *differences* do not imply a language disorder or a lack of intelligence. The language differences to be discussed in the following sections are those seen most frequently in African American English (AAE) and Hispanic or Latino speakers. It is important to understand language differences when they exist. For example, there is greater classroom success for children who are AAE speakers when teachers are familiar with the characteristics of AAE (Delpit, 2006). In the case of Hispanic- or Latino-speaking children, familiarity with the speech and language patterns of these children assures that teachers identify them as having differences, rather than disorders.

African American English

There are differences associated with languages and dialects (Smitherman, 2000), with examples of this presented in Chapter 12. The rules for grammar derive from the languages that influenced AAE, such as West African languages, French, Native American, and English.

Given that AAE follows consistent rules, these productions do not constitute a disorder. In addition, there is variability in the use of AAE among speakers (see Chapter 12). There are also no major differences in the phonological processes for AAE speakers and Mainstream American English (MAE) speakers (Goldstein, 2000). The mean number of morphemes in a child's sentence production generally assesses morphosyntactic development. This approach is not predictive for AAE-speaking children (Seymour, Bland-Stewart, & Green, 1998). However, Seymour et al. found that AAE-speaking children with language disorders could be identified by deletion of articles (e.g., *the, a*), conjunctions (e.g., *and, but*), prepositions (e.g., *at, above*), and modals (e.g., *can, could, should*), along with difficulty using more complex sentences. In general, there are no significant differences in the language development of typically developing AAE and MAE speakers.

Hispanic and Latino Children

The first words produced by Spanish-speaking infants and toddlers are not significantly different from those produced by English-speaking children, as shown in the following examples: *cookie, sleep, thank you, baby, eat, soda, more, dog,* and *cat* (Goldstein, 2000, p. 33). Finally, there is no difference in the vocabulary development between bilingual Spanish/English-speaking and monolingual-speaking toddlers (Pearson, Fernandez, & Oller, 1993).

Differences must be embraced and understood as differences, not disorders. Spanish-speaking children learning English as a second language may produce sounds and words in English that are influenced by Spanish (Goldstein, 2000), with examples of this presented in Chapter 14.

The following section describes children who are at risk for language development. It is important that teachers are able to identify these children so that they may be given supports in the classroom and/or be referred for assessment or intervention to address these difficulties.

INFANTS AND TODDLERS AT RISK FOR LANGUAGE DEVELOPMENT

Children at risk are those who do not attain developmental milestones at the expected times. There are important milestones that support later language:

- Babbling: Provides the practice for the production of speech sounds and words

- Joint eye-contact between adult and infant: Provides the basis for word learning

- Vocabulary of 50 words by 24 months

We know that children should be able to combine at least two words and have a vocabulary of 50 words by 24 months of age (Paul & Alforde, 1993; Rescorla, 1989; Rescorla, Roberts, & Dahlsgaard, 1997; Rescorla & Schwartz, 1990). We also know that infants and toddlers who better understand words are those who have better vocabulary skills when they are older (Bates, Benigni, Bretherton, Camaioni, & Volterra, 1979; Bates, Bretherton, & Snyder, 1988). In fact, children may be identified as having language difficulties as early as 24 months (Scarborough & Dobrich, 1990; Thal, Tobias, & Morrison, 1991).

We also know that children are notoriously variable in their developmental progress. Consequently, there may be errors when identifying a child as language delayed or disordered at an early age. However, it is best to err on the side of caution by providing the supports needed to prevent difficulties in the emergence of the skills needed for academic success. To help identify typical versus atypical development, Table 7.3 contains features of infants' and children's language development and Table 7.4 contains their language milestones along with a checklist to help the classroom teacher identify children who may have difficulties. The subsequent section provides the classroom teacher and parent with strategies to develop children's language abilities.

Table 7.3	Highlights of Children's Language Development

Birth to 1 Year

Hearing and Understanding	Talking
Birth to 3 Months • Startles to loud sounds • Quiets or smiles when spoken to • Seems to recognize your voice and quiets if crying • Increases or decreases sucking behavior in response to sound	**Birth to 3 Months** • Makes pleasure sounds (e.g., cooing, gooing) • Cries differently for different needs • Smiles when sees you
4 to 6 Months • Moves eyes in direction of sounds • Responds to changes in tone of your voice • Notices toys that make sounds • Pays attention to music	**4 to 6 Months** • Babbling sounds more speech-like with many different sounds, including *p*, *b*, and *m* • Chuckles and laughs • Vocalizes excitement and displeasure • Makes gurgling sounds when left alone and when playing with you
7 Months to 1 Year • Enjoys games like peek-a-boo and patty-cake • Turns and looks in direction of sounds • Listens when spoken to • Recognizes words for common items such as *cup*, *shoe*, *book*, or *juice* • Begins to respond to requests (e.g. "Come here" or "Want more?")	**7 Months to 1 Year** • Babbling has both long and short groups of sounds, such as "tata upup bibibibi" • Uses speech or noncrying sounds to get and keep attention • Uses gestures to communicate (e.g., waving, holding arms to be picked up) • Imitates different speech sounds • Has one or two words (e.g., *hi*, *dog*, *dada*, *mama*) around first birthday, although sounds may not be clear

(Continued)

Table 7.3   (Continued)

1 to 2 Years

Hearing and Understanding	Talking
• Points to a few body parts when asked • Follows simple commands and understands simple questions (e.g., "Roll the ball," "Kiss the baby," "Where's your shoe?") • Listens to simple stories, songs, and rhymes • Points to pictures in a book when named	• Says more words every month • Uses some one- or two-word questions (e.g., "Where kitty?" "Go bye-bye?" "What's that?") • Puts two words together (e.g., "more cookie," "no juice," "mommy book") • Uses many different consonant sounds at the beginning of words

2 to 3 Years

Talking	Hearing and Understanding
• Has a word for almost everything • Uses two or three words to talk about and ask for things • Uses k, g, f, t, d, and n sounds • Speech is understood by familiar listeners most of the time • Often asks for or directs attention to objects by naming them	• Understands differences in meaning (e.g., "go-stop," "in-on," "big-little," "up-down") • Follows two requests (e.g., "Get the book and put it on the table") • Listens to and enjoys hearing stories for longer periods of time

Table 7.4   Developmental Milestones Checklist for Language Development in Infants and Toddlers

1. Babbles at about 8 months (e.g., "babababababa")
2. Produces two words at about 12 months
3. Uses gestures (e.g., waving) at 12 months
4. Produces early words by 15 months (e.g., "mama")
5. Produces about 20 words at 18 months
6. Imitates two-word utterances at about 18 months
7. Points to items of interest (e.g., dogs, bicycles, and toys) by 20 months
8. Understands simple directions at 21 months
9. Produces about 50 words and word combinations by 24 months
10. Can understand speech by 30 months

Strategies for Teachers and Parents

The strategies for developing language abilities for infants and toddlers depend on interaction to promote their exposure to words and literacy materials (American Speech-Language-Hearing Association, 2009).

Infants

- Imitate the infant's production of sounds.
- Play early social games, such as peek-a-boo and patty-cake.
- Use language to describe actions (e.g., your actions while cooking and shopping; the infant's actions while bathing or playing).
- Label things and actions as you are walking.
- Talk about the sounds animals make (e.g., "woof-woof," "moo," and "baa").
- Introduce book reading (e.g., use picture books and describe pictures with words).

Toddlers

- Talk about what's going on around the toddler.
- Point to things and talk about them, using simple words and short sentences.
- Play with rhyme (e.g., nursery rhymes and rhyme books).
- Ask the toddler to point to pictures or things and name them.
- Name things and ask the toddler to point to the thing that was named.
- Read stories with simple sentences and pictures that help the toddler associate words with things.

CASE STUDY REVISITED

As described at the beginning of this chapter, the 2-year old Mary was not producing words with consistency and she had not yet begun to produce multiword utterances (e.g., two words or longer).

CASE STUDY REVISITED: Delay in the development of expressive language

Mary's teacher encouraged her parents to consult with their pediatrician, who referred them to a speech-language pathologist (SLP). The SLP presented her parents with a questionnaire that examined children's early speech and language abilities. The SLP was concerned about the report that babbling had not occurred in early speech development, indicating difficulty in producing sounds at an early age. Assessment showed that Mary had difficulty producing syllables in sequence, such as the word *banana*. Sequencing syllables requires that a child is able to plan and coordinate the mouth movements to produce these syllables accurately. For example, when the SLP asked her to label a picture of a banana, Mary produced "naba" and "nababa." In other words, she had difficulty in sequencing these sounds.

Mary was diagnosed with a speech disorder termed childhood apraxia of speech (CAS). CAS is a disorder that presents difficulty in planning and sequencing sounds in words. Thus, a child would likely have difficulty with sequencing the syllables in a word such as banana. Syllables must be sequenced in a certain order to produce this word correctly. The human brain possesses the ability to plan this sequence. A history of babbling is frequently absent for children who are unable to produce these sequences correctly, given that babbling requires the ability to sequence syllables (e.g., "babagada"). The SLP developed a program targeting the ability to successfully sequence syllables, and Mary was, over time, able to produce words such as banana.

The teacher met with the SLP, who gave her suggestions for working with Mary in the classroom: developing a positive self-image in the classroom; providing a variety of pictures (with words) of items targeted in the classroom for lesson plans to help Mary point to the desired item when speech difficulties occurred; modeling slower speech patterns to help her understand this strategy, targeting vocabulary items most relevant to the child's life experiences (ensuring that these words would be used and heard in more than one situation); and using some sound games and books that target sequencing sounds and syllables in recurring patterns (e.g., rhyme books and stories). The collaboration between teacher, parent, and SLP continued throughout the school year with a positive outcome.

SUMMARY

This chapter introduced children's language development from birth to age 3. It is important to understand that the foundation for later language skills begins in infancy, when the infant and adult achieve joint focus and the adult provides a name for entities and events. At this point, the infant begins to learn that objects have names and appropriately associates those names and objects. It is important to understand that children's language development requires that environmental input be present for learning (e.g., books, play, experience with a variety of events and things, and being talked to and read to). You should also understand that there is diversity in children's development, based on gender, language background, and cultural differences.

While this chapter introduced the language development of infants and toddlers, the next chapter similarly presents language development of preschool-age children, ages 3 to 5. You should reflect on the factors in phonological, morphological, semantic, and pragmatic development that mark the differences between the children described in this chapter and those in the next. As you read the next chapter, keep in mind that the preschool children's language development is dependent on the factors described in this chapter. Thus, it is important to identify children who require support and/or intervention early to assure that development and learning in the classroom are maximized.

KEY WORDS

Accommodation	Decontextualize	Intentional
Adaptation	Deferred imitation	Intonation
Assimilation	Equilibrium	Jargon
Cognitive dissonance	Innate	Joint attention

Joint focus

Organization

Overextension

Overgeneralization

Perceive

Performatives

Phonetically consistent
  forms

Phonological processes

Process

Quasiresonant nuclei

Reduplicated babbling

Reflexive

Schema

Semantic relations

Semantic roles

Semantics

Speech acts

Speech perception

Symbolic
  functions

Syntax

Variegated babbling

Vocables

STUDY QUESTIONS

1. What is the connection between cognition and play? What tasks would you use to improve children's play skills?

2. If a 3-year-old has difficulty combining two words to form a simple sentence, how would you help this child develop these skills?

3. If there was a child in your preschool classroom with language difficulties, at what point would you contact the children's parents?

4. Describe at least three methods that you might use to identify a 2-year-old and a 3-year-old with language difficulties.

5. Explain the reason that mean number of morphemes cannot be used to assess AAE-speaking children.

PROJECTS

1. Arrange to observe infants at different stages of development: 0 to 3 months, 3 to 6 months, and 6 to 12 months of age. Note the interaction between caregiver (e.g., mother, father, or other) and the infant. Analyze the response of the caregiver to the infant's sounds or eye contact.

2. Arrange to observe children at different stages of development (1 year, 2 years, and 3 years of age) to describe the main characteristics of their play behaviors. Use the information in this chapter to describe the language produced during their play. Next, note the differences in the language used during play that differentiates these stages of development. Specifically, do you notice any connection between the complexity of their play and their language?

3. Observe a child close to 2 years of age and a second child close to 3 to describe the characteristics of the words produced. Use the information in this chapter that describes phonological processes. Note the processes associated with their productions and the differences between the phonological processes of 2-year-olds and 3-year-olds.

STUDENT STUDY SITE

Visit the Student Study Site at **www.sagepub.com/levey** for these additional learning tools:

- Video Links
- Self Quizzes
- E-Flashcards

- Sample Forms and Assessment Tools
- Recommended Readings
- Web Resources

SUGGESTIONS FOR FURTHER READING

Baron, N. S. (2000). *Growing up with language: How children learn to talk.* Cambridge, MA: Da Capo.

Gallaway, C., & Richards, B. J. (1994). *Input and interaction in language acquisition.* Cambridge, UK: Cambridge University Press.

Golinkoff, R. M., & Hirsh-Pasek, K. (2000). *How babies talk: The magic and mystery of language in the first three years of life.* Boston: Penguin.

Gopnik, A., Meltzoff, A. N., & Kuhl, P. K. (2001). *Scientist in the crib: What early learning tells us about the mind.* New York: HarperCollins.

Martin, S., & Berke, J. E. (2006). *See how they grow: Infants and toddlers.* Florence, KY: Cengage Learning.

CHAPTER 8

Language Development From Ages 3 to 5

Deena K. Bernstein

CASE STUDY: Limits on speech sound production

Brian's parents were aware that his ability to communicate was not developing the same way that their older daughter's had developed. At 3 years of age, it was clear to the family that Brian was bright and could follow directions easily. However, his expressive language was limited to two- to three-word utterances that were not full sentences. For example, he frequently omitted auxiliary verbs (e.g., *is, are, was*), producing sentences such as "Where you going?" versus "Where are you going?" Additionally, he had difficulty naming pictures and objects, did not enjoy listening to his teacher read stories to the class, and had some difficulty with certain sounds in words.

Initially, their pediatrician told them that "boys are slower" to talk than girls, but when Mrs. Lane got a full-time job, she decided to place Brian in a 4-year preschool program. Mrs. Lane's report to the preschool teacher was that Brian was a typical child and that he was "normal" in every way and had limitations only in communications. Brian had no serious illnesses, and the results of a hearing screening were normal. The Lanes believed that Brian understood everything but that he had trouble expressing himself. They also said that they had trouble understanding what he said and that Brian became angry when he was not understood.

What strategy or strategies should Brian's classroom teacher use to improve his sentence production? On what information and experiences did you base your answer?

INTRODUCTION

The goal of this chapter is to introduce the classroom teacher to the language development of preschool-age children, ages 3 to 5. While this chapter describes the development of language at the preschool stage, the language skills described in Chapter 7 provide these children with a foundation for success in preschool. This chapter also attempts to provide classroom teachers with strategies to support children's academic development through methods of supporting children's literacy development in the classroom. Most children learn language and communication naturally and without formal instruction for the most part. For example,

> Mack rarely napped even as a baby. Now, at 3 1/2 years of age, when his mommy suggests he takes a nap during the day, he questions her by saying, "It's not dark out and the sun is not sleeping. Why should I?"

Children's creative abilities are evident in Mack's response to his mother. He invented a rationale for not napping, arguing that the sun was "not sleeping." Mack had never heard anyone use this phrase. Consequently, he was able to create a unique argument for not napping based on his own creative use of language.

Early in children's language development, they communicate their **intentions** (wants and needs) by using **eye gaze**, **gestures**, and **vocalizations**, and they assess the results of their communication by the effect they have on the behavior of others. Later, they use single words and multiword utterances to convey their intentions. Between a child's first and third birthday, the language input that caregivers provide, the child's social interaction with other adults and peers, the child's play behaviors, and the child's cognitive development all play a vital and dynamic role in the child's communication development. Although children come biologically equipped to learn language, all the factors noted above play an active role in the language acquisition process.

As noted in Chapter 3, language is composed of overlapping components: **form**, **content**, and **use**. While **phonology**, **morphology**, **syntax**, **semantics**, and **pragmatics** operate together, we will treat each component separately while pointing out their relationship with other components when appropriate. Five aspects of preschool language development form the focal point of this chapter: phonological growth, morphosyntactic development, the development of meaning, the elaboration of pragmatic skills, and emergent literacy.

The next section presents a general overview of language development during the preschool years. After that, a section that highlights the forms, meanings, and communication functions acquired by preschoolers follows. The last section discusses those aspects of language that will influence the child's ability to read and write.

As you read this chapter, it is important for you to keep in mind that later stages of language development are dependent on earlier factors and that the rates that children learn or develop language are variable and depend on differences in their intellect, learning style, ethnicity, socioeconomic factors, cultural environment, and language spoken in the home. It is also important to point out that language development is a gradual process and that there is relationship between the phonological, morphological, syntactic, semantic, and pragmatic development of oral language and the acquisition of literacy skills.

PRESCHOOL LANGUAGE DEVELOPMENT: AN OVERVIEW

As children advance from the one- and two-word utterance stage, their utterances become longer and more complex. They gradually elaborate the way they say things by adding more details to their utterances. They fill in words and word endings that were missing from their earlier utterances. These "missing items" now take the form of articles (e.g., *a*, *the*), prepositions (e.g., *in*, *on*), pronouns (e.g., *he*, *she*), noun endings (e.g., *-s* to indicate plurality), and verb endings (e.g., *-ed* to indicate past tense). The inclusion of these forms in children's speech makes their utterances more adult-like and less like a telegram. Below are some examples of typical developments in children's speech as they progress from being toddlers to being preschoolers:

Toddlers	*Preschoolers*
"More milk."	"I want more milk."
"Mommy car."	"Mommy is going in the car."
"Man car."	"The man is in the car."

From toddlerhood and all through the preschool period, children's vocabulary continues to grow. They learn new concepts and learn how to code these concepts linguistically. They learn to map their ideas onto various sentence types. By age 4, children's syntax is nearly adult-like (Owens, 2008).

During the preschool period, children learn more complex language for social interaction.

During the preschool years, typically developing children use more complex ways of communicating socially, and they begin to develop **discourse** skills, such as participating in a conversation and providing descriptions about events and people (Logan, 2003). By the time children enter the first grade, they can use language to describe past events and use experiences to demonstrate, instruct, reason (Tough, 1979), and tell simple stories "of their own and others authorship" (Owens, 2008, p. 231). Last, during the preschool period, children learn about the nature of print. The emergence of **preliteracy** or **emergent literacy skills** will set the foundation for learning to read and write. In the following sections, there is a detailed discussion of each area that composes language, along with examples of growth.

COGNITION, LANGUAGE, AND PLAY

As noted previously, much of a child's language develops within the context of social interaction, both with adults and peers. However, the importance of play as a vehicle for the development of language is often overlooked (Patterson & Westby, 1998; Sachs, 1984). Play is an ideal vehicle for the development of language because games involve turn taking (similar to conversations), shared topics, attention, and little or no stress (Owens, 2008).

Early in their development, toddlers' play is simple, concrete, and depends on the here-and-now. This means that children are more aware of objects present in their environment than they are of objects that are absent. However, as children mature cognitively, their play becomes more complex and less concrete.

During the preschool years, children's play begins to involve **themes** and **scripts** (Nelson, 1986; Patterson & Westby, 1998). These scripts are about familiar situations (e.g., going shopping and playing in the park). At first, the child represents himself or herself as part of the script, but later, he or she can project roles onto other people or dolls.

Initially, preschoolers prefer very functional and/or explicit props such as a phone, a car, or a shopping cart to use in their scripted play. As they mature cognitively, they can participate in play that is more imaginative and can use props that are more ambiguous. For example, a block can represent a car, and a checker piece can represent a coin to pay for food in the store (Pellegrini & Perlmutter, 1989). With more developed social and cognitive skills comes the ability to use language to assign meaning to these props (e.g., "This will be the car" and "This will be the money") and to different roles they delegate to the participants during play (e.g., "You be the daddy"). During this type of play, language is used to negotiate (e.g., "If you are the mommy, I'll be the baby") and to clarify (e.g., "You can't do that if you are the baby").

By age 5, children do not need props to engage in play and they can use only language to maintain their play activities (Bernstein & Levey, 2009). Although preschool children are too young for team games, they do enjoy group activities and can actively participate in songs, rhymes, and finger play that many preschool teachers use.

PHONOLOGICAL DEVELOPMENT

Children usually produce their first recognizable words between 1 and 1 1/2 years of age. However, many of their utterances are not clearly understood because they do not accurately produce the sounds or sound sequences that constitute words. Without knowing the child or the context in which the utterance is produced, it would be difficult to recognize "gawgi" for *doggy,* "dut" for *juice,* or "gikin" for *chicken.*

To master the sound system of the English language, children must acquire an inventory of sounds. The sequence of English consonant acquisition shows a great deal of variability in the ages at which different sounds are mastered (Sander, 1972). Table 8.1 lists a sequence of ages by which 90% of children use a sound correctly.

Table 8.1	Normative Articulation Development
24 months	*n*
28 months	*m, p, h*
32 months	*t, k, y* (e.g., *you*)
36 months	*f, w, ng* (e.g., ha*ng*), *b, g, d*
40 months	*w*
> 48 months	*l, r, sh, ch, z, v, z, zh* (e.g., *treasure*), *th* (e.g., *thumb* and *these*)

Phonological Processes

When learning to produce the English sound system, children often simplify the words produced by adults. The simplifications that children use as they attempt to produce adult-like speech are **phonological processes**. Some processes fade out of children's speech by age 3 or 4, while others continue through the preschool period. The most prevalent phonological processes found in the utterances of preschool children follow:

- Consonant cluster reduction: reducing two consonants (e.g., *sp*) to only one consonant (e.g., *p*)
  - "poon" for *spoon*
  - "tee" for *tree*

- Final consonant deletion: omitting the final consonant in words
  - "ka" for *car*
  - "hah" for *hat*

- Weak syllable deletion: omitting the unstressed (weak) syllable in a multisyllabic word
  - "nana" for *banana*
  - "fant" for *elephant*

As previously noted, these processes usually disappear in the speech of typically developing children by age 3 or 4 (Schwartz, Leonard, Folger, & Wilcox, 1980). Late talkers—that is, those children who fail to meet developmental milestones in terms of the size of their vocabulary and the length of their utterances—often continue to use the phonological processes noted above past the age of 5 (Paul & Jennings, 1992). They also exhibit proportionally smaller consonant and vowel inventories. For example, the inventory of their consonant sounds consists primarily of nasals (e.g., /m/ and /n/), glides (e.g., /j/ as in *yet,* /w/, and /l/), and voiced stops (e.g., /d/ and /g/). The preschool teacher may expect children to display consonant cluster reduction, final consonant deletion, and weak syllable deletion until 3 to 4 years of age.

MORPHOSYNTACTIC DEVELOPMENT

During the preschool years, a major change occurs in children's acquisition of morphology and syntax; they increase the length and complexity of their utterances. **Morphemes** acquired during the preschool period are shown in Table 8.2. The stages of **morphosyntactic development** of typically developing children, as well as examples of these changes, are shown in Table 8.3 (Brown, 1973).

Table 8.2 Grammatical Morphemes at Ages 3 to 5

Age	Morpheme	Example
3	Regular plural	The boy**s** are playing.
3	Possessive '*s*	That is the girl**'s** hat.
3	Uncontractible copula	She **is** (in response to "Who is pretty?").
3	Articles	I have **a** ball. Mommy pulled **the** wagon.
4 to 5	Regular past tense	He kick**ed** me.
4 to 5	Contractible auxiliary	Daddy**'s** eating.

Table 8.3 Morphosyntactic Development at Ages 3 to 5

Age 3	Declaratives	"<u>I'm hungry</u>."
	Interrogatives	"<u>Where</u> is daddy?"
	Imperatives	"<u>Push me</u>."
	Negatives	"<u>No</u> more milk."
	Quantity use	"I have <u>two</u> cookies."
	Adjective use	"Give me the <u>red</u> ball."
	Adverb use	"Run <u>fast</u>."
Ages 3 to 5	Embedded phrases	"The man <u>in the car</u> is my daddy."
	Subordinate clauses	"<u>Before you go</u>, put on your hat."
Ages 4 to 5	Conjunctions	"I play the guitar, <u>and</u> he plays the drums."
		"He cried <u>because</u> he dropped his ice cream."
		"I want to play with him, <u>but</u> he won't play with me."

Note that at age 3, new morphological forms are evident in the language of typically developing children. These include the use of the present-progressive morpheme -ing, the prepositions in and on, and the regular plural /s/. At age 3, children produce the basic sentence form, consisting of the subject-verb-object construction (e.g., "She drinks milk"), as well as constructions with subject-copula-compliment (e.g., "She is pretty") (Brown, 1973). At age 4, preschool children's utterances become longer, with the appearance of **embedded phrases** as well as **subordinate clauses**. In addition, subordinate clauses are introduced by **conjunctives** (e.g., after, although, and since) and **relative pronouns** (e.g., that, which, who, and whose).

Typical preschoolers not only include all the constructions mentioned above, but they also use complex sentences by age 5. Typical children's development of linguistic forms follows the direction of longer utterances and increased phonological, morphological, and syntactic complexity. It is important to note that children's elaboration of linguistic form is the result of their need to express more complex ideas in a greater variety of social situations. Table 8.4 provides examples of utterances from a typically developing 5-year-old.

Table 8.4   Shanna's Sentences at Age 5

Utterances	Examples of New Constructions
"Gimme the big red ball."	Expanded noun phrase
"He pushed me down the steps."	Expanded verb phrase
"I won't do it."	Negative sentence
"Can you eat the cake?"	Yes/no question
"What's in the box?"	WH question
"He didn't get a prize 'cause he was bad."	Causal construction
"If I pick up my toys, I can watch the videos."	Conditional construction
"When he'll come, he will get a surprise."	Temporal construction

Returning to the case study presented at the beginning of this chapter, it is clear that Brian, at age 3, should be able to produce basic sentence forms that included the auxiliaries is and are. Consequently, his mother's recognition of limitations in communication is supported by evidence from studies of children's typical development. We now turn our attention to preschoolers' semantic development, with an emphasis on the meanings they learn to express.

SEMANTICS: THE DEVELOPMENT OF MEANING

As noted in Chapter 7, semantics is the component of language that is concerned with meaning. Without meaning, there would be no point to language. People talk in order to express meaning, and they listen in order to discern the meaning of what others say.

Linguistic meaning is conveyed at the word, sentence, or discourse level. The meaning of some words can also be learned from the nonlinguistic context.

During the preschool period, children are able to classify and group words into broad categories (e.g., *doll, wagon, ball* = *toys*). They also begin to learn relational terms (e.g., *in front of*) and terms that code physical properties, time, and kinship.

Lexical Acquisition: Vocabulary Growth

The most familiar sense of meaning is **lexical** meaning. It is concerned with the meaning of words and the characteristics of the category to which a word belongs. The preschool period is one of rapid lexical growth. In fact, Nelson (1998) has referred to the young preschool child's brain as a sponge that soaks up several new words each day. Baumann and Kameenui (1991) state that from 18 months of age, typically developing children learn about eight to nine words each day. By the time they enter first grade, they have a vocabulary (lexicon) of more than 2,000 words (Owens, 2008). These words are learned through a child's natural daily interaction with caregivers and peers, along with conversations they have with others in their environment.

During this period, as children develop cognitively, they are better able to define words by including different types of information in their definitions. In addition, they learn to use different approaches to organize words. Their definitions are concrete and are usually descriptions of the appearance or function of the object to be defined, as shown in the examples below:

Teacher:	What is a spoon?
Ellie (age 3 1/2):	You eat with it.
Teacher:	What is a car?
Tzvi (age 5):	You ride in it, it has four wheels, a motor, and you drive it. You put in a key and you go. You can keep it in your driveway or in your garage. You put gas in it to go.

Relational Meanings

In addition to the acquisition of lexical knowledge that specifies referents, children acquire meaning that codes relationships at the word level and at the sentence level. During the preschool years, typically developing children not only code meaning of existence, nonexistence, and recurrence using simple sentences, but they also code more complex **concepts**. These include concepts of time, space, causation, and the sequencing of actions using more complex linguistic forms and a variety of sentence types. Table 8.5 lists some of the **semantic relations** expressed by preschoolers. The more advanced relationships are mapped, but also note the complex syntax that is used to express these relationships.

Concepts

We now turn our attention to the development of concepts, terms that code location (locatives), time, kinship, and physical properties. The typically developing child's syntactical

Table 8.5	Semantic Relations Expressed by Typically Developing Preschoolers	
Semantic Relation	**Age**	**Example**
Temporality	3	"Now I wash my hands, then I eat."
Conditionality	3 1/2	"I wear this when I walk."
Temporal sequence	3 1/2 to 4	"I'll make a car after I finish this."

development, as well as the amount of exposure the child has to these terms, influences his or her acquisition. While some concepts are acquired before entering preschool (e.g., *big/little*, *on*, *in*), the acquisition of more complex concepts is not evident until school age. The order of acquisition of some of these concepts is summarized in Table 8.6.

Table 8.6	Acquisition of Locational, Physical, Temporal, and Kinship Terms		
Age	**Locational Relationship**	**Physical**	**Kinship Term**
3 to 4	Under	Big/little Heavy/light	Mommy/daddy
4 to 4.6	Next to Behind In back of In front of	Tall/short Long/short Hard/soft	Mother/father Sister/brother
School age	Right/left	Deep/shallow	Uncle/cousin

Vocabulary Differences

Some children from low socioeconomic backgrounds or from culturally and linguistically diverse backgrounds enter kindergarten having not learned nearly as many different words as children from monolingual families or children from higher-income families. From age 2 on, large differences may exist in the vocabulary knowledge between two groups (Hirsch, 2001): monolingual children from higher socioeconomic families and children from low socioeconomic families, or those who come from culturally and linguistically diverse backgrounds. The gap between these two groups usually occurs because children from the second group may not have been exposed to and may not be familiar with unusual or low-frequency words (e.g., *reluctant*). Teachers of preschool children should be mindful of this "original vocabulary gap" for the following reasons (Hirsch, 2001, p. 3):

- Researchers have found that to understand spoken language, a person needs to know about 95% of the words heard, while the other 5% can be inferred from context.

- If a preschool child comes from a monolingual, high-income family, he or she understands 95% of the language directed at him or her by the preschool teacher.

- Thus, that child gains new knowledge from the teacher's remarks and is also learning "new meanings" by inferring meaning from the other 5% of the words.

- This "advantaged child" has gained new "word knowledge as well as world knowledge."

Such is not the case for the child from a low socioeconomic group or the child who comes from a linguistically and culturally diverse background. From the start, many of these children in preschool classrooms may not have a vocabulary robust enough to understand the language directed at them by the teacher. They therefore fail to gain "world knowledge" and also fail to learn "new word meanings" from context. This double loss is compounded even more as a child loses interest, self-confidence, and motivation to learn. Thus, preschool teachers should focus on the teaching of vocabulary directly and indirectly and through context (e.g., the introduction of new words connected to relevant situations).

Returning again to the case study at the beginning of the chapter, we see that Brian's inability to identify some pictures and objects may be due to difficulty acquiring vocabulary. Thus, this is an area that may indicate a language disorder in children who are slow at learning new words.

PRAGMATIC DEVELOPMENT

Typically developing preschoolers master and improve their conversational skills and increase the intentions (meanings) that they code and learn. Their goal is to become more aware of social settings and the interactions within them. During this period, preschoolers learn to describe objects and events removed from the immediate context. They not only talk about the here-and-now but also about the there-and-then. Thus, they use language effectively not only to convey their wants and needs but also to talk about past and future events.

Preschoolers learn to ask and answer a variety of questions. They also learn to take turns in a conversation, to stick to a conversational topic, and to contribute new and relevant information to a discourse (Owens, 2008). Some of the communicative functions that preschoolers use are described by the examples in Table 8.7. Note that by age 5, typically developing children not only express a wide variety of **communicative intentions**, but they also do so by expanding their linguistic forms (i.e., the sentences that they use to express these intentions).

Conversational Skills

Typically developing children learn language within a natural context as they interact with their caregivers and peers. Between 3 and 4 years of age, the typically developing child begins to gain a better awareness of the social aspect of conversation. The child begins to adapt language to the needs of her or his listeners. With the realization that other people's perspective must be taken into account (presuppositional ability) comes language that is well-adapted to the listener. That is not to say that the typical preschooler is always successful in getting his or her message across. Children are often unable to reformulate a

| Table 8.7 | Communicative Functions: The Typical Preschooler |

Communicative Function	Example
Requesting information (using a variety of questions)	"What's that?" "Can I go now?" "Is he eating candy?" "Where are you going?" "Why can't I have it?"
Responding to requests (answering a question or supplying information)	"It's in my closet." "I don't want it." "I didn't do it." "He did it."
Describing events, objects, or properties	"It's a red truck." "He's building it slowly." "That's a tractor." "There's a crane."
Stating facts, feelings, attitudes, and beliefs	"I feel sick." "Ghosts are not real." "I don't like it."
Encoding from a picture book	"The boy and the girl got into the van, and the van took them to the train."
Describing a plan	"First I'll build the tracks, then I'll make the train."
Describing a past experience	"She pushed me so hard I fell down and hurt myself."
Complaining	"You always give the big one to him."
Criticizing	"Your picture is yucky."
Annoying	"I'll do it again and again and again and again."
Threatening	"Give it back or I will tell Mommy."

message in response to a facial expression of noncomprehension. In other words, preschoolers are not always able to "read" a listener's face. Consequently, it is necessary to ask children to clarify a message that was not understood. The most common way preschoolers repair their messages is to repeat what they have said. A typical interaction illustrates a preschooler's method of "clarifying" a message:

Child (3 years, 5 months):   "He took it away from me!"

Teacher: "What?"

Child: "He took it away from me!"

Teacher: "Who did what?"

Child: "He took it away from me!"

Teacher: "Who took what away from you?"

Child: "Tommy took my toy."

Although preschool-age children learn to take turns in conversation, their conversations are short and the number of turns they take, as speaker and listener, is limited. As a child advances during the preschool years, he or she not only begins to acknowledge the conversational partner but also gains the ability to maintain a topic. This results in fewer new topics introduced into a conversation. By 5 years of age, more than half of typical children can sustain certain topics through about a dozen turns, while occasionally filling their turn with "yeah" or "uh-huh."

The ability to respond to a specific request for clarification (e.g., Teacher: "What?") does not usually develop until first grade. In sum, during the preschool years, typically developing children become better conversational partners by using a greater variety of linguistic forms to attain their end. They are more aware of social roles at age 5 than at age 2 and can even simplify their language when talking to a baby. Although they take turns in a conversation without prompts, they tend to make more coherent contributions to a conversation if they are talking about an activity in which they are actively engaged (Justice, 2008; Owens, 2008).

Development of Narrative

Narratives are a form of discourse. They contain sentences and statements that are logically connected to reflect causal and temporal relationships. When they are babies and toddlers, typically developing children are exposed to narratives and stories in picture books and television. They also begin to relate stories early in the preschool period. There are two types of narratives in the typically developing preschool child's repertoire: the **personal narrative,** in which the child shares a factual event that has occurred in his or her life, and the **fictional narrative,** in which the child shares a made-up event. Both types of narrative contain a thread that links event sequences that are either temporally or causally related. Examples of these types of narratives are shown below.

Personal Narrative

Jimmy (age 4 1/2): "I wanted to watch TV so I told my mommy I cleaned up the toys. Then I watched *Superman*." (causal narrative)

Sara (age 5): "First he went to the store, and then he showed the man which toy he wanted. He gave the man money and took the toy home." (temporal narrative)

Fictional Narrative

Lilly (age 4 1/2): "There were three pigs. They built houses, and the big bad wolf huffed and puffed. Then the house came down."

The three components of language (linguistic form, content, and use) appear in children's productions of narratives. For example, a typically developing child must use complex linguistic skills to order ideas and words (linguistic form), use vocabulary to specify events and people (content), and recognize how much information to share with the listener (use). Some of the major achievements of narratives by typically developing preschool children are presented in Table 8.8.

Table 8.8   Narratives in Preschoolers

Age	Narrative Type	Example
3	Primitive	Has a concrete core with minimal detail
4	Unfocused chains	Presents a story; drifts off at times
5	Focused chains	Has a main character and a series of events
5+	True narratives	Has thematic bonds and complex syntax that holds narratives together; stories contain setting information, a series of events, as well as consequences and motivations

It is important for preschoolers to master narrative skills because it is one of the best predictors of later school achievement. To produce a successful narrative, one must move beyond the concrete here-and-now. Researchers believe that this may be a critical link to the acquisition of literacy skills and subsequent school success (Paul & Smith, 1993; Peterson, Jesso, & McCabe, 1999).

EMERGENT LITERACY

Within the past 2 decades, educators and researchers have used the term *emergent literacy* to describe the knowledge of print that youngsters possess before they begin formal reading and writing instruction. The emergent literacy perspective asserts that oral and written language are interdependent, that oral language supports literacy, and that there is a strong relationship between oral language, later literacy, and academic achievement (Catts & Kamhi, 1999; Gallagher, Frith, & Snowling, 2000). It is important to note that the U.S. Department of Education (1997) indicates that preschoolers with language disabilities and other risk factors (e.g., poverty or family history of learning and language disabilities) experience difficulties in learning to read and write and make up the largest segment of children identified as learning disabled in the school-age years.

Thus far, our discussion has focused on typical language development in preschoolers. Now the focus will shift to some of the literacy challenges that children experience. There are several areas of knowledge that compose emergent literacy. Some of the key indications of emergent literacy include knowledge and development of print awareness, phonological awareness, and metalinguistic awareness. In addition, vocabulary and narrative structure development and knowledge are also factors that support emergent and later literacy abilities.

Print Awareness

Print awareness emerges when children begin to understand that print has meaning (Bernstein & Levey, 2009). By age 4, they recognize their names in print. It is not until 5 to 7 years of age that they learn the correlation between sounds and letters in words.

Metalinguistic Awareness

Metalinguistic awareness is a typically developing child's ability to manipulate subsystems of language independently of the meaning conveyed in the message. Armed with metalinguistic awareness, the typically developing child can think and talk about language as an object in itself. Consider the following example:

Pearl (age 4): "Mommy, talk and walk. It matches."

Ray (age 5): "My teacher told me to stick out my tongue and make a *th* sound when I say 'baf.'"

During the preschool years, children learn about the nature of print.

Phonological Awareness

Phonological awareness is a metalinguistic skill that allows the typically developing child to manipulate the sound structure of spoken language. Typically developing preschoolers engage in a variety of activities at home and in their preschool settings that require phonological awareness. These include:

- rhyming—for example, *bake* and *take;*
- segmenting words into their individual sounds—for example, *fish* = *f-i-sh;* and
- isolating sounds—for example, *cat* = *c-a-t.*

One of the phonological awareness skills most closely related to literacy acquisition is phonemic awareness. Phonemic awareness is the knowledge that spoken words consist of individual sounds and that a speaker can manipulate these sounds. Because early reading requires children to be able to map individual speech sounds onto their corresponding letters, it is this ability that enables children to decode the written word (print). In addition, phonemic awareness is required so that the child can learn to **encode**—that is, to map sounds onto letters or letter combinations. This ability enables the child to spell different words. Thus, phonemic awareness enables children to develop the **alphabetic principle**, which states that the letters in written words correspond to sounds in written words. Basic reading and spelling skills depend on the knowledge of the alphabetic principle.

Research has shown that successful readers are those children who perform well on phonological awareness tasks, while those who perform poorly often have difficulty with reading and spelling. This difficulty exists regardless of other factors such as IQ or socioeconomic status (Adams, 1990). The best single predictor of reading and spelling achievement in first and second grade is phonological awareness (Cooper, Roth, Speece, & Schnatschnedier, 2002; Roth, Speece, & Cooper, 2002).

Phonological awareness, receptive and expressive vocabulary, and narrative abilities all play vital roles in typically developing children's literacy acquisition. The next section discusses the other factors that influence the development of reading and writing skills.

Children at Risk for Literacy Challenges

As noted previously, most preschool children who exhibit a typical pattern of language development have acquired a wide range of emerging literacy abilities—awareness of the relationship between oral and written language, as well as recognition of the forms and function of print. These abilities include early phonological awareness; knowledge that words are separate units of language; ability to use context to figure out print (e.g., a STOP sign at a road intersection); and knowledge about books, stories, and other forms of print (e.g., magazines, letters, and lists).

Unfortunately, some children do not acquire the basic emergent skills that are the precursors to formal literacy instruction. Delays in this area are prevalent in children whose disability is language impairment—children with the diagnoses of specific language impairment, cognitive impairment, autistic spectrum disorders, hearing impairment, attention-deficit disorder, attention-deficit hyperactivity disorder, and children with motor disabilities. There are also a group of children who do not have these disabilities but are at risk for language and literacy challenges. These are children who have limited access to print or are limited English proficient.

Preschool educators and other professionals working with children at risk for literacy difficulties must promote opportunities for children to have meaningful and successful interaction with language and print. Collaboration between teachers, families, speech-language pathologists (SLPs), and administrators ensure that these young children have many high-quality opportunities to participate in language instruction, as well as receiving emergent literacy opportunities.

Identifying children who are vulnerable to language and literacy learning activities in preschool settings will enable educators to implement programs that will foster growth in literacy. Thus, early intervention will increase the likelihood of successful learning and academic achievement in higher grades. Along with signs to identify children at risk for literacy challenges, there are other signs to alert the classroom teacher to potential difficulties: limited vocabulary, limited play, lack of interest in books, and limited social interaction with peers. Other potential danger signals include a limited attention span and reluctance to ask questions to learn about unfamiliar concepts (Bernstein & Seiger-Gardner, 2008; Nelson, 1993, 2010). Another danger sign may be difficulty understanding spoken language and expressing ideas.

Using a *preventive* model means taking a proactive stance to identify children with difficulties before they enter the first grade and are unequipped to maintain the pace of instruction encountered in grade school (Justice, Invernizzi, & Meier, 2002).

Book Reading Strategies for Teachers and Parents

Book reading has a strong potential for fostering the type of language development linked to literacy. It is one of the usually scheduled preschool activities when language is front-and-center and when words are central to the activity. During book reading, children must attend to the language of the book and integrate it with information from their experiences as they construct and interpret the "world of the story." Children especially challenged in this situation are those with limited experience with book reading at home, given that book reading relies on language that is not connected to an ongoing activity. As children become familiar with the language of books, they are able to

- learn new concepts and vocabulary,

- become familiar with different kinds of stories and information in books, and

- learn strategies for extracting meaning from books.

The suggestions offered in the next section are points for teachers who want to ensure that using books will capture their students' interest and expand their language skills in the preschool classroom.

Suggestions for Classroom Teachers

There are several suggestions for classroom teachers to provide supports for literacy development (Dickenson, 2001). First, teachers should schedule sufficient time for book reading during the day: In a full-day program, read aloud three times a day for a total of 45 minutes, and in a half-day program, read aloud one to two times per day for a minimum of 10 minutes each time. There should also be a time for children to look at books alone or with a friend. The classroom should provide individual and small-group reading experiences each day, and the classroom teacher should never withhold book reading as a punishment.

There are also suggestions for the use of thoughtful book discussions. When you decide on a book to be read, identify the important vocabulary words and concepts you want the children to grasp. In addition, tell children word meanings you think they do not understand. When introducing a new word, try to use that word in another context. Finally, ask the children about their experiences related to an event that occurred in the story.

Children should be given meaningful and successful interaction with language and print to support literacy development.

Children's reading development is also enhanced when they are given the chance to read and reread various types of books. For example, favorite books may be read several times. Their interest may be engaged when they read books related to a theme (e.g., holidays, seasons, events, and class trips). The classroom teachers should seek out books that convey important information and varied vocabulary. As the academic year progresses, try to stretch children's attention by reading longer books. Look for opportunities to extend children's comprehension by asking questions about the plot or the characters that have not been discussed in previous readings.

It is critical for teachers to point out the importance of having print (e.g., books, magazines, and nameplates) in caregivers' homes, as well as print artifacts (e.g., crayons, markers, and pencils) (Zevenbergen & Whitehurst, 2003). While reading storybooks, preschool teachers should also use and model such techniques as **semantic contingency (**staying on a topic introduced by the child and related to the story being read), routines (reading about predictable situations that occur frequently in children's lives), scaffolding (structuring the teacher's linguistic input as well as the nonlinguistic context), questioning (encouraging students to think about what has been read), discussion (allowing students to discuss their ideas), and writing or drawing (encouraging students to write or draw about what they have read).

These strategies will help children learn to appreciate book reading. Other strategies noted in the literature include using an animated, dramatic, and lively style while reading and using the **dialogic approach** (Zevenbergen & Whitehurst, 2003). This technique differentiates between younger preschoolers (the 3-year-olds) and older preschoolers

(4- to 5-year-olds). For the younger group, this approach involves two assignments given 2 to 3 weeks apart. The first assignment consists of the following elements:

- Ask "what" questions.
- Follow answers with a question.
- Repeat what the child says.
- Help the child as needed.
- Praise and encourage.
- Follow the child's interest.
- Have fun.

The second assignment for the 3-year-olds, to be given 2 to 3 weeks after the first assignment, includes the following elements:

- Ask open-ended questions.
- Expand on what the child says.

When used with 4- to 5-year-olds, this approach is more complex:

- Completion prompts (e.g., "When daddy brought presents, Mary was _____")
- Recall prompts (e.g., "What happened when Mary hit Johnny?")
- Open-ended prompts (e.g., "Tell me what happened next")
- "Wh" prompts (e.g., "Where did Tommy hide? How did Marty feel? Why was Johnny sad?")
- Distancing prompts (e.g., "Did you ever go to the circus?")

Book reading and a structured interactional approach to book reading have positive effects on language development and provide support for the later development of reading skills (Bernstein & Levey, 2009; Valdez-Menchaca & Whitehurst, 1992).

LANGUAGE DIALECTS AND DIFFERENCES

A language dialect is a variation of a language that "is shared by a particular speech community for the purposes of interaction" (Battle, 2009, p. 544). Dialects are associated with cultural groups; may differ according to geography; and may differ in pronunciation, syntax, or vocabulary from other dialects of the same language.

African American English

At age 3, the speech of children exposed to African American English (AAE) includes the same sounds and patterns as that of children from homes where Mainstream American

English (MAE) is spoken (Stewart-Bland, 2003). Thus, the consonants *n, m, b, t, d, k, g, f, h,* and *w* are in the repertoire of typically developing children in homes where MAE or AAE is spoken. Similarly, at age 3, the phonological processes noted previously in this chapter are spoken by children exposed to MAE or AAE.

There are, however, certain consonants that distinguish typically developing children exposed to AAE and MAE, and these differences are usually not evident until after 5 years of age (Battle, 2009). This difference occurs in *th* and *v* words. Thus, the 5-year-old AAE-speaking child may say "free" instead of *three,* "baff" instead of *bath,* and "balentine" instead of *valentine.*

In the area of syntax and morphology, there is similarity in typically developing children from homes where AAE or MAE is spoken up to the age of 3. For example, they produce well-formed multiword constructions and other simple sentences similarly. As they progress through the preschool period, children exposed to AAE often lack the past-tense marker (*-ed*), the possessive (*'s*), and the inflection for the verb *be*. Examples consist of "walk" instead of *walked,* "Danny" instead of *Danny's,* and "He be ___" instead of "He is___." To learn more about AAE, refer to Chapter 12.

Hispanic and Latino Children

While Spanish is the most common language other than English spoken in the United States, there are many dialects of Spanish. In the United States, the most common dialects of Spanish are Mexican and Caribbean Spanish (i.e., Puerto Rican and Cuban). There are several English consonants that are not present in Spanish. They include the /v/ and /w/. There are consonants in Spanish not present in English. They include the trilled /r/ and /n/. There are also several English vowels absent from Spanish. These vowels consist of *cot, paw, bet, bat, put, look,* and *bit.*

In the area of morphology, typically developing children from Spanish-speaking homes who are acquiring English must learn that they do not have to learn the gender of common nouns (as they must do in Spanish). They must also learn the differences in marking verb tense in Spanish versus English. Table 8.9 presents some of the differences between MAE

Table 8.9 Morphological Differences: MAE and Spanish-English Speakers

	MAE	Spanish English
Past tense (*-ed*) (regular)	"Yesterday, I walk**ed**."	"Yesterday, I walk."
Plurals (*-s*)	"The girl**s** are pretty."	"The girl are pretty."
Possessive (*'s*)	"My sister'**s** coat."	"My sister coat."
Negative	"She does **not** cook."	"She no cook."
Interrogative (question inversion)	"**Is** Juan going?"	"Juan is going?"

and Spanish English. Note the differences in the order of the morphological markers in Spanish English, namely the placement of noun-modifying negation markers and the absence of plural noun markers.

Research indicates that there is often misdiagnosis of language disorders in Spanish-speaking children learning English as a second language (Paradis, 2005). It is important for the teacher to be cognizant of language dialects, language differences, and the acquisition of language by typically developing children. Chapters 13 and 14 discuss these differences further.

CASE STUDY REVISITED

At the beginning of this chapter, we met Brian, a 3-year-old whose expressive language was limited to short and incomplete sentences and who exhibited vocabulary problems in naming certain objects, difficulty producing certain sounds, and disinterest when books were read to the class.

CASE STUDY REVISITED: Limits on speech sound production

Brian's teacher, Ms. Wilson, observed Brian closely during his first 3 months in her classroom. She noticed that he could follow simple directions and played appropriately with the other children during free play but that he rarely volunteered information during circle time. He spoke in three-word utterances but did not use full sentences, had great difficulty naming various pictures, paid little attention during book reading, and had trouble pronouncing many sounds, relying mostly on consonants and vowels in the words he attempted. Ms. Wilson decided to seek approval from Brian's parents for psychological and educational evaluations, as well an evaluation by an SLP.

Following assessment, the SLP recommended intervention with the need for improved awareness of sounds in words to increase his speech abilities for word production and improved vocabulary to develop sentence production and support his development of reading skills. She saw him once a week in individual sessions and twice a week in a small group with two other children his age with higher language skills. She developed games to improve his ability to produce sentences in the group, which helped him in the classroom. Over time, Brian's speech and language skills improved, as did his interest in reading. His teacher and parents agreed with the recommendation that intervention continue throughout the year to support continued progress.

SUMMARY

By the time children enter kindergarten, they have acquired a great deal of language. During the preschool period, the foundation for continued growth has been set. They have expanded their linguistic forms, increased their vocabulary, and learned to use language in many different social contexts. The gains preschoolers make in spoken language, as well as the emergent literacy skills they have acquired, will aid them in the more complex task of learning to read and write.

It is important for preschool teachers to be aware of the stages of typical language development so that they may better identify preschool children with language-learning challenges. In this case, it is appropriate to refer these children to professionals for guidance and services while providing the appropriate supports for language and learning development in the classroom. When both SLPs and classroom teachers work collaboratively with parents around home-based activities that can reinforce and extend the ongoing language development plan, the likelihood for improvement is strengthened. This will help ensure that these children achieve academic success during the school-age years so that they can become literate and productive citizens.

This chapter addressed emerging literacy in preschool children and provided strategies to address preschoolers at risk for language and literacy challenges. The following chapter discusses language and communication skills with respect to older children and adolescents. Cognitive growth, use of more complex syntax, increased vocabulary development, use of figurative language, and social communicative competence are areas associated with increased performance expectations for older children and adolescents. Chapter 9 focuses on the extent to which these students are able to meet expectations. The next chapter also offers strategies for classroom teachers and parents to address language development.

KEY WORDS

Alphabetic principle	Gestures	Pragmatics
Communicative intentions	Intentions	Preliteracy
Concepts	Lexical	Relative pronouns
Conjunctives	Metalinguistic awareness	Scripts
Content	Morphemes	Semantic contingency
Dialogic approach	Morphology	
Discourse	Morphosyntactic development	Semantic relations
Embedded phrases		Semantics
Emergent literacy skills	Narrative	Subordinate clauses
Encode	Personal narrative	Syntax
Eye gaze	Phonological awareness	Theme
Fictional narrative	Phonological processes	Use
Form	Phonology	Vocalizations

STUDY QUESTIONS

1. What are the main differences in language (form, content, and use) between toddlers and preschool-age children?

2. What are three approaches you would use to address Brian's difficulties in the classroom?

3. What is the importance of vocabulary in children's language development? How would you help a child who has weak vocabulary?

4. If a 4-year-old has difficulty understanding embedded phrases and subordinate clauses when you are reading, how would you help him or her understand these sentences?

5. If there was a child in your preschool classroom with language difficulties, at what point would you contact the child's parents?

PROJECTS

1. Present preschool-age children (3-, 4-, and 5-year-olds) with a short story from a storybook appropriate for their age. Read the story to them and ask children to retell the story. Analyze and describe their narratives using the descriptions of narrative types in this chapter.

2. Show preschool-age children of different ages pictures of common objects. Ask the children to describe the object. Note the children's language skills at different stages of development. Note the differences in morphology, sentence length, and vocabulary.

3. Show 5-year-olds early sight words of different levels of complexity. First, present them with the words *cat, dog, cow, hop, dad,* and *go.* Next, present them with the words *exit, stop,* and *McDonald's*). Describe their accuracy. Note the manner of decoding, such as sounding out words. Write a short paper describing their word identification.

STUDENT STUDY SITE

Visit the Student Study Site at **www.sagepub.com/levey** for these additional learning tools:

- Video Links
- Self Quizzes
- E-Flashcards

- Sample Forms and Assessment Tools
- Recommended Readings
- Web Resources

SUGGESTIONS FOR FURTHER READING

Bernstein, D. K., & Levey, S. (2009). Language development: A review. In D. K. Bernstein & E. Tiegerman-Farber (Eds.), *Language and communication disorders in children* (6th ed., pp. 28–100). Boston: Allyn & Bacon.

Christie, J. F., Enz, B. J., & Vukelich, C. (2002). *Teaching language and literacy: Preschool through the elementary grades* (3rd ed.). Boston: Allyn & Bacon.

Helm, J. H., Beneke, S., & Steinheimer, K. (1997). *Windows on learning: Documenting young children's work.* New York: Columbia College Press.

Morrow, L. M. (2007). *Developing literacy in preschool.* New York: Guilford.

Roskos, K. A., Tabors, P. O., & Lenhart, L. A. (2004). *Oral language and early literacy in preschool: Talking, reading, and writing.* Newark, DE: International Reading Association.

Tabors, P. O. (2008). *One child, two languages: A guide for early childhood educators of children learning English as a second language.* Baltimore: Paul Brookes.

C H A P T E R   9

Language Development From Age 6 Through Adolescence

Cheryl Smith Gabig

CASE STUDY: The importance of understanding complex concepts

Ms. Spencer was concerned about Henry, a student in her ninth-grade science class who appeared disengaged and disinterested in the content of the class. She noticed that he did not participate in any class discussions and handed in homework assignments late or not at all. When assignments were completed, the product was substandard, with incomplete answers, poor spelling, and misuse of science vocabulary. During class, Ms. Spencer noted that Henry kept his head down, often laying it on the desk. He also did not look up or at her during class lectures or demonstrations. When called on, he hesitated when trying to explain the concepts covered, often using short, simple sentences. Ms. Spencer also noted that Henry had difficulty pronouncing and using the science vocabulary covered in each unit. She wondered if Henry did not understand the concepts covered in the class discussions and in the text or if he was simply not applying himself. Could there be an intrinsic explanation as to why Henry was failing? Was he not able to understand the complex language and science vocabulary used in the science text?

Do you think that Henry does not understand the concepts in the class discussion or that he is just not applying himself? On what information and experiences did you base your answer?

INTRODUCTION

This chapter focuses on language development in early and late childhood (6 to 12 years) and adolescence (13 to 19 years). A great deal of language change and linguistic refinement occurs during childhood and adolescence that allows an individual to function in academic, social, and vocational settings. A useful way to think about language development in childhood and adolescence is to consider the factors found in primary and secondary language development.

Primary Language Development

Primary language development includes the acquisition of the speech sound structure, sentence types, basic vocabulary, and social-pragmatic functions of language by the age of 5 years. (See Chapter 3 for an introduction to and definitions of these concepts.) By 5 years of age, most typically developing children display clear speech with good articulation, speak in complete sentences about the here-and-now (as well as the past and future), engage in conversations with an adult or peer, and easily acquire the meaning of words heard through conversation and social interaction.

Secondary Language Development

Secondary language development refers to the continued refinement and growth in the primary language system—beyond the basic competence seen in children at 5 years of age—with the protracted or extended development of additional competence in syntax, semantics, discourse, and pragmatics in school-age children and adolescents (Nippold, 2007).

The purpose of this chapter is to (1) identify the cognitive-linguistic sources of language input that influence the ongoing acquisition and refinement of the primary language system for school-age children and adolescents; (2) describe changes in language ability across form, content, and use of language; and (3) suggest questions that may help classroom teachers identify students at risk for underachievement, with explanations as to why a student is not achieving in the classroom.

EARLY SCHOOL-AGE LANGUAGE DEVELOPMENT

During the early grades, children's language abilities continue to develop, allowing them to accomplish the more abstract academic skills required in later grades. Beginning in kindergarten, children with intact language skills enjoy listening to stories in a group, are able to follow spoken directions, and can maintain their attention and focus on tasks (Peth-Pierce, 2000). Children with intact language skills are able to hear differences between sounds as they learn the names and sounds of alphabet letters and numbers.

In the first grade, children expand their vocabulary, develop the ability to write when they learn that written text represents spoken language, and begin to read and respond to a variety of literacy materials (e.g., books, magazines, and the Internet). In the second grade, children continue to develop their listening, speaking, reading, and writing skills. They are also more interactive participants in conversations and discussions. In the third grade, children begin to use critical-thinking skills, which allow them to determine meaning and distinguish truth from falsehood. Children are now able to read fluently enough to compose and write stories, and their vocabulary skills continue to develop.

These early grades provide children with the foundational language knowledge needed to succeed in later grades, discussed in detail in this chapter. See Figure 9.1 for an overview of language development from kindergarten to third grade.

| **Figure 9.1** | An Overview of Language Development: Kindergarten to Third Grade |

Kindergarten

- Follows one- to two-step directions in sequence
- Listens to and understands stories read to the class
- Answers simple yes/no and WH questions (e.g., "What did you . . . ?")
- Produces clear speech
- Asks for information
- Participates in and initiates conversation
- Understands reading from top to bottom and left to right
- Understands words that rhyme
- Can match words based on their sounds
- Matches some sounds with letters
- Has sight word recognition for some words
- Prints names
- Draws a picture to tell a story

First Grade

- Understands and can recall information
- Follows two- to three-step directions in sequence
- Answers more complex questions
- Can tell and retell stories with logical order of events
- Produces a variety of sentence types and supplies directions
- Stays on topic during a conversation
- Asks and answers WH questions (i.e., *who, what, where, why*, and *when*)
- Can match spoken with written words and can identify sounds in shorter words
- May sound out unfamiliar words when reading
- Prints words and spells frequently used words correctly
- Can write short stories

Second Grade

- Follows three- to four-step directions
- Understands concepts that involve location and time
- Can answer questions about a story
- Produces more complex sentences
- Can explain words and ideas
- Uses language in more complex ways (e.g., to inform, persuade, and entertain)
- Maintains topic and turn taking in conversation

(Continued)

(Continued)

- Displays intact phonological awareness for the correspondence between sounds, syllables, words, and longer spoken utterances with written forms
- Has expanded sight word recognition
- Monitors reading accuracy by rereading
- Can explain the main ideas of a story
- Writes clearly and uses a range of sentence types
- Moves from inventive to accurate spelling

Third Grade

- Shows good listening skills and continued progress in conversation skills
- Can summarize, predict, and explain when working with reading tasks
- Displays prediction and mastery of phonics in reading skills
- Uses learned information to learn new topics
- Uses topic-specific vocabulary in conversation and classroom discussion
- Can explain material that has been learned in the classroom
- Can ask and answer questions related to material learned in the classroom
- Makes continued progress in monitoring reading accuracy
- Composes stories and spells simple words correctly while using details in writing
- Asks and answers questions about reading materials
- Rereads and corrects errors
- Spells most words correctly

SOURCE: Reprinted and adapted with the permission of Wellman Owre and Kennedy Brennan (2002).

SOURCES OF LANGUAGE LEARNING IN LATE CHILDHOOD AND ADOLESCENCE

Later language development in children and adolescents can be traced to three sources of language input that stimulate and expand the knowledge and use of the primary language system acquired in the younger years. These aspects and demands include

- the source of complex language input,
- changes in cognitive processing, and
- growth in social experience and pragmatic knowledge of how to use language.

The interrelated aspects of cognitive development and demands of language processing also contribute to the changes and refinements in the language of older children and adolescents.

Late childhood through adolescence is an important developmental period in which children show advances in language abilities.

Source of Complex Language Input

Language development at any age requires input in order to learn and expand one's knowledge of language structure, vocabulary, or pragmatic functions. For young children, parental- and caregiver-spoken language is the main source of input for sentence structure, vocabulary, and social conventions of the language system (Hoff-Ginsberg, 1985, 1986, 1990; Hoff-Ginsberg & Shatz, 1982; Huttenlocher, Haight, Bryk, Seltzer, & Lyons, 1991).

The source of language input for later language development in older children and adolescents is different. By 9 to 10 years of age, children rely on written language for a great deal of input about vocabulary, figurative language, and complex sentence structure. According to Chall, Jacobs, and Baldwin (1990), beginning around the fourth grade, the language demands of textbooks, educational materials, and the curriculum increase dramatically as older children encounter more difficult concepts, vocabulary, complex syntax, and text organization.

Intact reading abilities are the main source of language input that stimulates the continued growth and acquisition of higher-level language, which includes abstract vocabulary and figurative language, complex sentence structure, and knowledge of narrative and expository text structures (Beck, Perfetti, & McKeown, 1982; Cain & Oakhill, 2007; Cunningham & Stanovich, 1997; Nippold, Allen, & Kirsch, 2001; Oakhill & Cain, 2007; Perfetti, 1994).

Changes in Cognitive Processing

In addition to proficient reading abilities that foster the acquisition and refinement of more complex language, cognitive development aids older children and adolescents in their ongoing language development. Beginning around 11 years of age, children begin to engage in more abstract thinking as they move into the stage of cognitive development called formal operational thinking (Inhelder & Piaget, 1958).

Abstract thinking is the ability to think beyond the immediate concept being talked about or the event taking place. Older children who have transitioned into Piaget's stage of formal operations are able to acquire abstract propositions and expand their vocabulary knowledge to include the broader scope of meaning of intangible words such as *freedom* or *liberty,* state and test hypotheses, understand and use logical operations in the construction of complex sentences, and engage in the understanding and use of figurative language such as metaphors, idioms, and proverbs.

The shift in cognitive development from concrete to abstract thinking also plays a role in the development of critical thinking skills, defined by Abrami et al. (2008) as "the ability to engage in purposeful, self-regulatory judgment" (p. 1102). The growth of critical thinking in older students, especially in adolescents, is particularly useful in history, language arts, mathematics, and social studies, where content vocabulary and specific issues and concepts related to the discipline must be actively acquired.

Leung and Kember (2003) argue that a student deeply involved in thinking and learning searches for the meaning inherent in the text or the intent of the author, theorizes and forms hypotheses about the content being acquired, and integrates aspects of a task or content into a whole. Students who use critical thinking and self-regulatory judgment actively engage in the metalinguistic analysis of word structure (e.g., prefixes, suffixes, and roots), sentence and text structure, the underlying meaning of specific content, and analysis of author intent if engaged in thinking about prose.

Growth in Social Experience and Pragmatic Knowledge

The older child and adolescent's growth in social competence is another source of language input with peers and in academic and social settings. Adolescents have increasingly more independence in elective coursework and engage in other social experiences, such as extracurricular activities and pursuits outside the immediate school and family. These changes also stimulate growth in the understanding and use of language. For example, an adolescent may choose to volunteer for a political action committee during an election, acquiring vocabulary specific to the political process—such as *constituency, ideology,* and *voter registration*—as well as learning how to speak about a candidate and the political issues. Another student may elect to take a course in auto repair or mechanics, acquiring vocabulary items such as *hydraulics, catalytic converter,* and *piston*. Such individualized social experiences promote the development of linguistic individualism (Nippold, 2007), along with acquisition of new concepts and experience associated with different social contexts.

GROWTH IN LANGUAGE FORM: THE USE OF COMPLEX SYNTAX AND DERIVATIONAL MORPHOLOGY

During late childhood and adolescence, there are subtle yet significant changes in the child's understanding and use of the form or structure of the language system. Recall that the term **form** refers to how words and sentences are formed or constructed, consisting of phonology, morphology, and syntax. While the speech and phonological aspects of language are well developed by late childhood, two other aspects of language continue to develop. These two aspects are the use of more complex syntax in both spoken and written language and the acquisition and use of complex word structures, or derivational morphemes, with the appearance of prefixes and suffixes in both spoken and written language.

The Development of Complex Sentence Structure

Children continue to increase the length of their utterances as they move from kindergarten to later grades (Bernstein & Levey, 2009). Syntactic skills increase with the production of modal auxiliaries (e.g., *can, could, shall, should, will, would, do, did, may,* and *might*), allowing children to produce indirect requests (e.g., "Can I have a cookie?").

The most obvious growth in language abilities in older children and adolescents is the comprehension and use of more complex sentence structures that express a variety of semantic relations. As children advance through later elementary grades and into middle school and high school, they understand and use more complex sentence structure in spoken and written language. Throughout the early and later grades of elementary school and into adolescence, children continue to modify and expand their knowledge of sentence structure through elaborating and expanding the basic structure of sentences. This is termed **intrasentential growth**, the use of more complex sentence patterns such as those incorporating conjunctions and subordinate and dependent clauses, along with the combination of simple sentences.

Children's spoken utterances and written sentences get longer with age, especially with the use of **subordinate dependent clauses** for communicating complex **propositions** or meanings (Hunt, 1970; Klecan-Aker & Hedrick, 1985; Loban, 1976; Scott & Stokes, 1995). To help you understand what aspects of complex sentence structure children acquire in late childhood and adolescence, a brief review of basic concepts and terminology of sentence structure is warranted.

Basic Sentence Types

There are four types of sentence in English: **simple**, **compound**, **complex,** and **compound-complex**. Table 9.1 outlines the four sentence types and how speakers or writers can modify basic, simple sentences to create more complex sentence structures.

Putting Words Together: Simple and Compound Sentences

To recognize how words are combined to make sentences (whether simple, compound, complex, or compound-complex), it is important to understand the concept of a simple sentence. A simple sentence is a sequence of words containing a subject and a predicate (e.g., subject + verb), expressing a complete thought. The simple sentence "The worm is eating the apple" contains a subject (*the worm*) and a predicate verb (*is eating*) and is able to stand alone as a complete thought.

To relay a more complex thought or proposition, children or adults combine simple sentences by using one of a group of words called **conjunctions.** A conjunction serves to coordinate or combine two simple sentences into a compound sentence. The compound sentence "The girl drew a picture and gave the picture to her mother" is made of two simple sentences that can stand alone. Each sentence is a complete thought and these sentences are combined using the conjunction *and* to form a compound sentence composed of (a) "The girl drew a picture" and (b) "(the girl) gave the picture to her mother." The subject (*the girl*) in the second sentence is omitted to avoid redundancy (e.g., "The girl drew a picture and **the girl** gave it to her mother").

Table 9.1	Basic English Sentence Types		
Simple	**Compound**	**Complex**	**Compound-Complex**
At least one *independent clause* Example: "The worm is eating the apple."	Two independent clauses joined by a *coordinating conjunction* Example: "We went to the movies, and we got some popcorn."	At least one independent clause and at least one *dependent clause* joined by a *subordinating conjunction* Example: "We will call you tonight when we get home."	Two independent clauses and at least one dependent clause Example: "Billy came home since it was raining and the baseball game was cancelled."
An independent clause is a sentence containing a subject and a verb. An independent clause is able to stand alone as a complete thought.	A coordinating conjunction is a connective device such as *and, but,* or *so* used to join two independent clauses. Each clause is a complete thought and can stand alone: • "We went to the movies." • "We got some popcorn." Coordinating conjunctions include *and, but, because, for, or, so,* and *yet.*	A dependent clause is a group of words that contains a subject and a verb but cannot stand alone as a complete thought: • "when we get home" This is not a complete thought and cannot stand alone. Subordinating conjunctions include *when, although, as, as if, before, than, unless, whether, because, in order, though, while, since, whenever,* and *where.*	The two independent clauses are • "Billy came home" and • "The baseball game was cancelled" The dependent clause "since it was raining" is not a complete thought and cannot stand alone.

Expanding and Embedding Meaning:
Complex and Compound-Complex Sentences

A complex sentence is formed with a simple sentence that contains phrases or groups of words that add critical meaning but cannot stand alone as a complete sentence. This is called a **dependent clause.** The meaning of the dependent clause is not apparent unless it is attached to the main sentence (Hunt, 1970; Loban, 1976; Nippold, 2007; Scott, 1988). In the sentence "We will call you tonight when we get home," the dependent clause ("when we get home") cannot stand alone as a complete thought. Its meaning is dependent on the main simple sentence, "We will call you tonight."

A compound-complex sentence is the most complex kind of sentence, formed by combining two or more simple sentences with a dependent or subordinating clause. The subordinating clause is signaled by a group of words called **subordinating conjunctions** (e.g., *when, although, as, as if, before, than, unless, whether, because, in order, though, while, since, whenever,* and *where*). Subordinating conjunctions do not appear in the speech and writing of younger school-age children but begin to appear at approximately 9 to 10 years of age in the fifth grade. Their usage peaks in grades 11 and 12 (Loban, 1976).

The use of **subordination** is a more difficult syntactic form than the use of parallel simple sentences linked by the simple conjunctions *and* or *but*. Subordination involves the construction of **embedded** dependent clauses, as in the sentence "The man who lives near the church is an American Indian and the oldest member of the community." This compound-complex sentence contains an embedded, dependent clause, "who lives near the church," and combines structural elements from both a compound and a complex sentence to create additional, embedded meaning. The sentence is syntactically more mature because it combines two simple sentences ("The man is an American Indian"; "The man is the oldest member of the community") with an embedded, dependent clause ("who lives near the church"). This creates a more coherent organization of the intended meaning than simply linking parallel simple sentences, as in "The man is an American Indian and the oldest member of the community and he lives near the church." The embedded clause adds additional meaning to the sentence but cannot stand alone as a complete thought.

We have described four sentence types: basic, compound, complex, and compound-complex. A **basic sentence** structure is the foundation for constructing the other sentence types. A compound sentence is two basic sentences with a simple conjunction (e.g., *and*), while the two more complex sentence types require either more advanced use of subordinating conjunctions (e.g., *when, although, as, as if, before, than, unless, whether, because, in order, though, while, since, whenever,* and *where*) or the strategy of embedding a clause within a basic sentence. Sentences get longer and more complex during late childhood and adolescence in both their spoken and written forms.

QUANTITATIVE MEASURES OF SYNTACTIC GROWTH IN LATER CHILDHOOD AND ADOLESCENCE

A number of quantifying indicators can chart the growth and use of more complex syntax by older children and adolescents. One indicator measures the growth in the number of words in a sentence, called average **sentence length**. Another method measures the number of clauses used in spoken or written language. This method measures growth in syntax. The approach is to divide sentences and clauses into separate strands, each called a **communicative unit,** or **C-unit**. A final method is to analyze the type of dependent clauses or subordinating devices used by older children and adolescents.

Average Sentence Length

Average sentence length is the average number of words per sentence, calculated by counting the number of words in each written or oral sentence and then dividing the total number of words by the total number of sentences. Spoken and written language becomes more complicated during late childhood and adolescence with the use of complex sentence structures.

Scott (1988) examined the spoken and written sentences produced by children in elementary grades and into high school, confirming the steady growth of average sentence length over time in the number of words per sentence. For example, an 8-year-old writer produces an average of 6.5 words per sentence, a 13-year-old 7.7 words per sentence, and an adult 11.5 words per sentence.

Communicative Units (C-Units)

Another method used to document growth in syntactic complexity is to segment the written sentences or spoken utterances into C-units, defined by each independent, simple sentence and by any dependent or subordinating clauses. For example, the sentence "The boy / who lives nearby / is my best friend" contains three C-units, indicated by the slant marks.

Loban (1976) studied the oral and written language of 211 children from kindergarten through grade 12, with focus on the number of dependent (e.g., subordinate) clauses in C-units as an index of growth in sentence maturity and complexity. For older students in grades 5, 7, 9, 11, and 12, Loban reported the average number of dependent clauses per C-unit in oral language to be 8.8, 9.8, 10.9, 11.2, and 11.7, respectively, while written language averages were similar: 8.7, 8.9, 10, 10.7, and 13.3. There is a steady growth in the use of dependent (subordinate) clauses in the spoken and written language of students in grades 5 through 12. Grade 12 students show the greatest command and use of dependent clauses, especially in the context of written language, which tends to be more formal than spoken language.

There is a steady growth in the use of subordinating, dependent clauses in the oral and written language of older children and adolescents. Older children and adolescents expand their knowledge and use of complex sentences by building on basic sentence structure through either the use of conjunctions or embedding a meaningful proposition within a basic sentence.

DERIVATIONAL MORPHEMES

Another aspect of form development during late childhood and adolescence is the appearance and use of **derivational morphemes** in oral and written language. Derivational morphemes are prefixes and suffixes that are used in combination with root words to form new words, as in *disestablishment* (made of the root word *establish* and two derivational morphemes, *-dis* and *-ment*). Derivational morphemes often change the part-of-speech of a root word. For example, the verb *teach* is changed to a noun by the addition of the suffix *-er* (*teacher*). Suffix additions are derivational morphemes (or suffixes) that are added to a root word to change the meaning of this word, as well as the part-of-speech (e.g., verb to noun).

The Development of Derivational Morphemes

Over the past 20 years, investigators have been interested in why some children learn effortlessly when and how to apply derivational morphemes (especially suffixes) to a word, along with being able to easily read, spell, and determine their meaning, while others do not (Carlisle, 1987, 1988, 2000; Henry, 1988, 1993, 2008; Moats & Smith, 1992). Children begin to use derivational morphemes in spoken and written language in later grades, beginning around fourth grade, when textbooks and reading material contain many more varied vocabulary forms (Carlisle, 1988, 2000; Henry, 1988).

Certain derivational morphemes emerge between 4 to 5 years of age with production of the comparative *-er* (e.g., *bigger*) and between 5 to 6 years of age with the superlative *-est* (e.g., *biggest*) (Norris, 1998), while there is a developmental trend in fourth-, sixth-, and eighth-graders in their ability to use suffix-addition rules in spoken language and in spelling derived forms (Carlisle, 1988). Children's metalinguistic awareness of the structure of complex words is also related to good reading comprehension abilities (Carlisle, 2000).

THE RELATIONSHIP OF DERIVATIONAL MORPHEMES TO ACCURACY IN SPELLING

Learning to spell words that contain derivational morphemes depends on knowledge of when and how to apply the appropriate morpheme, as well as how much a base word changes when the morpheme or suffix is added (Carlisle, 1988). Bernstein and Levey (2009) provide examples of children's spelling skills that show the increased awareness of the correspondence between sounds and letters over time as children attempt to spell the word *dragon:* MPRMRHM (kindergarteners), GAGIN (first-graders), and DRAGUN (second-graders). By the third or fourth grade, children are able to write more complex sentences and are able to proof and revise their written work (Bernstein & Levey, 2009).

There is a developmental trend between fourth-, sixth-, and eighth-grade students' knowledge of derivational morphology and their ability to spell words containing suffixes that shift a word significantly away from its root or base word. This shift or change in how a word is pronounced or spelled from its base, or root word, is called a **transformation**. Difficulties understanding the meaning and correctly spelling complex words arise when a root word, or base word, undergoes multiple transformations or changes. Carlisle (1988) identified four types of transformation between the base word and the derived form:

- No change: There is no change in the pronunciation or spelling when the suffix addition is used (e.g., *good* to *goodness*).

- Orthographic change: There is a change in the spelling of the derived form but no change in the phonology, or pronunciation, of the word (e.g., *beauty* to *beautiful*).

- Phonological change: There is a shift in the pronunciation or underlying phonological structure of the word when the derivational suffix is added (e.g., *magic* to *magician*).

- Both change: There is a transformation in the pronunciation or underlying phonology of the base word, as well as a change in the spelling or orthographic pattern of the base to derived form (e.g., *decide* to *decision; college* to *collegial*).

Carlisle (1988) found a developmental trend from the fourth to eighth grades in the ability to generate orally and spell derived forms using suffix additions. Learning derivational morphemes and the spelling of derived words is related to the relative complexity of the type of transformation needed between the base word and its derived form. Students made more errors on words requiring a phonological change and on words that required both phonological changes and an orthographic shift.

Latin and Greek Roots

High school students and adult learners continue to acquire and use more complex word structure with an added focus on words containing Latin and Greek roots and morphemes. Latin and Greek layers of language provide additional semantic meaning to the student than what is portrayed in words of Anglo-Saxon origin (Henry, 2008). Science, social studies, and mathematics textbooks in the upper grades contain a significant amount of vocabulary words with Latin and Greek morphemes, such as *anthropoid, anthropology, autoimmune, biodiversity, chromium, evolution, aggregate, technology, pterodactyl, synergy,* and *hexagram.* Older students' metalinguistic awareness of derivational morphemes, coupled with skills in recognizing additional meanings contained in words with Greek and Latin roots, is associated with reading comprehension and verbal scores on the college entrance exam (Mahoney, 1994).

Older school-age children and adolescents demonstrate increased language refinement and learning of language forms by acquiring more complex syntax abilities and knowledge of derivational morphology to derive additional word meanings. This knowledge contributes significantly to reading comprehension, written language, and spelling in older school-age children and adolescents.

GROWTH IN LANGUAGE CONTENT: VOCABULARY

Children substantially improve their vocabularies during their school years. School children between 3rd and 12th grade increase their vocabulary by 3,000 words per year (Nagy, Herman, & Anderson, 1985). By 12th grade, the estimated averages range from 8,000 to 50,000 words (Stahl & Nagy, 2006). This process consists of acquiring knowledge of word meanings, not simply acquiring a sight vocabulary for reading (Stahl & Nagy, 2006).

Development of New Vocabulary

Acquiring word meaning follows a gradual and incremental course, with partial meaning acquired first in a process called fast mapping. Carey and Bartlett (1978) demonstrated that children quickly develop some sense of the meaning of a new word from a single exposure. In a similar manner, older school-age children may have only a partial meaning of a new vocabulary word when it is initially encountered in listening or while reading text. With repeated exposure to a vocabulary word across a variety of linguistic contexts, the meaning can be continuously refined and expanded to include an in-depth knowledge of the semantic aspects of the word's meaning.

Beck and McKeown (1991) noted three levels of depth of word knowledge in school-age children: full concept knowledge, partial concept knowledge, and verbal association knowledge. A fifth-grader who knows the word *grim* to mean "appearing stern" has a verbal association level of knowledge of the word's meaning. In contrast, the student who knows that the adjective can also be applied to something uninviting (e.g., a *grim* task) and that it is related morphologically to *grimace* (meaning "a twisting or distortion of the face") has a broader and more fully developed conceptual formation of the word's meaning.

Children's understanding of more complex language also depends on intact vocabulary abilities. For example, children's understanding of jokes and riddles depends on their ability to understand ambiguity, or when words have more than one meaning. Consequently, children must have intact language skills to understand certain jokes. Westby (1998) reports that different types of jokes present children with more or less difficulty based on the different types of ambiguity. For example, phonological ambiguity is understood at 6 to 7 years of age (e.g., "Why did the clock go to the doctor? Because he had a tick."), but lexical ambiguity is understood later (e.g., "What happened to the girl's feet? She had bare feet."). In order to be able to interpret humor, children need well-developed language skills.

The Influence of Reading on Vocabulary

Perhaps the single most important factor in the continued and expansive development of vocabulary in the older school-age child and adolescent is reading skills. There is a relationship among knowledge of vocabulary, reading comprehension, and academic success (Anderson & Freebody, 1981; Beck et al., 1982; Medo & Ryder, 1993). Word reading accuracy and fluency has a strong association with vocabulary, reading comprehension, and scores on measures of verbal intelligence (Cain & Oakhill, 2006; Perfetti, 1994; Stanovich & Cunningham, 1992, 1993).

Reading abilities have a profound effect on vocabulary development and academic success, with reading skills in younger grades influencing reading performance and greater engagement in reading activities in older elementary grades through high school (Cunningham & Stanovich, 1997). First-graders are focused on recognizing words, and it is not until the third grade that children's reading becomes more automatic. Good reading skills continue to influence children's engagement in literacy activities, both within and outside school for older children and adolescents, while contributing to higher scores on measures of vocabulary and verbal intelligence (Cain & Oakhill, 2006).

There is substantial growth in vocabulary during late childhood and adolescence, influenced by reading accuracy and fluency. Moreover, children and adolescents may acquire a partial knowledge or simple association of a word's meaning when it is first encountered but will gradually alter and develop a more fully conceptualized understanding of the word's meaning with repeated encounters in a variety of language contexts. Vocabulary knowledge has been linked to academic success as well as achievement scores and measures of verbal intelligence.

GROWTH IN LANGUAGE CONTENT: FIGURATIVE LANGUAGE

Figurative language refers to a specific type of language that is meant to impart complex meaning other than the literal interpretation of the words and includes the understanding and use of dual-function words, metaphors, similes, proverbs, and idioms. Each of these types of figurative language has its own developmental trajectory, with dual-function words, metaphors, and similes being understood and used by children and adolescents before the full appreciation and use of idioms and proverbs.

Types of Figurative Language

Dual-function words are terms that have a primary, physical meaning and a secondary, psychological meaning used to describe emotional aspects of people, such as *cold, warm,* or *hard.* Dual-function words are used when the primary psychological or physical meaning is symbolically extended, as in "She looked up with a cold stare."

A full metaphor is a figure of speech in which a term or phrase is applied to some other thing to suggest a comparison or resemblance, as in "Life is a bowl of cherries." The usual form of a metaphor is "A is B."

A simile is a variation that makes a comparison explicit by inserting the word *like* or *as,* as in "He eats like a bird." An idiom is a phrase used to express complex meaning in a concise way, as in "Her financial problems are only the tip of the iceberg." Finally, a proverb is a short saying or adage used within a specific linguistic culture to express a common truth or familiar experience, as in "A little knowledge is a dangerous thing" or "Birds of a feather flock together."

Figurative Language in the Classroom

Children's exposure to figurative language in school-related activities begins in the early elementary grades and continues through middle school. Understanding figurative language is essential, given that teachers frequently use figurative language when speaking to students in class (Lazar, Warr-Leeper, Nicholson, & Johnson, 1989). Lazar and colleagues found that kindergarten teachers used idioms or multiple-meaning expressions using dual-function words in 4.65% of their utterances; by eighth grade, 20% of teacher's utterances contained a dual-function word or idiomatic expression. For example, teachers may say, "See if it comes back to you," meaning "to recall" a piece of information that was previously taught, or "We've been touching on letter writing," meaning that letter formation is being taught (Lazar et al., 1989). Nippold (1991) noted that idiomatic expressions are more likely to appear in printed materials used in the classroom, beginning in the third grade.

Development of Figurative Language

The ability to understand figurative language is not fully realized until later childhood and early adolescence, when cognitive development and metalinguistic abilities enable a child to make explicit comparisons between the literal use of terms and the secondary, implied meaning (Chan & Marinellie, 2008; Cometa & Eson, 1978; Douglas & Peel, 1979; Nippold & Fey, 1983; Winner, Rosensteil, & Gardner, 1976).

Winner et al. (1976) examined the responses from children ages 6 to 14 years old to metaphors in a story that contained dual-function words. Responses were scored as magical, metonymic, primitive metaphoric, or genuine metaphoric. In their study, children interpreted the metaphor "The guard was hard as a rock" in the following ways:

- Magical responses were explanations based on face value (e.g., "The king had a magic rock, and he turned the guard into another rock").

- Metonymic responses were explanations that showed some association between the comparison terms in the metaphor (e.g., "The guard worked in a prison that had hard rock walls").

- A primitive response focused on an incidental aspect of one of the terms in the metaphor but did not make a comparison between the terms (e.g., "The guard had hard, tough muscles").

- A genuine metaphoric response was one that abstracted the dimensional comparison shared by the two terms of the metaphor (e.g., "The guard was mean and did not care about the feelings of the prisoners").

Young children between 6 and 8 years old provided significantly more magical or metonymic responses to metaphors. By 8 years of age, some children were able to provide a primitive interpretation of the metaphor, although 10-year-olds provided this type of response significantly more. The oldest group, the 12- to 14-year-old children, was able to provide genuine metaphoric responses.

The Later Development and Use of Idioms and Proverbs

Idiom and proverb understanding shows a gradual and protracted developmental trend well into adolescence and adulthood (Nippold, 1991; Nippold et al., 2001; Nippold & Duthie, 2003; Nippold & Haq, 1996; Nippold & Martin, 1989; Nippold & Rudzinski, 1993). Idioms pose difficulty because the meaning of the individual words in the idiom—for example, "It's raining cats and dogs"—provides little assistance in understanding the figurative interpretation—that it's raining heavily (Nippold & Duthie, 2003).

Factors Influencing the Understanding of Idioms

The variables that influence the understanding of the figurative meaning of idioms include

- the **semantic transparency** of the idiom,

- the role of **context** in assisting in comprehension, and

- the individual's past exposure to the expression (Nippold & Duthie, 2003).

Semantic transparency refers to idiomatic expressions in which the figurative and literal meanings of the individual words are closely related, as in "Paddle your own canoe." If heard in context, an older child or adolescent may be able to discern the mental imagery and figurative meaning of the expression to mean "to accomplish on your own." Idioms that are not semantically transparent are called opaque. These are more difficult to interpret because the vocabulary does not assist in the nonliteral interpretation, as in "Paint the town red," meaning "to celebrate" (as opposed to the literal interpretation of actually painting the town with a brush).

Nippold and Rudzinski (1993) proposed the **metasemantic hypothesis,** which states that individuals learn the figurative meaning of idioms by examining the vocabulary contained in the idiom. Therefore, transparent idioms are learned earlier than opaque idioms. Nippold and Duthie (2003) found that older school-age children ages 11;7 to 12;9 (years;months) and adults ages 19;3 to 55;6 reported more relevant mental images for transparent idioms, also finding these idioms easier to comprehend than the opaque expressions.

The Role of Culture in Understanding Proverbs

Proverbs are a form of figurative language linked to a shared value or belief of a culture or society (Hirsch, Kett, & Trefil, 1988). The proverb "Birds of a feather flock together" means that people with similar behaviors or beliefs tend to socialize or interact with one another. The proverb "Don't bite the hand that feeds you" admonishes a person to not hurt or offend someone who employs or takes care of him or her.

Proverbs are more difficult to comprehend than idioms and metaphors, especially for children and adolescents from a different cultural or linguistic background, perhaps because of the significant tie to cultural references (Roseberry-McKibbin, 2007). Proverb understanding gradually improves in late childhood into adolescence and adulthood and follows a similar developmental process as idioms, with more familiar, transparent proverbs understood before less familiar, more opaque or abstract proverbs (Nippold & Haq, 1996).

THE ROLE OF COGNITIVE DEVELOPMENT IN UNDERSTANDING FIGURATIVE LANGUAGE

The gradual and protracted development of the ability to comprehend all types of figurative language has been explained by changes in cognitive development. Beginning at approximately 11 years of age, children enter a stage of cognitive development called **formal operations**, characterized by the emergence of abstract thinking. This marks the ability to consider alternate solutions to problems, an aspect of hypothetical-deductive reasoning (Inhelder & Piaget, 1959; Piaget, 1959). In this stage, a child can employ higher-level reasoning processes, including

- analysis (identifying the root causes of a problem or the issues that need to be addressed),
- synthesis (identifying possible solutions along with strategies and actions), and
- judgment (decisions to aid in the comprehension of metaphoric meaning).

Prior to this stage of development, a child is more concrete in his or her thinking, using more literal interpretations of figurative language forms. An understanding of metaphor and dual-function words emerges earlier, followed by comprehension of idioms and the understanding and appreciation of the cultural and semantic subtlety of proverbs (Douglas & Peel, 1979). Research shows a developmental process, with younger children providing more literal interpretations for all types of figurative language and older school-age children continuing to acquire a more comprehensive understanding of figurative language through adolescence and adulthood (Nippold & Duthie, 2003; Winner et al., 1976).

GROWTH IN PRAGMATIC LANGUAGE USE: SOCIAL AND COMMUNICATIVE COMPETENCE

The **pragmatic** aspect of language refers to both the linguistic (verbal behavior) and non-linguistic (nonverbal behavior) used by individuals when engaged in social communicative interaction. We use language in social contexts in order to accomplish or obtain a desired functional outcome, such as requesting information or commenting on an event. Moreover, when we communicate, we engage in organized rules of conversation and interaction that signal to others our intent or interest in the communicative exchange. In this way, we demonstrate the ability to perceive both the speaker and the listener role appropriate to the context (Prutting & Kirchner, 1987). A smooth interchange between a speaker and listener depends on the following verbal and nonverbal behaviors:

- Turn taking in conversation

- Pausing appropriately

- Maintaining the topic

- Using vocabulary appropriate to the context

- Using appropriate eye gaze, body posture, and facial expression

Since the pragmatic aspect of language is inherently linked to social interaction, the concept of social competence in older school-age children and adolescents becomes increasingly more compelling, especially when we consider developmental changes in social pragmatic language skills and the relationship between social competence and academic performance.

Social Competence

Social competence refers to a child's proficiency in social functioning with peers and adults, evident in the demonstration of pro-social skills and behaviors rather than outcomes of social functioning, such as peer status (Rydell, Hagekull, & Bohlin, 1997). Social competence is also linked to acceptance by peers and teachers and is consistently related to academic achievement (Cavell, 1990; Wentzel, 1991).

Middle childhood and adolescence is a period of refinement of pro-social verbal behaviors reflective of emerging social competence (Nippold, 1993; Rydell et al., 1997; Selman, Beardslee, Schultz, Krupa, & Podorefsky, 1986). The ability to use language to detect problems and negotiate solutions is finally consolidated during late adolescence (Selman et al., 1986).

> Henry did not make eye contact with peers when students were engaged in conversations or group learning activities. He also rarely, if ever, initiated conversations with peers. Ms. Spencer decided to initiate role-play in the classroom that provided models of a variety of communicative events that required verbal and nonverbal problem solving (e.g., returning an overdue library book).

INTERPERSONAL NEGOTIATION STRATEGIES

A pro-social verbal behavior of interest to psychologists, educators, and parents is the older child and adolescent's ability to engage in conflict resolution or interpersonal negotiation in various contexts of social interaction. Social competence in late childhood and adolescence is conveyed by how well the child or adolescent relates to and interacts with others in his or her home, school, or community (Cavell, 1990; Rydell et al., 1997; Selman et al., 1986; Wentzel, 1991). As previously noted, there is significant growth in social competence during middle and late childhood into adolescence, largely as a result of the expansion of successful communication skills and negotiation strategies to resolve potential conflicts with parents, teachers, and peers (Cavell, 1990; Rydell et al., 1997; Selman et al., 1986).

During adolescence, children are able to use language to detect problems and negotiate solutions.

The communication skills associated with successful negotiation and conflict resolution include

- defining a problem or conflict,

- proposing and justifying an action strategy to resolve the conflict, and

- evaluating the impact of the action strategy on others' feelings (Selman et al., 1986).

Adolescents are better at each of these three overt communication behaviors associated with successful conflict resolution or negotiation and are considered to be more socially competent (Selman et al., 1986).

In a study of three groups of school-age children—late childhood (11 to 13 years), middle adolescence (14 to 16 years), and older adolescence (17 to 19 years)—researchers asked each student to listen to a short statement containing a problem or quandary for one of the participants in the situation. Next, they asked the children to provide an explanation of and any solution to the stated predicament (Selman et al., 1986).

Findings were that the oldest group of adolescents (17 to 19 years) was better at recognizing and defining the inherent problem and proposing and justifying a solution or negotiation strategy. They were also better able to empathize and express more complex feelings for the hypothetical participants in the story (this ability is tied to *theory of mind*, as described in Chapter 2). Moreover, the girls in the older adolescent group were better communicators at each of the three levels of successful negotiation than males of the same age group. Younger children and adolescents were less likely to provide an action or interpersonal negotiation strategy, suggesting that ability in interpersonal negotiation as a form of pragmatic language functioning is still developing in late childhood into adolescence.

NONVERBAL COMMUNICATIVE BEHAVIORS IN ADOLESCENTS

Older children and adolescents demonstrate certain overt nonverbal social interactive behaviors during conversation with peers and adults: the use of gaze, facial expression, and gestures (Cavell, 1990). Along with nodding while listening and waiting for a turn, these behaviors provide evidence for the level of engagement in the social interaction during conversational exchanges (Turkstra, Ciccia, & Seaton, 2003).

STRATEGIES FOR THE CLASSROOM

Older children and adolescents navigate among several separate classrooms for each content area. During their navigations, they interact with many different teachers. Consequently, there is no primary-contact teacher who knows how the student functions across curriculum content areas or settings. For older school-age children and adolescents, the role of each educator becomes critical in noting and evaluating underachievement in the classroom.

This section provides a list of questions that teachers of any content area may ask when faced with an older school-age child or adolescent who is not achieving, and this list may serve to help problem-solve potential reasons for classroom underachievement. It is beyond the scope of this chapter to provide a full summary of scientifically based differentiated curriculum and evidence-based intervention strategies to meet the needs of those students who are at risk or who are underachieving in content-area classrooms.

Regardless of the specific content area (e.g., mathematics, social studies, science, or language arts), an educator may want to focus on each of the information-processing systems that we use when comprehending or producing language—including listening, speaking, reading, and writing—and ask themselves the following questions when faced with a student who is not achieving in the classroom.

Listening

- Does the student understand the content of the subject matter being taught?

- Does the student have the necessary background knowledge or world knowledge to understand the curriculum content?

- Is the vocabulary of the content area a possible source of difficulty?

- Does the vocabulary of the content area contain specific derivational morphology that may be contributing to a lack of understanding by the student?

- Does the student demonstrate pro-social listening behaviors during classroom lectures or discussions—including eye gaze, body posture, and positive facial expression toward the speaker—indicating that he or she is engaged in the communicative exchange?

Speaking

- Does the student use the vocabulary of the content area being taught?

- Is the vocabulary used correctly, including its pronunciation and meaning, indicating a basic understanding?

- Does the student speak in full sentences?

- Do the sentences used by the student contain examples of complex sentence structure, including subordinating clauses?

- Does the student orient toward the listener when speaking and use appropriate eye gaze, body posture, facial expression, and turn-taking strategies that signal social competency?

- Is the student able to articulate the problem under investigation and provide possible solutions or outcomes?

Reading

- Can the student read fluently, with few word-decoding errors, in grade-level texts?

- Does the student correctly pronounce the content area vocabulary when reading?

- Does the student comprehend the specific content material when reading?

- Does the content area text include figurative language, such as metaphors, idioms, and proverbs? If so, does the student understand the abstract meaning implied by the metaphoric use of language?

- Does the student have the necessary background knowledge or world knowledge to understand the text of the specific curriculum content area?

Writing

- Does the student complete all writing assignments within the expected time frame?

- Does the student correctly use the vocabulary of the content area in the writing assignment?

Significant vocabulary expansion occurs during late childhood and adolescence.

- Does the student demonstrate a range of vocabulary choices using complex morphological structure?

- Are examples of metaphoric language seen in the writing assignments?

- Does the student use complete and complex sentences, including examples of subordination, in writing assignments appropriate to the content area?

- Do the writing assignments include a significant number of spelling errors?

CASE STUDY REVISITED

We return to Henry, who you initially met at the beginning of this chapter. He is failing in the class, and his teacher, Ms. Spencer, is not sure whether he is not interested and not applying himself or whether there is some other reason for the following observed behaviors: Henry does not participate in the classroom during discussions, fails to do his homework, and consistently shows below-average performance on assessment measures. Henry seems bright enough. He also has many friends and is active on the school basketball team.

CASE STUDY REVISITED: **The importance of understanding complex concepts**

The school psychologist informed Ms. Spencer that Henry has a history of early speech and language learning difficulty and had received speech-language intervention until the fourth grade. He had also received special education services for a specific reading disability from second grade through fifth grade. With this new information regarding Henry's developmental and learning history, Ms. Spencer examined the upcoming science unit on Earth Processes and Cycles to determine the key concepts and student outcome expectations.

To see information on Content Standard 3: Earth Processes and Cycles, go to **www.sagepub .com/levey.**

Ms. Spencer immediately noted that the science unit was rife with complex vocabulary and demanding learning outcomes. This unit required the use of cognitive processes for logical deductive reasoning, along with specific language abilities such as describing, relating, and explaining the information in each task. Ms. Spencer had noted that Henry did not participate in any class discussion, often keeping his head down. When called on, he hesitated when trying to explain concepts covered, often using short, simple sentences. He was not accurate in his pronunciation or use of the scientific vocabulary.

By using these guidelines to help determine the reasons for Henry's lack of participation and underachievement in the science classroom, Ms. Spencer was able to make a number of curriculum adjustments to help Henry achieve classroom goals. Her strategies included helping Henry understand

- the meaning of the prefixes/suffixes and pronunciation of the complex vocabulary in tasks,

- the use of graphic organizers to help him compare/contrast concepts being taught, and

- the need for practice for fluent reading of the vocabulary items in the science text within the class.

Using the questions provided earlier to guide her careful assessment of Henry's academic abilities throughout the semester; Ms. Spencer was able to provide the ongoing adjustments in her teaching of the curriculum content. These adjustments were presented to the entire class but targeted especially to benefit Henry. Following these classroom adjustments, Henry was able to understand the underlying meaning of complex science vocabulary terms, organize his thinking processes to understand how concepts were or were not related, and use practice to achieve fluent reading of the vocabulary items in complex science texts.

SUMMARY

Late childhood and adolescence is a particularly important developmental period for children, characterized by advances in cognitive/intellectual ability, increased social awareness and skills, and consolidation of a number of aspects of language and communication. These aspects include refinements in syntax, semantics, and the pragmatic use of verbal and nonverbal behaviors in social contexts.

Significant achievements in cognitive/intellectual development, language processing and understanding, and social interaction prepare the older child and adolescent for successful transition into the adult community. Older children and adolescents become increasingly more metalinguistic and engage in purposeful, self-regulatory behavior, using critical-thinking skills to analyze the structure of texts, the intent of the author, the meaning of prefixes and suffixes in vocabulary, and the underlying meaning of abstract, figurative language.

In addition, significant changes in understanding and using complex sentence structure are noted with the appearance of complex subordinating clauses in spoken and written syntax during late childhood and into adolescence. For example, subordinating conjunctions (e.g., *when, although, as if, before, than, unless, whether, because, in order, though, while, since, whenever,* and *where*) begin to appear at approximately 9 to 10 years of age and peak in their usage in grades 11 and 12. Average sentence length becomes longer and more complicated in spoken and written language with the use of complex sentence structures and subordinating devices such as gerunds, participles, and infinitives.

Significant vocabulary expansion occurs during late childhood and through adolescence, the product of accurate and fluent reading and understanding of and exposure to complex vocabulary containing suffix additions, or derivational morphemes. There is a developmental trend between fourth, sixth, and eighth grade in the ability to use suffix addition rules in spoken language and in spelling derived forms. Learning to spell words that contain derivational morphemes depends on the student's knowledge of when and how to apply the appropriate morpheme, as well as how much a base word changes when the morpheme, or suffix, is added.

There is a gradual and protracted process in the development and understanding of figurative language, including the understanding of dual-function words, metaphors, idioms, and proverbs from later childhood and into early adolescence.

Finally, the development of social competence, evidenced by the use of pro-social verbal and nonverbal behaviors, allows the student to be a fully participating member of the classroom learning environment or the community.

In this chapter, we learned about the language and communication skills of late childhood and adolescence. In Chapter 10, we will learn about the relationship between oral language, reading, and writing in normal literacy development from preschool through school-age.

KEY WORDS

Basic sentence	Dual-function words	Sentence length
Communicative unit (C-unit)	Embedded	Simple
Complex	Figurative language	Social competence
Compound	Form	
Compound-complex	Formal operations	Subordinate dependent clause
Conjunctions	Intrasentential growth	Subordinating conjunctions
Context	Pragmatic	
Dependent clause	Proposition	Subordination
Derivational morphemes	Semantic transparency	Transformation

STUDY QUESTIONS

1. What are the three main sources of language refinement or change in older school-age children and adolescents?
2. Define the term *subordinating clause* and provide an example. When do children acquire the use of subordinating clauses?
3. How does vocabulary change in school-age children and adolescents? What is the influence of derivational morphology on vocabulary growth?
4. What are the differences among metaphors, idioms, and proverbs? When are these types of figurative language fully learned by school-age children?
5. Explain what is meant by *social competence* and provide an example of either verbal or nonverbal pragmatic behavior that is indicative of social competence.

PROJECTS

1. Record school-age children at different grade levels explaining a game with which they are familiar. Analyze the sentences produced by these children in terms of complexity (e.g., clauses, conjunctions, and vocabulary). What language differences did you find for different grade levels?
2. Ask school-age children at different grade levels to write a short story describing a vacation. Using the information in this chapter, note the use of derivational morphemes in terms of prefixes and suffixes in both spoken and written language. Also, note the vocabulary items used by children at each grade level. What morphological and vocabulary differences did you find for different grade levels?

3. Ask school-age children at different grade levels to give a list of words that mean the same thing as *happy* or any other words you choose. The goal is to determine the ability to provide a word list of synonyms to assess their vocabulary skills. What vocabulary differences did you find for different grade levels? Did you find any other differences?

STUDENT STUDY SITE

Visit the Student Study Site at **www.sagepub.com/levey** for these additional learning tools:

- Video Links
- Self Quizzes
- E-Flashcards

- Sample Forms and Assessment Tools
- Recommended Readings
- Web Resources

SUGGESTIONS FOR FURTHER READING

Fisher, D., & Frey, N. (2008). *Word wise and content rich, grades 7-12: Five essential steps to teaching academic vocabulary*. Portsmouth, NH: Heinemann.

Hinchman, K. A., Sheridan-Thomas, H. K., & Alvermann, D. E. (2008). *Best practices in adolescent literacy instruction*. New York: Guilford.

Ivey, G., & Fisher, D. (2006). *Creating literacy-rich schools for adolescents*. Alexandria, VA: Association for Supervision & Curriculum Development.

Nippold, M. A. (1998). *Later language development: The school-age and adolescent years*. Austin, TX: Pro-Ed.

Wallach, G. P. (2007). *Language intervention for school-age students: Setting goals for academic success*. Philadelphia: Elsevier Health Sciences.

CHAPTER 10

Supporting the Development of Literacy Skills From Infancy Through School Age

Sylvia Diehl

CASE STUDY: Literacy and spelling development

Carla is a fourth-grade student who has moved three times in her short school career. Because of missed school days and different approaches to teaching reading, she struggled to learn sound symbol correspondence. She did finally master it last year at the end of third grade at her previous school. However, Carla is anxious about spelling and sounds out each sound in a word and translates it literally to a written letter. She lacks confidence and tends to simplify her written work so that she can use words that she can spell easily.

Teacher: "Carla, why are you looking upset. Is it because you are having difficulty writing your story about what happened yesterday?"

Carla: "I can't spell the big words that I want to use in my story. When I put in the words that I can spell, my story isn't very good. See, I don't know how to spell *apartment* or *argument* or *jewelry*. I used *house*, *fight*, and *ring*, and it just doesn't sound right."

What are the factors that contribute to a child's spelling development? Given this difficulty, what could you infer about Carla's overall literacy development? On what information or experiences did you base your answer?

INTRODUCTION

Literacy is the ability to read, write, speak, listen, and think effectively (Meltzer, Smith, & Clark, 2001). Traditionally, it was conceived that the early years of life are focused on learning to speak and listen, while the early years of school shift to learning to read and write

(Teale & Sulzby, 1986). It is now acknowledged that the abilities to read, write, speak, and listen are inextricably interlocked from an early age. The connections between language and literacy nurture one another. Oral language feeds the development of reading and writing, while growth in reading and writing promotes growth in oral language.

This chapter explores the relationship between oral language, reading, and writing in normal literacy development from preschool through school age. This chapter also offers suggestions and methods recommended by the literature to support normal literacy development through strategies to help teachers connect reading, writing, listening, and expressive language skills. Finally, we address literacy development in children whose primary language is English. For more information about bilingual learners, refer to Chapters 12, 13, and 14.

THE DEVELOPMENT OF LITERACY

At birth, children begin learning the essential abilities for reading and writing. Well before age 3, children are aware of print. They see books, magazines, grocery lists, and even television shows that feature print on a daily basis. They listen to wordplay, stories, songs, and rhymes that all form a foundation for emergent literacy.

Emergent Literacy

Emergent literacy refers to the knowledge, abilities, and attitudes about reading and writing that young children acquire before they experience formal literacy instruction. Some say it starts at birth, but it is usually associated with the preschool years (Storch & Whitehurst, 2001; Whitehurst & Lonigan, 1998).

Emergent literacy involves a child's development of a thinking process *about* language, a **metalinguistic** sensibility. This is a change from a child's earlier ability to use language to think, rather than thinking about language. Phonological awareness, which includes phonemic awareness, requires metalinguistic knowledge.

As discussed in Chapter 8, the term **phonological awareness** is an encompassing term that involves skills such as the ability to manipulate, count, and identify linguistic units at the phoneme, word, or syllable level. In the same way that language and literacy complement each other, phonological awareness abilities and the development of reading and spelling reciprocally benefit each other (Adams, 1990; Blachman, 1994; Catts & Kamhi, 1999; Wagner & Torgesen, 1987).

LITERACY IN THE PRESCHOOL YEARS

At age 3, children are beginning a metalinguistic journey that will help guide their literacy learning for a lifetime. Children pay attention to the sounds in words and enjoy the rhythm in songs and chants. See Table 10.1 for an illustration of pre-kindergarten (pre-K) and kindergarten (K) literacy development.

Additionally, they begin to realize that groups of letters have meaning. They may even know that the letters in their name are "special." Their use of vocabulary expands tremendously, and they become more fluent in their language use each day. They interact with books by labeling and using repetitive sentence forms (Stadler & Ward, 2005). They are able to relate

Table 10.1 Pre-K and K Literacy Development

Grade	Print Concepts	Phonological Awareness	Spelling	Vocabulary	Fluency	Comprehension	Writing
Pre-K	• Realizes that groups of letters have meaning • Turns pages one at a time • Looks from left to right and top to bottom	• Pays attention to sounds in words • Enjoys rhythm in language and can say words that rhyme by age 4 • Can separate sentences into words and words into syllables • Knows words are made of sounds	• May use letter symbols but no sound symbol correspondence • May be able to spell name • Understands direction of writing on page • Sees some letter sound matches	• Has an ever-expanding vocabulary for words in his or her environment • Vocabulary continues to expand • Uses more complex sentences	N/A	• Retells stories • Relates stories to personal experience • By 4, answers WH questions about read-aloud stories	• Starts scribbling, which turns into writing that looks like letters and words • Will interpret writing for others
K	• Knows the parts of books, such as chapter, table of contents, and index • Knows written letters in words correspond with specific sounds	• Knows when words do not rhyme • Knows sounds of letters • Names all upper- and lowercase letters • Identifies same beginning sounds • Can separate onset and rime (e.g., *k* followed by *-ing*)	• Spells a few words, including name • Puts series of letters together with some awareness of letter sounds • May spell whole word using one letter	• Expands vocabulary using more words not in immediate environment	• Sight reads high-frequency words and some consonant-vowel-consonant words	• Predicts what's next in stories • Answers more involved questions about read-aloud stories	• Uses drawing with writing • Writes in lines generally from left to right and top to bottom • Uses some spacing • Writes uppercase and lowercase letters legibly

SOURCES: Chall (1996). Moats and Tolman (2009), Shipley and McAfee (2009), and Tompkins (2003).

personal experiences and retell stories that have been read to them. They are beginning to form an underlying structure for beginning conversations and how stories are told.

Four-year-olds continue to enjoy rhyme and alliteration (repeating the same consonant sound at the beginning of several words). Their development of phonological awareness starts with larger sound segments (words) and progresses to smaller ones (individual sounds) (Moats & Tolman, 2009).

Four-year-olds look from left to right and top to bottom when using print products and know that words are made of sounds and name letters when they see letter shapes. They may not name the right letters all the time but should know about 7 to 10 letters of the alphabet by their entrance into kindergarten. Their vocabulary and sentence forms continue to expand and are used to talk about the world around them.

They begin to tell stories that remain on topic but resemble lists of topically related items rather than typical story structure (Stadler & Ward, 2005). Their storytelling not only supports oral language but also provides underlying information about *storiness*. This knowledge of storiness translates into knowledge of narrative text structure, which supports literacy growth (Hedberg & Westby, 1993).

Four-year-olds can answer simple WH questions about the stories that are read aloud to them. Their writing is usually accompanied by talking and drawing (Dyson, 2000). They use oral language to support and explain their early use of print. They are able to use drawing, print, and speech together to form meaning.

STRATEGIES TO SUPPORT LANGUAGE AND LITERACY IN THE PRESCHOOL YEARS

The preschool years are important in the development of literacy. We know that children do not just wait to be "ready" for formal reading instruction (Teale & Sulzby, 1986). Children who have rich language and literacy experiences in the preschool years come to formal instruction with a sturdy developmental foundation. It is important to ensure that the preschool child's environment supports meaningful and functional activities that involve emergent literacy skills in a variety of ways. This section explores supporting literacy skills through creating a literacy-rich environment, vocabulary and thematic units, dialogic book sharing, play, phonological awareness, and prewriting. Each of these topics is discussed individually and followed by an application example from the vignette below.

Miss Carol teaches 3- and 4-year-old children. She is moving her class into a new classroom. She has taught for 2 years but just graduated from the university. She wanted to use what she learned in her education classes to ensure language and literacy success in her classroom. What do you think she thought about?

Creating an Optimal Environment for Literacy Acquisition

A print-rich environment influences the literacy acquisition of young children (Neuman & Roskos, 1990; Reutzel & Wolfersberger, 1996; Strickland, Snow, Griffin, Burns, & McNamara,

Very young children become aware of literacy when they are exposed to literacy artifacts such as books, magazines, letters, and grocery lists.

2002). The physical arrangement and the availability of materials set the stage for functional encounters with reading and writing. Many researchers have demonstrated the impact of a literacy-rich environment on children's literacy knowledge (Neuman & Celano, 2001; Roskos & Neuman, 2001).

Wolfersberger, Reutzel, Sudweeks, and Fawson (2004) proposed the "Classroom Literacy Environmental Profile" as a guide for teachers to evaluate the environmental design of a classroom, the arrangement of furnishings and other literacy props, and the provisioning of classrooms. See Table 10.2 for the ingredients in a literary-rich environment.

Children should have a wealth of literacy tools available that allow them to see print applied in many different ways. Experimentation with producing various print products should be encouraged. The environment should consider arrangement of desks or tables that is conducive to opportunities to collaborate with others. Platforms should be provided for children to share and celebrate their written work, and teachers should keep individual and group records of achievement. Print-rich classrooms demonstrate that literacy is a vital and useful part of life.

> Miss Carol made sure that there were books and reference sources in a variety of places in and the classroom. She put a selection of books in the quiet time corner and a calendar and class roster for birthdays on the wall. Cubby holes had each child's name and a special symbol that told something about that child. There were classroom directions in various places around the room. Miss Carol made sure that there was a writing center with many different writing choices, such as crayons, washable markers, colored paper, magic slates, and stamps.

Vocabulary and Language Supported by Thematic Units

Every time a child interacts with language, the interaction influences vocabulary development and reading abilities (Dickinson & Neuman, 2006). Both the quantity of language and quality of these language interactions matter to the literacy development of the child. Children who scored highest in reading in later years were exposed to the most language as young children (Hart & Risley, 1995). The frequency of exposure to a word isn't enough. Relational information that explains how the word connects to other ideas is an important part of vocabulary learning. The words and contexts that children hear in oral language eventually become the

Table 10.2 Ingredients in a Literacy-Rich Environment

Abundance of literacy tools is available	Contain print	• Books of different genres (e.g., fiction, nonfiction, poetry, contemporary, classic, and reference) • Books in plentiful amounts (e.g., books, magazines, newspapers) • Books in a range of levels (e.g., spanning multiple grade levels) • Organizational print items (e.g., class rules, menus) • Informational print items (e.g., alphabet strips, key words, charts)
	Produce print	• Writing utensils (e.g., pencils, pens, crayons, markers, chalk, stamps) • Surfaces for writing (e.g., whiteboard, chalkboard, easels, paper, chart paper, Post-It notes, blank books) • Publishing materials (e.g., tape, glue, stapler, stencils, stickers)
	Support literacy events	• Technology resources (e.g., CD player, television, computer, video camera, camera, printer) • Furnishings (e.g., beanbags, rugs, rocking chairs, student-sized desks, tables for projects) • Storage and display containers (e.g., chart stand, bookshelves, cabinets, bulletin boards, book racks) • Accessories (e.g., mailboxes, clipboards, clipart, puppet stage, flannel board)
Written communication is displayed	Commercially published	For example, books, posters, charts
	Adult-authored	For example, announcements, directions, word walls, achievement charts, thoughtful sayings
	Student-authored	For example, notes, poems, student-made books, student work samples
Literacy products	Short-term	Completed in one school day
	Long-term	Taking more than one school day to complete
	Informal	For example, personal messages, homework lists, thank-you notes
	Formal	Final copy, published (e.g., class newspapers)
	Shared	For example, work displayed on bulletin board, shared with other classes, student-authored bookshelf
Data keeping	Records of student achievement	For example, number of books read, time spent reading, portfolios, journals

SOURCE: Adapted from Wolfersberger et al. (2004).

words they will see in written language. Therefore, conversations that serve to make connections between the word meaning and associative relational information reap profound benefits in vocabulary and consequently in literacy learning.

The use of thematic units enables children to learn vocabulary and relational knowledge in authentic and meaningful ways (Lipson, Valencia, Wixson, & Peters, 1993; Schubert, 1993). Burns, Roe, and Ross (1992) defined thematic units as an effective way to teach language, organized around a central topic, idea, or theme that uses related activities and experiences. Children become more engaged when their learning is organized into conceptual units so that patterns are readily provided and they are given connections between what is being learned and events in their everyday lives (Reutzel, 1997). The goal of using thematic units is to allow the children to grasp larger relationships and understandings (Tunnell & Ammon, 1993). By comprehending the word meanings within the concepts in which they operate, children of all ages develop connections that will help them in comprehending the written word (Neuman & Dwyer, 2009).

Miss Carol decided that the first topic for her thematic unit would be the grocery store. She chose related books such as *Maisy Goes Shopping* (Cousins, 2001) and *Signs at the Store* (Hill, 2003) and related songs such as "A Shopping We Will Go" and "In the Corner Grocery Store" by Raffi. She asked her parents to send in empty containers and food coupons to make a classroom grocery store with various types of literacy-related play materials for learning key concepts and vocabulary (Tompkins, 2003). She used a planning matrix to ensure that she had embedded the literacy-related skills throughout the day. She simply listed her schedule on the left-hand side and the important literacy areas across the top.

 To see the Half-Day Infused Planning Matrix for Grocery Store Unit, go to **www.sagepub .com/levey.**

Dialogic Book Sharing

Dialogic book sharing involves a process of sharing book reading with a young child in which the more experienced reader and the young child interchange roles. The young child is encouraged to gradually become the storyteller, while the experienced reader serves as an active listener and questioner (Whitehurst et al., 1994). Dialogic book reading increases the foundations of print, promotes the growth of vocabulary, and supports children in their use of language to share ideas (Bus, van Ijzendoorn, & Pellegrini, 1995; Huebner, 2000; van Kleeck, 2008). A critical piece in successful storybook reading is a discussion between the novice reader and the experienced reader (van Kleeck, 2006).

Miss Carol decided to incorporate the recommendations made by the literature into her book-sharing practices (Beck, McKeown, & Kucan, 2002; van Kleeck, 2006; van Kleeck & Vander Woude, 2003; Zevenbergen & Whitehurst, 2003). She also held a special parent night to introduce the practice of book sharing to the parents of the children in her room. She made a parent handout that incorporated instructions related to the evidence-based practice. She reviewed the information on the parent handout seen in "Book-Sharing Handout for Parents" and modeled shared book reading using one of the books from the ocean theme.

 To see the Book-Sharing Handout for Parents, go to **www.sagepub .com/levey.**

Play

Play is an essential component in emergent literacy development. Wilford (2000) delineates five literacy goals that are supported through play. First, play supports the development of symbolization. In symbolic play, an object can represent something else, an important link to understanding that the written word can stand for the spoken word.

Second, play fosters language growth, which is directly tied to literacy achievement. Drama and discussions during play allow children to expand their vocabularies, learn about discourse rules and social roles, and learn to develop multiple schemes inside a story.

Third, play supports the ability to solve problems in meaningful contexts. To meet the cooperative goals involved in play, children must learn to tolerate trial and error, which is important when a child needs to persevere through a challenging text or a creative writing assignment.

Fourth, play promotes the motivation to persist in literacy activities. Unlike **decontextualized learning trials**, play provides the context in which to practice a story or area of interest repeatedly, which is key to the development of lifetime literacy learning and writing.

Fifth, play provides joyful engagement as children enter the world of literacy learning involving speaking, listening, reading, and writing.

> With the help of the parents' contributions, Miss Carol made a pretend grocery store play center. She role-played while retelling the book *Maisy Goes Shopping*. She also modeled how the children could take the roles of cashier, bagging helper, and shopper. She was particularly careful to stress the use of new vocabulary words in her modeled play.

Phonological Awareness

As emphasized in Chapter 8, it is crucial to focus on phonological awareness in preschool activities to provide children with adequate phonological skills to be successful when formal reading instruction begins (Phillips, Clancy-Menchetti, & Lonigan, 2008). Yopp and Yopp (2009) recommend that teachers introduce books, poems, songs, and games that play with sound to increase phonological awareness. They also stress the importance of collaborating with families in areas involving play, books, family stories, and school activities, which they believe cumulatively impact literacy learning. Yopp and Yopp assert that, while teachers should appreciate that phonological awareness activities are serious work, young children should learn phonological awareness as an extension of play so that the "riddles, games, singing, and dramatization will bring on laughter, silliness, and experimentation" (p. 8).

> In her planning, Miss Carol already identified time in the class schedule for phonological awareness activities. She realized that books that focus on alliteration, as well as silly songs that focus on sound play, are an excellent source of phonological awareness fun as described by Yopp and Yopp (2009). Miss Carol made up a clapping game using the targeted vocabulary to help the children begin to understand syllabication.

Prewriting

Print interest and prewriting abilities can be fostered in multiple ways. Teachers can

- model or display written applications,
- co-construct written products with the child, or
- provide independent prewriting experiences in the classroom.

In modeling or displaying written applications, teachers clearly highlight instances when they are using writing functionally in the classroom. Simple remarks such as "I may forget that, so I need to write it down" carry the message that writing is important.

In co-construction of a story or a written product, the teacher and child both contribute to the written product, representing a shared experience. This allows the child to actively participate in the writing experience and to benefit from the more experienced adult writer.

Last, writing centers and play centers provide independent prewriting experiences, allowing children to explore the writing process as it relates to them (Neuman & Roskos, 1992; Tompkins, 2003). The writing experiences in these contexts can provide opportunities for children to use writing to depict what they are learning, connected to themes and events in the classroom. The "Classroom Literacy Environmental Profile" (Wolfersberger et al., 2004) delineates the many materials that can be used in a writing center (see Table 10.2 for examples of materials that support a literacy-rich environment).

> Miss Carol also planned special ways to foster prewriting skills related to the grocery theme. For instance, she made certain that the writing center was stocked with pictures to make grocery lists, coupons, labels, and stickers that could be used in the school store. These additions to the writing center connected writing to something the children see in everyday life.

LITERACY IN THE ELEMENTARY SCHOOL YEARS

In the elementary school years, the child moves from identifying some letters at the beginning of kindergarten to reading fluently in a variety of literature by fifth grade. This section discusses development through the literacy-related areas of phonological awareness, vocabulary, spelling, fluency, comprehension, and writing. Because literacy development across the elementary grades involves many interrelated areas, multiple literacies are developing across skill areas and grades, as illustrated in Tables 10.1, 10.3, and 10.4.

Phonological Awareness

Children become aware of the sounds of language in two ways: the size of the unit focused on (e.g., sentence, word, sound, or letter) and the way that unit is used in a given context (e.g., matching, blending, segmenting, substituting, and deleting) (Yopp & Yopp, 2009).

Table 10.3 Early Elementary Literacy Development

Grade	Phonological Awareness	Spelling	Vocabulary	Fluency	Comprehension	Writing
1	• Identifies syllables in words • Blends sounds into words • Changes sounds by adding, deleting, or substituting phonemes	• Knows words have correct spelling • Represents phonemes in words with letters • Uses some invented spelling	• Knows words have antonyms and synonyms	• Creates meaning while reading • Rereads to get words right	• Provides information learned while reading • Follows simple written instructions	• Writing is self-centered • Begins with capital letter • Ends with period • Spacing irregular
2	• Continues to blend skills with phonics • Tries to decode longer words using phonic abilities • Reads words with one and two syllables	• Phonetic spellings reduce and traditional spellings increase • Uses short vowel sounds • Uses consonant blends and digraphs • Uses some morphological structures	• Uses context of reading to help decode words • Uses root words, prefixes, and suffixes to decode words	• Reading speed increases	• Provides main ideas, sequence events of story, story grammar elements • Answers questions found in written material • Uses context clues to aid comprehension	• Writes simple fiction and nonfiction with model • Uses variety of sentence types • Writing has beginning, middle, and end • Writing is legible • Uses regular spacing
3	N/A	• Uses primarily conventional spelling • Uses long vowel and r-control vowel spelling patterns • Uses complex consonant patterns • Uses diphthongs	• Vocabulary continues to be enriched through reading	• Reads at 114 words per minute • Uses word analysis skills when reading	• Monitors self while reading for comprehension • Asks for clarifying information • Knows fact/opinion • Knows cause/effect	• Writes narratives, letters, simple expositories • Sentence length increases with more clauses used

SOURCES: Blachman (1997), Chall (1996), Shipley and McAfee (2009), and Tompkins (2003).

Table 10.4 Late Elementary Through Adolescent Development

Grade	Phonological Awareness	Spelling	Vocabulary	Fluency	Comprehension	Writing
4 to 6	N/A	• Recognizes and can correct misspellings by using orthographic knowledge • Follows rules for applying inflectional endings • Uses syllabication • Uses homophones	• Uses vocabulary effectively in writing	• Reads fluently in a variety of literature types	• Follows written instructions • Makes inferences from text • Can summarize and paraphrase	• Uses narrative and expository writing • Organizes writing into beginning, middle, and end to convey main idea • Uses character and plot development • Revises and edits work
7 to 10	N/A	• Alternates consonants • Alternates vowels • Knows Latin and Greek affixes and root words • Knows etymologies	• Gains content-area vocabulary	• Reads for learning and entertainment	• Reads to obtain new knowledge and specific information	• Sentences are longer than spoken sentences and more linguistically complex • Uses expository writing to provide explanations and descriptions

SOURCES: Chall (1996), Shipley and McAfee (2009), and Tompkins (2003).

Phonological awareness begins holistically with the enjoyment of the rhythms and sounds of language, followed by the ability to separate words from a sentence. By kindergarten, phonological awareness development begins to move from the larger parts of words to smaller segments, such as sounds. As shown in Table 10.1, the child is able to identify the first sound of a spoken word and separate it from its rime (e.g., *king* begins with /k/), along with being able to blend sounds together to form words (Moats & Tolman, 2009).

Through first and second grade, phonological awareness abilities continue to grow (see Table 10.4) and children are able to manipulate words through matching, blending, segmenting, substituting, or deleting. In the first grade, children can match words and understand compound word deletion (e.g., "Say *hot dog*. Now say it without the *hot*") and syllable deletion (e.g., "Say *carpet*. Now say it without the *car*").

By second grade, children can delete sounds in the initial and final positions of words (e.g., "Say *gate*. Say it again without the /t/) and can count the phonemes in a word. The second-grader begins using strategies to read other than sounding and blending each phoneme. They use learned word patterns to read new words and may even self-correct. Tasks involving analysis, such as counting, segmenting, and deleting, are thought to be more challenging and develop later than tasks involving recognition (e.g., matching) or synthesis (e.g., blending and adding).

Vocabulary and Reading Comprehension

Vocabulary is strongly tied to reading comprehension. Cunningham and Stanovich (1997) reported that vocabulary size in the 1st grade strongly predicts reading comprehension in the 11th grade. Thus, the size of the vocabulary and the concepts that they convey provide a strong foundation for later reading success, as much as a full 10 years later. By kindergarten, a child is able to discuss vocabulary and ideas that are decontextualized.

At home, much of what is discussed is present. For instance, when the child is asked to set the table, a parent may be stirring something on the stove and there may be cooking smells coming from the kitchen. In contrast, when the child enters school, the child learns and talks about zebras, even though there is not a zebra present in the classroom. During kindergarten, children also relate oral stories or narratives, but they are not in typical story form. They are connected topically from one sentence to another but are usually reported as a sequential order of events rather than presented in episode form (Stadler & Ward, 2005).

After first grade, children learn about 3,000 words per year (Carlisle & Katz, 2005). By first grade, the child knows between 2,000 and 3,000 words; knows antonyms and synonyms; can use pictures, titles, and headings to gather comprehension clues; and can tell oral narratives with a plot (Stadler & Ward, 2005). By second grade, context clues, along with root words, prefixes, and suffixes, are used to help decode words. At this point, their narratives are more fully developed with settings, characters, plots, and resolutions. By third grade, children know between 4,000 and 6,000 words and are beginning to understand nonliteral language such as idioms. By fifth grade, children know between 5,000 and 8,000 words. Their comprehension skyrockets to 15,000 words because of their ability to understand words that contain inflections such as *-ed* and *-ing*.

Spelling

To be an accurate speller, children must use three types of linguistic knowledge. The first is their phonological knowledge of sounds to make a connection between sounds and

Literacy begins with early exposure to books and other literacy materials.

letters. The child learns that certain letters go with certain sounds. The second is **orthographic** knowledge, which is the understanding that the same sound can be spelled or can look different ways in print. For instance, the *ay* in *pay* can also be spelled as *eigh,* as in the word *neigh*. The last is **morphological** knowledge. This knowledge helps the child know how to add inflections such as *-ed* and *-ing*. Although children primarily use phonological knowledge first, followed by orthographic knowledge and then morphological knowledge, the stages of spelling development are not distinctly in that order. Spelling development involves an integration of all these types of linguistic knowledge.

From kindergarten to first grade, children generally depend on their knowledge of the connection between letters and sounds to spell (Ehri, 2000). In other words, they primarily depend on their phonological abilities to spell. At first, the word *car* may be spelled "kr." Children then begin to spell some consonant-vowel-consonant words with short vowels and may be able to use consonant blends and digraphs correctly.

At the end of first and second grade, children become more aware that there are many ways to spell the same sound. For instance, a long ē may be represented by *ee* as in *bee* or by *ea* as in *beak*. They may struggle with these alternative spellings. As they are exposed to more words in print, they depend on their orthographic knowledge to determine how a word should look to pick the correct alternative spelling (Wright & Ehri, 2007). Some ability to mark inflections using morphology appears in this stage, such as the use of *-ed* to mark the past tense of a verb and *-s* to mark plurals (Carlisle, 1988; Walker & Hauerwas, 2006).

The use of morphological knowledge generally blossoms in the third grade. Spellers use syllables and affixes consistently in their spelling (Tompkins, 2003). These spellers are applying their **chunking** ability to multisyllabic words. They learn to break syllables into words, use inflectional endings such as *-tion* or *-ment,* and use **homophones**. They experiment with the rules relating to joining syllables. Letter-doubling errors are common, such as understanding that words such as *matter* are not spelled as "mater." Children are constantly using all three linguistic abilities in concert on their journey to become proficient spellers.

Reading Fluency

The National Reading Panel (2000) defines **fluency** as the ability to read a text quickly, accurately, and with proper expression. When children first learn to read, they read primarily by using their phonological abilities to sound out a word phoneme by phoneme. This method is a good beginning but will not result in fluent reading. It is too slow and laborious to sound out each sound. As in spelling, fluent reading requires the integration of many linguistic skills: phonological, orthographic, morphological, and semantic. Phonologic skills are used to sound out words. Orthographic skills are used to memorize whole words for quick recognition and for decoding words when different grapheme (written) combinations represent the same phonemes. Morphologic knowledge is used to quickly identify prefixes and suffixes. All this knowledge then needs to connect with word meaning or semantic knowledge. The integration of these linguistic skills aids in quick word identification to keep meaning intact.

Additionally, a fluent reader also knows how to group words together in appropriate phrasing and to vary the melody of the language to help it make more sense. Because reading is so complex, our ability to read fluently develops over time. By third grade, most students have moved from word-by-word reading and are on their way to becoming fluent readers. Fluency is greatly influenced by familiarity with or complexity of the reading material, and even a skilled reader may have difficulty with unfamiliar technical material. Improvements in fluency continue into adulthood.

Writing

A child's first written word is often his or her name (Bloodgood, 1999). When children are aware of some letters within their names, they will begin to use these letters in their writing (Harste, Woodward, & Burke, 1984). This early writing is often combined with drawing. By kindergarten, children's writing reflects a beginning knowledge of sound and letter correspondence. They may use **invented spelling** and follow basic rules of writing such as staying in the lines and flowing from left to right and top to bottom. Some evidence of spacing may be indicated but with a great deal of variability. By first grade, most upper- and lowercase letters are written legibly.

In first grade, children begin to follow some writing conventions such as beginning sentences with a capital letter and ending with a period. Writing is primarily used to express personal experiences or feelings and is written for a specific audience, such as their parents or teacher. As children get more exposure to different forms of writing, they continue to refine and add different genres to their writing. They tell stories through narratives and use expository writing to share information. As the forms of writing diversify, their awareness of audience develops accordingly. By the end of elementary school, the ability to convey multiple perspectives begins to develop and the child starts to write persuasive essays.

Throughout elementary school, the complexity of children's oral language increases. With the increased development of oral language, the complexity of children's writing skills also increases. As the writing complexity grows, children learn to use words that tie sentences together (e.g., *and then*, *because*) in a cohesive manner. These cohesive ties help their writing become more coherent and help maintain clarity as the complexity increases (Dyson & Freedman, 1991). This ability continues to grow throughout the school years into adulthood.

STRATEGIES TO SUPPORT LANGUAGE AND LITERACY IN THE ELEMENTARY SCHOOL YEARS

The elementary school-age child goes through incredible changes in his or her literacy ability from kindergarten to fifth grade, and much of the basic tenets of instruction remain the same throughout the grades. This section explores supporting literacy skills through phonological awareness, vocabulary, reading comprehension, fluency, and writing. Each of these is discussed individually and followed by an application example from the vignette below.

> Mr. Bouchard teaches a third-grade class. His class is particularly enjoying reading about the ecosystems of the animals in the Southwest, especially the gila monsters, desert snakes, and coyotes. Most of Mr. Bouchard's students were doing well on their journey to become fluent readers, but three children seemed to be struggling. They were laboring to blend the words that they were sounding out, so decoding was not becoming automatic. What teaching strategies might help these students?

Phonological Awareness

The main focus in teaching phonological awareness is to teach the ability to analyze the sound structure of syllables and words in a conscious manner. The more automatic this process becomes, the more resources can be used for integrating meaning. Phonological awareness is still important in first and second grade but is not usually a focus by third grade (see Table 10.4). In first grade, the focus of phonological awareness training is on sound blending to sound out new words. In second grade, the focus moves to segmentation to decode more quickly and efficiently.

Four evidence-based practices should be incorporated into meaningful reading activities when teaching the ability to hear and manipulate sounds, or phonemic awareness (National Reading Panel, 2000; Torgesen et al., 2007):

1. The use of engaging and motivating activities

2. A carefully planned focus on one or two phoneme manipulation skills, such as blending and segmenting phonemes

3. Clarification of the connection of the sound to the grapheme correspondents in all activities involving phoneme manipulation

4. Teaching of phonemic awareness over time within a balanced program (i.e., teaching of phonemic awareness as one part of a program that supports all aspects of literacy)

Students come to school with different background knowledge, language abilities, learning preferences, and interests, and not all children learn to read at the same rate or in the same way. Subsequently, it is vital that teachers embrace the concept of differentiated instruction in their literacy programs (Walker-Dalhouse & Risko, 2009). Differentiation can take many forms in the classroom according to student needs. Teachers may differentiate content (i.e., what is taught), process (i.e., how it is taught), or product (i.e., how learning is assessed) to maximize the learning potential of every student.

> Since three of his students were struggling with sound blending, he decided to use a game that would help review the new vocabulary related to Southwest animals along with some sound blending and segmenting practice. He chose eight of the animals they had been reading about and placed their pictures on the edge of the whiteboard. Next, Mr. Bouchard would say, "I am thinking of a Southwest desert animal. The animal is a g-i-l-a. Who can tell me what you heard?" The children would then choose the animal, and the class would spell it together on the whiteboard. In this way, Mr. Bouchard gave much-needed phonemic awareness practice to his struggling students within an activity that supported vocabulary and spelling development for the whole class.

Fluency

To read fluently, children must be able to quickly identify most of the words and have an efficient process for decoding novel words. The amount of time spent reading provides the practice needed to develop automaticity. Students who read books that are challenging but not too difficult gain the increased practice and repeated exposure that fluency requires.

Stahl and Kuhn (2002) recommend that students are given opportunities to reread sentences and are encouraged to make their reading "sound like talking." They recommend that rereading begin as soon as children have mastered basic decoding, which is usually in first grade. The National Reading Panel (2000) recommends guided repeated oral reading to increase fluency and comprehension across grade levels. The factors that have been identified as predictors of fluency are

- the ability to identify individual words,

- the amount of time spent reading,

- the ability to retain text in their memories, and

- the ability to integrate those segments with other parts of the text (Mastropieri, Leinart, & Scruggs, 1999).

> Mr. Bouchard planned to work on fluency. He found a short three-paragraph play about living in the desert in the third-grade language arts text. The play had five animal characters. He made four sets of different colored cards, one set for each of the five animal characters. He gave each child a colored card with an animal character on it. This way, he could match the dialogue to the children's reading ability so all of them could be successful. After practice, the children were asked to read their parts for the class. It was videoed so that students could watch it at their computer stations. Parts of the videos were edited and shown at the next parent meeting.

Vocabulary

As we mentioned before, vocabulary is learned through listening to oral language and through reading written language. Whether through oral or written means, word knowledge develops from repeated exposure. Children move from the word being unknown to recognizing it as familiar to constructing an incomplete or general meaning to full word knowledge. Of the 3,000 words children learn in a year, only about 300 come from organized instruction (Nagy & Herman, 1985).

A great deal of children's word knowledge that is learned orally comes from incidental or embedded word learning. Since teachers cannot possibly directly teach all the words that students need to learn, they need to ensure that children are continuously exposed to new vocabulary items by embedding them into everyday classroom activities. Increasing **incidental learning** means increasing the frequency that the words are heard and used.

Children learn many words from reading (Nagy & Herman, 1985) and learn word knowledge through using the information surrounding the word to figure out its meaning (context clues). The most efficient context clues are those that give a definition. Unfortunately, many other types of context clues do not give enough information for the child to master the word. For this reason, teachers should model curiosity about word meaning and talk about word-learning strategies.

> Mr. Bouchard planned many repetitions of the new vocabulary through classroom discussions and peer group collaborations related to their readings on desert ecosystems. One day, he gave each student in the class a stack of sticky notes. He told the class to read the assigned text and use the sticky notes to mark the text information that they would like to talk about or had questions about. The students were then broken into cooperative groups for a round robin discussion of the sticky note points.

Reading Comprehension

Some recommended strategies from *Reading Next* (Snow & Biancarosa, 2004) are outlined below. The National Reading Panel (2000) suggests that these strategies are more effective when used in combination with one another than when used alone.

- *Awareness of text structure*: Students aware of the basic text organizations comprehend the information presented more readily, especially with repeated

To see Suggestions to Support Reading Comprehension and Writing Through Cooperative Discussion, go to **www.sagepub .com/levey.**

exposure to a variety of text structures. They use the information as a framework to understand and remember information (Pearson & Camperell, 1994).

- *Activating prior knowledge*: Students who think about what they know related to the reading topic (schema) or who explore related information before reading have increased comprehension (Dole, Brown, & Trathen, 1996), especially for expository text structures (Ehren, 2005).

- *Questioning*: Both question asking and question answering increase comprehension. Use this step with reading questions before the reading task to prime them for the information.

- *Self-monitoring*: This is a form of self-questioning. Good comprehenders ask themselves questions about how well they understand the material as they read. This allows them to stop and repair misunderstandings.

- *Summarization*: Readers who summarize have better reading comprehension (Malone & Mastropieri, 1992). This step is used after a reader has completed the reading or during the reading to capsulate smaller sections of the text. Summarization is the mark of a good reader, and readers who are struggling might have difficulty combining the smaller ideas to make a whole.

Mr. Bouchard knows that using more than one recommended strategy is more effective than using the strategies alone. One of his favorite activities to support this notion is KWLH (Ogle, 1986; Weaver, 1994). He knows that in using KWLH, he is using two of the recommended strategies that support reading comprehension. In the KWLH strategy, four steps are highlighted. The first two steps—(1) What I **know** about a topic and (2) What I **want to know**—are brainstormed before reading. These steps serve to activate prior knowledge. The last two steps—(3) What I **learned** and (4) **How** we can learn more—are completed after reading. These steps allow for summarization on the part of the student.

Writing

The importance of writing can't be overstated. It is vital for learning and for future success in life. However, many children struggle to meet the standards expected by school and those needed for later life. The 2002 National Assessment of Education Progress indicated that most students in 4th, 8th, and 12th grades had only partly mastered the writing skills demanded at their grade level (Persky, Daane, & Jin, 2003). These findings suggested that perhaps our teaching of writing could be improved.

A meta-analysis by Graham and Perin (2007) suggests teaching strategies to improve the teaching of writing for students from 4th to 12th grade. Graham and Perin recommend teaching children strategies for planning, revising, and editing writing compositions. They also recommend including sentence combining and summarization. See Table 10.5 for these and other classroom suggestions that support the writing process.

Table 10.5	Evidence-Based Writing Strategies	
Strategy	**Purpose**	**Brief Description**
Self-regulated strategy development	Helps students master higher-level cognitive processes that make up skill in the planning, production, revising, and editing of writing Helps students in further developing their ability to monitor and manage their own writing	SRSD involves six basic stages: 1. Activating background knowledge 2. Discussing the strategy benefits and expectations 3. Cognitive modeling of the strategy 4. Memorization of the strategy 5. Collaborative support of the strategy 6. Independent performance
Sentence combining	Helps children generate more complexity in their writing and supports writing fluency	Sentence combining teaches students to construct more complex and sophisticated sentences through exercises in which two or more basic sentences are combined into a single sentence.
Peer assistance	Improves writing through active academic responding, collaborative practice, and immediate feedback	Students work together to plan, draft, and/or revise their compositions; less-skilled and more-skilled writers learn from each other.
Summarization	Children learn to condense what is learned into manageable chunks of information. They learn to distinguish between important and trivial information and identify main ideas along with supporting details.	Explicit and systematic instruction on how to summarize texts

SOURCE: Graham and Perin (2007).

Mr. Bouchard felt that Self-Regulated Strategy Development instruction (Harris, Santangelo, & Graham, 2008) was a great fit in his classroom. It has proven to be effective in teaching writing strategies not just for able writers but also for struggling writers. As much as possible, Mr. Bouchard carved out uninterrupted time to write. He activated their background knowledge with brainstorming discussions and encouraged the children in his class to think and discuss their writing topics, as well as their compositions. He was careful to model how to give encouragement and support to other writers. He created a class newspaper so that the children would have a purpose and an audience for their writing. In this way, the process of planning, rewriting, and editing seemed natural and applied. He made sure to include self-regulation by having them set writing goals for themselves and used a self-questionnaire and a peer review process on their compositions before announcing them ready for publication.

LITERACY IN THE ADOLESCENT YEARS

Even though children are fluent readers in their adolescent years, literacy development is still active. Children in seventh grade and up continue to learn vowel and consonant **alternations.** An alternation is a change that is repeated in a regular pattern. It is no surprise that English is not a totally phonetically spelled language (e.g., *rafter/laughter/slaughter*), but there are rule regularities that address change (e.g., *electric/electricity; public/publicity*) that can be learned.

Adolescents also learn the **etymologies** (the origin of words) and meanings of Latin and Greek contributions. Their vocabulary continues to grow, especially in content areas, as they read to gain new knowledge or specific information for assignments. Their ability to analyze text structures (e.g., comparison/contrast, cause/effect, chronological order, argument/support, lists, technical manuals, editorials) continues to grow through content area readings.

Adolescents are able to take multiple critical perspectives and understand the use of **figurative language** (e.g., simile, metaphor, personification, hyperbole). Writing becomes increasingly more complex in structure and is now longer than their spoken sentences and much more linguistically complex. The ability to generate different text structures also continues to expand, including note taking, procedures, directions, editorials, résumés, and business letters.

The faculty of Shepherd Middle School participated in an online discussion group that focused on educational practices for adolescents. In their planning, they took into account their students' background experiences and social pressures that abound in middle school. The school was divided into teams to form smaller learning communities (Perks, 2006). This helped ensure that all children had adult advocates and also instilled a sense of belonging in the students. Teachers recognized the value in oral discussions, so learning-centered conversations were featured in every classroom. A bank of evidence-based reading strategies was shared with all teachers, and these strategies were supported in all content areas. Teams regularly communicated about the effectiveness of the strategy use. Similarly, writing strategies were supported across subjects. Time was allotted for writing in every class at least twice a week. Students were expected to keep portfolios of their work to demonstrate their writing progress. These portfolios were checked and evaluated on a regular basis. Do you think that their planning was adequate to meet the needs of their students?

STRATEGIES TO SUPPORT LANGUAGE AND LITERACY IN ADOLESCENCE

Supporting literacy in the adolescent population takes planning and knowledge. The transition to the teen years can sometimes threaten a child's self-esteem in a way that impacts his or her literacy development (Snow, Porche, Tabors, & Harris, 2007). If they have had difficulty in school in the past, children are less likely to trust that instructors know best how to teach them, which can further damage their self-esteem. The combination of these issues may mean reduced motivation and effort on the part of the adolescent (Ehren, Lenz, & Deshler, 2004). Biancarosa and Snow (2004), in their report *Reading Next: A Vision for Action and Research in Middle and High School Literacy*, outlined elements of effective adolescent literacy programs.

Identifying areas of interest around which instruction can be developed can help engage students in reading who would otherwise not be interested in typical classroom assignments. It is up to teachers to take these recommendations of best practice and blend them with the culture of the adolescent and the classroom. These recommendations are summarized below, along with tips for applying these principles in the classroom.

Children have already learned many things that support literacy learning before 3 years of age, such as labels for objects in their environments.

- *Direct and explicit reading comprehension instruction that emphasizes comprehension processes and strategies.* The reading comprehension strategies discussed under elementary school reading comprehension are all effective with adolescents but should be adapted to content areas.

- *Effective instructional principles embedded in content area learning that provide practice in reading and writing specific to the content area.* Content area texts are significantly different than texts that cover literature. It is important that students are supported in applying their reading and writing strategies across content area genres and that content vocabulary is specifically taught (Snow & Biancarosa, 2004).

- *Intensive writing connected to the types of writing in which students will have to perform well for high school and beyond.* The writing strategies of summarization, sentence combining, and peer supports are all evidence-based approaches that are appropriate for this population (Graham & Perin, 2007; Snow & Biancarosa, 2004).

- *Interdisciplinary teacher teams that meet on a regular basis to talk about students and align instruction to their needs.* This allows teams to plan together to coordinate literacy strategies and connections across content areas.

- *In-depth professional development that is long term and ongoing. Reading Next* suggests that in-services are not enough to bring about lasting positive change. Teacher knowledge and practice must be informed by science and supported by collaboration on a continuous schedule (Snow & Biancarosa, 2004).

- *Formative assessments are critical to inform instructional adjustments based on student progress* (Snow & Biancarosa, 2004). This is best characterized as an ongoing "feedback loop," which continues to refine instruction based on assessment data.

CASE STUDY REVISITED

At the beginning of this chapter, you met Carla, a fourth-grade student who had difficulty spelling and writing. She could not spell the words *apartment*, *argument*, and *jewelry*.

Case Study Revisited: Literacy and spelling development

Her teacher used a strategy to help Carla spell correctly. First, she used chunking in multisyllabic words. She asked Carla what word she would like to spell. Carla chose the word *apartment.* Her teacher asked her how many syllables were in the word *apartment.* Carla said, "Three." Next, her teacher asked her to show the three syllables. Carla was able to show her the three syllables: *a-part-ment.* Carla´s teacher then showed her several other words that had the inflectional morphological *-ment* (e.g., *agreement* and *department*). This helped Carla spell *apartment* and *argument.* In fact, she was able to recognize that the word *argue* was in the word *argument.* Next, they worked on the word *jewelry.* Her teacher asked her to see if she could find another word in the word *jewelry* that she could spell. Carla was excited to find the word *jewel.* After this, Carla was able to spell many multisyllabic words. She worked with her teacher to learn to identify root words and become familiar with other common prefixes and suffixes. Knowing these helped her feel more confident when spelling words that are more complex. When Carla had difficulty, she knew she could break the word apart and if necessary, see her teacher for help.

SUMMARY

This chapter reviewed the development of literacy from preschool through adolescence, with emphasis on the connections between reading, writing, speaking, and listening. It also reviewed supportive practices for teaching in the literacy-related areas.

- Before the age of 3, children have already learned many things that support literacy learning.

- Evidence-based practices for supporting literacy in preschool includes supporting language through play; shared book reading; phonological awareness through songs, books, and rhymes; and rich prewriting experiences.

- A large part of literacy development in early elementary school is devoted to becoming more automatic with the connections between letter sounds and their written counterparts.

- Children learn new vocabulary from listening and from reading.

- Reading comprehension is enhanced by knowledge of text structure, activating prior knowledge, questioning, self-monitoring, and summarization.

- Adolescent literacy instruction must consider self-esteem and motivational issues.

KEY WORDS

Alternations

Chunking

Decontextualized
   learning trials

Etymologies

Figurative language

Fluency

Homophones

Incidental learning

Invented spelling

Metalinguistic

Morphological

Orthographic

Phonological awareness

STUDY QUESTIONS

1. Describe the relationship between language and literacy.

2. You are moving from teaching preschool to kindergarten. How would your teaching be different? What would be the same?

3. How do the developments of spelling and writing inform each other? What does that mean for your teaching?

4. If you had a child in your class who had trouble making connections to what he reads, how would you support his reading comprehension?

5. How would you promote a print-rich environment in the older grades? How is literacy learning different in middle and high school than it was in elementary?

PROJECTS

1. Observe a child's speech in both single words and in phrases and sentences. Do this for both English and Spanish. What percentage of the time can you understand him or her in single words? In phrases? In sentences? Is it the same or different for each language?

2. Observe vocabulary words that a child uses in both English and Spanish. Bilingual children are sometimes more likely to know colors in English and household items in their home language. Include words from both languages in final vocabulary word counts. Write down what sounds you heard the child use in both Spanish and English, if possible.

3. Observe a speech-language pathologist (SLP) working with a bilingual child with a speech problem. Write your observations of the session, answering questions such as "Did the SLP use both languages in therapy or only one?" "Was the child able to respond in both languages?" "How often could you understand the child in each language?" Ask the SLP to share his or her thoughts about providing therapy to a bilingual child.

STUDENT STUDY SITE

Visit the Student Study Site at **www.sagepub.com/levey** for these additional learning tools:

- Video Links
- Self Quizzes
- E-Flashcards

- Sample Forms and Assessment Tools
- Recommended Readings
- Web Resources

SUGGESTIONS FOR FURTHER READING

Clay, M. M. (2001). *Change over: Time in children's literacy development*. Portsmouth, NH: Heinemann.

Fisher, D., Brozo, W. G., & Ivey, G. (2006). *50 content area strategies for adolescent literacy*. New York: Prentice Hall.

Frey, D., & Frey, N. (2007). *Improving adolescent literacy: Content area strategies at work*. New York: Prentice Hall.

Harvey, S., & Goudvis, A. (2007). *Strategies that work: Teaching comprehension for understanding and engagement*. Portland, ME: Stenhouse.

Tovani, C., & Keene, E. O. (2000). *I read it, but I don't get it: Comprehension strategies for adolescent readers*. Portland, ME: Stenhouse.

Wilhelm, J. D., & Smith, M. W. (2007). *You gotta BE the book: Teaching engaged and reflective reading with adolescents*. New York: Teachers College Press.

CHAPTER 11

Educational Implications of Narrative Discourse

Lynn S. Bliss and Allyssa McCabe

CASE STUDY: **The ability to describe events and stories in narratives**

Joshua is 8 years and 7 months old. His classroom teacher, Ms. Smithfield, received the results of standardized tests of language development. She found that his scores on these tests place his understanding and speaking skills below average abilities. She also found that his reading and writing abilities are lower than those of the other children in the class. These scores explain the problems noted within the classroom. For example, Joshua is unable to produce coherent descriptions of real events or fictional stories. When writing, his descriptions are short and do not exhibit an organized sequence. Joshua is in a special school for children with learning disabilities. He also receives special speech and language intervention. His teacher began to search for strategies to help his understanding and speaking in the classroom, along with his writing.

What strategies could Joshua's classroom teacher use to support his description of real events? On what information or experiences did you base your answer?

INTRODUCTION

Narrative discourse is important because of its contribution to social relations, effective communication, and literacy. There are two main types of narratives: personal and fictional. A **personal narrative** is a description of a past event, experienced by the speaker or by someone the speaker knows. A **fictional narrative** consists of an imaginary story, either from a book or spontaneously created by a speaker. Narratives of either kind typically present a chronological sequence of events within a cultural context.

This chapter focuses on personal narratives because of their importance in daily communication activities and because of the fact that they tend to be better structured than fictional narratives (McCabe & Bliss, 2003). Children use personal narratives frequently to describe their experiences and relate to others. The following passages highlight the differences between a fictional narrative and a personal narrative produced by a 9-year-old boy with language impairment who is from a European North American background.

Personal Narrative Prompt

Have you ever had a pet?

> One time we had a rat in our attic. Well, we, we, umm, we smelled it. There was, there was like this awful smell, and it was there for a couple, few days. And, and till the the, um, animal control came, and he said he, he put like a trap. So the, so the, umm, **so** [emphasis ours] the rat couldn't . . . was dead. Dead in the attic. The, umm, the pet control guy, umm, grabbed it with his net, and he put it in his, put it in his back of his truck, and drove it away.

Fictional Story Prompt

The child looked at a wordless picture book called *Frog, Where Are You?* (Mayer, 1969). The child was then asked to tell the story of this book.

> First there was this boy, and his dog, and his turtle. And he goes off. He, he's sleeping. He's sleeping. And when he wakes up he puts on his boots. And was barefoot. . . . He's barefoot. So he's gotta put on his socks and, and put on his boots. And then the dog falls. And then be, bee hive, bees. And there's the, there's the beehive. And that is the hole. I guess it's the beaver hole. And (points to hole) squirrel. No squirrels live in trees. I'm mistaken. Gopher (pointing to picture of the hole). A gopher. And the beehive plops down. And the all the bees come out. Mad. And if they're mad they want to sting. If they're happy they don't sting. There's the bees. My gosh. . . . They're gonna catch, **they're gonna catch the dog. Until, until, until the man, the man goes like this (motion)** [emphasis ours]. And then owl starts . . . the owl is swooping, swooping that way (motions). And, and this is the antlers. And, and out comes the deer. And, and the deer gallops him in the place. He's onto the, to the deer's neck. And the deer, and the deer lets, lets. . . . There's this like big hill. And the boy, the boy doesn't loses his balance. And he (laughing) and he and he falls down. And then . . . and then he's in the lake. He's in the lake where the duckies, where the duckies are. And the boy says, "Shhh." And and then the boy gallops. The boy, the boy, umm, crawls on the log. And he's balancing on the log until he sees the frog. That's the end.

The personal narrative has a **coherent** structure, while the fictional account is merely an **incoherent** description of the pictures from a wordless picture book. The speaker does not attempt to create a story from the pictures. The major differences follow:

Narrative discourse is essential to support development in language and literacy.

- The personal narrative was produced in the past tense and included specifically related **causal** events (e.g., "so the rat was dead" because of being entrapped).

- The fictional narrative is produced in the present tense, and its contents are confined only to picture description.

- Event sequencing and causal relations between events are absent in the fictional narrative. A series of disconnected actions just happens for no apparent reason. The only potentially causal action (bolded in the above account) is not explicitly **articulated** (it includes a contextualized gesture) and so cannot be assumed to actually be causal.

The following section highlights the importance of personal narratives in functional discourse.

THE IMPORTANCE OF NARRATIVE DISCOURSE

A personal narrative serves to help speakers make sense of an experience. They put into words a description of something that has happened to them. For example, an individual who has just been in a car accident may initially describe the event disjointedly because exactly what happened in the accident may not seem clear to the person. After retelling the narrative to listeners who ask pointed questions and received answers, the narrator's description becomes clearer and the component events make more sense to both the speaker and the audience. The narrator is now able to represent the events more logically. Personal narratives enable teachers and professionals to understand how a student conceptualizes an event and organizes information.

Narratives are critical in educational settings and are a prerequisite for full literacy acquisition. Preschool children with typical language development (TLD) begin to learn narrative structure and practice this form of communication. TLD refers to children who gain syntactic, semantic, and discourse abilities within normal developmental stages. Narrative skills of preschool children have been shown to be good predictors of *subsequent* literacy achievement (Bishop & Edmundson, 1987; de Hirsch, Jansky, & Langford, 1966; Tabors, Snow, & Dickinson, 2001; Snow, Porche, Tabors, & Harris, 2007).

School-age students often produce personal narratives when they *practice* writing. For example, they will describe in writing personal experiences of a summer holiday. High-stakes testing, mandated by the "No Child Left Behind" Act, often requires students to write personal narratives. Personal narratives have also been recommended as the basis for mastering writing skills so that students begin to write about what they know and in the process come to understand that their real lives are worthy of being written about (Calkins, 1994). Narrative discourse is challenging because of its decontextual nature. This feature is described below.

Decontextualized Narratives

Decontextualized narratives are descriptions of events that can be produced and understood without the benefit of pictures or text or extraordinary inference on the part of listeners. They do not include nonverbal gestures. Decontextualized narratives are valued in education as a means of relating to other people and engaging successfully in discourse experiences such as sharing time (Cazden, 1985; Peregoy & Boyle, 2005).

Children begin to use decontextualized narratives in the preschool years. Their use depends on questions asked by parents. Parents who ask many questions about *when* and *where* something happened between 26 and 43 months have children who produce significantly more decontextualized orientative information to relative strangers when they are 3 or more years of age (Peterson & McCabe, 1994).

Personal narratives are important in other aspects of our lives. For example, in medical settings a patient needs to describe to a doctor the origins of a problem (Charon, 1993). A physician might ask, "How did you hurt yourself?" The answer would require a personal narrative. The physician needs to be able to understand the specific cause in order to treat the patient. Legal testimony is another area in which personal narratives are important (Barry, 1991). Witnesses need to be able to describe events clearly in order for justice to be served.

Personal narratives constitute an important component of daily communication. Therefore, it is critical for teachers to be able to understand how they are formed and how to help students use this discourse genre.

THE STRUCTURE OF NARRATIVE DISCOURSE

To see Types of Narratives and Examples, go to **www.sagepub .com/levey.**

Personal narratives can be described by their overall structure, content, and manner of production. There are six general structures for personal narratives (McCabe & Rollins, 1994; Peterson & McCabe, 1983). See "Types of Narratives and Examples" on the companion website for examples of the narratives shown below:

- *A one-event narrative* has only one specific past-tense action.
- *A two-event narrative* is characterized by two actions.

School-age students produce personal narratives when they practice writing.

- *A leap-frog narrative* includes events that are not sequenced appropriately and/or omits major events so that the listener must infer a logical causal sequence and any missing events.

- *A chronological narrative* contains a chronological sequence or listing of events without much coherence and/or evaluation; so it sounds like a travel itinerary.

- *An end-at-the-high-point narrative* builds up to a high point (i.e., the most important part of the experience, as signaled by evaluation) and then ends abruptly, without resolution of the high point events.

- *A classic narrative* is complete, in that the narrator orients the listener to who, what, when, and where something occurred, builds actions up to a high point, and then resolves the action.

Teachers need to be aware of whether a student is able to provide an overall structure to a narrative. It may not be necessary to categorize the narrative by one of these structures, but it is necessary to be able to recognize if a child uses or does not use an appropriate narrative structure.

Personal narratives can also be evaluated for content and manner of production. The following five dimensions characterize this aspect of narration (McCabe & Bliss, 2003; Miranda, McCabe, & Bliss, 1998):

- *Topic maintenance:* the relation of utterances to a central theme
- *Informativeness:* the completeness or sufficiency of information of a narrative
- *Event sequencing:* the chronological or logical ordering of events
- *Referencing:* the identification of people, places, and events
- *Fluency:* the manner of production of a narrative

To see the Narrative Assessment Protocol, go to **www.sagepub .com/levey.**

The "Narrative Assessment Protocol" on the companion website presents a chart that can be used to evaluate all these dimensions.

An example of a well-formed narrative produced by a 6-year-old European North American boy with typical language development is presented below. He described an experience with a broken bone.

> I broke my arm. . . . I was, well, the day . . . 2 days ago. I was climbing the tree. And I, well see, I went towards the low branch. And I and I got caught with my bathing suit? I dangled my hands down. And they got bent because it was like this hard surface under it? Then they bent like two triangles. But luckily it was my left arm that broke. . . . I had to go to the hospital and get mm. . . . It was much worser than you think because I had to get, go in the operation room. And I had to get my, and I had to take anesthesia. And I had to fall, fall asleep. And they bended my arm back. And I have a cast on.

This is an example of a classic narrative because there is a high point (the broken arm) and a resolution (surgery). The narrative is appropriate for all the dimensions that have been described. Children with TLD are able to chronologically sequence events around a focal event at about age 5 (McCabe & Bliss, 2003). Cultural variations occur in narrative discourse. It is important for readers to be able to identify different cultural styles so that they are not misinterpreted as language impairments.

CULTURAL VARIATIONS OF NARRATIVE DISCOURSE

Students from culturally and linguistically diverse communities use alternative structures and dimensions in their personal narratives. This point is critical because students who use different narrative styles should not be judged as having a discourse impairment. Instead, their discourse may represent cultural patterns. Departures from classic narratives may be a cultural difference rather than a deficit. Teachers need to understand cultural differences in narration so that they can better address the needs of their students.

These differences are best illustrated by the research of Sarah Michaels (1991). She observed a class in which sharing time was occurring. This activity required the 7-year-old children to relate a personal experience. An African American child produced a narrative in a style that was unfamiliar to the teacher from the mainstream community. During the presentation, the teacher often interrupted the child and later told the examiner that the child may be learning disabled. When interviewed, the child expressed her frustration at not being able to spontaneously communicate her experiences in her own style. There was a cultural mismatch between the communication styles of these two individuals. If the teacher had been more aware of cultural variations in her student's discourse, she may have been more accepting of the child's communication style.

The predominant discourse patterns from African American, Spanish, and Japanese communities are described in this chapter. These cultural patterns were selected because of their prominence in school settings. Further information on cultural patterns may be obtained from other sources (see McCabe, 1996; McCabe & Bliss, 2003).

Some students from African American communities may produce **topic-associating narratives** (Heath, 1983). These narratives can be identified by relatively lengthy descriptions of several situations that are linked semantically rather than chronologically and by emotional terms that are used to express ideas (Champion, 2003; Heath, 1983; Hyon & Sulzby, 1994; Michaels, 1991). Chapter 12 presents more examples of this type of narrative. An example of a topic-associating narrative produced by an 8-year-old African American girl with TLD follows (McCabe, 1996).

> We went to the dentist before, and I was gettin' my tooth pulled, and the doc, the dentist, said, "Oh, it's not gonna hurt." And he was lying to me. It hurt. It hurted so bad I coulda gone on screamin' even though I think some. . . . I don't know what it was like. I was, in my mouth like, I was like, "Oh that hurt!" He said no, it wouldn't hurt. 'Cause last time I went to the doctor, I had got this spray. This doctor, he sprayed some spray in my mouth and my tooth appeared in his hand. He put me to sleep and then, and then I woke up. He used some pliers to take it out, and I didn't know. So I had told my, I asked my sister how did, how did the man take (it out)? And so she said, "He used some pliers." I said, "Nah, he used that spray." She said, "Nope he used that spray to put you to sleep, and he used the pliers to take it out." I was like, "Huh, that's amazin'." I swear to God I was so amazed that, hum. . . . It was so amazing, right? that I had to look for myself, and then I asked him too. And he said, "Yes, we, I used some pliers to take out your tooth, and I put you to sleep, an, so you wouldn't know, and that's how I did it." and I was like, "Ooouuu." And then I seen my sister get her tooth pulled. I was like, "Ooouuu," 'cause he had to put her to sleep to, hmm, to take out her tooth. It was the same day she got her tooth pulled, and I was scared. I was like,"EEEhhhmmm." I had a whole bunch cotton in my mouth, chompin' on it 'cause I had to hold it to, hmm, stop my bleeding. I, one day I was in school. I took out my own tooth. I put some hot water in it the night, the, the night before I went to school. And I was taking a test. And then it came out right when I was takin', when I finished the test. And my teacher asked me, was it bleeding? I said, "No it's not bleeding, 'cause I put some hot water on it." And so my cousin, he wanted to take out his tooth, and he didn't know what to do, so I told him, "I'm a Pullin' Teeth Expert. Pull out your own tooth, but if you need somebody to do it, call me, and I'll be over."

In this topic-associative narrative, the child described events around pulling teeth. The narrative is lengthy and includes considerable emotion pertaining to the following semantically related events:

- Lying dentist extraction
- Previous painless extraction

- Sister's extraction
- Tooth falling out in school
- Cousin's request

Another cultural style in narrative discourse is reflective of speakers whose first language is Spanish. It should be noted that there are many different versions of Spanish and different variations in communicative styles for Spanish-speaking individuals. Generalizations cannot be made for all cultures in which Spanish is primarily spoken (McCabe, Bailey, & Melzi, in press; Silva & McCabe, 1996). However, some general trends can be described. The following attributes of this cultural style have been identified as

- broad topic maintenance;
- conversationally focused narrative, rather than a narrative produced as a monologue;
- information presented by descriptive statements (e.g., "There were three men") rather than action statements (e.g., "Three men drove the car");
- optional use of redundant agents or subjects of utterances; and
- disruptions in fluency, representing attempts to identify an appropriate English word.

The following example is from an 8-year-old Mexican American girl with TLD who scored as English dominant on the James Language Dominance Test (James, 1974). It was told in English to a bilingual member of her California community.

Adult: Tell me about the time you went to El Salvador.

Child: Uh, not that fun (in reference to experimenter's prior comment about how getting a scorpion bite was not fun). But I, they were talking about the waves. They say there come a monster and all that stuff that do the waves. I go, "Get real." I got in the, a swimming pool and then when they took the picture somebody got, something got up. And it wasn't the waves or nothing. We took the picture, I'm like, "Mom, what's that?" "I don't know." I then, I felt like something pull my leg. And I just drowned like, "Help! Help!" I called my mom and they got me those thing, I'm like, "I don't need it. It's just that I need help. I'm trapped!" She hold me, got up and said, "Don't get in the swimming pool anymore." I go, "Why?" "Because, because you're going to drown again." "Okay." I got into the waves. Now that's when I drowned. I got in and like the waves got on top of me. And it was like too high for me 'cause I got all the way to like 3 feet. I and my my cousin got in. He helped me. But then my my brother got in. He went like 4 feet. So my mom went to help him. And then nobody got in the pool, the swimming pool. We left and everything that we see is green, pure green. I'm like, "Why is everything green around here?" We slept on my dad's room. And the phone just keeped on ringing, ringing, ringing. My dad wouldn't answer it. [Adult: No?] And so I answered it. I was, "Who is this?" "Is Martha there?" "Yes,

> who is it?" "Her friend." "Mom, they want you on the phone." "Who is it?" "I don't know. He won't tell me his name." "Is it a boy?" "Yes." My dad got mad. And he's all, "Who is it?" "I don't know. You tell him. He won't tell me." My mom got the phone, and he said, "Who is it?" And he goes it's um, "Is David there? It's a friend of his." And my my brother said, "Who is it?" And I go, "I don't know and I don't care. Let's go to sleep. We got asleep. The phone rings again. I just unplug it. And my mom plug it back on. We're I just plug it—She plugs it, I displug it. We stayed like that. And then until I got, until I cut it. And it wouldn't work anymore. I'm like, "Yes no more phone for the whole week!" And then um I needed to call my friend. The phone's broken, man. I had to go to the public phone. I couldn't find none. [Adult: No public phones?] My dad go like, "See what you get for cortando . . . cutting the . . . telephone?" I go, "Not my fault it kept on ringing." I couldn't get some sleep. And then we went to the beach. And we slept there . . . on the beach.

This speaker seamlessly links several incidents in a swimming pool in El Salvador with a phone conversation that she acts out in reported speech and the phone ringing during the night and her struggle to stop the ringing and get some sleep. This excerpt is lengthy.

Several dimensions are influenced by the child's Spanish background in this narrative. For example, it is characterized by broad-topic maintenance. The speaker includes information about her family, including her father, mother, brother, and cousin. Informativeness is adequate—listeners do not feel that key events are omitted from the various experiences narrated. Referencing is variable. Sometimes the speaker identifies her **referents** and other times assumes the listener knows them. The child is generally fluent throughout this lengthy narrative.

There are numerous speakers from Asian cultures in the United States. They do not use the same narrative discourse style. This section will focus mainly on Japanese children who have been in this country for less than 2 years. Some salient aspects of their narratives are

- descriptions of similar experiences in one narrative rather than a focus on only one event,
- minimal information because of the value of concise discourse, and
- omittance of referents because of the value of brevity.

The use of multiple experiences and conciseness is also evident in the narratives of Chinese and Korean children (Minami & McCabe, 1991). An example from an 8-year-old Japanese girl who gave this narrative in her native language follows. She was asked if she had ever been cut by a knife or other sharp object (Minami & McCabe, 1996).

> When [I was] in kindergarten. Got leg caught in a bicycle. Got a cut here, here and. . . . Wore a cast for about a month. Took a rest for about a week. And went back again. Had a cut here. Fell off an iron bar. Had two mouths (means a big wound).

The child describes two experiences and chooses not to use the redundant agent "I" in an effort to achieve conciseness.

The samples that have been presented highlight some cultural variations in personal narrative discourse that can help teachers address each student's instructional needs. In addition, the samples help avoid possible cultural mismatches between the discourse styles of teacher and student.

DIFFERENTIATING IMPAIRED VERSUS CULTURALLY DIFFERENT NARRATIVE DISCOURSE PATTERNS

Students with language impairments produce a variety of symptoms of impaired narrative discourse. They do not produce the well-formed narratives of their peers of the same chronological age (Miranda et al.,1998). Some of the more prevalent difficulties associated with language impairment, such as reduced topic maintenance, informativeness, referencing, event sequencing, and fluency, are described in this section.

One common trend is production of a **leapfrogging narrative**. In this type of discourse, events are not presented in chronological order and salient information is omitted. Students with language impairments may not always maintain the topic of the discourse. They may provide extraneous information or use a stream of consciousness type of production. They do not appear to be able to limit their discourse to one topic.

Informativeness is another dimension that is usually impaired. They do not provide the listener with enough information for the message to be easily and fully understood. Event sequencing may be impaired because speakers do not sequence events in chronological order. They have difficulty with the dimension of referencing, as evidenced by failing to appropriately identify people, places, and locations. Children with language impairments may not adequately link utterances; so their discourse may be choppy or difficult to understand. Finally, their narratives exhibit many disruptions in fluency. These disruptions may reflect a reduced ability to plan, monitor, and/or revise utterances (Peterson & McCabe, 1983).

Many of these impairments are reflected in the narrative below. It was produced by a 9-year-old student from a European North American background. He was diagnosed as language impaired from standardized test results. He is describing going to the hospital (Bliss & McCabe, 2008).

Yeah, I had a X-Ray because they they're checking on my leg and I was scared that I was going up there. And they gave me a balloon and I went to um Toys "R" Us and gave me a toy but I never. . . . Uh, I just broke my leg and I just fall down on my bike because I got hurt and my bandaids on me . . . put their off and I jumped out of my bike and I. . . . I flied and then I jumped down.

Adult: You jumped down?

Child: Uhhuh, on the grass . . . and I, um, our grandma, um, she died. She, um, she was getting older. Our grandma and she died and the, uh, funeral. . . . My ma and dad went to the funeral. And then Aunt Cindy was there too. And we, uh, they, um, um, everyone was sad that, um, uh, that died. . . . And on my birthday I went on my bike. I, uh, um . . . I just jump on my bike. I just balance on my. . . And I did it with, uh, I did do it with only my hands. I didn't do it without my hands, and I, uh, um, one hand too.

The overall structure of this narrative is a leapfrogging one. The speaker changes the topics by talking about his experiences in a hospital, bike riding, and his grandmother. In addition, the discourse dimensions are compromised. For example, he does not provide sufficient information about any experience for the listener to understand the events. Some of his referents are vague (e.g., *there, it*), while others are used appropriately (e.g., *grandmother* and *father*). This child has difficulty producing fluent utterances.

Narrative impairments are different from culturally influenced discourse behaviors. Speech-language pathologists identify symptoms of impaired narrative discourse, including word-finding deficits, lack of informativeness, inappropriate referencing, inability to construct a narrative, and reduced discourse coherence.

EXAMPLES OF NARRATIVES FROM SELECTED LANGUAGE DISORDERS

In this chapter, several frequently occurring disorders and typical narrative patterns are presented. The disorders are **attention-deficit hyperactivity disorder (ADHD), learning disabilities,** and **Asperger Syndrome.** They were selected to demonstrate a wide range of impairments. Teachers need to understand narrative patterns of children with these disorders so that they can recognize impairments and refer children to speech-language pathologists. Professionals can identify and remediate narrative discourse impairments that are typically found in these disorders.

Attention-Deficit Hyperactivity Disorder

ADHD is frequently identified in school-age children (Westby & Watson, 2004). It is increasing in prevalence; in America, approximately 3% to 5% of the school-age population receives this diagnosis (Westby & Watson, 2004). Discourse impairments consist of lack of discourse organization, off-topic utterances, abrupt topic shifting, verbosity, and impaired register (Westby & Cutler, 1994; Westby & Watson, 2004). Children with ADHD have difficulty maintaining a topic. They may shift topics quickly because they cannot attend to what they are discussing. In addition, their discourse may be dysfluent, because they do not plan what they want to say. For example, excessive pauses and revisions may indicate that a speaker is talking extemporaneously without prior planning.

The following sample is from a 9-year-old child diagnosed with ADHD. He is on medication to control his attention and impulsive behaviors. He frequently interrupts others and blurts out remarks that do not have any immediate meaning (e.g., "You're fired!"). He is not popular and is not asked to engage in social play activities because he continually tries to change the activity and does not concentrate on what his peers are doing. He tends to be isolated and at times is teased or bullied by his classmates. He is enrolled in a regular classroom. He does not do well in school because he cannot concentrate on a task for a sustained amount of time. Here is his personal narrative about his visit to a hospital after his dog bit him:

> Well, he was chewing up something and I did not like it. But you know what? He was being such a . . . such a . . . he was being so sick. He was just chewing it up, sucking. I got

> mad at him and . . . and . . . then I . . . just I just tried to spank him. And he really didn't notice who was behind him. And and I, and I was playing Nintendo, you know. . . . But then, well I was fixin' to jump so he could just scratch the table. . . . But . . . but . . . um . . . before I could even jump, he bit me right on my lip, right here. Can you see the scar here still? But, you know what? When I had to get the stitches out. . . . You wanna know about the really stupid lady? I hope she got fired. You know why? She was so stupid? You know what she did? Well you see, umm . . . umm. . . . Well, not the stupid lady, these people that were trying to take out my stitches. . . . They were, umm, umm. . . . No matter how strong they are. . . . They're so stupid . . . 'cause they just . . . you know. . . . But, you know what? You know how they were taking my stitches out? They just like, when they put them it. . . . Uhmm, even when they, you know . . . they were just pull them all up like that. And then like that (gestures in a pulling direction) and then like that (more gestures) or something. And then I just couldn't hold still, um . . . so then they get this one dopey lady to come hold me down. And then . . . ummm, she hold me down so hard. . . . Uum . . . when I got out of there in the park . . . in the parking lot, there was . . . I had this big bruise on my cheek. She grabbed me that hard.

This narrative is characterized by deficiencies in topic maintenance, informativeness, and fluency. These features have been previously described in the discourse of children with ADHD.

Learning Disabilities

Learning disabilities are generally identified in children who have narrative discourse deficits both in comprehending and producing narratives (Bishop & Edmundson, 1987; Roth & Spekman, 1986; Westby, 1994; Wright & Newhoff, 2003). They cannot understand subtle or abstract meanings or make inferences from unstated information. Their narratives are short, lack detail, and are disorganized. There is a close link between preschool narrative ability and later academic achievement (Bishop & Edmundson, 1987; de Hirsch et al., 1966; Tabors et al., 2001).

The following sample is from a 9-year-old child with a learning disability. He is enrolled in a regular classroom in middle school. His reading is 2 years below grade level, and his writing abilities are impaired. Samples of his written and oral storytelling abilities are presented below.

Written Description of One Frog Too Many

The spelling and grammar replicate his work.

> The got got a gift. it was a frog. he took the frog out the other frog bet [bit] the other frogs leg. the boy was mad. the frogs were on the turtle. the other frog poosh the little frog off. the boy left the biggst frog behind. the boy went on the fog that was left bhind was onto be there. the biggst frog pusht the frog in the water. the boy did not now [know] the tutle [turtle] went to the boy to tell. they look erverwar but they can not hine [find] him. the boy went home crying. the dog was with him. the little frog jamp [jump] in the window and land on the other frogs head. they were frends [friends].

He has difficulty with spelling, punctuation, and grammar. His writing is diminished compared to other children of his age and is below age level. Note also that he is attempting to sound out words phonetically (e.g., "poosh" for *push*), although these efforts are inconsistent (e.g., "pusht"). Note also that such invented spelling is more typical of a 5- or 6-year-old TLD child than a 9-year-old.

Oral Personal Narrative About a Visit to the Hospital

My brother broke a thumb. Um, we had a cedar chest. And our mom left it open. But this was when he was kinda little. Um, he was looking inside of it. And he had his thumb like that (shows the clinician). And it went ppsshhh. Well, had to go to the emergency room. One time he, we were playing on his wimple. And we he said when the time to get our mom say, "It's time to get off." So he didn't let me do a submarine. Submarine, when you go straight down. He did it in the shallow end. Hit his head on the bottom. He started screaming in the water. Well, had to call the . . . uh, the ambulance out. After a while he felt better. First I thought he broke his head open because he went down fast. We can go down fast. And if . . . we have a 8 foot deep pool. And the deep end, the very deep end, we can swim down there. And, uh, can swim up in like, um, half . . . , no wait 12 seconds.

His oral personal narrative is stronger than his written abilities. He described two hospital events and went off topic at the end of his discourse. He did not provide complete information about each event. Event sequencing, referencing, and fluency were appropriate.

Asperger Syndrome

Asperger Syndrome is the final disorder that we will describe. This impairment is on the Autism Spectrum. Discourse deficits include verbosity, pedantic discourse style, reduced ability to modify a message according to the attributes of a listener, off-topic discourse, **perseveration** on one topic, and failure to shift topics (Rubin & Lennon, 2004; Safran, Safran, & Ellis, 2003; Tsatsanis, 2004). The oral discourse (not a narrative despite the fact that he was asked to tell a narrative) from an 8-year-old child diagnosed with Asperger Syndrome is presented below. He is also enrolled in a regular classroom. He rarely initiates interactions with his peers and prefers to play alone on the computer. He does not make eye contact and speaks in a monotone and with rapid speech. During this sample, he refused to leave the computer.

I'm building a bug. Yeah, I'm building a bug. And I'm gonna print it out. If I tell my dad that I eaten in Mrs. B's class, and I tell him, I'm gonna stay in this class, Dad is really gonna be mad because I had eaten in Mrs. B's. ("Jason" was punished and therefore could not eat in the cafeteria with other children.) And I was supposed to eat at the cafeteria. Can you help me print this? ("Jason" cannot print the page.) I can't print this thing. Mrs. S, can I use your computer? (She indicates no.) But the printer does not work. (Again, indication of no.) It's not fair! Mrs. S can't let us use this computer. I forgot to tell you Ethan is my friend. When can I go with you and look for him? I'll just show you what Ethan looks like. (He begins to draw a picture of a boy.) And on the back [of the paper], I'll describe him. See this is Ethan (pointing to his drawing). Will we have time to find him? Can we go see if we can find Ethan? What else can I do when I'm done with this [picture]? I always have to play with Jeremy. How am I gonna get out of this [computer program]?

This sample is characterized by impaired topic maintenance. This child had a stream of consciousness type of discourse that focused on him. His discourse was fluent. The other narrative dimensions cannot be applied to this sample because "Jason" did not produce a narrative.

EDUCATIONAL IMPLICATIONS FOR FOSTERING COHERENT NARRATIVES IN THE CLASSROOM

Teachers can play a critical role in identifying possible impaired narration and referring students to speech-language pathologists. Teachers can plan to elicit personal narrative discourse in regular classroom routines, either with a sharing time or other types of activities. Personal narratives are easily elicited with the conversational map procedure. First, the teacher provides a brief description of a personal experience (e.g., a spilling accident or going to a hospital). Next, the student is asked to describe an experience on the same topic. When the student stops talking, the teacher encourages the child to elaborate on the personal narrative through the use of neutral prompts (e.g., repetition of child's last utterance or saying, "Uh huh" or "Tell me more"). A teacher can listen to the student's discourse and evaluate whether the structure, content (e.g., informativeness, event sequencing), and manner of production (e.g., fluency) are appropriate.

In the analysis of a child's narrative, the cultural differences that have been described should be considered. If a teacher feels that the narrative discourse is impaired, the child should be referred to a speech-language pathologist for a complete evaluation. Teachers make accurate referrals to speech-language pathologists when they consider discourse criteria (Damico & Oller, 1980).

Teachers can employ effective strategies to foster narrative discourse coherence and enhance the work of speech-language pathologists. The teacher can encourage effective storytelling by telling his or her own personal narratives to students as a model for them, using role playing to enable students to relate personal narratives, and encouraging students to share their own personal experiences. Some educational activities that can be implemented in the classroom follow (adapted from McCabe, 1996):

- Read, write, and/or summarize newspaper articles that pertain to real-life situations (e.g., events that occurred in the community).

- Encourage students to create their own articles based on their experiences.

- Use sharing time with preschool and elementary school children so that they can describe their experiences over the weekend or on vacation.

- Tell or have students read stories from different cultures (references available in McCabe & Rollins, 1994).

- Enable students from the cultures to then describe a personal experience that embodies some of the cultural practices of the story.

- Encourage preschool and elementary children to draw what happened to them before they either tell the story or write it. This procedure is based on the educational practices described by Calkins (1994).

  - Enable students to tell and/or write about their personal experiences based on emotions (e.g., "Have you ever felt really: happy, afraid, proud, or embarrassed? Tell me a story about one time you felt this way").

  - Encourage students to tell personal stories based on photos or photo albums.

Teachers can identify possible narrative discourse deficits in their students, but teachers need to appreciate differences between culturally influenced narration and narrative impairments. They can foster narrative growth by developing a variety of educational activities. There should be a close working relationship between teachers and speech-language pathologists.

A teacher can encourage a child to elaborate on the personal narrative through use of neutral prompts, such as saying "Tell me more."

CASE STUDY REVISITED

The case study presented at the beginning of this chapter described Joshua, a schoolchild who is 8 years and 7 months old. The classroom teacher has developed a set of strategies to help him express and write about personal narratives, along with offering these strategies to the other children in the class.

CASE STUDY REVISITED: **The ability to describe events and stories in narratives**

First, Ms. Smithfield modeled a personal narrative, telling about having to give her pet dog a pill that he kept spitting out. She then encouraged students to share their own personal experiences, writing some examples on the board to give them ideas. Once children began to express these personal narratives, she found that she needed to ask Joshua and some other children to expand. To this end, she asked "Then what happened?" and "What else can you tell us?" to encourage children to develop their narratives. Over a short period of time, Joshua became more successful at producing personal narratives, with less need for cues to expand. When children had achieved this goal, Ms. Smithfield encouraged students to write their personal experiences, with the goal of developing articles for a classroom book. To help them develop their ideas, she again gave them some ideas and topics from which to choose, such as what happened over the weekend (what they did or something they saw) or what they did while on vacation over the summer. She also encouraged children to draw to express these personal narratives. Joshua especially enjoyed drawing to describe his experiences, along with writing a few lines. Over time, Joshua's writing became longer and he was also able to talk and write about these experiences with more coherence and organization.

SUMMARY

This chapter focused on narrative discourse—personal narratives in particular. Personal narratives are recounts of past experiences and are important for typical language development for social and academic success as well as in medical and legal contexts. There are six types of personal narrative structures that range from simple, one-event descriptions to classic narratives that orient the listener to the main events of an experience and the consequences of actions. Five dimensions characterize personal narratives. These dimensions include topic maintenance, informativeness, event sequencing, referencing, and fluency.

Personal narratives vary according to a speaker's cultural and linguistic background. We described the features of narratives used by African American speakers and speakers whose first language is Spanish. These features should not be mistaken for signs of a deficit in discourse.

Symptoms of impaired narrative discourse include lack of information and event sequencing. We also presented examples of narratives produced by children with language disorders. The symptoms are not unique to one disorder. Teachers are encouraged to elicit personal narratives from their students, and a checklist is included for this purpose. Educational strategies for improving narratives are presented, including modeling narratives, summarizing real-life situations, and having children read and tell stories from other cultures.

Earlier chapters described children's language development, beginning with infants and toddlers in Chapter 7, moving to preschoolers in Chapter 8, and ending with later school-age children in Chapter 9. It is important to understand that the precursors for narrative discourse begin in these earlier ages, with children's exposure to the structure of stories in books.

In Chapter 11, you learned about the nature and structure of discourse, including the impact of culture on discourse patterns. Chapter 12 discusses African American English and how it may contribute to the achievement gap often described with respect to minority children. This next chapter also provides strategies for narrative development and dialect use.

KEY WORDS

Articulated

Asperger Syndrome

Attention-deficit hyperactivity disorder (ADHD)

Causal

Coherent

Decontextualized narratives

Fictional narrative

Incoherent

Leapfrogging narrative

Learning disabilities

Narrative discourse

Perseveration

Personal narrative

Referents

Topic-associating narratives

STUDY QUESTIONS

1. Explain the main difference between the personal narrative structure and the fictional account structure.

2. List the eight general structures that characterize personal narratives.

3. Describe the importance of the awareness of cultural differences in narrative scripts.

4. List some general trends associated with Spanish speakers' narrative styles.

5. Describe the impaired narrative characteristics associated with a language impaired child's narrative skills.

6. What would you do to help a child who does not produce a narrative discourse?

7. Why would a child who exhibits impaired narrative discourse also exhibit disruptive social skills?

8. Why should cultural consideration be taken into account in evaluating narrative discourse?

PROJECTS

1. Ask children of different ages to describe personal experiences they have had that relate to one of the following topics: a scary experience, a happy event, a vacation, or a trip to the doctor or hospital. You may model a personal narrative about one of these experiences first. Ask children to expand on their initial narratives by asking elaborative questions (e.g., "Then what happened?" "What else can you tell us?"). Using this chapter as a guide, analyze children's narrative skills at different ages.

2. Ask children to role-play events, such as explaining why they were late to school, taking a pet to the vet, what happened when a pitcher of milk was spilled, or how a child broke his or her

leg. You can expand the discourse with elaborative questions such as those presented above. Using this chapter as a guide, analyze children's responses.

3. Ask children to reenact fictional stories that include multiple characters and dialogue. Children can play different roles and then switch roles. You can serve as a model for the dialogue and also expand the children's discourse by asking elaborative questions. Using this chapter as a guide, analyze the language in their stories.

STUDENT STUDY SITE

Visit the Student Study Site at **www.sagepub.com/levey** for these additional learning tools:

- Video Links
- Self Quizzes
- E-Flashcards

- Sample Forms and Assessment Tools
- Recommended Readings
- Web Resources

SUGGESTIONS FOR FURTHER READING

Bliss, L. S., & McCabe, A. (2008). Personal narratives: Cultural differences and clinical implications. *Topics in Language Disorders, 28*(2), 162–177.

McCabe, A. (1996). *Chameleon readers: Teaching children to appreciate all kinds of good stories.* New York: McGraw Hill.

McCabe, A., & Bliss, L. S. (2003). *Patterns of narrative discourse.* Boston: Allyn & Bacon.

McCabe, A., & Rollins, P. R. (1994). Assessment of preschool narrative skills. *American Journal of Speech-Language Pathology, 3*(1), 45–56.

Peterson, C. A., & McCabe, A. (1983). *Developmental psycholinguistics: Three ways of looking at a child's narrative.* New York: Plenum.

C H A P T E R 12

African American English in the Classroom

Julie A. Washington and Monique T. Mills

Case Study: Understanding African American English

Jasmine and Imani are 6 years old in the same first-grade classroom in an urban school district. Jasmine and Imani are both African American and from low-income households.

Jasmine: Jasmine's teacher is impressed with how articulate she is in comparison with the other children in the classroom. Although Jasmine uses African American English (AAE) dialect, her dialect use is low and her teacher, Mrs. Steiner, barely notices it. She is also a great narrator. Mrs. Steiner recently described Jasmine's narratives as clear and organized.

Imani: Mrs. Steiner is concerned about Imani. She seems to have trouble with grammar. She leaves the endings off words, her sentences seem incomplete, and she is sometimes hard to understand. Imani's use of AAE dialect can be characterized as high. Mrs. Steiner also recently shared with a fellow teacher that Imani's stories are long and very unorganized and that she seems to be making things up when she tells stories. Mrs. Steiner recently requested that Imani receive an evaluation from the school speech-language pathologist.

What inferences can you draw about the differences in language abilities of these two children? On what information or experiences with children's productions did you base your answer?

INTRODUCTION

The focus of this chapter is to describe the role that language plays in the performance of African American children in the classroom. In addition, this chapter presents the language variations that African American children often bring to school, the potential impact of this variation on learning, and strategies and implications for the classroom teacher. We present a discussion of **language variation** as it relates to dialectal variation, along with the cultural linguistic gifts that African American children bring to the learning contexts through their unique and culturally driven narration and linguistic style. The importance of this information is its impact on increased academic success in classrooms where teachers are aware of the features of AAE (Delpit, 1996).

Although there are many other languages and cultures found in the classroom, this chapter focuses on the features of AAE because these children make up a significant portion of the school-age population when compared with other languages and cultural groups. The other well-represented language and cultural group in U.S. schools today is made of Hispanic speakers and second-language learners. This population is addressed in Chapters 13 and 14.

Directly addressing AAE in a textbook on language difference and disorder is appropriate because language facility and failure to use standard English are factors that may bias how student achievement is viewed. By explaining the features of AAE, teachers from other linguistic and cultural groups can better understand how these language differences impact student success in various academic contexts.

Language is a critical developmental skill, and intact language abilities support efforts to teach children a wide range of skills, from active listening to proficient reading and writing. Children who have strong language skills are also more likely to be strong readers and writers (Kamhi & Catts, 2005). When young children enter school, there is an expectation that they will arrive with sufficient language skills to support the learning process. When children lack the skills that are compatible with those needed to support learning, both teacher and student are challenged.

Any number of variables can influence the language skills that children bring to early learning, including poverty (Fazio, Naremore, & Connell, 1996; Hart & Risley, 1995; Washington & Craig, 1998), a home language other than English (Hardin, Roach-Scott, & Peisner-Feinberg, 2007), or family and community differences in language use (Washington & Thomas-Tate, 2009). This challenge can seem particularly daunting for children who enter schools speaking languages or dialects that differ from the Mainstream Classroom English (MCE) that they will encounter in textbooks and classroom instruction.

In addition to the need to focus their cognitive resources on learning to read, write, and master mathematics, these students face the additional task of learning to understand and utilize the new and different language of the classroom. It is important for children to learn that, while their language may appear different and may not be standard, these differences do not mean that they are less bright or less capable. The teacher has a significant role to play in making sure these children feel just as capable at learning as anyone else in that class. To achieve this goal, the teacher needs to communicate that language is something that is contextually governed—what is appropriate in one setting may not be appropriate in another—and that everyone uses unique vocabulary and phrases that come directly from our families of origin.

AFRICAN AMERICAN ENGLISH

AAE has been studied extensively by scholars in various disciplines, including communicative sciences and disorders, linguistics, and education (Craig & Washington, 2006; Green, 2002; Labov, 1972; Thomas-Tate, Washington, & Edwards, 2004; Wolfram, 1971;

Children who speak diverse languages and dialects are common within the classroom.

Wolfram & Thomas, 2002). AAE is the community language of most, but not all, African Americans in the United States. AAE impacts the morphology, syntax, and phonology of American English in predictable ways. Table 12.1 presents the major features and examples of AAE spoken by African American children in northern dialect regions.

The Social Perception of African American English

Although AAE is spoken in varying degrees by African Americans from both low- and middle-socioeconomic backgrounds, it is used primarily by low-income and working-class African Americans (Delpit, 2006; Green, 2002). As such, AAE has developed as a highly stigmatized (i.e., socially unacceptable) variety of American English. In fact, early discussions of AAE focused on debating the legitimacy of the dialect, with linguists finally agreeing that AAE is a rule-governed variation of American English, rather than an ungrammatical variant (Labov, 1972; Wolfram, 1971).

Language is one of the overt indicators of class membership (Purcell-Gates, 2002). As such, it is not uncommon for listeners to make judgments about a speaker's educational background or income level based on the speaker's use of language. This tendency is not unique to Americans (Macaulay & Trevelyan, 1973; Milroy & Milroy, 1974), nor is it solely directed at African Americans.

In her exposition on the relationship between social class and language, Purcell-Gates (2002) described teachers' disparaging comments and lowered expectations directed toward her white, impoverished students who used **Appalachian dialects** that were associated with poverty and rural living. Teachers and others outside the students' linguistic

Table 12.1	Morphosyntactic Features of African American Child English

AAE Features	Example
Zero copula/auxiliary	*My brother hungry. / We makin' a cake.*
Subject-verb agreement	*They was outside playin'.*
"Fitna"/"sposeta"/"bouta"	*We fitna go in the house. / They bouta go to the park.*
Undifferentiated pronoun case	*Him goin' over him house.*
Multiple negation	*I don't know nobody who got no toys for Christmas.*
Zero possessive	*My mama found my brother shoe outside.*
Zero past tense	*He said he already call his mama.*
Invariant *be*	*He be goin' to the movies all the time.*
Zero *to*	*He wanted his dog __ run.*
Zero plural	*His hand fit in his gloves.*
Double modal	*I'm am lookin' for my truck.*
Regularized reflexive	*He rode his bike all by hisself.*
Indefinite article	*I saw a elephant at the zoo.*
Appositive pronoun	*My mama she was tired.*
Remote past *been*	*I been knowin' how to swim.*
Preterite *had*	*He had went outside to play.*
Completive *done*	*I done had enough already.*

community frequently stereotyped these children based on their linguistic skills and lowered their expectations accordingly. Purcell-Gates found that teachers made these judgments within minutes of hearing these students talk.

Similarly, Stubbs (2002) asserted that, as members of a language community, we hear language through a powerful filter of social values and stereotypes, resulting in linguistic stereotyping. These stereotypes impact our expectations and beliefs about these speakers (Delpit, 2002). It is when these beliefs impact teachers' interactions with, expectations of, and beliefs about their students that they become especially harmful. It is important that teachers begin to recognize these language variations as differences and not interpret them as deficits.

African American English and the Academic Context

Most African American children speak AAE at the time of school entry. Craig and Washington (2006) found that more than 90% of their African American preschool and kindergarten study participants spoke AAE at the time of school entry, regardless of socioeconomic status (SES), as shown in Table 12.1. This table illustrates the wide variety of AAE features produced by African American children from preschool through fifth grade.

The language forms used by children as they enter school provide a window into the language of the communities in which they live. Thus, the language that students use at home will be the language that teachers see reflected in the classroom environment (Delpit, 1996; Hart & Risley, 1995). The **density of dialect use** in children varies widely (density is defined as the overall number of AAE tokens or types in a language sample divided by the number of words or utterances). This is true even when children live in the same neighborhoods. Washington and Craig (1994) found that children's use of AAE ranged from quite low (less than 10% of utterances impacted) to quite high (more than 50% of utterances impacted) in a sample of low-income, African American preschoolers residing in the same neighborhood in metropolitan Detroit. Consequently, some children entered school with oral language skills that differed greatly from MCE, while others produced only a small number of AAE forms that varied only slightly from MCE. It is the group whose language use differs greatly from MCE that appears to be at highest risk academically.

Table 12.2 provides an example of utterances produced by two kindergartners: one whose dialect use was low and one who exhibited a high density of dialect use. These samples were obtained from two 5-year-old females from low-income families who were both describing the same picture.

Although both of these children are AAE speakers, 54.5% of utterances include an AAE feature for the child whose AAE use is high, while 7% of utterances (one utterance) include an AAE feature for the child whose AAE is low. These examples demonstrate the difference in the amount of dialect that may be used even by low-income African American children and how the standard sample more closely resembles MCE.

Despite differences in dialect used by the children in Table 12.2, both are skilled users of complex syntax. Craig and Washington (1994) found that at these young ages, low-income children who used the most dialect also produced language that was more syntactically complex than children who were low or moderate dialect users. Unfortunately, as children move through the grades to high school, high dialect use rapidly loses its advantage (Craig & Washington, 2006). For example, high use of dialect has been found to

Table 12.2   Samples of High- and Low-Density AAE Speakers

High-Density AAE	Low-Density AAE
everybody are getting hurt / ++	the boy is going to the hospital /
somebody gotta get run over car /	and this is the grownup /
then they fell /	and this is the man /
then the peoples in the car is smashed / ++	and the lady is sitting right there /
then they hurt in the car / ++	and she got a little wrap over her head/
and the hospital had to come and get them up /	and she got some shoe-s on /
the kid's on the street 'cause the car gonna get him / ++	and it-'is a broke-en bike /
and his papers all falling / ++	the car is smashed /
the crossing guard she whistling to him to make the car stop and / ++	and the lady and the man and the little man is try-ing to get the little boy out / ++
so the boy can get his papers /	and the officer is blowing his whistle and stopping his hands /
	and the officer girl is telling him to stop (be)cause a car is coming /

NOTE: ++ signifies utterances that include an AAE feature.

mask listener perceptions of the linguistic complexity in young children's language samples (Craig & Washington, 1994). Washington and colleagues continue their research on the use of dialect in the classroom and its potential impact on the academic achievement gap.

THE ACHIEVEMENT GAP

The significant gap in educational achievement that exists by race and ethnicity in the United States is well documented and widely referenced (Cooper & Schleser, 2006; Foster & Miller, 2007; Kieffer, 2008; Mattison & Aber, 2007; Neuman & Celano, 2006; Yeung & Pfeiffer, 2009). Termed the *achievement gap*, these disparities in academic performance are characterized by significantly below-average performance among underrepresented minority groups, including Hispanic American, African American, and Native American students.

Although there have been gaps identified for most academic subject areas, the poor reading performance of underrepresented minorities has been widely discussed as a critically important contributor to the presence and persistence of the achievement gap. Without question, reading is connected to all academic subjects, with the relationship of language skills and reading outcomes being well-established (Kamhi & Catts, 2005; Restrepo & Dubasik, 2008; Snow & Griffin, 1998).

Source of the Achievement Gap

There is no debate on the existence of the achievement gap. What is widely debated is the source(s) of this gap. The National Assessment of Educational Progress, an annual nationwide assessment that has been called the nation's report card, has documented a consistent, intractable gap in achievement between minority children and their peers since 1971. The most recent report documents promising gains in reading performance for African American children but a troubling decrease in performance for Hispanic students (Planty et al., 2009).

Several social, educational, and demographic variables have been implicated: poverty, racial discrimination, low teacher expectations, cultural mismatch, and language skills (Cooper & Schleser, 2006; Foster & Miller, 2007; Kieffer, 2008; Mattison & Aber, 2007; Neuman & Celano, 2006; Yeung & Pfeiffer, 2009). The prevailing view is that some combination of these factors is likely responsible for the gap.

EDUCATION AND DIALECT

In school settings, AAE-speaking students frequently experience communication breakdowns with teachers who are unfamiliar with this variety of American English (Delpit, 1996). This is primarily because "teaching and learning are rooted in and are dependent upon a common language between teacher and student" (Hilliard, 2002, p. 89).

Craig and Washington's (2006) research on low-income AAE-speaking children demonstrated that these children may face academic challenges secondary to an inability to **code-switch** between AAE and MCE. Code-switching refers to the ability to alternate between the use of two wholly different languages, as well as the alternation between varieties within a language (Auer, 1999). Over time, it is expected that the use of AAE in the classroom will decrease as children learn to code-switch to use of classroom language.

Connor and Craig (2006) found evidence of code-switching in a small group of low-income African American preschool children. Children who were able to code-switch at this young age had language and phonological skills that were excellent compared to their low-income peers who had not yet begun to code-switch. Children in their sample who used the most dialect also had the best emergent literacy skills.

The children in the Connor and Craig (2006) study who showed evidence of code-switching represent the youngest group in which this important metalinguistic skill has been documented. More commonly, some African American children begin to code-switch near the end of their kindergarten year (Craig & Washington, 2006; Washington & Thomas-Tate, 2009). The use of AAE by children from both middle- and low-socioeconomic backgrounds decreased significantly between kindergarten and second grade for the participants in the Craig and Washington (2006) samples. Findings were that, after third grade, there was very little evidence of code-switching. Approximately two thirds of children code-switched before third grade, whereas one third appeared to be "code resistant" and did not learn to code-switch spontaneously (Craig & Washington, 2006; Washington & Thomas-Tate, 2009).

Craig, Washington, Thompson, and Potter (2004) found that children unable to code-switch between AAE and MCE may face academic challenges. Specifically, they found that children who did not code-switch by the end of third grade were likely to be one or more grade levels behind in their reading abilities by the fourth grade (Craig & Washington, 2006; Craig et al., 2004). This may provide some insight into why the third grade appears to be the grade in which the most referrals for special education evaluation occur.

Reading and Writing

The specific mechanisms underlying the relationship between AAE and reading (and writing) are not well understood despite many decades of investigation. Early investigations of the reading difficulties of African American children, related to their use of AAE (known as Black English at that time), examined the mismatch between AAE and text as a potential source of difficulty for African American children learning to read (Baratz & Shuy, 1969; Bereiter & Engelmann, 1966). It has been hypothesized that the distance between AAE and the language of text is wide enough to have a negative impact on learning to read (Delpit, 2001; Washington & Craig, 2001). This notion is not new and has been implicated in reading problems in other languages and dialects as well (Saiegh-Haddad, 2003; Yu Cho, 2002).

Tests of this **mismatch hypothesis** (Cecil, 1988) have yielded mixed results. Charity, Scarborough, and Griffin (2004) examined the reading performance of low-income children who were confirmed speakers of AAE who evidenced the use of MCE in their oral language. They found that students with more knowledge and use of MCE had fewer mismatches between their oral language and the language encountered in text. They further discovered that this knowledge significantly impacted the expectations and perceptions of their teachers, with children having more MCE knowledge being viewed more favorably.

In another test of the mismatch hypothesis, Connor and Craig (2006) examined the relationship between AAE dialect and emergent literacy skills in low-income preschoolers. They hypothesized that if the mismatch hypothesis was correct, the use of AAE would negatively impact emergent literacy skills. In contradiction to the mismatch hypothesis, Connor and Craig found that children who were moderate to high dialect users exhibited stronger phonological awareness, letter-word recognition, and sentence imitation skills than peers who used little dialect. These outcomes are similar to the findings related to complex syntax (Craig & Washington, 1994).

Similar to bilingual children, it appears that proficient use of the language spoken in the child's community serves to benefit African American children when young. However, as they get older, knowledge of MCE becomes more predictive of literacy success than the use of AAE (Charity et al., 2004). Consequently, AAE becomes problematic for reading achievement (Craig & Washington, 2006; Craig et al., 2004). Following the comprehensive discussion of narrative development in Chapter 11, which examined the predominant discourse patterns from African American, Spanish, and Japanese communities, we will now examine the African American oral tradition.

ORAL NARRATIVES

African American Oral Tradition

The African American oral tradition is characterized by emotional vitality, realness, and interrelatedness (Van Keulen, DeBose, & Weddington, 1998). Emotional vitality is demonstrated in dramatic prosodic patterns and nonverbal behaviors, such as body posture and gestures. Lively verbal dueling is also common among young adults in urban speech communities (Dandy, 1991; Smitherman, 2000; Taylor, 1982). The African American oral tradition is set in an interactive communicative context with continuous audience validation, participation, and influence (Collins, 1985).

Narratives

Traditionally, narration—an interactive practice of sharing oral and signed stories (Banks-Wallace, 1998)—has been a very good technique for reaffirming the oral tradition of many racial/ethnic minorities, particularly African Americans (Baber, 1992). Oral narration has been used as a means for transmission and preservation of culture in both African societies and African American communities. The **griots,** West African entertainers whose performances included tribal histories and genealogies, held the special role of transmitting cultural mores and histories through oral narration in African societies (Baber, 1992; Banks-Wallace, 2002).

Champion, Katz, Muldrow, and Dail (1999) found that identity, social relationships, and entertainment are three common themes in the oral narratives of African American preschoolers. In addition, young children often embed a moral message or judgment in their narrative structure, which is similar to trickster tales, sermons, and personal anecdotes found within the African American community. According to Champion, Seymour, and Camarata (1995), these moral-centered stories appear to have links to African American culture and possibly to West African cultures.

Topic-Associating and Topic-Centered Narratives

A narrative is something that has happened, is happening, or will happen (Engel, 1994). It includes an event or series of events that involves people, places, and actions. Generally, narratives are encompassed by boundaries of time and space but not always (Banks-Wallace, 1999). Narratives, which are told intentionally, have either an implicit or explicit feeling of sequence and convey meaning by their perspective or point of view. Those that have an implicit feeling of sequence have been referred to as **topic-associating narratives,** while those that have an explicit sequential order have been called **topic-centered narratives** (Champion et al., 1999; Michaels, 1981).

Topic-associating events are related because several things happen that, when described together, reveal a common theme. Topic-centered events in narratives are related because one happening leads to another. Topic-associating narratives do not adhere to a linear pattern of organization. Rather, they reflect other structural and thematic patterns (Hyon & Sulzby, 1994). Conversely, topic-centered narratives follow a linear organizational pattern, with a clear beginning, middle, and end. Examples of the structure of these narratives are presented below (de Villiers & Burns, 2003).

Topic-Centered Structure

- Organized around a single topic or closely related topics
- Uses main characters and temporal/locational grounding that remain constant and are lexically explicit
- Uses clear thematic progression with beginning, middle, and end

Topic-Associating Structure

- Organized around loosely linked topics with implied (associative) connections
- Exhibits frequent shifts in key characters and temporal/locational grounding
- Does not adhere to a linear pattern of organization

Michaels (1981) found that African American first graders used a topic-associating narrative style that is characterized by a series of anecdotes connected with *and* and an implicit theme, topic, or event. Topic changes were systematically signaled by shifts in pitch contouring and tempo, often accompanied by a time marker. For people accustomed to a topic-centered style, these narratives may give the impression of having no obvious structure and hence, no point. Children who use this style may appear to roam around the "important" aspects of the narrative and miss the "point" because they do not present information in a linear fashion.

Foster (1987) described the discourse style of an African American college teacher as she led lively discussions in her classroom. This teacher described good narrators as people who can simultaneously teach, entertain, hold the attention of an audience, and, if necessary, solicit audience participation. This perception of a "good" narrative differs from factual renditions preferred in elementary school classrooms (Heath, 1983). Examples of these two types of narrative produced by school-age children are presented below (de Villiers & Burns, 2003).

Example of Topic-Associating Narrative

(Girl, age 8 years and 5 months)

1. I live on Lyme street.
2. It's a nice place.

3. I got a- my auntie lives up there.

4. I was gonna go to my- another school.

5. This year I'm going to a different new school.

6. So I might be happy there.

7. But about my house.

8. I just love being at my house.

9. My cousins come over to play with me.

10. An' sleep over sometimes.

11. Sometimes I have slumber parties.

12. Great!

13. An' then in the morning sometimes my mother takes us- my grandpa take us to the park.

14. Get us McDonald's or, ummm, all of that.

15. Sometimes he take us to the zoo.

16. An' see all the animals.

17. It was fun at the zoo.

18. I saw the animals, bears.

19. It was great!

Example of Topic-Centered Narrative

(Girl, age 6 years and 10 months)

1. One day I was going over aunt's house.

2. Then me and my cousin Jenea, we wanted to go to the library.

3. Then we got there and I was reading books.

4. And then I wanted to, um, go on computers.

5. So I signed up.

6. But then we . . . which.

7. Uh, then a magic show was, um, startin' to come on.

8. Then this guy, he was just, he didn't know where his magic hat was.

9. So he made a hat with big balloons like clowns.

10. And then after he made a hat he made, um, the duck out of balloons.

11. Um, it was like that duck that's on Michael Jordan.

12. He made that of balloons.

13. An' then he, he had helpers.

14. But he didn't pick me.

15. An' then he, whoever go, whoever did the job he gave them a wand.

16. An' then when the magic show was done we, they had snacks.

17. They had cracker fishes, cookies, and juice.

18. Then I wanted to go a computer.

19. But I forgot that I had to go on the computer.

20. Then we left.

Performative Narratives

A close relative of the topic-associating narrative is the **performative narrative**. Performative narratives have been said to have high tellability, with the ability to capture something notable or outstanding stylistically. This is in contrast to dialogic, sense-making narratives with low tellability (Ochs & Capps, 2001). Performance, a communicative event in which there is a relationship between performer, audience, and stylized material (Foster, 1995; Hymes, 1972), is another example of the emotional vitality characteristic of the African American oral tradition.

Many stories told in the oral tradition of African Americans are humorous, moral centered, and performative (Champion, 1998). Humorous stories are made even more so by colorful embellishment and exaggeration. Sound effects, alliteration, exaggeration, and gesture are devices performative narrators use to (re)capture an event (Dyson, 1993; Heath, 1983; Ochs & Capps, 2001) and to connect with their audience.

Champion (1998) found that African American school-age children in her study used performative structure indicated by a heavy use of paralinguistic strategies, including tempo, intonation contours, pause, rhythm, vowel elongation, and stress. Teachers may expect students to communicate in an informative rather than a performative mode in the school context (Dyson, 1993). Therefore, performative narratives may not be welcomed in the official classroom setting.

Education and Oral Narration

Studies of teacher-child collaboration (Michaels, 1984; Michaels & Cazden, 1986) indicate that African American teachers applaud both the topic-associating and the topic-centered styles of oral narrative while European American teachers find topic-associating narratives lacking in cohesion. Moreover, topic-associating narrators are deemed communicatively incompetent and are provided fewer opportunities to linguistically engage in classroom learning opportunities. Indeed, topic-associating narratives may be regarded as bad narratives that are difficult to follow.

Narratives that African American children tell are not exclusively topic associating (Champion, 1998; Hester, 1996; McGregor, 2000). Champion (1998), in her study of African American school-age children, found that the narrative structures children produced varied by elicitation task. Hyon and Sulzby (1994), who used a different elicitation task than Michaels (1981), showed that African American kindergartners produced more topic-centered narratives than topic-associating narratives. Further, Hester (1996) found that topic association varied according to the topic, speaking task, listener characteristics, and the communicative intent of the speaker. Moreover, Hyon and Sulzby (1994) showed that African American kindergartners produced more topic-centered narratives than topic-associating narratives.

Narrative Style Variation

African American narrative style varies as a function of age and communicative context, similar to the findings for the use of AAE. This pattern supports the notion that African American students produce a varied repertoire of narrative structures. Some narrative structures produced by African American preadolescents are more consistent with the African American oral tradition (moral centered and performative), while others are more consistent with the mainstream American oral tradition (topic centered) (Champion, 1998). Moreover, the narrative productions of school-age African American children reportedly reveal a kind of complexity that traditional narrative analyses such as highpoint and story-grammar are unable to capture (Champion et al., 1995).

It is unfortunate that these rich and varied narrative productions are often undervalued in school contexts where linear, factual narratives are valued. Similar to AAE, explicit instruction in a narrative style that may be second nature to their mainstream peers may be necessary for some, but not all, African American children. The following strategies may be useful for encouraging the production of a variety of narrative types when this skill is not present.

STRATEGIES FOR THE CLASSROOM TEACHER: NARRATIVE DEVELOPMENT

The classroom teacher can promote metalinguistic awareness by allowing students to lead discussions or recount events in AAE and in MCE. Similar to the contrastive analysis approach, this strategy increases student awareness of the differences in narrative styles, and the contexts within each might be appropriate.

The teacher should allow students to engage in varied oral language practices (e.g., interviews with one another, poems, oral reports, oral narration, and raps). Embracing these different cultural and social manifestations of narratives promotes acceptance of diverse styles and practices for both students and teachers.

The teacher should also work with students to write and perform a play on a topic of their choosing. Again, encourage students to become proficient in the use and performance of varied styles. Baker (2002) supports the notion of making older students "trilingual," such that they are well-versed in the language styles necessary to succeed in three of the most important contexts in our lives: home, school, and, eventually, work. This is an excellent strategy because it encourages children to recognize what language styles are appropriate in varied contexts. Learning to make these discriminations and varying language use accordingly will enhance students' overall communication effectiveness.

Oral narration is a cross-cultural practice and is a significant source of variation among African American children in the classroom. Narratives have been examined for their differences and the cultural influences on these differences, as well as their potential to inform assessment and showcase the linguistic skills of African American children.

African American children often bring language variations to school.

STRATEGIES FOR THE CLASSROOM TEACHER: DIALECT USE

It is important for the classroom teacher to realize that, from a linguistic perspective, all dialects are created equal and teachers need to get educated about the dialects of their students! However, AAE is a **socially marked dialect** (Purcell-Gates, 2002), meaning that it is spoken by marginalized groups. Consequently, these socially marked dialects are associated with many negative outcomes for speakers, such as low educational attainment, poverty, and underemployment. Despite the negative outcomes, it is important to recognize that these dialects reflect language differences and not allow them to cloud your thinking or cause you to stigmatize your students.

Fogel and Ehri (2006) described an intervention that successfully changed teachers' perceptions of AAE. This was based on providing them with information about the child's language system. This strategy is based on providing children with explicit instruction in MCE grammar. Krashen (2003) distinguishes conscious learning from unconscious acquisition,

Encouraging students to engage in interviews with one another promotes understanding and acceptance of diverse communication styles.

where conscious learning refers to explicit instruction and unconscious acquisition refers to learning language through exposure in the social setting. Unconscious acquisition seems to govern the MCE learning of approximately two thirds of African American children, but approximately one third will require explicit instruction on grammatical rules, particularly syntax and morphology. Students need instruction in and experience with the language of the school.

Fogel and Ehri (2000) advocated using a contrastive approach to teach African American students to use MCE. In this strategy, students were systematically taught to translate sentences from AAE to MCE. In a similar vein, Wheeler, Denham, and Lobeck (2005) started with AAE as a model and taught students to compare and contrast AAE and MCE in an effort to encourage **bidialectism** in their students. Contrastive approaches are effective without denigrating AAE and succeed in teaching students to code-switch at a metacognitive level. Another strategy involves role play, creating situations in which AAE or MCE would be the preferred dialect. Students will choose to use the appropriate oral language system if they understand what it is (Purcell-Gates, 2002).

CASE STUDY REVISITED

We presented a description of Jasmine and Imani at the beginning of the chapter. Mrs. Steiner was very pleased with Jasmine's progress but was concerned about Imani. She contacted the speech-language pathologist with her concerns.

Case Study Revisited: **Understanding African American English**

Mrs. Steiner's school district offered a district-wide professional development workshop on language use in African American children. Since she had several African American children in her first-grade class, she decided to attend. The presenter talked about AAE, which she had never heard of, and about narrative traditions in African American children. When the speaker gave examples of AAE, Mrs. Steiner recognized the features from her African American students. When the speaker talked about high- and low-density use, she immediately realized that this was the factor that distinguished Jasmine from Imani: Imani was a very high-density dialect user, but Jasmine used only a few features.

Mrs. Steiner realized at that moment that Imani did not have a speech and language impairment. She also learned from the speaker that she should help Imani learn MCE. She made a mental note to speak to the speech-language pathologist about observing Imani instead of assessing her and decided to ask for suggestions about some effective strategies for helping her acquire MCE. The speaker's focus on oral narration also helped Mrs. Steiner understand that Imani's narratives were not unorganized; rather, she was using topic association in her narratives, which was a cultural narrative style. She realized that Jasmine had learned to tell the kinds of stories with which Mrs. Steiner was more familiar. Mrs. Steiner decided that she would begin to encourage many different types of narration in her classroom but would also teach Imani and the rest of the class to tell topic-centered stories, since that is the kind of story usually expected at school.

SUMMARY

AAE has been written about more than any other American English dialect (Wolfram & Thomas, 2002). When there are discussions of language variation among African Americans, from either a linguistic or an educational vantage point, AAE quickly becomes the focus. It is important for the classroom teacher to understand that AAE is spoken by most African American children, regardless of their socioeconomic backgrounds, and that middle-SES children appear to code-switch from the use of AAE to MCE more easily than their low-SES peers. However, children who do not learn to code-switch frequently encounter difficulty learning to read, and, not surprisingly, their continued use of dialect negatively impacts expectations for their performance (Charity et al., 2004; Delpit, 2001, 2006).

The goal of this chapter was to introduce the classroom teacher to the features of AAE so that classroom teachers who interact with AAE-speaking children learn to recognize and appreciate AAE (Fogel & Ehri, 2006). Fogel and Ehri found that teacher responses to students' use of AAE were more positive when they were more aware of the forms that AAE could take. This could certainly have an impact on the success of these children in the classroom.

While Chapter 12 focused on African American English and the extent to which culture influences language and student achievement, Chapter 13 discusses the impact of culture and second-language learning of English in terms of dual-language systems and student achievement.

The upcoming chapter investigates bilingualism, stages of second-language learning, principles and practices for effective teaching of second-language learners, and conferencing with parents and other professionals to provide support to second-language learners. These strategies are useful for classroom application.

Familiarity with the growing number of language differences found in classrooms in the United States is essential to support these children's language and learning abilities to enhance their academic achievement and positively address and narrow the achievement gap.

KEY WORDS

Appalachian dialects	Griot	Socially marked dialect
Bidialectism	Language variation	Topic-associating narratives
Code-switch	Mismatch hypothesis	Topic-centered narratives
Density of dialect use	Performative narrative	

STUDY QUESTIONS

1. Describe at least three main differences between topic-associating and topic-centered narratives.

2. Describe the differences between high- and low-density AAE speakers.

3. Describe the implications of literacy development for AAE-speaking children.

4. Explain the importance for classroom teachers to understand AAE. How would you explain the language patterns associated with AAE to other classroom teachers to help them understand that this is not a disorder?

5. Explain code-switching. Describe the relationship between AAE and academic skills. Observe a classroom and note instances of code-switching that occur.

6. Create an assignment that uses a contrastive approach to help students learn to use MCE.

7. Describe the creation of an activity that encourages your students to use a variety of oral narrative styles.

PROJECTS

1. Collect spontaneous writing samples from the African American students in your class. Identify the examples of AAE used by these students in their writing. In particular, pay attention to *errors* that are developmental and demonstrate emerging writing skills and try to distinguish these from the *differences* that characterize AAE.

2. Select three to five AAE features described in this chapter. Observe your students interacting with one another in the classroom or on the playground. Listen for the features that you have chosen

from the list and write them down when you hear them. Use this activity periodically to increase your sensitivity to language forms that are dialectal.

3. Audiotape the oral narratives of a focal student each week. You should record stories told to the entire class and peers. Ask the student to transcribe his or her narratives. Together with the student, decide whether the narratives are topic-centered, topic-associating, performative, or some combination. Use this activity to help students develop a repertoire of narrative skills.

STUDENT STUDY SITE

Visit the Student Study Site at **www.sagepub.com/levey** for these additional learning tools:

- Video Links
- Self Quizzes
- E-Flashcards
- Sample Forms and Assessment Tools
- Recommended Readings
- Web Resources

SUGGESTIONS FOR FURTHER READING

Champion, T. B. (2003). *Understanding storytelling among African American children: A journey from Africa to America.* Mahwah, NJ: Erlbaum.

Craig, H. K., & Washington, J. A. (2006). *Malik goes to school: Examining the language skills of African American students from preschool–5th grade.* Mahwah, NJ: Erlbaum.

Delpit, L. (2006). *Other people's children: Cultural conflict in the classroom* (Rev. ed.). New York: New Press.

Gee, J. P. (2009). "Decontextualized language" and the problem of school failure. In C. Compton-Lilly (Ed.), *Breaking the silence: Recognizing the social and cultural resources students bring to the classroom.* Newark, DE: International Reading Association.

Washington, J. A., & Thomas-Tate, S. (2009). How research informs cultural-linguistic differences in the classroom: The bidialectal African American child. In S. Rosenfield & V. W. Berninger (Eds.), *Implementing evidence-based academic interventions in school settings* (pp. 147–164). London: Oxford University Press.

C H A P T E R   1 3

Bilingual Language Acquisition and Learning

Henriette W. Langdon

Case Study: Learning English as a second language

Clara is a 5-year-old attending a monolingual kindergarten in New York. This is Clara's first experience in school, as she had no preschool experience in Puerto Rico. Clara's teacher contacted her parents after 3 months because Clara does not speak to any children, even those who are Spanish speakers. She also appears to have some difficulty listening in the classroom, attending more to off-task noises and movements of the other children than to the teacher. She completes written work, such as writing her name, copying words, coloring, and completing crafts projects, with no reminders. Her play skills are adequate, and she occasionally joins other children to play ball and use the swings during recess, although, even in these situations, her interaction with others is minimal. Clara and her family emigrated 1 year ago from a rural area of Puerto Rico, and Spanish is the main language spoken in the home. Her parents completed elementary school and both worked in farming in their homeland. The family came to join some relatives who have been living in New York for more than 10 years.

What can Clara's teacher do to help her become more fluent in English, increase her attention and listening skills, and interact more in class with the other children? On what information and experiences did you base your answer?

INTRODUCTION

There are as many as 6,912 different languages spoken in the world (Gordon, 2005). Of the people living on this planet, 5 billion speak 30 of these languages, while 1.5 billion others speak 6,888 of these languages. Accelerated migration from country to country for political or social issues in the past half century makes it certain that many individuals have been exposed to more than one language or culture. In fact, 300 different languages are spoken in the United States, 820 in New Guinea, 297 in Mexico, and 145 in Canada.

The United States is home to 5 million children who attend K–12 programs and whose primary language is one other than English. These children are frequently termed **English-language learners**. The language most commonly spoken by these students is Spanish (79%), followed by Vietnamese (2.9%). Other languages spoken by children in the United States are Hmong (1.8%), Korean (1.2%), Arabic (1.2%), Haitian Creole (1.1%), and Cantonese (1%). Another 100 languages are spoken by less than 1% of children in this country (Office of English Language Acquisition, 2002). Each language has its own structure and rules, and each speaker has an individual language-learning history that includes using his or her first language and acquiring English.

The United States is home to 5 million children whose first language is not English.

The classroom teacher must understand the process of learning English as a second language and the factors that are associated with this process: the length of exposure to English, the type of exposure to English, the level of development of the child's first language, and the motivation for learning a second language. These are the factors that the classroom teacher must consider to determine whether the child is experiencing typical problems related to learning a second language or if the child has a language disorder.

The purpose of this chapter is to enable teachers to differentiate a language *disorder* from a language *difference* when working with children who are learning a second language. In this chapter, L1 (first language) refers to the child's native, dominant language spoken in the home and L2 (second language) refers to English.

DEFINITIONS OF BILINGUALISM AND RELATED TERMS

There are several terms associated with L2 learning: *bilingual*, **bilingualism**, **primary** or **dominant language**, *language proficiency*, *learning* a language versus *acquiring* a language, and *language dominance*, as well as *bilingual programs*. The term *bilingual* is defined, by some, as the ability to communicate orally and in writing in more than one language and, by others, to include the ability to communicate about a variety of topics. *English-language learner* is also a term that has been used to designate a category of bilinguals (Langdon, 2008; Roseberry-McKibbin, 2008).

There are also terms that refer to the age of L2 learning. For example, children who acquire two languages prior to age 3 are referred to as *simultaneous bilingual learners*, as they are acquiring both L1 and L2 simultaneously. Children who acquire two languages after that age are referred to as *sequential bilingual learners*, as they are learning these two languages in sequence (i.e., first L1, then L2). These terms do not define the individual's level of proficiency, as a student might be more proficient in speaking about certain topics in one of the two languages but more proficient in writing in the other language due to more experience in that language.

In very few cases, bilingual (or multilingual) individuals display a balanced competence in all their languages (Baker, 2006; Baker & Prys Jones, 1998; Bialystok, 2001). In terms of competence, Kohnert's (2009) definition of *bilingual* is operational and practical: Bilinguals can be defined as individuals who have systematic experience with two or more languages to meet present or future communication needs.

One important consideration is the distinction between how a language is learned. Learning a language implies a conscious process, which takes places in a classroom. Acquiring a language implies a more naturalistic process in all contexts (e.g., home, play, and school) that includes communicating with parents, family members, and friends (Krashen, 1981). To summarize this difference, the acquisition of a language is defined by the natural development of a language as opposed to the intentional learning of that language.

Terms such as **proficiency** and **dominance** are commonly used to quantify and qualify the level of mastery of the first or second language. Proficiency refers to the degree of mastery of the individual's linguistic ability for listening, understanding, speaking, reading, and writing. Dominance indicates which language (or languages) is (are) mastered with greater competency. For example, which language (L1 or L2) is stronger?

Because the first language is spoken in the home, it is not uncommon for students who are learning a second language at school to be more familiar with terms related to the home, such as utensils or furniture. Thus, expecting equivalent knowledge of vocabulary or competence across two languages may not be a realistic goal when working with L2 learners. No single test or series of tests can capture all the elements of the concepts of proficiency or dominance.

Other concepts related to the interaction between two or more languages include *code-switching* and *language loss* when discussing issues regarding bilingualism. In bilinguals, **code-switching** is a common phenomenon. It consists of using a word, phrase, or sentence from one language while communicating in the other language. Language loss occurs when someone loses proficiency in a language. There are many causes of this phenomenon, such as loss of exposure to and practice of the first language (Anderson, 2004).

Both code-switching and language loss should be considered in deciding whether a student has a language difference or a language disorder in the L1 or L2. An important first step is to evaluate the student's communicative proficiency in both L1 and L2.

STAGES OF SECOND-LANGUAGE LEARNING

The learning of an L2 develops in stages. Five stages of L2 development have been identified and are briefly described below (Krashen & Terrell, 1983). Even though these stages were first described almost 3 decades ago, they are still referred to in the current research literature.

Stage I: The Silent/Receptive or Preproduction Stage

During this period, the learner has a vocabulary of about 500 words. This period may last from the beginning of exposure to the language to 6 months after first exposure. During this time, the child may not say much, which is why it is referred to as the "silent period." This silence is natural, as the child is not yet comfortable taking risks to produce words or sentences in the new language.

This stage has implications for Clara, the student we met in the case study at the beginning of the chapter. Clara's teacher has already contacted her parents after 3 months. Should her teacher wait another 3 months to see if Clara can progress beyond Stage I before considering other options?

Stage II: The Early Production Stage

This period may last for another half a year. During this stage, the learner may communicate with one- or two-word phrases and understands a number of different questions: yes/no, either/or, and who/what/where questions.

Stage III: The Speech Emergence Stage

This stage can be one more year. During this time, the learner can use short phrases and simple sentences to communicate. In addition, the learner can engage in dialogues and may use longer sentences, but errors may be evident.

Stage IV: The Intermediate Language Proficiency Stage

This stage lasts another year, and the student may use more complex sentences but may still need to ask for clarification.

Stage V: The Advanced Language Proficiency Stage

During this stage, learners are using specific vocabulary and can participate successfully in the classroom. This stage lasts 3 to 5 years.

What is most important to understand is that it may take an L2 learner at least 3 years to become proficient in the new language. In the next section, we present a framework for understanding communicative proficiency.

A FRAMEWORK OF COMMUNICATIVE PROFICIENCY

Cummins (1981, 1984, 1989, 2008) proposed a model to differentiate two types of language proficiency: (a) the language proficiency noted in a context-embedded, face-to-face situation, referred to as **basic interpersonal communicative skills (BICS),** and (b) the language proficiency acquired in a context-reduced (academic) situation, which is referred to as **cognitive academic language proficiency (CALP).**

BICS refers to the language skills needed for social interaction on the playground and school bus, along with playing sports and talking on the telephone. Consequently, these contexts are less cognitively demanding. CALP refers to formal academic learning that requires the language abilities to listen, understand, read, and write in the context of classroom material requirements. These contexts are cognitively demanding. These concepts are demonstrated in the following examples:

BICS: "Open your books to page 5." (Less complex)

CALP: "Explain the character's motivation in the story we just read." (More complex)

L2 learners usually acquire BICS within 2 years of contact with the second language, while they may require 5 to 7 years of exposure before CALP is achieved. Although it may take an L2 learner up to 5 years to catch up to the level of a monolingual peer's academic performance, the school team does not have to wait this long to determine if an individual is experiencing a language problem. Thus, early intervention may be initiated in the presence of a genuine language disorder.

The difference between BICS and CALP can be applied to the case study presented at the beginning of this chapter. For example, Clara and her family have been in the United States for only 1 year. Consequently, she may be in the process of achieving BICS.

BILINGUAL PROGRAMS

The term *bilingual program* designates different types of academic programs that vary in scope and practice for teaching and using (a) two languages or (b) only English. The scope of programs range from not offering any support for their L2-learning students (**submersion**) to two-way bilingual programs in which speakers of both languages are learning together (also referred to as **dual immersion** or **two-way immersion**).

Between these models, transitional programs offer instruction in the two languages for 2 or 3 years, with initial emphasis on the first language. Students are dismissed once they attain sufficient proficiency to learn in an English-only classroom. No further instruction or support is offered for children's first language after that time.

Developmental bilingual programs are geared to prepare students to become bilingual and biliterate (Brisk, 2005; Herrera & Murry, 2005). These programs are composed of the following models: the **Specifically Designed Academic Instruction in English (SDAIE),** the **Sheltered Instruction Observation Protocol (SIOP)**, and the **Cognitive Academic Language Learning Approach (CALLA)** (Reed & Railsback, 2003). These instructional approaches are employed in bilingual classrooms and are also utilized by mainstream teachers.

The SDAIE approach consists of teaching content subjects in English while ensuring that the language used is comprehensible to the student in lesson plans following the SDAIE model. Some of the features of the SDAIE model are as follows:

- Teacher models

- Focusing on engaging the children's interest

- Teaching of vocabulary, idioms, and double meaning (e.g., *red/read*)

- Slow speech rate and clear articulation

- Gestures and facial expressions
- Writing and listening

The SIOP model was created by observing guidelines and standards for L2-acquisition programs in the United States (Echevarría, Vogt, & Short, 2004). The SIOP model is similar to the SDAIE model. This model focuses on providing strategies and pedagogical tools for classroom teachers. The key features of the SIOP model include the following:

- Lesson preparation
- Strategies
- Interaction
- Practice/application
- Lesson delivery
- Review/assessment

Finally, the CALLA model follows four foundational beliefs: active learners learn best, students can self-identify the most effective learning strategies for themselves, strategy instruction is more effective for academic learning, and strategy training can help facilitate transfer of learning to new tasks. CALLA is organized around five phases of instruction: preparation, presentation, practice, evaluation, and expansion. Ongoing assessment is used in each phase to help continuously plan appropriate instruction (Herrera & Murry, 2005).

The classroom teacher must understand the process of learning English as a second language and the factors that are associated with this process.

ASSESSING SECOND-LANGUAGE DEVELOPMENT

It is important for teachers to determine the stage of their students' second-language development. Krashen (1981) states that students should be exposed to situations in which they can comprehend what they hear while being challenged to continue developing their linguistic skills. For example, if a student can understand and respond to "what-doing" questions, they are challenged to provide a reason for an action. A typical session may ask, "What is the lady doing?" If she is buying fruit, the student may respond that she is using the fruit to make a salad or that she wants to keep it for a snack.

Before any intervention can be planned, assessment of the student's oral and written language in his or her first and second languages needs to be completed, along with a history of his or her educational background. Collaboration of parents and classroom teachers is critical. This is because parents can provide additional information about a student's progress over time (Gutiérrez-Clellen & Kreiter, 2003; Langdon, 2008; Restrepo, 1998; Roseberry-McKibbin, 2008).

To see more information on Obtaining Language and Schooling History, go to **www .sagepub .com/levey.**

Information is collected to determine which language might be dominant for which specific tasks. Using a three-tiered approach, as found in the next section ("Response to Intervention"), school personnel are able to assess, intervene, and document each student's progress in the least restrictive environment (American Speech-Language-Hearing Association, 2009). To determine the best approach to children's language and learning abilities, we will next review the **Response to Intervention (RtI)** approach.

RESPONSE TO INTERVENTION

In the past, an L2-learning student who was experiencing difficulties received some accommodations in the general-education classroom, with or without direct consultation from specialized personnel such as a **speech-language pathologist (SLP)**, **special educator**, **adaptive physical educator (APE),** or other specialist. Progress was not always consistently documented, and referral for full testing was one of the more consistent solutions to the student's learning problem.

The RtI model challenges pullout service, allowing the mainstream and L2-learning student to receive more quality instruction in the classroom with timely interventions. RtI is a systematic model that blends general-education and special-education approaches, emphasizing the importance of good instruction over time and documenting its efficacy via curriculum-based measurement.

RtI was created as a prereferral procedure to intervene before students met with failure. Not only do students receive tailored support, but frequent assessment is required to document progress. Only when the most appropriate, research-based interventions are used and progress is not evident can a referral for full evaluation to the Child Study Team go forward.

RtI was the answer to over-referral of students for special-education evaluation. The accountability component of RtI is what makes this approach different from previously used models of prereferral intervention. RtI consists of three tiers (National Association of School Psychologists [NASP], 2007).

Tier 1: High-Quality Instructional and Behavioral Supports for All Students in General Education

Research-based, quality education using ongoing universal screening, progress monitoring, and assessment to design instruction is provided to all students in the general-education setting.

The basis of RtI is the delivery of high-quality instruction by a qualified teacher using evidence-based instruction in the general-education setting. Teachers should implement a variety of research-supported teaching methods and approaches. Teachers of culturally and linguistically diverse students should use teaching methods and approaches that are research-supported for these populations and should receive the training they need to be qualified teachers of diverse students. (NASP, 2007, p. 3)

Tier 2: Targeted Supplemental Services for Students Whose Performance and Rate of Progress Are Below What Is Expected for Their Grade and Educational Setting

Based on comprehensive evaluation, interventions are provided to students with intensive needs.

Identified students receive additional strategies and supports that are provided by general- and special-education teachers, and support services. . . . Further outcomes on critical achievement variables are monitored to determine the degree of responsiveness. Judgments of degree of responsiveness take the student's cultural and/or linguistic diversity into account. Lack of progress at this point indicates the need for intensive instruction and supports. . . . For students with cultural and/or linguistic diversity, lack of satisfactory progress may not constitute a learning disability if the language of Tier 2 services was not accessible for the student or if the services were inappropriate for the student's culture. (NASP, 2007, pp. 3–4)

Tier 3: Intensive, Individualized Intervention That Has Been Designed Based on Comprehensive Evaluation Data From Multiple Sources

Students who are indentified as at-risk or who fail to make adequate progress in general education receive interventions. At this level, there is a "clear need for more intensive, specialized services, [and] a special education evaluation is usually conducted" (NASP, 2007, pp. 4–5). For all students, including L2 learners, the evaluation should include assessments in various academic and language areas, including input and observations from parents and teachers involved in the education of the student. In deciding eligibility for special education, the team must determine if instruction was adequate and if interventions and assessments were culturally sensitive.

APPLICATION OF THE RTI MODEL TO LANGUAGE INTERVENTION

Each student presents with a specific set of needs and level of performance with respect to his or her L1 and L2. In applying the RtI model, the recommendations need to be made very carefully, as there are differences from case to case depending on the age of the student and his or her own language and experience history. Some illustrations of how the RtI model can be applied to different student needs follow:

- Parents report that their child had delayed language development in the L1. This will result in a possible slower rate of development of the L2. This does not mean that the child has a learning difficulty or that he or she might not be able to acquire two languages. However, this may mean that the child may need more time provided via Tier 1 to reach criterion on any given task.

- Parents report a significant medical history, such as multiple ear infections at a young age. This may result in delayed language development in the L1 and indicate that this child needs special instruction and accommodations, beginning with interventions at Tier 2 rather than Tier 1.

- Teachers and parents report that the student has had more difficulty than siblings and/or peers in keeping up with language and academic learning, even in the L1. In this case, beginning interventions suggested for Tier 2 would be more appropriate.

- Parents report that the child has moved a great deal from school to school due to economic hardships. Recommendations for Tier 1 would be preferable before proceeding to Tier 2.

RtI recommends types of intervention and specific instructional approaches. The adequacy of instruction is a critical concern when evaluating the performance of L2-learning students. Whether these students had the most appropriate instruction in L2 acquisition based on their current level of language function is a serious concern. This is because general education teachers, for the most part, have not experienced sufficient professional development in evidence-based best practices in assessment and instruction of L2-learning students. To help you achieve better understanding of these practices, the next section details principles for professional development that promote positive L2 learning and how these principles guide best practices.

PRINCIPLES FOR PROMOTING POSITIVE SECOND-LANGUAGE LEARNING

Crockett (2004) described five effective principles for promoting positive L2 learning, not only for higher achieving students but also for those who may experience a learning difficulty. First, teachers should identify the elements that need to be learned and demonstrate these elements with examples. Second, teachers should provide students with strategies and multiple opportunities to apply those strategies. One approach is to have the students participate in small-group interactions. This may provide the opportunity for some L2 learners to interact as tutors. The small-group interactions also enable teachers and students to offer ongoing feedback on skill development. Third, activities presented to students should be meaningful and relevant. Fourth, students with reading and writing difficulties may benefit from explicit instruction in word decoding and spelling. Fifth, all students benefit from the effective instruction provided to students with language-learning disabilities. Examples of these strategies are presented in the following sections.

Increase Comprehensibility

Students benefit from content that is supplemented with pictures, along with objects, demonstrations, gesture and intonation cues, or peer tutoring techniques. Activate schema (e.g., ideas, mental images, and associated meanings) and preteach key vocabulary (vocabulary to be used in lengthier texts). The use of choral responses with other students can also help increase comprehension.

Increase Interaction

Structure cooperative learning opportunities in which students learn to use language to achieve goals to complete a given project. Selecting children for each group who can support the L2 learner and work effectively from a technical standpoint is key.

Increase Thinking/Study Skills

Teachers can engineer activities that ask higher-order thought questions (e.g., "What would happen if . . . ?"). Teachers can also model "thought language" by thinking aloud (e.g., "What did he or she *think, believe*?"). In other words, teachers can explicitly teach and reinforce study skills.

Use Student's Native Language to Increase Comprehensibility

Using verbal rehearsal in a student's native language to support L2-acquisition goals can help with recall. Verbal rehearsal can be done in both the child's first and second language, strengthening the connections in both language systems.

Total Physical Response

The total physical response (TPR) method was developed in the 1960s as a language-learning tool based on the relationship between language and its physical representation or execution (Asher, 1966, 1969, 1972, 2000). TPR emphasizes the use of physical activity to increase meaningful learning opportunities and language retention. A TPR lesson involves a detailed series of consecutive actions accompanied by a series of commands or instructions given by the teacher. Students respond by listening and performing the appropriate actions. This method needs to be adapted to students' level of English-language skills. TPR is an especially good technique for L2-learning students in Stage I, since it does not rely on oral production.

Language Experience Approach

The language experience approach is also known as the dictated stories approach (Carrasquillo & Rodríguez, 2002). The student dictates a personal experience to a teacher or aide. Subsequently, the student uses the text that has been dictated as reading material. This is a very effective strategy not only for addressing L2 fluency but also for increasing reading and vocabulary skills.

Dialogue Journals

The dialogue journals approach is also known as the interactive journals approach. A written dialogue between teacher and student that mirrors everyday communication is a powerful way to develop communication skills. The teacher does not evaluate the form of the student's written skills. Instead, the teacher focuses on the intent (meaning) of the student's communication effort.

Many of the strategies suggested in this section would be appropriate for the teacher in the case study presented at the beginning of this chapter. In the next section, we present more specific strategies that have been utilized in teaching content material to L2-learning students. We selected these strategies because they should be incorporated in every classroom where there are children learning English.

The classroom can be structured to enable students to interact cooperatively with one another and with the teacher.

SPECIFIC STRATEGIES FOR TEACHING CONTENT MATERIAL

The seven strategies listed below are those most frequently mentioned by researchers as being useful for instructing L2-learning students. These strategies are (1) use of a thematic approach, (2) explicit teaching of learning strategies, (3) use of various media, (4) incorporation of the students' experiences in the learning process, (5) vocabulary building, (6) teacher discourse, and (7) **scaffolding**.

Use of a Thematic Approach

In this approach, a consistent theme is used to reinforce a topic throughout the curriculum to develop growth in oral and written language skills (Beaumont, 1992). For example, if a curriculum's goal is to examine the formation of clouds and rain, the topic can be addressed through the selection of an appropriate book that describes this process. Next, words connected to the formation of clouds and rain can be listed, followed by the definition of each word. In social studies, students can apply concepts by interpreting a weather map or by following weather in other cities.

Farr and Quintanar-Sarellana (2005) indicate that thematic instruction has an effect on motivation, engagement, and sense of purpose. They argue that encouraging students to work together on projects develops their language skills through asking questions, solving problems, negotiating, and interacting with peers.

Explicit Teaching of Learning Strategies

In this model, specific instruction about the material to be learned is provided in terms of the "why and how" of events in the classroom. Prior to initiating a unit, a discussion about what the students already know about the material takes place and points to be covered in the classroom session are written on the board. Before reading a textbook, students are taught to preview the text by examining chapter headings and subheadings, diagrams, and pictures, along with discussing the text's content. Students are assisted in learning to tap metacognitive and cognitive understanding achieved through awareness, reflection, and interaction. A graphic organizer (referred to as a K-W-L Chart) can be created that lists what students already know about the topic (K), what they want to learn based on the chapter preview (W), and then—after concluding the chapter—what they did learn (L). (For more information on explicit teaching of learning strategies, see Duffy, 2002; Facella, Rampino, & Shea, 2005; and Savaria-Shore & Garcia, 1995.)

Utilization of Media

Teacher Robin Liten-Tejada, featured in the video *Profile of Effective Teaching in a Multilingual Classroom* (Silver, 1995), enhances her students' ability to use and demonstrate their knowledge through sociodramatic play and other media such as art. Sociodramatic play is also helpful for school-age children who need practice in the pragmatic aspects of language, such as making requests, being specific, and repairing communication breakdowns.

Ruíz (1988) noted a significant improvement in special-education students' oral language skills when sociodramatic play was used, in comparison with their performance in more structured academic tasks. As children discussed key elements of their play (e.g., scene, actors, and props), their ability to negotiate meaning improved. The negotiation process may require the use of particular language structures, such as turn taking, convention, and message repair (Beaumont, 1992).

Incorporation of Student's Experience in the Learning Process

In this approach, the focus is on engaging students in bridging academic content with their experiences and culture. Not only cultural content can be tapped in this approach but also culturally based modes of learning and communication (Doherty, Hilberg, Pinal, & Tharp, 2003; Farr & Quintanar-Sarellana, 2005). This method enables the student to learn to recognize words already in his or her speaking vocabulary but not yet in his or her reading vocabulary. Similarly, dictated stories can be used to help the student connect his or her experiences with a reading lesson (Carrasquillo & Rodríguez, 2002).

Vocabulary Building

To assist students in expanding their vocabulary, the weekly vocabulary list should be linked to the content that is being taught. Echevarría et al. (2004) provide suggestions for increasing knowledge of vocabulary, such as clarifying the meaning of a word by offering a synonym or cognate.

In Liten-Tejada's video (Silver, 1995), she asks students to remember a word (*creek*) that they learned the previous week. They are then asked to connect it to a newly learned word (*stream*). Students can be encouraged to create dictionaries and develop a "word wall" using the relevant vocabulary from a given lesson.

TEACHER DISCOURSE AND TEACHING STYLE

At the heart of all instruction is the teacher's style of content delivery. Langdon (1989, 2008) and Short (1991) argue for collaboration between SLPs and teachers to provide students with discourse and interaction strategies such as the ones that follow:

- Speak more slowly and enunciate clearly.

- Emphasize important words and use body language when needing to make a point.

- Use students' names instead of pronouns.

- Clarify the meaning of unfamiliar words; if a student does not understand something, rephrase what you said using simpler syntax. Ask the student to rephrase what he or she understood to ensure that the information was correctly comprehended.

- Use visuals (e.g., pictures, videos, real objects) to increase comprehension of ideas and concepts.

- Do not "correct" students, but focus on meaning with respect to both receptive and expressive language. Model conversations during the student-to-student or student-to-teacher interaction.

- Allow for additional wait time to enable the student to process and formulate an answer.

SCAFFOLDING

Scaffolding is an instructional strategy to facilitate the students' acquisition of skills. The goal is to ensure that the student can learn new material more independently and is consistent with the **zone of proximal development (ZPD)** described by Vygotsky (1962). (See Chapter 2 for a full discussion of this model.)

The scaffolds are used to move the student from his or her current level of skills to the level of the classroom target skills. This can be done with models from more advanced peers through group projects. The next section provides additional strategies to advance the student's skills within these group-learning contexts.

STRUCTURING THE CLASSROOM

The classroom should be structured to enable students to interact cooperatively with one other and with the teacher (Calderón, 2001; Kagan, 1994; Slavin, 1995). Cooperative learning activities offer students the opportunity to listen, negotiate turn-taking rules, ask questions, clarify information, repair miscommunications, initiate and maintain topics, change roles, explain, persuade, record, summarize, and apply social skill conventions when joining and taking leave of a group. For Clara, our case study student, cooperative groups for games and projects would foster opportunities for increased interactions and for language learning from peers.

After working in small groups, students can conduct a debriefing session to evaluate both the product and the process followed. This debriefing assists them in developing functional communication skills and metalinguistic awareness. The group work provides experience in highly contextualized here-and-now activities that are more frequently associated with home cultures. It also enhances practice in school language skills, such as planning and reflecting.

The information presented in this section has outlined the best strategies suggested by researchers and teachers for teaching L2-learning students. The most important main points are to consider the learners' (and their families') experiences with teaching and learning processes in their home culture or country, consider that L2 learning develops in various stages, and consider the warning signs of language-learning problems. The RtI model also requires an ongoing record of student performance so that progress (or lack of progress) can be clearly documented. We next review language proficiency tests.

LANGUAGE PROFICIENCY TESTS

The most commonly used assessments for L2-learning students are known as language proficiency tests. The purpose of each proficiency test is to classify the English-language learner's language proficiency skills into five different levels, which range from "nonspeaker" to "fluent speaker," and to provide more appropriate language instruction to the learner. What is assessed in tests is mostly oral and written grammar, syntax, story retelling, and vocabulary but it is not related to ability to learn new academic material in a second language.

More recent tests, created by various states, are available only in English. For example, the California English Language Development Test, first implemented in 2001, assesses English listening, speaking, reading, and writing abilities. This test was created to determine the proficiency of L2-learning students in each of the four language areas. Specific standards are listed for each curriculum area and at five levels of proficiency: beginning, early intermediate, intermediate, early advanced, and advanced. Exit criteria for each level are also delineated for each one of the language areas (listening, speaking, reading, and writing).

Many of the proficiency tests were developed to provide quick measures of these students' proficiency. This tends to sacrifice the accuracy of the results; therefore, the outcomes may be available only as guides for placement, and they do not offer practical suggestions for the teacher. Consequently, classroom teachers need to supplement these statewide language tests with a performance-based instrument that they can use on a regular basis to document their students' growth and development in English (Kuhlman, 2005). For a listing and brief review of each of the proficiency tests that are commonly used, see Langdon and Cheng (2002) and Langdon (2008).

This chapter has provided some foundational knowledge about English-language learners, how a second language is learned, and how best to teach and assess these students. Let's see how the text material has shaped your recommendations for Clara, the student presented in the case study at the beginning of this chapter.

CASE STUDY REVISITED

Clara is the 5-year-old child from a Spanish-speaking family residing in New York whose kindergarten teacher is concerned about her lack of verbal participation in both English and Spanish. The best way to proceed is to have a parent conference and obtain information about her language development using Table 13.1. The following questions would assist in determining if Clara might have difficulty developing English and learning skills.

- Do the parents note any problems in communicating with her in Spanish? If yes, describe the nature of the problem. If she was delayed in developing language in Spanish, what is the status of her communication skills at the present time? If there are concerns, a screening in Spanish may be warranted. If no problems are noted, then we know that her Spanish skills are likely to be intact.

- Did Clara suffer from any ear infections or problems? If the answer is positive, was this a chronic problem? What is the hearing status at this time? If unsure, recommend a hearing screening or more in-depth audiological assessment.

- Does Clara play with other children in her neighborhood? If the answer is no, ask the reason. For example, if parents report that Clara does not engage in play with other children, this behavior may stem from lack of experience in interacting with peers. Recall that this is the first time that Clara is attending a school program.

Case Study Revisited: **Learning English as a second language**

A family conference with parents that addresses these questions was initiated to help determine the action to take. Clara was also given time to get used to the school atmosphere and to instruction in an English-only environment. Her teacher remembered that it was not unusual for children to be silent for a while when learning L2. In addition, the teacher ensured that the information presented in the school environment was comprehensible to Clara and to other children who are learning English. Clara was also grouped with other children to complete projects. The teacher considered the academic traits possessed by the other children that would support Clara's needs. During this interaction, she was encouraged to respond by using means other than verbal when verbal communication presented her with difficulty. In the meantime, her parents were advised to continue to dialogue with her in Spanish, along with increasing her vocabulary skills by providing labels for objects and actions. Several studies have demonstrated that concepts learned in one language can be readily transferred to another language (Oldin, 1989, 2005).

After 3 months, the school team and Clara's parents reconvened to review her language and school progress. The teacher noted that Clara had begun to be more comfortable in dialoguing with the other children in Spanish, but many of her peers made fun of her because she could not pronounce the /r/ sounds, as in *pera* and *rosa*, and had difficulty producing the /l/ sound. She also pronounces her name incorrectly, saying "Claa." Clara's parents had thought that this was normal for children her age. They discussed the recommendation for referral for speech-language intervention. The teacher has noted that Clara is now able to answer yes/no questions in English and she is intermittently using one- to two-word phrases. The latter is commensurate with Stage II in English-language development.

The team also suggested that Clara be integrated into the bilingual speech-language therapy program for a period of 2 months. In this case, suggestions for intervention would be moved from Tier 1 to Tier 2. Even though the /r/ sounds in Spanish may not be completely developed until age 6 or 7, the sound interfered with intelligibility at times and was a source of ridicule from peers. Parents would participate in the sessions and practice with her at home.

Clara's case illustrates how the school team can proceed when bilingual students are referred. Close collaboration with the classroom teacher is critical. To be effective, team members need to be knowledgeable about bilingual language development and best teaching techniques. In addition, the RtI model, if implemented effectively, is very helpful in offering services that will ultimately contribute to the student becoming a more successful language and academic learner.

SUMMARY

This chapter offered the reader some strategies on how to approach bilingual children when it is unclear whether they are not progressing due to an L2 development issue or because of a possible language-learning disability. This dilemma is not easily solved and requires time and specific knowledge in understanding how individuals develop an L2. Referring bilingual children for evaluation and service is the last step the classroom teacher should resort to after attempting many different strategies within the classroom. The very purpose of this text is to reinforce the notion that there are stages of L2 acquisition that may take varying lengths of time for each child.

This text does not maintain that L2 learners should typically be referred for evaluation and classification as special-education students. Rather, this text advocates that each child needs to be served as an individual, ensuring that each child gets what he or she needs. Adopting this perspective moves the question of how best to serve bilingual and/or L2 learners away from a political agenda.

This chapter offered a review of important terms such as *bilingual*, *proficiency*, *dominance*, and *bilingual programming*. In addition, it compared and contrasted types of language proficiency, detailing the difference between basic interpersonal communication skills and cognitive academic language proficiency.

Moreover, this chapter highlighted the differences between a more basic, nonacademic level of communication and the language that is required in a more formal academic setting. A brief review of various stages of L2 development was outlined as well. The chapter continued with a description of the RtI model and some preferred teaching strategies for L2-learning students. Finally, this chapter applied key foundational concepts to a case study of a bilingual child and outlined a process for intervention.

Chapter 14 continues to focus on L2 learners. This next chapter is devoted to describing the characteristics of typical speech development in bilingual children and bilingual children with speech disorders and suggesting evidence-based assessment and intervention approaches that aid in correctly identifying bilingual children in need of intervention.

KEY WORDS

Adaptive physical educator (APE)

Basic interpersonal communication skills (BICS)

Bilingualism

Code-switching

Cognitive Academic Language Learning Approach (CALLA)

Cognitive academic language proficiency (CALP)

Dominance

Dual immersion

English-language learner

Primary or dominant language

Proficiency

Response to Intervention (RtI)

Scaffolding

Sheltered Instruction Observation Protocol (SIOP)

Special educator

Specifically Designed Academic Instruction in English (SDAIE)

Speech-language pathologist (SLP)

Submersion

Two-way immersion

Zone of proximal development (ZPD)

STUDY QUESTIONS

1. Discuss the implications of language proficiency and language dominance in assessing an L2 learner's linguistic and academic performance.

2. Request to participate in an RtI conference discussing the needs of an L2-learning student. What were the issues and how were they resolved? What was similar to or different from the information presented in this chapter?

3. Observe the instruction of a classroom in which the majority of students are L2 learners. Were any of the strategies that were listed in this chapter used? Did you think the teaching methodology was effective? Explain your answers.

4. If you were the classroom teacher, how do you think you could best collaborate with other professionals in your building if you had a student like Clara?

5. List the key concepts and strategies that were new to you in reading through this chapter.

PROJECTS

1. Take and record a sample of a bilingual, Spanish-English preschool or kindergarten child who has been exposed to English for 1 year interacting with a native speaker in each language (English and Spanish). Select similar topics, such as favorite stories or activities, otherwise you will have difference due to the context. Observe vocabulary words that a child uses in both English and Spanish. Bilingual children are sometimes more likely to know colors in English and household items in their home language. Include words from both languages in final vocabulary word counts. Write down what sounds you heard the child use in both Spanish and English, if possible.

2. Observe an SLP working with a bilingual child with a speech problem. Write your observations of the session, answering questions such as "Did the SLP use both languages in therapy or only one?" "Was the child able to respond in both languages?" "How often could you understand the child in each language?" Ask the SLP to share his or her thoughts on providing therapy to a bilingual child.

STUDENT STUDY SITE

Visit the Student Study Site at **www.sagepub.com/levey** for these additional learning tools:

- Video Links
- Self Quizzes
- E-Flashcards
- Sample Forms and Assessment Tools
- Recommended Readings
- Web Resources

SUGGESTIONS FOR FURTHER READING

Bialystok, E. (2001). *Bilingualism in development: Language, literacy, and cognition.* New York: Cambridge University Press.

Genesee, F., Paradis, J., & Crago, M. (2004). *Dual language development and disorders: A handbook on bilingualism and second-language learning.* Baltimore: Paul Brookes.

Kohnert, K. (2008). *Language disorders in bilingual children and adults.* San Diego, CA: Plural.

Langdon, H. W. (2008). *Assessment and intervention for communication disorders in culturally and linguistically diverse populations.* Clifton Park, NY: Cengage.

Roseberry-McKibbin, C. (2008). *Multicultural students with special language needs: Practical strategies for assessment and intervention.* Oceanside, CA: Academic Communication Associates.

Bilingual Speech Sound Development and Disorders

Leah Fabiano-Smith and Brian A. Goldstein

CASE STUDIES: Speech sound development in children learning English as a second language

CASE STUDY 1

Rosario is a 5-year-old, bilingual, Spanish-English–speaking child in Mr. Jones' kindergarten class. Mr. Jones knows that Rosario's older brother is in third grade and speaks English at school. Since Rosario speaks very little English in the classroom, Mr. Jones assumes that Spanish is the only language spoken in the home. Rosario participates in classroom activities but does not communicate much with the other children. She follows directions in English, but Mr. Jones is not sure how much of the academic information Rosario is absorbing. When Rosario speaks in English, she is difficult to understand. What should Mr. Jones do?

CASE STUDY 2

Javier is a 7-year-old, bilingual, Spanish-English–speaking child in Mrs. Clark's first-grade class. Javier has been in an English-only school for almost 2 years. Mrs. Clark has noticed that both she and the other children in the class find it difficult to understand Javier when he speaks in English. Mrs. Clark is not sure what languages are spoken in Javier's family and is concerned that he might not be getting enough exposure to English. Javier seems to be struggling academically as well; his reading and writing skills are not on par with the rest of the children in the class. What should Mrs. Clark do?

Based on your reading of these case studies, what do you think the classroom teachers should do? On what information or experience did you base your answer?

INTRODUCTION

It is estimated that 5.2 million bilingual school-age children live in the United States (National Center for English Language Acquisition and Language Instruction Education Programs, 2005). The growing bilingual population, combined with the relative lack of research in bilingual speech development, leaves teachers with little information when they are concerned if a bilingual child is developing his or her two languages in a typical fashion. As a result, teachers may find it difficult to determine when a bilingual child needs to be referred to the school speech-language pathologist (SLP) for a speech evaluation.

We attempt to address this problem by outlining research that currently exists in the area of bilingual speech development and disorders and applying that research to guidelines for referral to an SLP. The purpose of this chapter is to (1) describe characteristics of typical speech development in bilingual children, (2) describe characteristics of bilingual children with speech disorders, and (3) suggest evidence-based assessment and intervention approaches that aid in correctly identifying bilingual children in need of intervention. We will use examples from Spanish-English bilinguals throughout the chapter; however, the principles explained can be applied to speakers of *any* two languages.

Many children in classrooms are learning English as a second language.

BILINGUALISM

The term *bilingual* is defined by Wei (2001):

> The term "bilingual" primarily describes someone with the possession of two languages. It can, however, also be taken to include the many people in the world who have varying degrees of proficiency in and interchangeably use three, four, or even more languages. (p. 7)

For many years, the view that bilingual children were the exception, rather than the rule, has dominated American society. A number of researchers in the area of **bilingualism** have pointed out that there is a growing number of bilingual speakers (de Groot & Kroll, 1997). More specifically, one in three people worldwide speak two or more languages (Wei, 2001).

As Wei (2001) points out in his definition, the degree of **proficiency** (the level of competence at which an individual is able to use language for both basic communicative tasks and academic purposes) varies from person to person. That is, bilinguals as a population are a heterogeneous group. Bilingual children have different language environments at home, school, and elsewhere (e.g., children who spend the school year in New York and the summer in Puerto Rico) that directly affect their exposure to and proficiency in each language. It is important to acknowledge that within each individual bilingual child, proficiency is not static; a bilingual child's ability to speak both languages changes frequently as the child's language environment changes (Genesee, Paradis, & Crago, 2004).

Changing language environments lead to constant changes in language proficiency. Variability in language proficiency within the bilingual population has important effects on bilingual language development. Information on a bilingual child's language proficiency allows educators to distinguish low proficiency in a language from an actual speech sound disorder. A **speech sound disorder** is defined as impairment in the structure and/or function of the speech and hearing mechanism (Bernthal & Bankson, 2004). However, before teachers can determine if a bilingual child has a speech disorder and requires a referral for speech therapy services, they must first have knowledge of typical speech development in this population.

BILINGUALISM AND TWO SPEECH SOUND SYSTEMS

It is widely accepted in the literature that bilingual children maintain two speech sound systems, one for each language, that periodically interact with each other (Keshavarz & Ingram, 2002; Paradis, 2001; Paradis & Genesee, 1996). According to de Groot and Kroll (1997), "the bilingual mind is not simply the sum of the cognitive processes with each of the two monolingual modes. . . . The two languages of the bilingual may interact with one another" (p. 2).

Very young bilingual children (1 to 2 years of age) who are exposed to two languages from birth are aware of what sounds (e.g., *p, b, t, s, z*) and syllables (i.e., consonant and vowel sound combinations) belong to each of their languages. For example, bilingual Spanish-English–speaking children understand that the Spanish trill *r* sound is specific to Spanish, as in the word *carro* (*car*), and the English approximant *r* sound is specific to English, as in the word *car*. Bilingual children who begin exposure to English in preschool have demonstrated similar characteristics after only a year of exposure to the new language (Fabiano & Goldstein, 2004).

As bilingual children grow, they may use the sounds or syllables from one language in productions of the other, but this occurs rarely (Fabiano & Goldstein, 2005). This demonstration of separation, with a few occurrences of interaction, indicates that bilingual children are not *confused* by the acquisition of two languages; rather, bilingual children appear to maintain a distinction between their speech sound systems early in development while at the same time utilizing interaction to manage the production demands of two speech sound systems.

A number of research studies have provided evidence for the presence of two separate speech sound systems that interact with each other. Most studies have examined **cross-linguistic effects** as evidence for interaction between bilingual children's two speech sound systems (Brulard & Carr, 2003; Johnson & Lancaster, 1998; Keshavarz & Ingram, 2002; Paradis, 2001; Schnitzer & Krasinski, 1996). Cross-linguistic effects occur when sounds, syllables, and stress patterns (i.e., the pattern of prominence given to a particular part of a word) that are specific to one language appear in the child's production of his or her other language (e.g., the trill *r* is specific to Spanish, while the English approximant *r* is specific to English). For example, a bilingual Spanish-English–speaking child may produce the word *carro* using the English *r* instead of the Spanish trill *r*. This constitutes an instance of cross-linguistic effects, because the English-specific sound was used in a Spanish production.

Cross-linguistic effects occur in a bidirectional fashion; both languages influence each other, causing English sounds to be found in Spanish productions and Spanish sounds to be found in English productions (e.g., the English word *rope* could be pronounced with the Spanish trill *r* instead of the English *r*). The findings from studies such as these indicate that the types of cross-linguistic effects cited above are typical in the speech production of bilingual children and are not indications that bilingual children are confused from learning two languages. This research also strongly supports the notion that bilinguals use information from both of their languages in speech production, while maintaining separation for language-specific characteristics (Brulard & Carr, 2003; Goldstein, Fabiano, & Iglesias, 2003; Keshavarz & Ingram, 2002; Paradis, 2001).

Knowledge of the organization of bilingual children's speech sound systems aids our ability to determine if a bilingual child has a speech disorder, because it allows us to distinguish a difference in speech production between monolingual and bilingual children. Due to the influence of one language on the other, bilingual children may sound different than monolingual children. This difference needs to be distinguished from an actual underlying language-learning disorder. If we know how speech sound systems are organized in typically developing bilingual children, it will be clear when a child presents with characteristics that deviate from that norm.

If we know that bilingual children maintain separation between their two speech sound systems, we know that we have to take into consideration the speech skills of bilingual children in *both* of their languages. If we examine only English, we are not including skills that a child possesses in his or her other language. By not considering skills from both languages, teachers and SLPs may either inappropriately refer or diagnose a typically developing child as disordered (overdiagnosis) or fail to diagnose an existing speech sound disorder (underdiagnosis).

Now that we are aware of what bilingual children *know* about their speech sound systems and how that knowledge is organized, we can move to how they *use* that knowledge. Research studies examining speech production in bilingual children are few; however, as educators, we must use the information that is available to determine when to refer bilingual children for a potential speech disorder.

TYPICAL SPEECH DEVELOPMENT IN BILINGUAL CHILDREN

Many studies have compared the speech skills of bilingual children to monolingual speakers of either language (Gildersleeve-Neumann, Kester, Davis, & Peña, 2008; Goldstein & Washington, 2001; Goldstein, Fabiano, & Washington, 2005) and to other bilingual children

(Fabiano-Smith & Barlow, 2009; Goldstein, Fabiano, Gildersleeve-Neumann, & Barlow, 2007). Both types of comparisons tell us important information on speech acquisition in typically developing bilingual children; however, it is especially important to compare bilingual children to other bilingual children in order to avoid either overdiagnosis or underdiagnosis of disorders in this population. Therefore, we will discuss characteristics of typical speech sound acquisition in bilingual children.

As noted in the previous section, it is widely accepted that bilingual children have two separate language systems by a very young age (Kaiser, 1994; Keshavarz & Ingram, 2002; Meisel, 1989) and that they interact with each other (Fabiano, 2006; Fabiano & Goldstein, 2005; Paradis, 2001). To account for the influence of one language on the other in speech production, Paradis and Genesee (1996) proposed two hypotheses about production accuracy in bilingual children: deceleration and acceleration.

Deceleration

The **deceleration hypothesis** predicts that speech sound development in bilingual children is sometimes slower than that of monolingual children and that this is *typical*. Evidence for this hypothesis has been found in studies that have compared bilingual children to monolinguals (e.g., Gildersleeve-Neumann et al., 2008; Swain, 1972; Vihman, 1982).

In one study, Gildersleeve-Neumann et al. (2008) examined the English skills of typically developing, bilingual, English-Spanish–speaking 3-year-olds. The results indicated that the bilingual children were not as easy to understand, made more consonant and vowel errors, and produced more uncommon error patterns than the monolingual English speakers. The bilingual children also exhibited error patterns in both languages that were not exhibited by monolingual English speakers. However, only the bilingual children's English skills were examined.

In another study that examined both languages of bilingual children, Goldstein and Washington (2001) found that despite overwhelming similarity of accuracy (i.e., a match between the child's production and the adult target) between monolingual and bilingual 4-year-olds, the bilingual children were much less accurate than monolingual speakers on some sounds, indicating deceleration in this area.

Fabiano-Smith and Goldstein (2010) examined eight bilingual Spanish-English–speaking 3-year-olds and compared them to their age-matched monolingual peers on sound accuracy. Overall, monolingual children were significantly more accurate than bilingual children in both languages; however, the accuracy level of bilingual children was still within the typical range for their chronological age. In addition, the low accuracy that was driving this significant difference was a result of specific types of sounds (e.g., *s*, *z*, *p*, *b*, and Spanish trill). These specific sounds (i.e., fricatives and trill), however, were difficult sounds for both monolingual and bilingual children.

Therefore, there is some evidence that the rate of acquisition for some skills in bilinguals is slower when compared with their monolingual counterparts. *However,* the accuracy level of bilingual children still falls within the typical range for monolingual speakers of that age. Therefore, we know that at certain times in typical development, bilingual children may demonstrate speech development that is slightly slower than that of monolinguals.

Acceleration

The **acceleration hypothesis** posits that speech skills in bilingual children could emerge earlier than would be the norm for monolingual children of the same age and that this is also typical. That is, it should be expected that bilingual children achieve some speech sound **developmental milestones** before monolingual children. Just as previous studies examining bilingual acquisition have found evidence for deceleration, some studies have found that acceleration may be occurring in bilingual acquisition (Gawlitzek-Maiwald & Tracy, 1994).

In Spanish-German bilingual children, Kehoe, Trujillo, and Lleó (2001) and Lleó, Kuchenbrandt, Kehoe, and Trujillo (2003) found that sounds at the ends of words were produced more frequently in the words of bilinguals than in the productions of monolinguals. This type of result shows that speech sound skills in bilinguals might be accelerated relative to monolinguals.

It is important to note that sometimes one skill can emerge more slowly while another is emerging faster; thus, deceleration and acceleration can occur at the same time on different skills. However, more often in the literature, we find evidence of bilingual speech skills that are *comparable* to monolingual speakers of the same age (De Houwer, 1990; Goldstein et al., 2005; Goldstein & Washington, 2001; Nicoladis, 1994; Padilla & Liebman, 1975).

Goldstein and Washington (2001) examined the English and Spanish skills of typically developing 4-year-old bilingual Spanish-English–speaking children and found that there were no significant differences between the two languages on the accuracy of speech sounds. The results indicated that the overall speech skills of these bilingual 4-years-olds were similar to those of monolingual children.

Goldstein et al. (2005) examined the speech skills of typically developing 5-year-old bilingual Spanish-English–speaking children and compared them with their age-matched monolingual peers. They found no significant difference between bilingual and monolingual children on their speech production skills. These findings demonstrate that even though bilingual children may demonstrate slower development at one point (e.g., at age 3), they will not always demonstrate slower development later (e.g., at age 5).

Paradis and Genesee (1996) define acceleration as a faster rate of acquisition in bilinguals *as compared with* monolinguals; however, it seems that bilinguals are utilizing information between their two languages, resulting in their ability to acquire two languages in the same time period as monolingual children acquire only one. Despite the demand of learning two languages, bilingual children have demonstrated age-appropriate speech skills in both languages when compared with their monolingual peers in many studies, possibly indicating a variation of the hypothesis of acceleration.

Bilingual children possess two separate speech sound systems, one for each language, that interact with each other. This interaction is observed in production in the form of (1) cross-linguistic effects (e.g., a Spanish-English–speaking bilingual child will substitute the *ch-* sound for the *sh-* sound because the *sh-* sound is not found in most dialects of Spanish; so, *she* will be pronounced as "che"), (2) at times a *slower* rate of acquisition when compared with monolinguals (e.g., a bilingual child might not produce the *r-* sound correctly in a word like *red*; whereas a monolingual child would), (3) at times a *faster* rate of acquisition when compared with monolinguals (e.g., a bilingual child might produce the *l-* sound correctly in a word like *lake*; whereas, a monolingual child would not), and (4) at times the *same* rate of acquisition as monolinguals (e.g., bilinguals and monolinguals accurately produce the *s-* sound at the same time). Thus, we know that differences in rate of development when compared with monolingual children are typical in bilingual speech development and are not indicative of a speech disorder.

IMPLICATIONS FOR THE CLASSROOM

The similarities and differences between monolingual and bilingual speakers hold implications for educators: (1) Teachers should not be concerned if bilingual children exhibit cross-linguistic effects in their speech, because they are the result of language interaction, not disorder, and (2) teachers should take into consideration the age of the bilingual child when making referrals because we expect slower development at younger ages and commensurate development with monolinguals as the bilingual child matures. Thus, these findings can be utilized as a foundation for teachers to decide which students require a referral to an SLP and which bilingual children are developing typically.

STRATEGIES TO IDENTIFY BILINGUAL CHILDREN WITH SPEECH DISORDERS

Now that we have established characteristics of typical speech development in bilingual children, we will move on to determining whether or not a bilingual child presents with a speech disorder. Even though only SLPs perform formal and informal speech and language assessments, classroom teachers can use some of these methods to aid in their understanding of a bilingual child's language development. It is important for all educators to know how to distinguish *differences* between monolingual and bilingual children caused by learning one versus two languages from actual underlying language-learning problems, or *disorders*.

Language Proficiency

All educators should have knowledge, typically gained through communication with parents, of each bilingual child's language history. If a parent is not available, either performing an in-depth interview with the child's teachers or examining the child's school records can aid in determining the child's language history. During a parent-teacher conference, teachers could ask parents for information on

- language history (when the child began exposure to each language and if exposure to both languages has been maintained),
- percentage of input in each language (how many hours per week the child *hears* each language), and
- percentage of output in each language (how many hours per week the child *uses* each language).

Ask parents what a typical day is like for their child. For each task, ask what language is heard and used by the child during that task, or if it is a mixture of both.

Remember, how often bilingual children hear and use each language is not static, as language environments change frequently depending on school settings and living situations. Updated information from parents should be obtained on a regular basis to gain knowledge of the child's *current* language environment. If a teacher observes a change in a bilingual child's language skills in the classroom, he or she should check with the child's parents for changes in the language environment in the home before considering a referral.

The issue of proficiency in each language is paramount to educators of bilingual children. Previous work has shown that bilingual children need at least 20% exposure in order to use a language (Pearson, Fernandez, Lewedeg, & Oller, 1997), so teachers want to determine that bilingual children are receiving enough exposure to each language before suspecting that poor language skills are indicative of a disorder. This knowledge will allow us to distinguish low *proficiency* in a language from poor speech skills due to a speech *disorder.*

Some children have not had enough experience with English yet to exhibit good speech skills. Children with low proficiency in English but typical skills in Spanish (or their other language) need support from an English as a second language (ESL) instructor, not from an SLP. These children simply need more experience with English. Children with poor speech skills in *both* languages require the help of an SLP to remediate an underlying language-learning problem, or disorder. This differentiation is critical to avoid overdiagnosis of speech sound disorders. Therefore, the classroom teacher should obtain information on a bilingual child's experience with *both* of his or her languages to make the appropriate referral to either the ESL teacher or the school SLP.

If a bilingual child is referred to an SLP due to a suspected speech disorder, both languages will be examined separately throughout the bilingual assessment. Examination of single-word samples, connected speech samples, and specific language skills, such as utterance length and vocabulary, will occur. If a child has a fundamental problem learning speech and language, it will be apparent across both languages. If only one language is assessed, it is impossible to make the differential diagnosis between (1) disorder and (2) low proficiency in either language. It is possible that some bilingual children with limited proficiency in one language may *appear* disordered (due to low proficiency in that language), but when their other language is assessed, typical skills are found. Without assessing across both languages, overall speech skills might be misinterpreted. Due to the separation that exists between the two speech sound systems of the bilingual child, assessment of both languages is critical to an appropriate differential diagnosis. If both languages are not assessed, bilingual children could be overidentified for speech-language therapy services. By taking into consideration both languages and determining how those languages interact, we can make a reliable and valid diagnosis and determine a child's strengths and weaknesses.

CHARACTERISTICS OF BILINGUAL CHILDREN WITH SPEECH DISORDERS

The way in which an SLP determines whether or not a bilingual child demonstrates a speech sound disorder is based on the same principles we use for monolingual children. The difference between diagnosis of a monolingual child and diagnosis of a bilingual child is that the SLP examines both languages for evidence of a speech sound disorder. The principles commonly used to diagnose a child with a disorder are delayed speech sound development, frequency of error patterns, and uncommon error patterns.

Delayed Speech Sound Development

Typically developing children demonstrate errors in their speech production throughout early speech development. However, when children demonstrate error patterns past the

Bilingual children maintain two speech sound systems that periodically interact with each other.

point in development that is considered typical, this is characteristic of disorder. For example, it is typical for both English- and Spanish-speaking 3-year-olds to omit one of the sounds in a consonant blend (e.g., *train* "tain"). However, if a child is still omitting one of the sounds in a cluster/blend at 6 years old, this is indicative of a speech sound disorder.

Frequency of Error Patterns

As stated in the previous section, typically developing children use error patterns in early speech sound development, and there are a variety of common patterns both English- and Spanish-speaking children use. For example, the patterns of simplifying consonant blends (e.g., *train* → "tain") and replacing more difficult sounds with easier sounds to produce (*ship* → "tip" or *duck* → "kuk") are found in the speech of preschool-age (i.e., 3- and 4-year-olds), typically developing children. However, the high-frequency use of error patterns and its effect on one's ability to understand the child's speech is cause to suspect a speech sound disorder. Additionally, there is cause for concern if the child's speech does not become more understandable over time.

Uncommon Error Patterns

We know that there are typical error patterns in the speech production of young children; however, in addition to those typical error patterns, children with speech sound disorders tend to use uncommon error patterns as well. For example, in both English and Spanish, the frequent deletion of initial consonants in words is characteristic of a speech sound disorder (e.g., *dog* → "og" for English; *sopa* (*soup*) → "opa" for Spanish) as is changing the production of sounds made in the front of the mouth to ones made in the back (*plate* → "plake" for English; *plato* (*plate*) → "plako" for Spanish). The frequency, as well as the type, of error pattern is used to determine the severity of a speech sound disorder. In bilingual children, the frequency and type of errors a child produces are examined across both of their languages.

LANGUAGE PROFICIENCY

From the information stated previously, we know that the first step for classroom teachers is to talk to a child's parents and determine what the language environment is like in the home. In terms of Case Study 1, we know that Rosario's brother speaks English at school, so he most likely uses English at home at times. Thus, we should not assume that the only language spoken in the home is Spanish. Determining what Rosario's language environment is like in the home will help us determine her language proficiency.

Bilingual children may not always *use* a language as much as they are *exposed* to a language (i.e., they may be exposed to two languages but speak primarily in one), so it is important to find out the actual input of each language from their parents. Knowledge of a child's language proficiency helps us decide whether a child requires ESL instruction or requires speech therapy services.

STRATEGIES TEACHERS CAN USE TO HELP BILINGUAL CHILDREN WITH SPEECH DISORDERS

Classroom teachers are extremely important in the identification and referral of children with speech sound disorders. Involving teachers in this process is commensurate with Response to Intervention principles in the following ways.

Just as in the case studies presented, if a teacher suspects there may be a problem with the speech development of a bilingual child in his or her class, the teacher can refer that child for further evaluation by the school's SLP. In addition, classroom teachers can collaborate with the school's SLP on strategies inside and outside the classroom that strengthen speech and language skills. This collaboration can take place before a child who is struggling is diagnosed.

Once the child is diagnosed, the classroom teacher can inform the SLP of topics and assignments being taught in the classroom, and the SLP can, in turn, reinforce those topics in speech-language therapy sessions. The classroom teacher can also work with the SLP on group activities in which the whole class can participate to strengthen speech and language skills.

STRATEGIES TEACHERS CAN USE TO SUPPORT BILINGUAL DEVELOPMENT

There are some strategies that classroom teachers and SLPs can use to support bilingual development. First, encourage a child's parents to speak to their child in the language that is most "natural" to them. Supporting parents in this way will provide a good model for *language* in general, whether it is English or another language. Having a good language model in the home will provide a good foundation for learning a new language in school. In addition, it supports cultural values and connections important for a child's psychosocial and linguistic growth.

Second, teachers and SLPs should allow bilingual children to speak to their bil peers in either of their two languages in the classroom. Often, this allows children to one another comprehend what is occurring in the classroom, thus aiding in their acquis of English. It allows bilingual children to compare what the teacher is explaining in Eng with how that concept is expressed in their native language.

Finally, teachers and SLPs can seek out the help of interpreters when needed, both for interactions that take place within the classroom and with family members during parent conferences. Often, the aid of an interpreter can clarify questions that both the teachers and parents have regarding a child's progress in school and help build a strong home-school connection.

CASE STUDIES REVISITED

Case Study Revisited: Speech sound development in children learning English as a second language

Case Study 1

Mr. Jones knows that Rosario speaks very little English in the classroom and that her English productions are often difficult to understand. He notes that she does participate in activities but does not communicate with the other children during these activities. She appears able to follow directions in English, but he is not sure how much of the academic information she absorbs.

Mr. Jones set up a parent-teacher meeting and found out that before entering kindergarten, Rosario was cared for primarily by her Spanish-speaking grandmother and that both of her parents are Spanish-English bilinguals. Her parents stated that both English and Spanish are spoken in the home. Since Rosario has been in an English-speaking kindergarten class for only 3 months, she is getting accustomed to using English more often. Her parents report that she has started to speak in English with her older brother at home. Thus, Rosario is exposed to both English and Spanish at home, even though she speaks almost exclusively in Spanish at this point in time.

Since Mr. Jones now knows that Rosario lives in a bilingual home but that she has been cared for almost exclusively by a Spanish speaker, he has a better idea as to why Rosario does not use English often and is difficult to understand. He also knows that Rosario has exposure to English at home and is starting to use it with her brother. Therefore, if her English doesn't improve over time, there might be cause for concern (i.e., she is receiving enough exposure to progress in her English proficiency).

Mr. Jones decides to talk to the school's ESL instructor to see if extra instruction in English will improve Rosario's language skills. If her skills do not improve by the end of the school year, Mr. Jones will refer her to the school SLP for further assessment.

Case Study 2

From the information stated previously, we know that the first step for classroom teachers is to talk to the child's parents and determine what the language environment is like in the home.

We know Javier has been exposed to English at school for 2 years, thus, he has experience with English. What his language environment is like in the home, however, is unknown.

Mrs. Clark met with Javier's mother and was told that only Spanish is spoken in the home. She also reported that the people in her family have a difficult time understanding Javier when he speaks in Spanish. She said that he doesn't sound like other Spanish speakers his age and that his speech sounds like that of a much younger child. She has concerns regarding his speech development in Spanish, just as Mrs. Clark has concerns about his speech development in English.

Now that Mrs. Clark knows that there are concerns about Javier's speech development in both languages and that Javier is receiving sufficient exposure in both English (at school) and Spanish (at home), she decides that he might have an underlying language-learning problem. Javier is referred to the school SLP for a full speech and language assessment to determine if he requires intervention for a speech disorder.

These case studies illustrate that teachers fill an important role in determining the needs of the bilingual children in the classroom. The information that teachers obtain through communication with parents and their observation of bilingual children in the classroom allows them to make appropriate referrals. This information, when provided to the SLP on referral, is also very important for assessment and diagnosis of speech disorders.

Teachers should allow bilingual children to speak to their bilingual peers in either of their two languages in the classroom to help one another understand what is being discussed.

SUMMARY

Identifying and treating bilingual children with speech disorders is neither simple nor straightforward. An appropriate referral for speech assessment and diagnosis develops from understanding the organization of the speech sound system in bilingual children. We know that bilingual children maintain two speech systems that interact with each other, resulting in

- acceleration: a more rapid rate of acquisition in bilinguals than monolinguals;

- deceleration: a slower rate of acquisition in bilinguals than monolinguals; and

- cross-linguistic effects: use of sounds in one language not found in the other.

Remember that these effects do not indicate that bilingual children are *confused* by the acquisition of two languages, nor does it signal the presence of a speech disorder.

A referral should be made to the speech-language pathologist for children experiencing speech problems in both languages. After the referral, the results of assessment can be translated into appropriate intervention for children with speech sound disorders or ESL instruction for those children with low language proficiency. Distinguishing language difference from language disorder will keep bilingual children with typical development from being overdiagnosed with speech sound disorders.

Speech-language therapy services can be provided in order to help bilingual children attain age-appropriate speech skills in both languages, making them good communicators in both languages and in all language contexts.

Chapter 14 presented issues related to language and literacy development, with the understanding that disorders are distinct from differences due to variations in cultural and linguistic environments. Chapter 15 is dedicated to preparing classroom teachers to help parents support their children's language and literacy development in the home, from infancy through adolescence. Training parents and engaging them as partners in their children's education is critical to giving every child an opportunity to be successful and can contribute greatly to closing the achievement gap.

KEY WORDS

Acceleration hypothesis	Deceleration hypothesis	Speech sound disorder
Bilingualism	Developmental milestones	
Cross-linguistic effects	Proficiency	

STUDY QUESTIONS

1. What is the definition of *bilingualism*?

2. What is a speech *difference*? What is a speech *disorder*?

3. Why is language proficiency important when deciding whether or not to refer a child for a speech evaluation?

4. What are some characteristics of a speech sound disorder in bilingual children?

5. Why is it important to consider the development of both languages in bilingual children?

PROJECTS

1. Observe a child's speech in both single words and in phrases and sentences. Do this for both English and Spanish. What percentage of the time can you understand him or her in single words? In phrases? In sentences? Is it the same or different for each language?

2. Observe vocabulary words that a child uses in both English and Spanish. Bilingual children are sometimes more likely to know colors in English and household items in their home language. Include words from both languages in final vocabulary word counts. Write down what sounds you heard the child use in both Spanish and English, if possible.

3. Observe an SLP working with a bilingual child with a speech problem. Write up your observations of the session, answering questions such as "Did the SLP use both languages in therapy or only one?" "Was the child able to respond in both languages?" "How often could you understand the child in each language?" Ask the SLP to share his or her thoughts about providing therapy to a bilingual child.

STUDENT STUDY SITE

Visit the Student Study Site at **www.sagepub.com/levey** for these additional learning tools:

- Video Links
- Self Quizzes
- E-Flashcards

- Sample Forms and Assessment Tools
- Recommended Readings
- Web Resources

SUGGESTIONS FOR FURTHER READING

Fabiano, L., & Barlow, J. A. (2009). Interaction in bilingual phonological acquisition: Evidence from phonetic inventories. *International Journal of Bilingual Education and Bilingualism, 6,* 1–17.

Fabiano, L., & Goldstein, B. (2005). Phonological cross-linguistic effects in bilingual Spanish-English speaking children. *Journal of Multilingual Communication Disorders, 3*(1), 56–63.

Fabiano, L., Goldstein, B., & Washington, P. S. (2005). Phonological skills in predominantly English-speaking, predominantly Spanish-speaking, and Spanish-English bilingual children. *Language, Speech, and Hearing Services in Schools, 36,* 201–218.

Goldstein, B. (2004). *Bilingual language development and disorders in Spanish-English speakers.* Baltimore: Paul Brookes.

Kloosterman, V. I. (2003). *Latino students in American schools: Historical and contemporary views.* Westport, CT: Praeger.

CHAPTER 15

Fostering Teacher and Family Partnerships in the Development of Language and Literacy

Susan Polirstok and Jo Hoffman

CASE STUDY: Parents and their impact on language development

Ms. Jones, a first-grade teacher, sits at her desk every morning before school to plan activities and differentiated instruction for her students. She muses about the language differences between two 6-year-old girls from middle-class families in her class. Both girls, Tanisha and Grace, are learning the basics of beginning reading without any apparent difficulties. While both girls appear to be developing literacy skills in typical fashion, Tanisha has better vocabulary and language structures than Grace. Ms. Jones wonders what factors in their early language development contributed to these observable language differences.

What factors in Tanisha's and Grace's early language development could have contributed to the differences observed in vocabulary and language structures? On what information or experiences did you base your answer?

INTRODUCTION

The focus of this chapter is to examine the role of the classroom teacher as a source and a resource for parents to support the language and literacy development of children. This chapter provides teachers with strategies based on the most recent research, along with activities that teachers can suggest that parents use to support the language and literacy development of their children as they grow from infancy to 12th grade.

THE ROLE OF THE TEACHER IN LANGUAGE AND LITERACY DEVELOPMENT

An important part of the teacher's role in children's language and literacy development is to help parents and families discover how virtually every activity can become a language-learning experience through the use of models such as **scaffolding,** a layered approach to the use of individualized supports for learning new concepts.

For teachers to be effective in the role of parent trainer, they must have a thorough knowledge of language development for infants and toddlers through later adolescence. Chapters 7, 8, and 9 of this text examine language and communication skills from a developmental and theoretical perspective for these age groups, comparing typical and atypical language development and providing instructional strategies for use at each developmental age, from infancy through adolescence.

Similarly, Bos and Vaughn (2002) detail strategies teachers can use to increase language skills, especially in those children with learning and behavioral challenges. These strategies include **chunking** (presenting information in understandable chunks) and **generalization** (applying learning in other settings). The teacher also needs to be aware of his or her importance as a language model, vocabulary developer, and director of classroom opportunities for student interaction.

Once this knowledge of language development is in place, teachers can educate parents and families about the importance of talking to children and the fact that books, newspapers, magazines, and other literacy objects and tools (including technology, such as computers) are significant factors in the development of children's communicative abilities. Parents need to understand that their support of language and literacy development provides a strong foundation for academic success over time.

This chapter discusses the role of the family in children's language and literacy development and the role of the teacher as a parent trainer and highlights models of parent and family training that teachers might adopt.

THE ROLE OF THE FAMILY IN EARLY LANGUAGE AND ACADEMIC DEVELOPMENT

The acquisition of language and **communicative competence** (the ability to use the full array of language skills for expression and interpretation) is a function of children's experiences and environment (Copple & Bredekamp, 2009). The family's role in promoting language development is critical, as evidenced in the areas discussed below.

Oral Language

In infancy, parents often speak to their child and encourage "babbling" (see Chapter 7). Interacting with **babbling** (infant's production of a series of connected syllables, such as "bababbababa") actually helps shape the development of real words. During the toddler stage (when children constantly ask "What's that?" or "Why?"), parents can respond to children's questions by providing labels for objects and events in the environment.

Young children's language expands rapidly through their toddler years. Between 18 and 24 months, it is common for children to add 10 or more new words a day to their

Teachers can provide families with suggestions to support their children's language and literacy development.

vocabulary (White & Coleman, 2000), while moving from two-word utterances to three- or more-word sentences by age 3 (Bernstein & Levey, 2009). See Chapters 7 and 8 for a full description of early language development.

Interaction and Play

Specifically, typically developing toddlers benefit from interaction with caregivers through talking, asking questions, listening, and having an adult read to them. Two-year-olds are continuously developing ideas about how things work. Consequently, caregivers can provide opportunities for children to explore, predict, and talk about things that have happened. Children who practice with rich and varied spoken language are able to develop extensive vocabularies (Copple & Bredekamp, 2009).

It is also important that children ultimately learn to express their ideas in complete sentences. The parent or caregiver is encouraged to respond to children's words or ideas by expanding them, by introducing new vocabulary or concepts, and by asking questions. Since play is of the utmost importance for toddlers, skillful caregivers can join in pretend play and make play a language-learning opportunity (Copple & Bredekamp, 2009).

Listening to Good Language Models

Listening to good language models, regardless of the spoken native language, is also important. Language develops by observing complex social interactions within the family

(Vukelich, Christie, & Enz, 2002) and the community, beginning in infancy and continuing through adolescence. This idea stems from the work of Vygotsky (1962) and Bandura (1986).

Teaching parents about strategies to enhance adolescents' communication can be valuable, especially stressing the importance of **active listening** (Polirstok, 1989). Interactions with family members and other caregivers require that the child is engaged by using prompts (e.g., "Look!"), objects, and/or toys to elicit responses using scaffolds (described in Chapter 2). Over time, scaffolding enables a child to learn basic conversation skills.

Additional opportunities for language learning present themselves every day in the home environment through children's educational programming on television (e.g., *Sesame Street*) and computer applications. Thus, a myriad of opportunities for acquisition of oral and receptive language that results in robust learning exists beyond reading and talking to children.

Reading

Research in children's oral proficiency shows a connection between children's oral language development and the amount of time spent reading storybooks (Vukelich et al., 2002). For example, reading to a child as young as 3 months of age can facilitate the infant's focus on pictures in the book while engaged in a **joint-attention activity** (Mandel Morrow, 2001).

At 6 to 9 months of age, an infant may try to turn a page of a book and be responsive to the reader's use of changes in intonation and/or movements related to the text. One-year-olds are responsive when being read to, along with demonstrating delight through smiles and physical movements when hearing familiar parts of the story recalled from previous readings. They may also use **jargon** (a sequence of unintelligible speech with the use of adults' intonational patterns) as a prelanguage response to the text.

At 15 months of age, infants can identify the front cover of a book as differentiated from the end cover, identify if the book is oriented correctly, and attempt to "read" along with the adult by producing sounds and words (Mandell Morrow, 2001).

When children reach kindergarten age, their language skills reflect their early language-learning experiences. Language development variations are most apparent in kindergarten, given that early conversational and literacy experiences vary greatly in children's experiences (Copple & Bredekamp, 2009). Hence, the teacher must recognize his or her role in addressing the variability in children's performance through direct instruction and engaging parents in learning and modeling strategies that will help strengthen the language and literacy development of their children.

THE ROLE OF THE TEACHER IN ENGAGING PARENTS IN THEIR CHILDREN'S LANGUAGE DEVELOPMENT

It is important that early childhood teachers recognize the difference between typical and delayed language development and possess the skills and strategies necessary to work collaboratively with young children and their families. Helping parents create a language-rich environment is essential. In such an environment, parents would focus on exposure to literacy artifacts such as television, radio, computer games, pictures (e.g., on the wall, on cups, on clothing), magazines, newspapers, and grocery lists. In preparation for academic learning, joint book reading introduces children to vocabulary, sentences, and narrative structure.

Classroom teachers can help parents understand that virtually every activity can become an opportunity to learn new words and concepts.

Children need to listen to complex sentence structures as well as lengthy language utterances to achieve readiness (i.e., adequate pre-literacy skills) for success in the early grades.

The teacher can play an important role here in helping parents understand how they serve as language models for their children. Using active modeling as a teaching technique, a teacher can model verbal interactions that are language-rich and expansive. This strategy can serve parents well and can go far beyond the early childhood years.

Looking across the K–12 literacy curriculum, the role of the teacher is to help identify the specific challenges each student may be facing and to communicate what strategies and resources are available for parents to support their children's language development. Trips to local museums, libraries, and family vacations can become rich opportunities for vocabulary and concept development.

Another strategy that teachers can encourage parents to use at home is family reading, where everyone in the family sets aside a specific amount of time each day or week to read and discuss what they are reading with one another. The idea here is to model that reading is important while creating opportunities for increased family interaction.

Recent research on the support of language development in the home (Tamis-LeMonda & Rodriguez, 2008) has identified five strategies that teachers can provide to parents that will have a positive impact on children's language and literacy skills. These strategies include

- early and consistent participation in routine learning activities, such as shared book reading;

- teaching letters and numbers;

- trips to libraries and other enriching destinations, while talking about objects and events;

- quality parent-child interactions characterized by varied and rich information about objects and events in the environment and, more broadly, in the community; and

- providing age-appropriate learning materials that support young children's language and learning.

WORKING WITH FAMILIES WHOSE NATIVE LANGUAGE IS NOT ENGLISH

Intensive language and literacy interventions can be helpful to families whose primary language is not English. This is especially true for parents who may not be able to read or write in either their native language or English. Young children striving to learn English need to hear and see their native language spoken and written to best support their language development (Copple & Bredekamp, 2009). It is important to assist and broaden the role of families in their children's oral language development and overall literacy learning (Ordonez-Jasis & Ortiz, 2006).

Teachers working with second-language–learning families should provide diverse literacy materials, use the parents' primary language in intervention, and offer strategies that are not dependent on the parents' ability to read and write (Ordonez-Jasis & Ortiz, 2006). See Chapters 12 through 14 for more information on second-language strategies.

Teachers can employ several strategies for second-language–learning families in a naturalistic way, without families incurring significant time or financial loss while learning a second language. For example, involving the entire family in learning English establishes the importance of learning a second language, along with multiple models for both the child and other family members. Making a commitment as a family to watch English television for at least 30 minutes each night—while following the basic interpersonal communication skills model discussed in Chapter 13—can be beneficial in learning English. Using English to talk about what was viewed can reinforce vocabulary, sentence structure, and understanding of the events in the show.

Trips to the grocery store or the department store can be another effective activity to learn the names of foods, clothing, and objects used daily in the home. Looking at labels and identifying letters and sounds can help reinforce what a child might be learning in school and can be useful to the parents as well. Buying an English newspaper or magazine for the house each week can be another English-learning opportunity. Naming the pictures in English, finding English words they know, and discussing the articles in their native language can help make strong connections between the first and second languages.

If there is a computer in the house, the teacher can use countless sites and activities to develop a home-based program in English for the entire family. Finally, the family can be encouraged to take advantage of opportunities in the community to learn English. These opportunities may include visiting the local library, participating in an English as a second language program, or participating in programs at the community-college level. The classroom teacher can act as a resource finder for services that are available in the community.

THE TEACHER AS PARENT TRAINER

Teachers play a pivotal role in training parents and families to become more aware of what they can do in the home to increase language development in their children. This section describes three models of parent training: the Parent-as-Teacher Model, the Parent-as-Trainer

Model, and the Mixed Model. In each of these models, the teacher's role is to effectively train parents to work with other parents using a trainer-of-trainer's model. In this section, we also explore specific strategies for language development that parents can employ.

Models of Parent and Family Training

With skillful planning of family workshops, early childhood teachers can provide important information and training for families to support their children's language development. Initially, teachers must understand families and their cultures. This is essential to know exactly how to support them and how to engage them in collaboration (Friend & Cook, 2003).

Teachers must also be knowledgeable of and skillful using strategies to engage parents positively in their children's learning. Whether the approach, as outlined by Hurwitz and Polirstok (1985), is the Parent-as-Teacher Model, the Mixed Model, or the Parent-as-Trainer Model, the aims of family learning programs are to develop the skills and knowledge of the adult and the child and to help parents and caregivers support their children's learning and development with greater confidence (Heydon & Reilly, 2007).

Parent-as-Teacher Model

In the Parent-as-Teacher Model (Hurwitz & Polirstok, 1985), parents learn about the types of language and literacy problems their children experience. They also learn from a teacher or a professional trainer techniques that they can implement at home. Modeling of these techniques for parents is critical to provide examples of effective teaching. Often, parents keep a journal of their teaching efforts, detailing how their child responded and what follow-up issues arose. In this way, the teacher can monitor parent and child progress and provide support as needed.

Parents may begin to see changes not only in the areas of language and literacy but in their child's behavior. The improved behavior often occurs simply because of increased positive parent attention (Tamis-LeMonda & Rodriguez, 2008). The model initially fosters dependency on the teacher or trainer. Over time, the goal is to help parents begin to function more autonomously with respect to their language and literacy activities at home.

Mixed Model

In the Mixed Model (Hurwitz & Polirstok, 1985), teacher-directed training in specific language and literacy skills occurs in the same manner as the Parent-as-Teacher Model described above. Parents keep a journal of their teaching efforts, detailing how their child responds and what follow-up issues arose. In this way, the teacher or trainer can monitor parent and child progress and provide support as needed.

An additional community component is included in this model, providing parents with knowledge and access to community resources and services in the community via a handbook that is typically developed for support. Hence, parents themselves might seek English as a second language training from a provider identified in the community. Additionally, if a child is interested in art, a children's art program in the community could foster language development and engage the child in his or her preferred activity.

In this model, the teacher is engaged in providing language and literacy training, working along with a social worker from the community to help parents in the group avail themselves of resources in the community.

Parent-as-Trainer Model

In the Parent-as-Trainer Model (Hurwitz & Polirstok, 1985), parents are trained to work effectively with other parents who are resistant to engage. By identifying another parent from the community as the group leader/organizer, parents may feel less threatened to participate than they would if a teacher or a social worker were the group facilitator. In terms of social, linguistic, and cultural factors, this may be an important consideration in increasing overall participation.

Using the framework of the Parent-as-Teacher Model, a parent who has learned the techniques to foster language and literacy development can function as a "turnkey trainer" of the other parents. For example, if a parent has received training in developing vocabulary in functional contexts, such as when visiting a grocery store, he or she can share that technique with another parent or parents.

The key here is to be sure that the parent has learned the technique well enough to explain it to another parent or parents. This model requires quality-assurance control, and the teacher or trainer must ensure that the individuals who will eventually serve as turnkeys have in fact learned these techniques and are able to explain them accurately to increase understanding.

From a cost-effective standpoint, this model can be very efficient and advantageous. In addition, classroom teachers may put parents at ease with a turnkey trainer who has a cultural identity more similar to their own (Polirstok, 1987).

STRATEGIES FOR SUPPORTING LANGUAGE AND LITERACY DEVELOPMENT IN THE HOME

Regardless of the model of parent and family education adopted, the key is communicating that strategies for supporting language and literacy development in the home can be fun (Strickland, 2004). Helping families understand their role and providing them with specific strategies is an integral role of the early childhood educator.

Strickland (2004) points to specific kinds of information that teachers and caregivers of young children can provide to the parents and families of those in their care. It is important for parents to understand that oral language and literacy develop together. What young children learn from listening and talking contributes to their ability to read and write and vice versa.

> Young children learn about the uses of language and literacy in their lives through their observations and interactions with others using language and literacy strategies as they go about their everyday lives. (p. 86)

Since children who fall behind in oral language and literacy development are less likely to be successful beginning readers, helping families learn to support development in this area is an important role for teachers of young children.

Strickland (2004) notes that parent programs are successful when they are sustained, consistent over time, highly accessible, and provide support for specific program activities with an environment of shared purpose among children, families, and teachers. This notion of shared purpose grows out of a commitment of the entire school staff to connect the home and school environments. Greater success results from combining family workshops on language and literacy development with other services, such as health and social services. It is also essential that teachers remember to be patient and flexible and acknowledge that parents have a great deal to contribute.

There is no mythical finish line in terms of engaging parents in their child's language and literacy development. At every grade level, parents have a contribution to make. Activities that provide motivation and contribute to a student's success in school include helping with organization or resources (including helping children learn to search online), taking trips to the local library, quizzing children for tests, and reviewing homework.

Teachers need to use a broad array of techniques to engage parents in the literacy development and school success of their children. There is a correlation between learning to read and using language effectively, which leads to success in later school grades and vocational contexts (Kauffman, 2004).

Home-Based Literacy Activities Involving Print and Digital Materials for Older Students

As the nature of reading changes from *learning to read* in early grades to *reading to learn* in later elementary grades, activities to promote literacy in the home setting are critical. The International Reading Association (IRA, 2008) suggests that parents can encourage their children to read for pleasure by helping them identify age- and reading-level–appropriate materials geared to the children's interests, both online and in print. The IRA also provides many resources for teachers and parents on its website.

The technology-rich world of the Internet (including social networks, cell phones, and gaming systems) is a valuable tool for literacy activities that parents and children can share, and teachers can make parents aware of the presence of literacy materials online to foster children's interest in reading.

Today's students operate in a world different from earlier generations. Kindergarteners to college-age students have been defined as "digital natives" or members of the first digital generation (Prensky, 2001). For example, in the later elementary grades, some children prefer reading digitally online rather than reading books or stories in print. Conveniently, age-appropriate novels, nonfiction reading materials, and magazines on any given topic can be found online, in addition to being available in libraries and bookstores. Consequently, it is essential to engage children in meaningful, interesting ways that capitalize on the use of technology in their everyday lives.

Web-Based Activities and Factors

Families can find resources online that will provide ideas, activities, and additional information for children of various developmental ages across the Pre-K–2 continuum. The Internet is a rich resource for learning more about supporting language and literacy development in children and adolescents. Internet reading provides many benefits for later-grade elementary students. For example, the IRA suggests that, unlike a printed book, the Internet offers interactive texts with audio and video links that can more easily match a reader's learning style. Reading online also offers comprehension aids—for example, context clues with interactive organizing structures such as subheads, diagrams, and definitions of content vocabulary. There are several good resources on the web for language development as well as organizations that provide support for language development.

For Examples of Online Websites That Address Language and Literacy Development Across the Pre-School to Grade 12 Continuum and Professional Organization Website Resources, go to **www.sage pub.com/levey.**

The Internet also frequently offers hypertext links that bring the reader to additional information related to the online text. According to the professionals at IRA, teachers and parents need to work collaboratively to encourage children to browse online for research and information related to assigned projects and/or hobbies and areas of interest.

As reading and writing typically develop together, teachers can suggest to parents that they encourage their children to express their thoughts in e-mails to friends and family members, thus offering reading and writing practice in an informal, low-stress setting.

Online author studies provide a wonderful opportunity for teachers and parents to collaborate. Initiated by teachers and followed-up by parents, children can read authors' websites and buy or borrow books from the library written by the authors studied.

Also, as some children may have problems with handwriting, learning to keyboard is an excellent compensatory strategy. In fact, for some children, learning to keyboard may help with fluency and ideation as they move beyond the physical limitations of handwriting.

STRATEGIES TO ENGAGE PARENTS OF ADOLESCENTS IN HOME-BASED LITERACY ACTIVITIES

Middle school teachers need to engage parents in partnerships in which they can learn how to help their adolescents continue literacy development. The role of parents includes providing homework support, organization, and study skills. First, teachers must stress to parents the importance of providing structure at home and expectations for academic success. Establishing a schedule for homework and study time is key.

Most adolescents need to have their homework monitored in terms of completion and accuracy, but parents trying to be homework tutors over an extended period can be quite problematic. Parents need to understand that they can provide some assistance, but if their adolescent needs extensive assistance, he or she should be encouraged to attend after-school homework help sessions, to develop a homework "buddy" who can be called in each of their classes, and to arrange for a tutor if needed.

Most parents report that homework time is extremely stressful. For adolescents who are in the process of trying to effectively separate from their parents, the fact that they may need parental help with their homework creates lots of frustration. Helping an adolescent without being overbearing is a skill parents need to develop. A teacher trying to engage parents needs to be mindful of all the contradictions and subtleties that working with adolescents poses.

Helping adolescents learn how to appropriately plan for a major paper or assignment is invaluable. Teachers need to be able to explain to parents and adolescents

- how to task-analyze an assignment into smaller components (i.e., break a task into smaller, sequenced steps that compose the overall task) and

- how to plan time each day to accomplish each of the components and ultimately complete the final paper or assignment on time.

It is necessary to teach these organizational and planning skills directly. The parent's role is to help the adolescent plan out when he or she can devote time to each component, using a calendar to help document this plan. Even if parents do not have much content knowledge related to the topic of a major assignment, their role can simply be to prompt

The Internet is a rich resource for learning more about supporting language and literacy development in children and adolescents.

their child to establish a planning process. Hence, their involvement appears as "managerial" rather than a "parent-as-teacher" role (Polirstok, 1989).

Finally, understanding current events in the context of modern culture involves reading newspapers and online news reports. Parents can provide opportunities to discuss these events at the family dinner table. Discussion of current events is a good strategy to help adolescents extend their **schema** (a mental representation of experience), vocabulary skills, and logical thinking. Establishing time for conversations is something teachers can impress on parents. These conversations can also include discussions of what family members are reading, interesting movies or television programs recently viewed, and events that occurred at school or work. The art of conversation, of sharing information using appropriate language, and of pondering solutions to problems both personal and global, can be a rich foundation for reading and writing (Nippold, 2000).

CASE STUDY REVISITED

Ms. Jones illustrates the kinds of roles that teachers play when enlisting parents and other family members in support of children's language and literacy development. At the conference with Grace's mother and grandmother, Ms. Jones talked with them about Grace's language development in the context of their family life. Through active modeling, she demonstrated how conversations with Grace can include more vocabulary and lengthier utterances.

Case Study Revisited: Parents and their impact on language development

Ms. Jones explained that Grace can learn new vocabulary words in everyday contexts, such as shopping in the supermarket. As an extension, a discussion about healthy foods seems like a wonderful way to build schema. She also suggested that Grace could be encouraged to organize the foods in the shopping cart into categories (e.g., meat, dairy, fruit, and vegetables).

Ms. Jones also emphasized the importance of setting aside a specific amount of time each day or during each week for family reading, where everyone in the family reads and discusses what they are reading with one another. They also talked about Grace's interest in nature. Ms. Jones helped them understand how to use Grace's interests as opportunities to enhance her language development. For example, Grace's family could take walks through the park, stopping to examine and discuss nature. New vocabulary, as well as concepts about nature, can begin from simply finding an acorn on the ground during their walk. Once at home, Grace can be encouraged to draw a picture or write a story about the events that took place in the park. Ms. Jones found a free educational Saturday-morning program led by the naturalists at the city park. Park programs geared toward children would be ideal for Grace, especially since she has such a keen interest in the outside world.

One of the areas in which Grace needed further support was in her ability to listen to lengthy utterances. Ms. Jones suggested that the family discuss television shows and movies, asking Grace to tell them about the things she most enjoyed about these events (including the things that actors said that interested her the most). Finally, Ms. Jones shared online resources for Grace's family to help support language development at home and some terrific websites on animals and insects for Grace to explore with her mother. Grace's family left the conference knowledgeable and empowered to be educational partners with Ms. Jones in Grace's language development.

SUMMARY

In typically developing young children, language acquisition occurs naturally in supportive environments at school and at home. This chapter outlined in-class, teacher-planned activities and three models of parent and family training that teachers can use: the Parent-as-Teacher Model, the Mixed Model, and the Parent-as-Trainer Model. In all cases, supportive environments provide language-learning experiences through conversations with family members, television viewing, computer games, local shopping trips in the community, and trips to museums and other local points of interest. Organization for study at home and planning and management of long-term assignments are areas in which teachers and parents can create meaningful partnerships to enhance the literacy development and academic success of children and adolescents.

As children mature through their school years, the role of teachers in the classroom with respect to language development needs to include modeling the use of language, promoting classroom conversation, presenting new content through use of chunking, relating new concepts to previously learned ideas and vocabulary, and teaching students to generalize learning across settings.

This chapter focused on preparing teachers with the ability to help parents support their children's language and literacy development from infancy through adolescence. Training parents and engaging them as partners in their children's education is critical to giving every child an opportunity to be successful and can contribute to closing the achievement gap.

KEY WORDS

Active listening	Communicative competence	Joint-attention activity
Babbling	Generalization	Scaffolding
Chunking	Jargon	Schema

STUDY QUESTIONS

1. Describe the role of the family in early language development. List three ideas to help teachers of toddlers collaborate with their students' families.

2. Discuss why it is essential for teachers to have a strong knowledge of language and literacy development. Discuss the most salient features of language development at each of these levels: early-elementary, late-elementary, and adolescent grades.

3. Write a scenario illustrating the expansion of conversation with a young child.

4. What are the models of parent training a teacher or professional can adopt? What are the pros and cons of each model?

5. Discuss three uses of technology to support language and literacy development in later-grade elementary students and adolescents.

PROJECTS

1. Using the information in this chapter, prepare a PowerPoint presentation for parents on the topic of typical and atypical language development and discuss user-friendly strategies that parents can employ in the home to support the language development of their children.

2. For your district's next professional development day, request permission to do a workshop on models of parent training to support literacy development at home. Use the information in this chapter to focus on different models of parent training, strategies parents can use to support literacy development at home, and various literacy resources available to parents.

3. When meeting with a parent of a special-needs student in your class, take time to review the Individual Education Plan with parents so that they understand the identified child's language and literacy goals. The classroom teacher can also use the information in this chapter to model strategies that the parent can use at home to support these goals.

STUDENT STUDY SITE

Visit the Student Study Site at **www.sagepub.com/levey** for these additional learning tools:

- Video Links
- Self Quizzes
- E-Flashcards

- Sample Forms and Assessment Tools
- Recommended Readings
- Web Resources

SUGGESTIONS FOR FURTHER READING

Angell, C. A. (2008). *Language development and disorders: A case study approach.* Sudbury, MA: Jones & Bartlett.

Dyer, L., Lansky, B., & Spellman, S. (2004). *Look who's talking: How to enhance your child's language development starting at birth.* Minnetonka, MN: Meadowbrook.

Endrizzi, C. K. (2008). *Teachers and families as literacy partners.* Urbana, IL: National Council of Teachers of English.

Phillips, L. M., Hayden, R., & Norris, S. P. (2007). *Family literacy matters: A longitudinal parent-child intervention study.* Calgary, AB: Detselig.

Swartz, S. L., Geraghty, C. A., & Pitchford, K. (2008). *Family literacy workshops: Preschool through grade 6.* San Diego, CA: Cavallo.

Glossary

Abstract thought Higher-level thinking processes that are characterized by organization and logic.

Acceleration hypothesis At certain points in development, bilingual children might demonstrate a faster rate of acquisition than their monolingual peers.

Accommodation 1. If a new event does not fit into a cognitive schema that already exists (e.g., *penguin*) there is a change in the existing schema (e.g., *birds*) to incorporate the characteristics of this new information. 2. As required by law (IDEA), the process of providing students with hearing loss reasonable assistance to enable them to function in the least restrictive environments, such as placement in the front row of a classroom (preferential seating) for students with mild hearing loss (20dB–30dB), use of assistive listening devices (such as FM system) for student with greater degrees of hearing loss (> 30dB) or unilateral hearing loss, use of sign language interpreting services for students who use sign language as their primary language (more likely in students with severe [70dB–85dB] to profound hearing loss [> 90 dB]).

Active listening An enhanced communication tool whereby the person who is the listener periodically reflects back his or her understanding of what is being communicated as a means of ensuring full comprehension.

Adaptation The tendency of an organism to change in response to the environment.

Adaptive physical educator (APE) A professional who adapts or modifies physical education to address the individualized needs of children and youth who have gross motor developmental delays.

Affricates Speech sounds produced by creating a stop-closure in the oral cavity and releasing it as a fricative. In American English, affricates appear in the first and last underlined sounds in *church* and the first and last sounds in *judge*.

Alphabetic principle This process describes the ability to recognize the correlation between phonemes (spoken sounds) and graphemes (alphabetics).

Alternations Changes that are repeated in a regular pattern. Spelling rules feature common alternations or change processes (e.g., *electric/electricity*; *public/publicity*), but most of these change patterns have exceptions in the English language (e.g., *version/versions*; *person/people*).

Alveolar ridge A bony prominence of the hard palate directly behind the upper incisors (teeth) that serves as an important place of articulation (a static or unmovable articulator) for the speech sounds /l/ in *left* and /t/ in *top*.

Appalachian dialects These dialects are called Southern Mountain Dialects by linguists. These dialects began with some of the first settlers in Appalachia: Scotch-Irish and Palatine Germans (origins in the Rhine Valley of Germany).

Approximants A class of sounds produced by bringing one articulator close to another without creating audible noise. The semivowels /j/ in *you*, /w/ in *wet*, and liquids /r/ in *red* and /l/ in *low* are examples of approximant sounds.

Articulated Produced by speech; spoken.

Articulation Movements of the vocal tract to produce speech sounds in a language.

Articulators Structures in the vocal tract that are used to create speech sounds. There are dynamic (movable) articulators, such as the tongue and lips, and there are static (unmovable) articulators, such as the alveolar ridge and teeth, to which movable articulators approximate (make contact) to produce speech sounds.

Asperger Syndrome A disorder on the Autism Spectrum that is characterized by challenges in social and pragmatic abilities with typical cognitive development.

Assimilation 1. In terms of cognition, this term applies to children's exposure to new information or a new event. In this case, the new entity can be incorporated into a schema that already exists when there is a good fit between the new information and the preexisting schema. 2. In the phonetic theory, this explains changing of a speech sound to become more similar to the sound of an adjacent sound.

Assistive listening devices (ALDs) Include a large variety of devices (e.g., Infrared, Induction Loop, FM amplification) designed to improve audibility in specific listening situations. Some are designed to be used with hearing aids or cochlear implants, while others are designed to be used alone. These devices have the same goal: to pick up a sound close to the source and make that sound stand out from among other background noises (specifically, improving the signal-to-noise ratio).

Attention Mental focus, serious consideration, or concentration.

Attention-deficit hyperactivity disorder (ADHD) An impairment characterized by excessive activity and distractibility.

Audiogram A standard method for representing hearing abilities or hearing loss.

Auditory feedback One of several sensory (afferent) feedback loops that assist young children who are developing speech determine the accuracy of their speech sound production.

The ability to monitor one's own speech sound production is extremely important to normal speech production. The absence of or alteration in auditory feedback will negatively affect the quality of speech.

Auditory processing disorder (APD) Historically known as central auditory processing disorder, it's a disorder in which peripheral hearing sensitivity is normal and yet the brain is not able to recognize and interpret sounds, most notably the sounds composing speech. Children with APD often do not recognize subtle differences between sounds in words, even when the sounds are loud and clear enough to be heard. These difficulties are exacerbated by background noise in the listening environment, and so use of an assistive listening device is often indicated to help the student with APD overcome his or her barriers to education.

Auditory-oral approach A method in which children learn to use whatever hearing they have, in combination with lip reading and contextual cues (speech reading) to understand and use spoken language. The goal is to give the deaf individual the necessary spoken language skills to be mainstreamed educationally and to function independently in the hearing world.

Auditory-verbal approach Uses strategies to integrate listening, speech language, and communication into children's daily routines and experiences to teach them to listen and learn that certain sounds have certain meanings.

Auditory-visual approach A method in which children with hearing loss (but who have residual hearing) learn to associate sound with the object that produces that sound (e.g., showing the child a truck and presenting the sound a truck makes). The goal is to provide the child with hearing loss a visual reference for the sound they are hearing (likely for the first time) to give them a sense of recognition of the meaning of that sound.

Axon A long fiber of a nerve cell (a neuron) that carries outgoing (efferent) messages.

Babbling Strings of nonreduplicated syllables expressed in varied syllable sequences (e.g., "babigaguda").

Basic interpersonal communication skills (BICS) Language skills needed in social situations. It is the day-to-day language needed to interact socially with other people.

Basic sentence Also called independent clauses, they contain a subject and a verb, expressing a complete thought.

Bidialectism Proficiency in using two dialects.

Bilingualism When an individual has proficiency in two languages. It may also describe individuals who have varying degrees of proficiency in three, four, or even more languages.

Brain The center of the nervous system in all vertebrate and in most invertebrate animals that controls the other organ systems of the body.

Brainstem The lower part of the brain, adjoining and continuous with the spinal cord.

Broca's area A region in the left frontal lobe of the brain associated with speech that controls movements of the tongue, lips, and vocal cords.

Causal An event that makes something happen.

Cell body Contains all the general parts of a cell, including the nucleus, which is the control center. The nucleus contains the cell's genetic material (DNA) located in chromosomes.

Cells The basic organizational units of all living organisms.

Central nervous system The part of the nervous system that consists of the brain and the spinal cord.

Cerebellum A region of the brain that plays an important role in motor control. The cerebellum does not initiate movement, but it contributes to coordination, precision, and accurate timing.

Cerebral cortex A thin area of grey matter covering the surface of each cerebral hemisphere that is responsible for the processes of thought, perception, and memory and serves as the seat of advanced motor function, social abilities, language, and problem solving.

Cerebral plasticity The ability of the brain to reorganize neural pathways based on new experiences, which allows the brain to acquire new knowledge and skills (also termed *neuroplasticity*).

Cerebrum The largest and uppermost portion of the brain. The cerebrum consists of the right and left cerebral hemispheres and accounts for two thirds of the total weight of the brain.

Chunking 1. Learning to spell by breaking multisyllabic words down into syllables. 2. A process to enhance short-term memory recall by grouping pieces of information together in manageable units that share some aspect of commonality. 3. Speakers may present information in smaller chunks or portions to help listeners understand this information.

Cochlear implant An electronic device that can help to provide a sense of sound to a person who is profoundly deaf or severely hard-of-hearing when hearing aids are of limited benefit. The implant consists of an external portion that sits behind the ear and a second portion that is surgically placed under the skin. An implant has the following parts: a microphone, a speech processor, a transmitter (these worn externally), and a receiver and electrode array (these internally implanted). The cochlear implant takes sounds and converts them to electrical impulses that are carried to the auditory nerve according to an algorithm to provide an organized representation of sounds in the environment. An implant does not restore normal hearing. Instead, it can give a deaf person a useful representation of sounds in the environment and help him or her understand speech.

Code-switch A code is a system of signals used for sending messages. Code-switching describes changing from one language or system to another.

Cognition The mental ability to acquire knowledge by the use of attention, working memory, reasoning, intuition, and perception to adapt to one's environment.

Cognitive Academic Language Learning Approach (CALLA) This model integrates academic language development, content-area instruction, and explicit instruction in learning strategies for both content and language acquisition.

Cognitive academic language proficiency (CALP) Formal academic learning that includes listening, speaking, reading, and writing about subject-area material.

Cognitive dissonance 1. A problem fitting an entity into an existing schema. 2. A condition of conflict resulting from discrepancy between one's beliefs and one's actions.

Cognitive functions A range of high-level brain functions, including the ability to learn, understand and use language, remember information, organize, plan, problem solve, and focus, maintain, and shift attention as necessary.

Coherent A narrative or conversational utterance that is clearly understood.

Communication 1. The exchange of information between people through speaking, writing, or using a common system of signs or behavior. 2. The vehicle for social interaction consisting of both verbal (words, sentences, narratives, and conversations) and nonverbal (eye gazing, gesturing, turn-taking in conversation, and facial expressions) acts.

Communicative competence A linguistic term that characterizes a person's knowledge of grammar, syntax, morphology, and phonology, along with an understanding of how and when to use this knowledge appropriately.

Communicative intentions 1. An individual's meaning reflected in asking questions, making requests, or contributing to a conversation. 2. A speaker has an intention to induce a listener's awareness of how an utterance is to be understood.

Communicative unit (C-unit) A method of separating spoken utterances or written sentences into distinct independent clauses (simple sentences) and any dependent or subordinating clauses; often used to measure growth in language ability with age.

Competition model A psycholinguistic theory of language acqusition and understanding.

Complex A sentence that contains an independent clause joined by one or more dependent clauses. A complex sentence always has a subordinator such as *because, since, after, although,* or *when* or a relative pronoun such as *that, who,* or *which.*

Compound A sentence that contains two independent clauses joined by a coordinator, such as *for, and, nor, but, or, yet,* or *so.*

Compound-complex A sentence made up of more than one main clause and at least one subordinate clause. It is the combining of a compound sentence with a complex sentence.

Concepts Children's understanding of the world and how the world develops. Concepts involve children's conception of themselves, other people, physical laws of time and motion, recognition of patterns (e.g., results that allow further prediction of patterns), and learning to think in abstract terms.

Conductive hearing loss (CHL) Occurs when there is a problem with the conduction of sound waves through the outer ear, tympanic membrane (eardrum), or middle ear (ossicles). This type of hearing loss may occur in conjunction with sensorineural hearing loss or alone.

Congenital Refers to a defect or condition in a fetus, present at birth, which may be inherited genetically or caused by some insult in utero.

Conjunctions Used to link words, phrases, and clauses with words such as *and.*

Conjunctives Words that connect elements of meaning and construction within sentences. Examples include *and, since,* and *therefore.*

Constriction A narrowing within the vocal tract that occurs during the production of fricative speech sounds (e.g., /s/ in *see*, /f/ in *fly*, and the *sh* sound in *shoe* and *push*). A constriction is formed by moving a dynamic articulator into close contact with another articulator to create a narrow passageway through which air is forced, creating a hissing sound.

Content 1. The meaning of an expression. 2. Linguistically, this term refers to semantics or rules that apply to assigning meaning in a language.

Context 1. Refers to spoken or written statements that precede or follow in spoken conversation or in a written passage, usually influencing its meaning or effect. 2. It also refers to the conditions or circumstances that are present.

Continuity hypothesis The child's understanding of language gradually emerges from the sounds produced in his or her babbling.

Conversational skills The ability of children to respond in reciprocal fashion to questions and comments by adults and peers with fluent responses that follow grammatical convention and use appropriate vocabulary.

Corpus callosum A structure of the brain in the longitudinal fissure that connects the left and right cerebral hemispheres; the white matter structure in the brain that facilitates communication between the two hemispheres.

Cross-linguistic effects The bidirectional influence of one language on the other in bilingual speech and language production.

Cytomegalovirus A herpes virus most frequently transmitted to a developing fetus. For infants who are infected by their mothers before birth, two potential adverse scenarios exist: 80% to 90% will have complications within the first few years of life that may include hearing loss, vision impairment, and varying degrees of mental retardation. Another 5% to 10% of infants who are infected but without symptoms at birth will subsequently have varying degrees of hearing and mental or coordination problems.

Deaf Full or partial inability to detect or understand sounds, which may be caused by a wide range of biological and environmental factors. The term *hearing impaired* is often used to refer to those who are deaf, although those who are deaf often prefer to be referred to as *deaf* and *hard-of-hearing.*

Deceleration hypothesis At certain points in development, bilingual children might demonstrate a slower rate of acquisition than their monolingual peers.

Decode 1. The process of transforming information from one format to another, the reverse of encoding. An example consists of being able to read something that is written. 2. An individual is able to comprehend or understand information from another source.

Decontextualize Separation of an object from the original context. This occurs when a child uses a word to represent an object or action that is absent from the child's view.

Decontextualized learning trials Learning that takes place in isolation without environmental clues to support meaning. For instance, using flash cards to help children learn to read common words.

Decontextualized narratives These are narratives that do not have meaning in a situation. The discourse cannot be understood by associated meaning in a situation.

Deep structure The underlying meaning of the sentence before it is transformed into the surface structure, expressed by a speaker.

Deferred imitation Imitation of an event after a period of delay showing that the child understands an expression. The child's utterance may be expanded or changed.

Dendrites The branched projections of a neuron that act to conduct the electrochemical stimulation received from other neural cells to the cell body of the neuron, from which the dendrites project. Electrical stimulation is transmitted onto dendrites by upstream neurons via synapses.

Density of dialect use The extent to which speakers use the features of their dialect.

Dependent clause A group of words that contain a subject and verb but do not express a complete thought. A dependent clause cannot be a sentence, while an independent clause is a group of words that contains a subject and verb and expresses a complete thought. In this case, an independent clause is a sentence.

Derivational morphemes Prefixes and suffixes that are added to a root word to create additional meaning. This often changes the part-of-speech of the root word, as in adding the suffix *-er* to the verb *teach* to create the noun *teacher.*

Developmental milestones Skills that children exhibit within a certain age range.

Dialogic approach Includes nine specific questioning/prompting strategies that caregivers can use to actively engage young children in storybook reading.

Diaphragm A major muscle of inspiration, the diaphragm is a dome-shaped muscle that separates the thorax and the abdomen. The lungs are attached to the diaphragm through the pleural lining. When the diaphragm contracts, the size of both the thorax and lungs increases, resulting in airflow into the lungs.

Diphthongs Vowel-like sounds that are produced with a gradually changing vocal tract shape. They are slightly longer in duration than single vowels (monophthongs). Examples of diphthong sounds are shown by the underlined letters in the words *cho<u>i</u>ce* and *m<u>ou</u>th.*

Discourse Linguistic term used to refer to a continuous stretch of (especially spoken) language that is longer than a sentence.

Discrimination A listener's ability to determine similarities and differences between items such as speech sounds in the language.

Dominance A task is performed with greater accuracy when comparing two languages.

Dual immersion a distinctive form of dual language education in which native English speakers and native speakers of another language are integrated for academic content instruction in both English and the partner language.

Dual-function words Sometimes called double-function terms. These are words that refer to both a physical and a psychological state, such as *bright.*

Duration The period of time that something lasts or exists. In phonetics, the meaning relates to the length of a speech sound.

Dynamic articulators Movable structures in the vocal tract, such as the tongue and lips, used to create speech sounds.

Educational audiologist (EA) Conducts hearing or speech and language evaluations in a school setting, assesses classroom acoustics, plans and monitors treatment programs, recommends assistive listening devices according to the child's nature of impairment and interacts with parents, teachers, and school nurses to work as part of an education team.

Egocentric speech Often called private speech, describes Piaget's concept of a child's inability to take another's point of view. The child's speech is not adapted to the listener's understanding of the child's expression.

Embedded Also called a dependent clause or a subordinate clause. Although it contains a subject and a predicate, it sounds incomplete when standing alone (e.g., "Wherever he goes, he makes friends").

Embedded phrases The process by which one phrase is included (embedded) in a sentence (e.g., "In the morning, I drink coffee").

Emergent literacy skills Skills and knowledge about literacy that a child acquires before learning to read. These skills consist of knowing that the print on a page contains information about the story.

Emergentism Language emerges from an integrated neural network that detects regularities in input from the environment. For example, children learn irregular verbs (e.g., *caught*) through observing patterns of language use (e.g., *catch/caught*).

Encode 1. Involves converting incoming information into meaning, such as spoken speech sounds into words. 2. The process of understanding incoming stimuli and converting information into meaningful units.

English-language learner An individual in the process of acquiring English and who has a first language other than English. Other terms commonly found in the literature include language minority students, limited English proficient (LEP), English as a second language (ESL), and culturally and linguistically diverse (CLD).

Environment The external events to which a child is exposed, such as people, things, and actions.

Environmental Relating to, or caused by, a person's surroundings.

Equilibrium The goal of fitting new information or input into an existing cognitive schema, also called cognitive balance.

Etymologies The study of the history, development, or origin of words.

Executive functions The management system of the brain that works together to have a major impact on the ability to perform such tasks as planning, prioritizing, organizing, paying attention to and remembering details, and controlling our emotional reactions.

Expansions The process of increasing an expressed sentence to include a broader variety of ideas.

Expiration The phase of the breathing known as exhalation, during which air is expelled from the lungs.

Expressive language The language an individual produces spontaneously, without imitating another's speech.

Eye gaze When a child stares or looks into someone else's eyes to gain or maintain their attention.

Fictional narrative A story in which the content is made-up, such as in storybooks or novels.

Figurative language When words are used in an abstract (conceptual) sense rather than a literal (factual) sense, such as in similes (e.g., *She is as light as a feather*) and metaphors (e.g., *He is bright*).

Fluency 1. The ability to read a text quickly, accurately, and with proper expression. It involves the ability to read with little effort and without conscious attention to the mechanics of reading. 2. The ability to speak, read, and/or write with no difficulty.

Form The structure of language as opposed to meaning (content) or social use (pragmatics).

Formal operations The formal operational stage begins at approximately age 12 and lasts into adulthood. During this time, children develop the ability to think about abstract concepts with the use of logical thought, deductive reasoning, and systematic planning.

Frequency modulation (FM) Method of transmitting radio signals by varying the frequency (speed) of the radio wave while the height (amplitude) of the wave remains constant. The FM wave is approximately 20 times wider than the wave in amplitude modulation (AM), accounting for the fact that the FM system has a finer tonal quality. However, FM signals do not carry for long distances. FM systems are one type of assistive listening device used to help people with hearing losses.

Fricatives A class of speech sounds formed by creating a significant constriction in the vocal tract by positioning two articulators close together. Examples consist of the sound /s/ in *sun* and /f/ in *fun*.

Frontal lobe An area in the brain located at the front of each cerebral hemisphere and positioned anterior to the parietal lobes and the temporal lobes. The left frontal lobe is involved in controlling language, and the right frontal lobe plays a role in nonverbal abilities.

Fundamental frequency Fundamental frequency (f_o) is determined by the rate at which the vocal folds vibrate during phonation. The faster the vocal folds vibrate, the higher the f_o. Fundamental frequency shifts are perceived as shifts in vocal pitch. For example, an adult male with a f_o of 100 Hz will be perceived as having a lower pitched voice than a female with an f_o of 200 Hz.

Generalization The transfer of training such that a learned behavior or skill in one context or setting will be demonstrated in a new context or setting.

Genetic inheritance Traits and qualities transmitted through genes that have been passed from parents to their offspring.

Gestures 1. Movements made with a part of the body to express meaning, emotion, or to communicate an instruction. 2. A term used in phonology for a matrix of features specifying a particular characteristic of a segment. For example, an oral gesture would specify all supraglottal characteristics (such as place and manner of articulation).

Glides Sometimes referred to as semivowels, these are vowel-like sounds that do not make up the nucleus of a syllable. Examples consist of the first sounds in the words _yellow_ and _white_.

Glottis The space between the vocal folds. When the vocal folds open, the size of the glottis increases. When the vocal folds are completely closed, the space between the vocal folds is eliminated and the glottis does not exist.

Grammar The rules that govern the composition of sentences, phrases, and words in any given natural language. The term refers also to the study of such rules, and this field includes morphology and syntax, phonetics, phonology, semantics, and pragmatics.

Grey matter The major component of the central nervous system that routes sensory or motor stimulus to interneurons of the central nervous system (CNS) to create a response to the stimulus through chemical synapse activity.

Griot A storyteller in West Africa who maintains the oral traditions and history of a village or a family.

Guided distributional learning A theory of language acquisition that describes children's finding regularities in input (i.e., spoken language in the environment) that they have been guided to notice. For example, one regularity consists of the distribution or order of words in expressed sentences, with subject or agent in the first position in sentences.

Habilitation technologies Use of assistive devices along with support personnel whose responsibility is to help individuals with significant hearing losses function in as normalized a manner as possible in all aspects of daily life.

Hard palate A bony structure that makes up the roof of the mouth, the hard palate is a static or unmovable articulator important to the production of speech sounds.

Hard-of-hearing Refers to having varying amounts of hearing loss, but usually not enough to be considered deaf.

Hearing aids Electronic devices that pick up and amplify sound to make communication easier for individuals who are hard-of-hearing. Hearing aids are prescriptively fitted according to the degree of hearing loss of the individual to maximize the use of the residual auditory area (that is, to prescriptively amplify sound into the region that is audible yet still comfortable for the person with hearing loss).

Heschl's gyrus Any of several small gyri that run transversely on the upper surface of the temporal area of the cortex and are involved in the processing of auditory stimuli.

Homophones Words that sound the same but are spelled differently with different meanings (e.g., *red* and *read*).

Incidental learning Learning that results from indirect activities rather than formal didactic teaching. It can occur through observation, social interaction, and problem solving.

Incoherent A narrative or conversational utterance that cannot be understood. The meaning is not clearly presented.

Inhalation The phase of the breathing cycle during which air is brought into the lungs. It is also known as *inspiration*.

Innate Qualities or abilities that are inborn.

Innateness theory The theory that children are born with the abilty to acquire language.

Input Information or a situation from the environment that enters the child's mind to be processed.

Inspiration The phase of the breathing cycle during which air is brought into the lungs. It is also known as *inhalation*.

Intentional The use of communication to indicate specific wants, desires, or needs.

Intentions The meanings conveyed by a speaker.

Intonation A prosodic feature of speech that is related to the fundamental frequency of vocal fold vibration (i.e., repetition rate of the vocal folds). During speech production, variations in fundamental frequency are perceived as changes in pitch. Changes in intonation can signal a question form (e.g., rising intonation) or a statement (e.g., rising-falling intonation).

Intraoral pressure Pressure developed in the oral cavity (mouth). In order to produce stop, fricative, and affricate sounds, it is necessary to increase the pressure in the oral cavity.

Intrasentential growth Syntactic development includes growth inside sentences (*intrasentential growth*) and between sentences (*intersentential growth*). Intrasentential growth is reflected in longer sentences, while intersentential growth is reflected in linking sentences and the use of grammatical connective devices.

Invented spelling Efforts to spell words when the standard spelling is not yet acquired. Attempts usually use the knowledge that is known by the beginning speller. *For instance, a child who is just learning sound/symbol associations may spell the word bird as "brd."*

Jargon 1. These are sequences of variegated babbling that have the intonational shape of the child's native language. 2. The language and vocabulary associated with a particular discipline, often confusing to novices and persons not familiar with that given discipline.

Joint attention or joint-attention activity The processes by which young children focus their attention on an object or event with a social partner through nonverbal communication. This may include joint gaze and pointing.

Joint focus When an infant and adult look at the same object or event, arising from the infant's interest, and the adult provides the label or name for that object or event.

Language A system of arbitrary symbols that is rule-based, dynamic, generative, and used as a social tool to communicate.

Language acquisition device (LAD) A theoretical component of the human mind that enables children to aquire any language. Language based on cognition. Language is acquired and understood through cognitive processes.

Language content The meaning of the message conveyed through speech. Language content is also referred to as *semantics*.

Language variation Language variation describes how language varies in different contexts, such as ethnicity, geography, speaker age, speaker gender, and socioeconomic status.

Larynx A set of structures that house the vocal folds.

Leapfrogging narrative A narrative in which the events are not presented in chronological or logical order. The events appear to be presented randomly.

Learning disabilities A disorder characterized by academic difficulties in reading, writing, mathematics, and other areas. This impairment may be accompanied by impairments in pragmatics or discourse.

Left brain The verbal communication center of the brain that processes information in an analytical and sequential way, first looking at the details and then putting them together to get the whole.

Lexical The individual words that make up the vocabulary of a language.

Liquids A class of speech sounds known as approximants. Examples are the speech sounds /l/ in the word low and /r/ in red.

Literacy The ability to identify, understand, interpret, create, communicate, compute, and use printed and written materials associated with varying contexts.

Memory The capability of the mind to retain learned information and knowledge of past events or experiences and retrieve that information and knowledge.

Meningitis An inflammation of the membranes that cover the brain and spinal cord (the meninges) caused by a viral or bacterial infection. This can result in ossification (growth of hard bone) of the cochlea and result in profound hearing loss.

Metacognition An important concept in cognitive theory that consists of monitoring one's progress as a learner and making changes and adapting one's strategies in relation to one's performance. Metacognition involves self-reflection, self-responsibility, initiative, goal setting, and time management.

Metalinguistic The ability to think about language use in a conscious manner. Just saying

the word *animal* does not require conscious knowledge, but knowing that it has three syllables, three vowels, and three consonants would require conscious ability to focus on its form rather than its meaning.

Metalinguistic awareness The conscious awareness of how language works.

Mismatch hypothesis The theory that there is a mismatch between the language found in texts and classrooms and the language spoken by AAE-speaking children.

Mixed hearing loss The result of both conductive and sensorineural hearing impairment.

Modal auxiliaries A type of auxiliary verb that is used to indicate grammatical mood, such as a necessity or a possibility (e.g., *could, should*, and *will*).

Models An expressed utterance or a behavior that is used to demonstrate the utterance or behavior.

Morphemes The minimal distinctive component of grammar. Morphemes are commonly classified into free forms (morphemes that can occur as separate words) or bound forms (morphemes that cannot occur by themselves, such as affixes). An example is the word *misguided*, consisting of three morphemes (i.e., *mis-guid-ed*).

Morphological Related to the patterns used to form words. This includes patterns used to change words to indicate a grammatical function. For instance, the past tense of *jump* becomes *jumped*.

Morphology A study of the system of rules for combining the smallest units of language into words.

Morphosyntactic development The addition of morphemes that expand a child's syntax or sentence length, with examples including determiners (e.g., *the*), present progressive (*-ing*), and plural (*-s*).

Myelinated A layer that surrounds only the axons of many neurons. The main role of a myelin layer (or sheath) is an increase in the speed at which impulses pass along the myelinated fiber.

Narrative A verbal description of events that are longer than a single utterance.

Narrative discourse Consists of two types of narrative: personal and fictional. Both play an important role in social and literacy skills.

Nasal cavity A cavity of the vocal tract that is important for the resonance of the nasal sounds.

Nasals A cavity of the vocal tract that is important for the resonance of the nasal sounds. Examples of nasal sounds are /m/ in _man_, /n/ in _no_, and the final sound in _hang_.

Noise-induced hearing loss (NIHL) The result of exposure to sound that is sufficient to damage the hair cells in the inner ear and can cause hearing loss, ear ringing, and distortion of sounds.

Object permanence 1. The knowledge that objects have an existence in time and space, independent of whether or not they can be seen or touched. 2. Ability to remember that an object exists even when removed from sight.

Occipital lobe The visual processing center of the brain.

Onset-rime _Onset_ refers to the initial consonant or group of consonants in a syllable (e.g., the _c_ in the word _cat_), and _rime_ refers to the remainder of the syllable (e.g., "at" in the word _cat_).

Oral cavity One of the continuous, air-filled cavities of the vocal tract (the mouth).

Organization A cognitive process based on the natural tendency to organize information into related and interconnected structures to aid in understanding.

Orthographic Pertaining to the written word.

Orthography Written system of a language, such as letters that compose written words.

Otitis media (OM) Otitis media is an inflammation or infection of the middle ear that typically occurs in the area between the eardrum (the end of the outer ear) and the inner ear, including the eustachian tube. Typically serous (clear) or purulent (pus-like) fluid is excreted by the mucous membrane that lines the middle ear, and this results in a conductive hearing loss.

Ototoxic drugs Medications that can result in a hearing loss as a side effect of taking that drug. Some drugs used with premature babies to sustain life are ototoxic.

Overextension A process in children's early word usage in which the meaning of a word is applied to more examples than in adult language. This may occur when a child perceives similarities in the characteristics of entities and calls them by the same name (e.g., all four-legged animals called "doggy").

Overgeneralization A process whereby children extend their use of grammatical features beyond the context of those in adult language. For example, children may overgeneralize the regular suffix _-ed_ to irregular verb forms (e.g., "eated" vs. _ate_).

Parallel distributed processing The theory that assumes the mind is composed of a great number of elementary units connected in a neural network. Mental processes are interactions between these units, which excite and inhibit each other in parallel rather than sequential operations. In this context, the connections are made between pairs of units that are distributed throughout the network.

Parietal lobe A lobe in the brain that integrates sensory information from different modalities that determine spatial sense and navigation.

Perceive To hear, understand, or interpret something in a particular way.

Performative narrative Used to entertain, and a speaker may use elaboration and exaggeration to make a story more amusing.

Performatives Speech acts that constitute a speaker's intention or meaning to a listener. Part of a number of speech acts, such as promises, greetings, and commands for action.

Perseveration The repetition of a word, phrase, or longer utterance.

Personal narrative A narrative that describes a past event experienced by the narrator or someone familiar to the narrator.

Pharynx Air-filled cavity of the vocal tract located between the larynx and the oral and nasal cavities.

Phonation The process of setting the vocal folds into vibration to produce sound.

Phoneme awareness The understanding that spoken words consist of individual phonemes, such as awareness that the word *boat* contains four phonemes, that the words *bee* and *ball* both begin with the phoneme /b/, that the words *pill* and *pot* both begin with the phoneme /p/, and that phonemes can be rearranged or substituted to make different words.

Phonemes The sounds of a language. The first sound in the words *finger* and *pharynx* is the phoneme /f/, for example.

Phonemic awareness The ability to hear and manipulate individual phonemes.

Phonetically consistent forms Expressions used to convey consistent meaning, such as "doggy" used only to label dogs.

Phonological awareness The ability to pay attention to the sounds of language separate from its meaning. It is a term that involves such skills as the ability to manipulate, count, and identify linguistic units at the phoneme, word, or syllable levels.

Phonological processes Rules that map sounds in the target language to phonemes in young children's limited production inventory, such as producing a /w/ for the *r* in *rabbit*

("wabbit") instead of the intended /r/. These processes are predictable (typical) developmental speech production errors that children make while learning to produce speech.

Phonological processing An auditory processing skill that involves detecting and discriminating differences in phonemes or speech sounds.

Phonology Rules for the combination of sounds to form words in a language.

Phrase structure rules Phrase-structure rules describe a language's syntax and sentence structure.

Place of articulation The anatomical location at which a sound is created within the vocal tract. For example, the place of articulation of the stop sound /b/ in *boy* is at the lips (bilabial). The place of articulation of the /f/ sound in *five* is the constriction made by the upper teeth and lower lip (labio-dental).

Power source The ventilatory system is the power source for a speaker's speech efforts.

Pragmatic Pragmatic behaviors are those that conform to appropriate communicative interaction or behaviors.

Pragmatics 1. The branch of linguistics that studies language use rather than language structure. 2. The connection between language development and the environment or the context in which communication occurs.

Prefrontal cortex The anterior part of the frontal lobes of the brain that is involved in planning complex cognitive behaviors, personality expression, and decision making and moderating correct social behavior.

Prelinguistic The period between birth and 13 months of age during which a baby uses sounds and gestures to communicate wants and needs before recognizable speech develops.

Preliteracy A period of development that occurs before a child is able to read or write.

Primary auditory cortex Located in the temporal lobe, it is the region of the brain that is responsible for processing auditory (sound) information.

Primary or dominant language The language most often used in communication.

Primary visual cortex Located in the occipital lobe, it is the region of the brain that is responsible for processing visual information.

Private speech Often called egocentric speech, this is Piaget's concept of a child's inability to take another's point of view. The child's speech is not adapted to the listener's understanding needs.

Process The ability to understand, interpret, or make sense of information.

Proficiency The relative ability to use a language for communication.

Proposition An idea unit or statement often expressing that something is true or false.

Prospective mental development What children need to learn with guidance.

Pruning Eliminates weaker synaptic contacts while stronger connections are kept and strengthened, with connections that have been activated most frequently preserved.

Quasiresonant nuclei Sounds produced by infants that approach the quality of real vowels and very brief consonants.

Recasts Sentence recasts are adults' corrections or modifications of children's utterances.

Receptive language The language that people comprehend or understand.

Reduplicated babbling Babbling that consists of repeated consonant-vowel pairs (e.g. "bababa").

Referents Objects, people, or events that a narrator mentions in conversation or a narrative.

Reflexive Without thought, such as an automatic or involuntary action.

Relative pronouns A pronoun that refers to a previously used noun, such as *he* or *it*.

Resonance A phenomenon in which a body of air, having a naturally tendency to vibrate at a particular frequency or frequencies, is set into vibration by another structure vibrating at or near those frequencies. In the example of vowel production, the air particles within the cavities of the vocal tract (body of air) will respond (vibrate) to the sound created in the larynx by the vibrating vocal folds. As the size and shape of the vocal tract are altered, the resonance characteristics will change, as will the quality of the sound produced.

Response to Intervention (RtI) A method of academic intervention used in the United States designed to provide early, effective assistance to children who are having difficulty learning using research-proven interventions.

Retrospective mental development What children can do by themselves, defined by independent problem solving.

Reverberation The echo of sound that results in persistence of the original sound in an enclosure or partially enclosed space after the source of sound has stopped.

Rhythm The pattern formed by stressed and unstressed syllables.

Rib cage Also referred to as the thorax, the rib cage is a barrel-shaped structure composed of 12 pairs of ribs that articulate (attach) to the sternum in front and to the vertebral column in back. The lungs are attached to the inside of the rib cage by the pleural lining.

Right brain Visual and processes information in an intuitive and simultaneous manner, first looking at the whole and then looking at details. Individuals who are right-brain dominant focus on aesthetics, feeling, and creativity.

Scaffolding An instructional strategy that involves supporting novice learners by limiting the complexities of the context through supports and gradually removing those supports as learners gain the knowledge, skills, and confidence to cope with the full complexity of language in different contexts.

Scaffolds Scaffolds consist of input from adults that provide children with cues and supports that allow them to acquire language.

Schema 1. According to Piaget, the basic psychological structure for organizing information. 2. An organizational or conceptual pattern in the mind used to catagorize objects or ideas.

Scripts A real or imagined piece of text that plans out what one is to say or do on a specific occasion.

Self-regulation The method or procedure that learners use to manage and organize their thoughts and convert them into skills used for learning. Self-regulation involves continuously monitoring progress toward a goal, checking outcomes, and redirecting unsuccessful efforts.

Semantic contingency The adult response is related to the child's meaning.

Semantic relations Relations between concepts or meanings.

Semantic roles The underlying relationship that a word has with the main verb in a clause, such as the relationship the agent *boy* has with the verb *go* in the sentence "The boy goes to school."

Semantic transparency The relationship of the range of potential meaning of a figurative use of language to its referent; often ranges from a more literal association that is easily understood, such as "a sunny disposition," to a more abstract, nonliteral association, as in "up a creek without a paddle."

Semantics 1. The component of language that refers to meaning and rules that govern the assignment of meaning to entities (e.g., people, animals, and things) along with activities or events. 2. A subdivision of linguistics devoted to the study of meaning in language and how the meaning in language is formed by the use and interrelationships of words, phrases, and sentences.

Sensorineural hearing loss (SNHL) Occurs when there is damage to the inner ear (cochlea) or to the nerve pathways from the inner ear (retrocochlear) to the brain.

Sensory information The ongoing reception and processing of sensory stimuli in the brain. Sensory reception of stimuli occurs through the senses: smell, sight, hearing, touch, and taste.

Sentence length The number of words in a spoken or written sentence· Sentence length increases as children's language abilities develop.

Sheltered Instruction Observation Protocol (SIOP) Professional development in the SIOP Model helps teachers plan and deliver lessons that allow English learners to acquire academic knowledge as they develop English-language proficiency.

Simple A sentence that contains only a subject and a verb.

Social competence Social competence refers to the social, emotional, and cognitive skills and behaviors that children need for successful social adaptation and social interaction.

Social interaction Any action that is shared with others and contains a shared symbolic system.

Socially marked dialect A dialect that has become much more marked than others as substandard or deficient.

Sociointeractional Describes a social relation or social interaction relationship.

Soft palate A muscular extension of the hard palate also known as the velum. The soft palate is lowered during production of the nasal sounds and is raised during production of all other English speech sounds.

Special educator A highly trained professional who provides specifically designed instruction and services to children with disabilities.

Specifically Designed Academic Instruction in English (SDAIE) A teaching approach intended for teaching various academic skills, such as social studies, science, or literature, through using English language with students who are still learning English. SDAIE requires that students possess intermediate fluency in English as well as mastery of their native language through material in their primary language.

Speech Spoken language, distinct from written language. The neuromuscular process by which humans turn language into a sound signal that is transmitted through the air (or another medium, such as a telephone line) to a receiver.

Speech acts Utterances in relation to the behavior of the speaker and hearer in interpersonal communication.

Speech-language pathologist (SLP) A professional sometimes called a *speech therapist* who is educated and trained to prevent, assess, diagnose, and provide intervention for disorders related to speech, language, cognitive-communication, voice, swallowing, and fluency throughout the life span.

Speech perception 1. The awareness of sounds spoken in the surrounding language. 2. How the brain processes speech and language to understand sounds and words of a native language.

Speech reading A method of using visual clues from a speaker's face to decode the contents of spoken language.

Speech sound disorder Speech acquisition that occurs in a delayed and/or deviant manner.

Spinal column An intricate structure of bones, muscles, and other tissues that form the posterior part of the body's trunk, from the skull to the pelvis, and that protects the spinal cord.

Static articulators Structures in the vocal tract against which dynamic (movable) articulators contact to produce speech sounds. For example, the tongue (a dynamic articulator) is placed in contact with the alveolar ridge of the hard palate (a static articulator) to produce the /t/ sound.

Stop-plosives A class of speech sounds produced by forming a complete closure in the oral cavity, building up pressure behind that closure, and suddenly releasing the closure to produce a brief noise burst. Examples of stop-plosives are the sounds /p/ in _pie_, /t/ in _top_, and /k/ in _key_.

Stops A term sometimes used synonymously with stop-plosive. These are sounds produced by forming a complete closure in the oral cavity without the noise burst that characterizes the release of a stop-plosive.

Stress A prosodic feature of speech related to the syllable. A stressed syllable tends to be longer in duration, higher in frequency (pitch), and of greater intensity (loudness) than an unstressed syllable. In the word *above*, the first syllable is unstressed, whereas the final syllable is stressed.

Subglottal pressure The pressure below the vocal folds. The generation and maintenance of a steady, positive subglottal pressure is critical to speech sound production.

Submersion When students who speak languages other than English receive no special language assistance. Submersion is a violation of federal civil rights law (*Lau v. Nichols*, 1974).

Subordinate clauses A group of words that has both a subject and a verb but (unlike an independent clause) cannot stand alone as a sentence as it does not express a complete thought. An example is the phrase "Until I find my keys" in the sentence "Until I find my keys, we can't leave."

Subordinate dependent clause Sometimes called a dependent clause and is usually introduced by a subordinating element such as a subordinating conjunction or relative pronoun.

It does not express a complete thought and requires the rest of the sentence to determine its meaning. It must always be attached to a main clause that completes the meaning (e.g., "After Mary ate the sandwich, she cleaned the table").

Subordinating conjunctions Join a subordinate clause to a main clause with words such as *after, although, because, until,* and *when.*

Subordination Writers use subordination to combine two ideas in a single sentence, such as "Mary read while she drank tea."

Surface structure A spoken sentence. The surface structure provides the syntactical and phonological component of the sentence that individuals hear.

Syllable A unit of spoken language that consists of one or more vowel sounds alone, a syllabic consonant alone, or any of these with one or more consonant sounds.

Symbolic functions A word used to represent an entity or activity through language.

Synapses Connections between neurons through which "information" flows from one neuron to another.

Syntax 1. Rules that govern the way words combine to form phrases, clauses, and sentences (and one of the major components of grammar). 2. The order or arrangement of words in a sentence.

Temporal lobe The lower lateral lobe of either cerebral hemisphere, located in front of the occipital lobe and containing the sensory center of hearing in the brain.

Theme A distinct, recurring, and unifying quality or idea.

Theory of mind (TOM) The ability to understand mental states, such as an individual's beliefs, intents, wishes, beliefs, and knowledge; to understand these mental states that may be different from one's own mental states.

Thorax See *Rib cage.*

Thought processing The ability to solve problems, plan, organize, predict, speculate, and hypothesize or infer.

Topic-associating narratives Lengthy narratives in which topics or themes are presented by semantic links rather than chronological ordering. A narrative style in which the main topic is not explicitly stated but is implied for loosely connected episodes.

Topic-centered narratives Related because one happening leads to another; a narrative style that refers to a linear progression of information with explicit sequential foundation.

Trachea A tubular structure of the lower respiratory system that extends from the larynx to the mainstem bronchi of the lungs.

Transformation A formal linguistic operation that shows a correspondence between two structures, such as an active sentence (e.g., *John kicked the ball*) and a passive sentence (e.g., *The ball was kicked by John*). In vocabulary, it's a change in a root word by the addition of either a prefix or a suffix to derive new meaning and change the part of speech. For example, the noun *family* is transformed to an adjective, *familiar,* via the addition of the suffix *-iar* to the root of the base word.

Two-way immersion A distinctive form of dual-language education in which native English speakers and native speakers of another language are integrated for academic content instruction with English and the partner language.

Use A linguistic term that defines the pragmatics of language or rules for using language in interaction.

Variegated babbling A stage in babbling characterized by varied sequences of sounds in syllables.

Velopharyngeal closure Occurs when the velum is raised and the pharyngeal walls close around the velum, thus sealing off the nasal cavity so that air and sound pass through the oral cavity.

Velum See *Soft palate*.

Ventilatory system The structures of the rib cage and diaphragm-abdomen responsible for the mechanical exchange of air into and out of the lungs (breathing).

Verbal reasoning The ability to understand facts and concepts or ideas expressed in words and to manipulate this information to solve a problem.

Vocables Word-like productions that emerge at about 10 to 12 months and that lack meaning but sound like real words.

Vocabulary The words one is typically familiar with and uses within a given language. There are several different types of vocabulary that include speaking vocabulary, listening vocabulary, reading vocabulary, and writing vocabulary.

Vocal cords A pair of muscular tissues in the larynx that are separated during inhalation and can be set into rapid vibration to produce sound (phonation). They are also known as the *vocal folds*.

Vocal folds See *Vocal cords*.

Vocal tract Air-filled interconnecting cavities within which some speech sounds are created and all sounds are resonated. The vocal tract consists of three interconnecting cavities: the pharyngeal cavity (pharynx), oral cavity (mouth), and nasal cavity.

Vocalizations 1. Any voiced sound; to use the voice to express something. 2. An utterance viewed as a sequence of sound.

Voiced sounds Sounds produced with vocal fold vibration.

Voiceless sounds Those sounds produced without vocal fold vibration.

Wernicke's area The region of the brain that is important in language development. Wernicke's area is located on the temporal lobe on the left side of the brain and is responsible for the comprehension of speech (Broca's area is related to the production of speech).

White matter The part of the brain that contains myelinated nerve fibers. The white matter is white because it is the color of myelin, the insulation covering the nerve fibers. The white matter is the tissue through which messages pass between different areas of grey matter within the nervous system.

Working memory Allows a child to understand and remember a series of directions.

Zone of proximal development The difference between what a learner can do without help and what he or she can do with help. The distance between the actual developmental level as determined by independent problem solving and the level of potential development as determined through problem solving under adult guidance or in collaboration with more capable peers.

References

CHAPTER 1

Bernstein, D. K., & Levey, S. (2009). Language development: A review. In D. K. Bernstein & E. Tiegerman-Farber (Eds.), *Language and communication disorders in children* (6th ed., pp. 28–100). Boston: Allyn & Bacon.

Boyer, E. (1991). *Ready to learn: A mandate for the nation.* Princeton, NJ: Carnegie Foundation for the Advancement of Teaching.

Hadley, P., Simmerman, A., Long, M., & Luna, M. (2000). Facilitating language development for inner-city children: Experimental evaluation of a collaborative, classroom based intervention. *Language, Speech, and Hearing Services in Schools, 31*(3), 280–295.

Owens, R. E. (2008). *Language development: An introduction* (7th ed.). Boston: Pearson Education.

Peets, K. F. (2009). The effects of context on the classroom discourse skills of children with language impairment. *Language, Speech, and Hearing Services in Schools, 40,* 5–16.

Quale, C., Peters, B., & Matkins, R. (2010). *Classroom techniques for students with language-learning disorders.* Retrieved May 22, 2010, from http://www.communicationconnects.com/articles/classroomTechniques.pdf

Rescorla, L. (1989). The language development survey: A screening tool for delayed language in toddlers. *Journal of Speech and Hearing Disorders, 54,* 587–599.

Secord, W. (2002, November). *Practical performance assessment.* Paper presented at the meeting of the American Speech-Language-Hearing Association, Atlanta, GA.

Sotto, C., & Prendeville, J. (2007, November). *Collaborative support for children's language/literacy skills using classroom performance data.* Paper presented at the meeting of the American Speech-Language-Hearing Association, Boston.

CHAPTER 2

Abbeduto, L., & Boudreau, D. (2004). Theoretic influences on research on language development in addition, intervention in individuals with mental retardation. *Mental Retardation and Developmental Disabilities, 10,* 184–192.

Astington, J. W. (1990). Narrative and the child's theory of mind. In B. K. Britton & A. D. Pellegrini (Eds.), *Narrative thought and narrative language* (pp. 151–171). Hillsdale, NJ: Erlbaum.

Baron-Cohen, S. (1993). From attention-goal psychology to belief-desire psychology: The development of a theory of mind, and its dysfunction. In S. Baron-Cohen, H. Tager-Flusberg, & D. J. Cohen (Eds.), *Understanding other minds: Perspectives from autism* (pp. 59–82). New York: Oxford University Press.

Baron-Cohen, S. (1996). *Mindblindness: An essay on autism and theory of mind.* Cambridge: MIT Press.

Bartsch, K., & Wellman, H. M. (1995). *Children talk about the mind.* Oxford, UK: Oxford University Press.

Bates, E. (1976). *Language and context: The acquisition of pragmatics.* San Diego, CA: Academic Press.

Bates, E., Camaioni, L., & Volterra, V. (1976). Sensorimotor performatives. In E. Bates (Ed.), *Language and context: The acquisition of pragmatics* (pp. 49–71). San Diego, CA: Academic Press.

Bates, E., & Elman, J. (1996). Learning rediscovered: A perspective on Saffran, Aslin, & Newport. *Science, 274,* 1849–1850.

Bates, E., Elman, J., Johnson, M., Karmiloff-Smith, A., Parisi, D., & Plunkett, K. (1998). In W. Bechtel & G. Graham (Eds.), *A companion to cognitive sciences* (pp. 590–601). Oxford, UK: Basil Blackwell.

Bates, E., & MacWhinney, B. (1982). Functionalist approaches to grammar. In E. Wanner & L. R. Gleitman (Eds.), *Language acquisition: The state of the art*. Cambridge, UK: Cambridge University Press.

Bates, E., & Snyder, L. (1987). The cognitive hypothesis in language development. In I. Uzgiris & J. Hunt (Eds.), *Infant performance and experience: New finding with the ordinal scale*. Urbana: University of Illinois Press.

Berk, L. E. (1992). Children's private speech: An overview of theory and the status of research. In R. M. Diaz & L. E. Berk (Eds.), *Private speech: From social interaction to self-regulation* (pp. 17–53). Hillsdale, NJ: Erlbaum.

Borden, G. J., Harris, K. S., & Raphael, L. J. (2003). *Speech science primer: Physiology, acoustic, and perception of speech*. Philadelphia: Lippincott Williams & Wilkins.

Bruner, J. (1972). Nature and uses of immaturity. *American Psychologist, 8,* 687–708.

Bruner, J. (1986). *Actual minds, possible worlds*. Cambridge, MA: Harvard University Press.

Bruner, J. (1990). *Acts of meaning*. Cambridge, MA: Harvard University Press.

Carter, A., Ornstein, A., Davis, N., Klin, A., & Volkmar, F. (2005). Social development in autism. In F. Volkmar, R. Paul, & D. Cohen (Eds.), *Handbook of autism and pervasive developmental disorders* (3rd ed., Vol. 2, pp. 312–334). New York: Wiley.

Chomsky, N. (1957). *Syntactic structures*. The Hague, Netherlands: Mouton.

Chomsky, N. (1959). A review of Skinner's verbal behavior. *Language, 35,* 26–58.

Chomsky, N. (1964). *Current issues in linguistic theory*. The Hague, Netherlands: Mouton.

Chomsky, N. (1965). *Aspects of the theory of syntax*. Cambridge: MIT Press.

Coleman, D. (1995). *Emotional intelligence: Why it can matter more than IQ*. New York: Bantam.

Conezio, K., & French, L. (2002). Science in the preschool classroom: Capitalizing on children's fascination with the everyday world to foster language and literacy development. *Young Children, 5,* 12–18.

De Villiers, J. G., & de Villiers, P. A. (2003). Language for thought: Coming to understand false beliefs. In D. Gentner & S. S. Goldin-Meadow (Eds.), *Language in mind; advances in the study of language and thought* (pp. 335–384). Cambridge: MIT Press.

Dore, J. (1978). Requestive systems in nursery school conversations: Analysis of talk in its social context. In R. Campbell & P. Smith (Eds.), *Recent advances in the psychology of language: Language development and mother-child interaction* (pp. 271–292). New York: Plenum.

Epstein, A. (2003). *How planning and reflection develop young children's thinking skills*. Retrieved May 22, 2010, from http://journal.naeyc.org/btj/200309/Planning&Reflection.pdf

Feinfeld, K. A., Lee, P. P., Flavell, E. R., Green, F. L, & Flavell, J. H. (1999). Young children's understanding of intention. *Cognitive Development, 14,* 463–486.

Fey, M. E., Long, S. H., & Finestack, L. H. (2003). Ten principles of grammar facilitation for children with specific language impairments. *American Journal of Speech-Language Pathology, 12,* 3–15.

Garhart Mooney, C. (2000). *An introduction to Dewey, Montessori, Erikson, Piaget, & Vygotsky*. St. Paul, MN: Redleaf Press.

Gathercole, S. E., & Baddeley, A. D. (1990). Phonological memory deficits in language disordered children: Is there a causal connection? *Journal of Memory and Language, 29,* 336–360.

Gentner, D. (2003). Why we're so smart. In D. Gentner & S. Goldin-Meadow (Eds.), *Language in mind: Advances in the study of language and thought* (pp. 195–235). Cambridge: MIT Press.

Gopnik, A., & Meltzoff, A. N. (1988). From people, to plans, to object: Changes in the meaning of early words and their relation to cognitive development. In M. B. Franklin & S. S. Barten (Eds.), *Child language: A reader* (pp. 60–69). New York: Oxford University Press. (Reprinted from *Journal of Pragmatics, 9,* 496–512)

Gopnik, A., & Meltzoff, A. N. (1998). *Words, thoughts, and theories*. Cambridge: MIT Press.

Gopnik, A., & Wellman, H. (1992). Why the child's theory of mind really is a theory. *Mind and Language, 7,* 145–171.

Guajardo, N. R., & Watson, A. C. (2002). Narrative discourse and theory of mind development. *Journal of Genetic Psychology, 16*(3), 305–325.

Hainline, L. (1978). Developmental changes in visual scanning of face and nonface patterns by infants. *Journal of Experimental Child Psychology, 25,* 90–113.

Haith, M. M., Bergman, T., & Moore, M. J. (1977). Eye contact and face scanning in early infancy. *Science, 198*(4319), 853–855.

Hale, C. M., & Tager-Flusberg, H. (2003). The influence of language on theory of mind: A training study. *Developmental Science, 6*(3), 346–359.

Halliday, M. (1975). *Learning how to mean: Explorations in the development of language.* New York: Edward Arnold.

Harris, P. L. (1971). Examination and search in infants. *British Journal of Psychology, 52,* 469–473.

Hirsh-Pasek, K., & Golinkoff, R. M. (1997). *The origins of grammar: Evidence from early language comprehension.* Cambridge: MIT Press.

Hirsh-Pasek, K, Golinkoff, R., & Hollich, G. (1999). Trends and transitions in language development: Looking for the missing piece. *Developmental Neuropsychology, 16*(2), 139–162.

Huitt, W. (2000). The information processing approach. *Educational Psychology Interactive.* Valdosta, GA: Valdosta State University. Retrieved June 12, 2002, from http://chiron.valdosta.edu/whuitt/col/cogsys/infoproc.html

Hulit, L. M., & Howard, M. R. (1997). *Born to talk: An introduction to speech and language development.* New York: Macmillan.

Jenkins, J. M., & Astington, J. W. (1996). Cognitive factors and family structure associated with theory of mind development in young children. *Developmental Psychology, 32,* 70–78.

Jones, W., Carr, K., & Klin, A. (2008). Absence of preferential looking to the eyes of approaching adults predicts level of social disability in 2-year-old toddlers with autism spectrum disorder. *Archives of General Psychiatry, 65*(8), 946–954.

Jusczyk, P. W., Friederici, A. D., Wessels, J., Svenkerud, V. Y., & Jusczyk, A. M. (1993). Infants' sensitivity to the sound patterns of native language words. *Journal of Memory and Language, 32,* 402–420.

Karmiloff-Smith, A. (1992). *Beyond modularity: A developmental perspective on cognitive science.* Cambridge: MIT Press.

Lantz, J. (2002). Theory of mind in autism: Development, implications, and interventions. *Reporter, 7*(3), 18–25.

Lohmann, H., & Tomasello, M. (2003). The role of language in the development of false belief understanding: A training study. *Child Development, 74*(4), 1130–1144.

McLeish, J., & Martin, J. (1975). Verbal behavior: A review and experimental analysis. *Journal of General Psychology, 93,* 3–66.

Miller, C. A. (2006). Developmental relationships between language and theory of mind. *American Journal of Speech-Language Pathology, 15,* 142–154.

Ninio, A., & Snow, C. E. (1996). *Pragmatic development: Essays in developmental science.* Boulder, CO: Westview Press.

Piaget, J. (1929). *The child's conception of the world.* London: Routledge & Kegan Paul.

Piaget, J. (1954). *The construction of reality in the child.* New York: Basic Books.

Piaget, J. (1967). Language and thought from the genetic point of view. In D. Elkind (Ed.), *Six psychological studies.* New York: Random House.

Piaget, J. (2007). *The language and thought of the child* (M. Gabain & R. Gabain, Trans.). London: Routledge. (Original work published 1923)

Pinker, S. (1994). *The language instinct: How the mind creates language.* New York: William Morrow.

Proctor-Williams, K., Fey, M., & Loeb, D. (2001). Parental recasts and production of copulas and articles by children with specific language impairment. *American Journal of Speech-Language Pathology, 10,* 155–169.

Prutting, C. A. (1982). Pragmatics as social competence. *Journal of Speech and Hearing Disorders, 47,* 123–134.

Schult, C. A. (2002). Children's understanding of the distinction between intentions and desires. *Child Development, 73*(6), 1727–1747.

Seidenberg, M. S., & Elman, J. (1999). Do infants learn grammar with algebra or statistics? *Science, 284,* 5413.

Shatz, M., Wellman, H. M., & Silber, S. (1983). The acquisition of mental verbs: A systematic investigation of the first reference to mental state. *Cognition, 14,* 301–321.

Skinner, B. F. (1957). *Verbal learning.* New York: Appleton-Century-Crofts.

Thompson, R., & Hixson, P. (1984). Teaching parents to encourage independent problem solving in preschool age children. *Language, Speech, and Hearing Services in Schools, 15,* 175–181.

Tomasello, M. (1999). *The cultural origins of human cognition.* Cambridge, MA: Harvard University Press.

Turkstra, L. (2007). Pragmatic communication disorders: New intervention approaches. *ASHA Leader, 12*(12), 16–17.

Vygotsky, L. S. (1935). *Mind in society: The development of higher psychological processes.* Cambridge, MA: Harvard University Press.

Vygotsky, L. S. (1986). *Thought and language.* Cambridge: MIT Press.

Vygotsky, L. S. (1988). Inner speech. In M. B. Franklin & S. S. Barten (Eds.), *Child language: A reader* (pp. 181–187). New York: Oxford University Press. (Original work published 1962)

Wellman, H. M. (1990). *The child's theory of mind.* Cambridge: MIT Press.

Westby, C. (2007, March 30). *Play and language: The roots of literacy.* Paper presented at the continuing education conference at Lehman College of the City University of New York, Bronx.

Wimmer, H., & Perner, J. (1983). Beliefs about beliefs: Representation and constraining function of wrong beliefs in young children's understanding of perception. *Cognition, 13,* 103–128.

Wellman, H. M., Cross, D., & Watson, J. (2001). Meta-analysis of theory-of-mind development: The truth about false-belief. *Child Development, 72,* 655–684.

Witt, B. (1998). Cognition and the cognitive-language relationship. In W. O. Haynes & B. B. Shulman (Eds.), *Communication development: Foundations, processes, and clinical applications* (pp. 101–133). Baltimore: Williams & Wilkins.

Zimmerman, B. J., & Rosenthal, T. L. (1974). Observational learning of rule-governed behavior by children. *Psychological Bulletin, 81,* 29–42.

CHAPTER 3

American Speech-Language-Hearing Association. (1993). *Definitions of communication disorders and variations* [Relevant paper]. Retrieved from http://www.asha.org/policy

American Speech-Language-Hearing Association. (2005). *Cultural differences in communication and learning styles.* Retrieved from http://www.asha.org/practice/multicultural/readings/reading_2.htm

Apel, K., Masterson, J. J., & Niessen, N. L. (2004). Spelling assessment frameworks. In C. A. Stone, E. R. Silliman, B. J. Ehren, & K. Apel (Eds.), *Handbook of language and literacy: Development and disorders* (pp. 644–678). New York: Guilford Press.

Baddeley, A. D. (1986). *Working memory.* Oxford, UK: Clarendon.

Baddeley, A. D., Gathercole, S. E., & Papagno, C. (1998). The phonological loop as a language learning device. *Psychological Review, 105,* 158–173.

Bernstein, D. K., & Levey, S. (2009). Language development: A review. In D. K. Bernstein & E. Tiegerman-Farber (Eds.), *Language and communication disorders in children* (6th ed., pp. 28–100). Boston: Allyn & Bacon.

Bornstein, M. H., Han, C.-S., & Haynes, O. M. (2004). Specific and general language performance across early children: Stability and gender considerations. *First Language, 24*(3), 267–304.

Brown, D. S., & Ford, K. (2007). *Communication strategies for all classrooms: Focusing on English language learns and students with learning disabilities.* Retrieved from http://www.readingrockets.org/article/19260

Caldera, Y. M., Huston, A. C., & O'Brien, M. (1989). Social interactions and play patterns of parents and toddlers with feminine, masculine, and neutral toys. *Child Development, 60,* 70–76.

Catts, H. W., & Kamhi, A. G. (Eds.). (2005). *Language and reading disabilities* (2nd ed.). Boston: Allyn & Bacon.

Cummins, J. (1984). *Bilingual education and special education: Issues in assessment and pedagogy.* San Diego, CA: College Hill.

Geschwind, N., & Galaburda, A. M. (1985). Cerebral lateralization. Biological mechanisms, associations, and pathology: A hypothesis and a program for research. *Archives of Neurology, 42*(5), 428–459.

Gillam, R. B., & Johnston, J. R. (1992). Spoken and written language relationships in language/learning impaired and normal achieving school-age children. *Journal of Speech and Hearing Research, 35,* 1303–1315.

Gillon, G. T. (2004). *Phonological awareness: From research to practice.* New York: Guilford Press.

Goldstein, B. (2000). *Cultural and linguistic diversity resource guide for speech-language pathologists.* San Diego, CA: Singular.

Gottardo, A. (2002). The relationship between language and reading skills in bilingual Spanish-English speakers. *Topics in Language Disorders, 22*(5), 46–70.

Huttenlocher, J., Haight, W., Bryk, A., Seltzer, M., & Lyons, T. (1991). Early vocabulary growth: Relation to language input and gender. *Developmental Psychology, 27,* 236–248.

Juel, C., Griffith, P. L., & Gough, P. B. (1986). Acquisition of literacy: A longitudinal study of children in first and second grade. *Journal of Educational Psychology, 78,* 243–255.

Justice, L. M., & Schuele, C. M. (2004). Phonological awareness: Description, assessment, and intervention. In J. E. Bernthal & N. W. Bankson (Eds.), *Articulation and Phonological Disorders* (5th ed., pp. 376–411). Boston: Pearson.

Kamhi, A. G., & Catts, H. W. (1991). *Reading disabilities: A developmental language perspective.* Boston: Allyn & Bacon.

Levey, S. (2004). The discrimination and the production of English vowels by bilingual Spanish/English speakers. *Perceptual and Motor Skills, 99,* 445–462.

Levey, S., & Schwartz, R. G. (2002). Syllable omission by two-year-old children. *Communication Disorders Quarterly, 23*(4), 169–177.

Limbos, M. M., & Geva, E. (2001). Accuracy of teacher assessments of second-language students at risk for reading disability. *Journal of Learning Disabilities, 34*(2), 136–151.

Moore, J., Yin, L., Weaver, T., Lydell, P., & Logan, S. (2007). Preschool caregiver perceptions of the effect of gender on literacy skills. *Reading Improvement, 44* (3), 132–148.

Nelson, N. W., & Van Meter, A. M. (2007). Measuring written language ability in narrative samples. *Reading and Writing Quarterly, 23,* 287–309.

Odom, S. L., McConnell, S. R., Ostrosky, M., Peterson, C., Skellenger, A., Spicuzza, R., et al. (1997). *Play time, social time: Organizing your classroom to build interaction skills.* Minneapolis: Institute on Community Integration, University of Minnesota. Retrieved from http://ici.umn.edu/products/curricula.html

Owens, R. E. (2008). *Language development: An introduction* (7th ed.). Boston: Pearson Education.

Rochet, B. L. (1995). Perception and production of second-language speech sounds of adults. In W. Strange (Ed.), *Speech perception and linguistic experience: Theoretical and methodological issues in cross-language speech research* (pp. 339–410). Timonium, MD: York Press.

Roth, F. P., & Troia, G. A. (2006). Collaborative efforts to promote emergent literacy and efficient word recognition skills. *Topics in Language Disorders, 26*(1), 24–41.

Sandall, S., McLean, M. E., & Smith, B. J. (2000). *DEC recommended practices in early intervention/early childhood special education.* Longmont, CO: Sopris West.

Shaywitz, B. A., Shaywitz, S. E., Pugh, K. R., Constable, R. T., Skudlarski, P., Fulbright, R. K., et al. (1995). Sex differences in the functional organization of the brain for language. *Nature, 373,* 607–609.

Siegel, L. (1993). Phonological processing deficits as the basis of a reading disability. *Developmental Review, 13,* 246–257.

Stanovich, K. E. (1994). Does dyslexia exist? *Journal of Child Psychology and Psychiatry, 35,* 579–595.

Stanovich, K. E., Cunningham, A. E., & Cramer, B. (1984). Assessing phonological awareness in kindergarten children: Issues of task comparability. *Journal of Experimental Child Psychology, 38,* 175–190.

Stanovich, K. E., & Siegel, L. S. (1994). The phenotypic performance profile of reading-disabled children: A regression-based test of the phonological-core variable-difference model. *Journal of Educational Psychology, 86,* 24–53.

Tommy, R. (2007). *Language disorders: From infancy through adolescence* (3rd ed.). St. Louis, MO: Mosby Elsevier.

Torgesen, J. K. (1999). Assessment and instruction for phonemic awareness and word recognition skills. In H. W. Catts & A. G. Kamhi (Eds.), *Language and reading disabilities* (pp. 128–153). Boston: Allyn & Bacon.

Torgesen, J. K., Al Otaiba, S., & Grek, M. L. (2005). Assessment and instruction for phonemic awareness and word recognition skills. In H. W. Catts & A. G. Kamhi (Eds.), *Language and reading disabilities* (pp. 127–156). Boston: Allyn & Bacon.

Treiman, R. (1993). *Beginning to spell: A study of first-grade children.* New York: Oxford University Press.

Troia, G. A. (2004). Phonological processing and its influence on literacy. In C. A. Stone, E. R. Silliman, B J. Ehren, & K. Apel (Eds.), *Handbook of language and literacy: Development and disorders* (pp. 271–301). New York: Guilford Press.

Tunmer, W. E., & Nesdale, A. R. (1985). Phonemic segmentation skills and beginning reading. *Journal of Educational Psychology, 77,* 417–427.

Vellutino, F. R., & Scanlon, D. (1987). Phonological coding, phonological awareness, and reading ability: Evidence from a longitudinal and experimental study. *Merrill-Palmer Quarterly, 33,* 321–363.

Wagner, R. K., & Torgesen, J. K. (1987). The nature of phonological processing and its causal role in the acquisition of reading skills. *Psychological Bulletin, 101,* 192–212.

Wong-Fillmore, L., & Snow, C. E. (2002). What teachers need to know about language. In C. T. Adger, C. E. Snow, & D. Christian (Eds.), *What teachers need to know about language* (pp. 7–54). McHenry, IL: Delta Systems.

CHAPTER 4

American Speech-Language-Hearing Association. (1997). *Guidelines for audiologic screening.* Rockville, MD: Author.

American Speech-Language-Hearing Association. (2002). *Guidelines for audiologic service provision in and for schools.* Rockville, MD: Author.

American Speech-Language-Hearing Association. (2005). *(Central) auditory processing disorders* [Technical report]. Retrieved from http://www.asha.org/policy

Anderson, K. L. (1989). *Screening instrument for targeting educational risk (SIFTER).* Retrieved from http://www.kandersonaudconsulting.com/uploads/SIFTER.pdf

Anderson, K. L., & Matkin, N. (2007). *Relationship of hearing loss to listening and learning needs.* Retrieved from http://www.kandersonaudconsulting.com

Arick, D. S., & Silman, S. (2005). Nonsurgical home treatment of middle ear effusion and associated hearing loss in children: Clinical trial. *ENT—Ear, Nose, and Throat Journal, 84,* 567–568, 570, 572–574, 576, 578.

Bellis, T. J. (2002). *When the brain can't hear: Unraveling the mystery of auditory processing disorders.* New York: Atria.

Bess, F. H., Dodd-Murphy, J., & Parker, R. A. (1998). Children with minimal sensorineural hearing loss: Prevalence, educational performance, and functional status. *Ear & Hearing, 19,* 339–354.

Blair, J. C., Peterson, M. E., & Viehweg, S. H. (1985). The effects of mild sensorineural hearing loss on academic performance of young school-age children. *Volta Review, 87,* 87–93.

Blamey, P. J., Barry, J. B., & Jacq, P. (2001). Phonetic inventory of development in young cochlear implant users six years post-operation. *Journal of Speech Hearing Research, 44,* 73–79.

Blumsack, J. T., & Anderson, K. L. (2004). Back to school! 13 facts revisited. *Hearing Review, 11*(10), 14, 16, 62–63.

Carney, A. E, & Moeller, M. P. (1998). Treatment efficacy: Hearing loss in children. *Journal of Speech and Hearing Research, 41,* 561–584.

Chermak, G. D., & Musiek, F. E. (Eds.). (1997). *Central auditory processing: New perspectives.* San Diego, CA: Singular.

Chermak, G. D., Tucker, E., & Seikel, J. A. (2002). Behavioral characteristics of auditory processing disorders and attention-deficit hyperactivity disorder: Predominately unattentive type. *Journal of American Academy of Audiology, 13,* 332–338.

Cherry, R. (1980). *Selective auditory attention test (SAAT).* St. Louis, MO: Auditec.

Cherry, R. (1992). The selective auditory attention test (SAAT): A screening test for auditory processing disorders in children. In F. H. Bess & J. W. Hall III (Eds.), *Screening children for auditory function* (pp. 361–371). Nashville, TN: Bill Wilkerson Center Press.

Cherry, R., & Rubinstein, A. (2006). Comparing monotic and diotic selective auditory attention abilities in children. *Language, Speech, and Hearing Services in Schools, 37,* 137–142.

Cole, E. B., & Flexer, C. (2007). *Children with hearing loss: Developing listening and talking birth to six.* San Diego, CA: Plural.

Crandell, C. C., Smaldino, J. J., & Flexer, C. (Eds.). (2005). *Sound-field amplification: Application to sound perception and classroom acoustics* (2nd ed.). Clifton Park, NY: Thomson Delmar.

Culbertson, D. (2007). Language and speech of the deaf and hard of hearing. In R. L. Schow & M. A. Nerboone (Eds.), *Introduction to audiologic rehabilitation* (pp. 197–244). Boston: Pearson Education.

DeConde Johnson, C., & Meinke, D. K. (2008). Noise-induced hearing loss: Implications for schools. *Seminars in Hearing, 29*(1), 59–66.

Eberhard, J. P. (2008). A place to learn: How architecture affects hearing and learning. *ASHA Leader, 13*(14), 26–27, 29.

Elfenbein, J. L., Hardin-Jones, M. A., & Davis, J. M. (1994). Oral communication skills of children who are hard of hearing. *Journal of Speech and Hearing Research, 37,* 216–226.

English, K. M. (1995). *Educational audiology across the lifespan: Serving all learners with hearing impairment.* Baltimore: Paul Brookes.

Flexer, C., & Madell, J. R. (2008). Why is hearing important for children. In J. R. Madell and C. Flexer (Eds.), *Pediatric audiology: Diagnosis, technology, and management* (pp. xix–xxii). New York: Thieme.

Folmer, R. L. (2008). Hearing loss prevention practices should be taught in schools. *Seminars in Hearing, 29*(1), 67–81.

Gravel, J., & Nozza, R. (1997). Hearing loss among children with otitis media with effusion. In J. Robert, I. Wallace, & F. Henderson (Eds.), *Otitis media in young children: Medical, developmental, and educational considerations* (pp. 63–92). Baltimore: Paul Brookes.

Hall, B. J., Oyer, H. J., & Haas, N. H. (2001). *Speech, language, and hearing disorders: A guide for the teacher* (3rd ed.). Boston: Allyn & Bacon.

Halliday, L. F., & Bishop, D. V. M. (2005). Frequency discrimination and literacy skills in children with mild to moderate sensorineural hearing loss. *Journal of Speech and Hearing Research, 48,* 1187–1203.

Hedge, M. N., & Maul, C. A. (2006). *Language disorders in children: An evidence-based approach to assessment and treatment.* Boston: Pearson, Allyn & Bacon.

Hicks, C., & Tharpe, A. M. (2002). Listening effort and fatigue in school-age children with and without hearing loss. *Journal of Speech and Hearing Research, 45,* 573–584.

Hidedecker, M. J. (2008). Noise-induced hearing loss in school-aged children: What do we know? *Seminars in Hearing, 29*(1), 19–28.

Irwin, L. (2009). *"Minimal" hearing loss: What does it mean?* Retrieved from http://www.handsandvoices .org/articles/tech/minimal.html

Jerger, J., & Musiek, F. E. (2000). Report of the consensus conference on the diagnosis of auditory processing disorders in school-aged children. *Journal of American Academy of Audiology, 11,* 467–474.

Joint Committee on Infant Hearing. (2007). Year 2007 position statement: Principles and guidelines for early hearing detection and intervention programs. *Pediatrics, 120,* 898–921.

Keith, R. (1986). *SCAN: A screening test for auditory processing disorders.* San Antonio, TX: Psychological Corp.

Kochkin, S., Luxford, W., Northern, J. L., Mason, P., & Tharpe, A. M. (2007). MarkeTrak VII: Are 1 million dependents with hearing loss in America being left behind? *Hearing Review, 14*(9), 10, 14, 16, 18, 19, 22, 24, 26, 31, 34, 36.

Kopun, J. G., & Stelmachowicz, P. G. (1998). Perceived communication difficulty of children with hearing loss. *American Journal of Audiology, 7,* 30–38.

Kuder, S. J. (2003). *Teaching students with language and communication disabilities* (2nd ed.). Boston: Pearson.

Moeller, M. P., Tomblin, J. B., Yoshinaga-Itano, C., McDonald, C., & Jerger, S. (2007). Current state of knowledge: Language and literacy of children with hearing impairment. *Ear and Hearing, 28,* 740–753.

National Center for Hearing Assessment and Management. (2007). *Universal newborn screening: Summary statistics of UNHS in the United States.* Retrieved October 10, 2008, from http:// www.infanthearing.org/status/unhsstate.html

National Institute of Deafness and Other Communication Disorders. (2008). *Noise-induced hearing loss.* Retrieved from http://www.nidcd .nih.gov/health/hearing/noise.asp

Nevins, M. E., & Chute, P. M. (1996). *Children with cochlear implants in educational settings.* San Diego, CA: Singular.

Niskar, A., Kieszak, M., Holmes, A., Esteban, E., Rubin, C., & Brody, D. (1998). Prevalence of hearing loss among children, 6 to 19 years of age. *Journal of the Medical Association, 279*(14), 1071–1075.

Northern, J. L., & Downs, M. P. (2002). *Hearing in children* (5th ed.). Baltimore: Williams & Wilkins.

Peng, S., Spencer, L. J., & Tomblin, J. B. (2004). Speech intelligibility of pediatric cochlear implant recipients with seven years of device experience. *Journal of Speech and Hearing Research, 47*, 1227–1236.

Reed, V.A. (2005). *An introduction to children with language disorders* (3rd ed.). Boston: Pearson, Allyn & Bacon.

Rosenfeld, R. M., Culpepper, L., & Doyle, K. J. (2004). Clinical practice guidelines: Otitis media with effusion. *Otolaryngology Head and Neck Surgery, 130*(5S), S95–S118.

Ross, M., Brackett, D., & Maxon, A. (1991). *Assessment and management of mainstreamed hearing-impaired children: Principles and practices.* Austin, TX: Pro-Ed.

Smoski, W. J., Brunt, M.A., & Tannahill, J. C. (1992). Listening characteristics of children with central auditory processing disorders. *Language, Speech, and Hearing Services in Schools, 23*, 145–149.

Smoski, W. J., Brunt, M. A., & Tannahill, J. C. (1998). *Children's auditory performance scale.* Tampa, FL: Educational Audiology Association.

Sorkin, D. L. (2008). Education and access laws for children with hearing loss. In J. R. Madell & C. Flexer (Eds.), *Pediatric audiology: Diagnosis, technology, and management* (pp. 218–231). New York: Thieme.

Thibodeau, L. M., & DeConde Johnson, C. (2005, September 27). Serving children with hearing loss in public school settings. *ASHA Leader, 6–7,* 36–38.

Tye-Murray, N. (2009). *Foundations of aural rehabilitation* (3rd ed.). Clifton Park, NY: Delmar.

Tye-Murray, N., & Kirk, K. I. (1993). Vowel and diphthong production by young users of cochlear implants and the relationship between the phonetic level evaluation and spontaneous speech. *Journal of Speech and Hearing Research, 36*, 488–502.

Yoshinaga-Itano, C. (2003). Early intervention after universal neonatal hearing screening: Impact on outcome. *Mental Retardation and Developmental Disabilities Research Review, 9*(4), 252–256.

CHAPTER 5

Atkinson, J. E. (1978). Correlation analysis of the physiological factors controlling fundamental voice frequency. *Journal of the Acoustical Society of America, 63*, 211–222.

Cavallo, S. A. (1999). Intervention planning for adults with voice disorders. In H. B. Klein & N. Moses (Eds.), *Intervention planning for adults with communication problems: A guide for clinical practicum and professional practice* (pp. 271–318). Boston: Allyn & Bacon.

Fujiki, M., & Brinton, B. (1984). Supplementing language therapy: Working with the classroom teacher. *Language, Speech, and Hearing Services in Schools, 15*, 98–109.

Guitar, B. (1998). *Stuttering: An integrated approach to its nature and treatment* (2nd ed.). Baltimore: Williams & Wilkins.

Kelso, J. A. S., & Munhall, K.G. (Eds.). (1988). *R. H. Stetson's motor phonetics: A retrospective edition.* Boston: College-Hill.

Kent, R. D. (1997). *The speech sciences.* San Diego, CA: Singular.

Levey, M., & Osterberg, A. (2009). *Anatomical figures.* New York: MicellaDesign.

Mackay, I. R. A. (1987). *Phonetics: The science of speech production.* Boston: Allyn & Bacon.

Netsell, R., & Daniel, B. (1979). Dysarthria in adults: Physiological approach in rehabilitation. *Archives of Physical Medicine and Rehabilitation, 60*, 502–508.

Shriberg, L. D., & Kent, R. D. (2003*). Clinical phonetics.* Boston: Allyn & Bacon.

St. Louis, K. O., Raphael, L. J., Myers, F. L., & Bakker, K. (2003, November 18). Cluttering updated. *ASHA Leader, 4–5,* 20–22.

CHAPTER 6

Baddeley, A. D. (1986). *Working memory.* Oxford, UK: Clarendon.

Barkley, R. A. (1997). Behavioral inhibition, sustained attention, and executive functions: Constructing a unifying theory of ASHA. *Psychological Bulletin, 121*(1), 65–94.

Baron-Cohen, S., Ring, H., Moriarty, J., Schmitz, B., Costa, D., & Ell, P. (1994). Recognition of mental state terms, clinical findings in children with autism, and a functional neuroimaging study of normal adults. *British Journal of Psychiatry, 165,* 640–649.

Berk, L. E. (1992). Children's private speech: An overview of theory and the status of research. In R. M. Diaz & L. E. Berk (Eds.), *Private speech: From social interaction to self-regulation* (pp. 17–53). Hillsdale, NJ: Erlbaum.

Bernstein, D. K., & Levey, S. (2009). Language development: A review. In D. K. Bernstein & E. Tiegerman-Farber (Eds.), *Language and communication disorders in children* (6th ed., pp. 28–100). Boston: Allyn & Bacon.

Binder, J. R., Frost, J. A., Hammeke, T. A., Bellogowan, P. S., Springer, J. A., Kauf, J. N., et al. (2000). Human temporal lobe activation by speech and nonspeech sounds. *Cerebral Cortex, 10,* 512–528.

Carpenter, P. A., Just, M. A., Keller, T. A., Eddy, W. F., & Thulborn, K. R. (1999). Time course of fMRI-activation in language and spatial networks during sentence comprehension. *NeuroImage, 10,* 216–224.

Chomsky, N. (2002). *On nature and language.* New York: Cambridge University Press.

Constantinidis, C., Williams, G. V., & Goldman-Rakic, P. S. (2002). A role for inhibition in shaping the temporal flow of information in prefrontal cortex nature. *Neuroscience, 5*(2), 175–180.

Denckla, M. (1996). A theory and model of executive function: A neuropsychological perspective. In G. R. Lyon & N. A. Krasnegor (Eds.), *Attention, memory, and executive function* (pp. 263–278). Baltimore: Paul Brookes.

Embick, D., Marantz, A., Miyashita, Y., O'Neil, W., & Sakai, K. L. (2000). A syntactic specialization for Broca's area. *Proceedings of the National Academy of Sciences, 97,* 6150–6154.

Friederici, A. D., Opitz, B., & von Cramon, Y. (2000). Segregating semantic and syntactic aspects of processing in the human brain: An fMRI investigation of different word types. *Cerebral Cortex, 10,* 698–705.

Geffner, D. (2007, November). *Managing executive function disorders.* Paper presented at a meeting of the American Speech-Language-Hearing Association, Boston.

Hécaen, H., & Albert, M. L. (1975). *Human neuropsychology.* New York: John Wiley.

Hirano, S., Naito, Y., Okazawa, H., Kojima, H., Honjo, I., Ishizu, K., et al. (1997). Cortical activation by monaural speech sound stimulation demonstrated by positron emission tomography. *Experimental Brain Research, 113,* 75–80.

Horwitz, B., Rumsey, J. M., & Donohue, B. C. (1998). Functional connectivity of the angular gyrus in normal reading and dyslexia. *Proceedings of the National Academy of Sciences, USA, 95,* 8939–8944.

Kleim, J. A., & Jones, T. A. (2008). Principles of experience-dependent neural plasticity: Implications for rehabilitation after brain damage. *Journal of Speech, Language, and Hearing Research, 51,* S226–S239.

Laine, M., Rinne, J. O., Krause, B. J., Teras, M., & Sipila, H. (1999). Left hemisphere activation during processing of morphologically complex word forms in adults. *Neuroscience Letters, 271,* 85–88.

Mildner, V. (2008). *The cognitive neuroscience of human communication.* New York: Erlbaum.

Otto, B. (2010). *Language development in early childhood* (3rd ed.). Saddle River, NJ: Merrill.

Owens, R. E. (2008). *Language development: An introduction.* Boston: Allyn & Bacon.

Penfield, D. W., & Roberts, L. (1959). *Speech and brain mechanisms.* Princeton, NJ: Princeton University Press.

Poldrack, R. A., Wagner, A. D., Prull, M. W., Desmond, J. E., Glover, G. H., & Gabrieli, J. D. (1999). Functional specialization for semantic and phonological processing in the left inferior prefrontal cortex. *NeuroImage, 10,* 15–35.

Rumsey, J. M., Horwitz, B., Donohue, B. C., Nace, K. L., Maisog, J. M., & Andreason, P. (1999). A functional lesion in developmental dyslexia: Left angular gyral blood flow predicts severity. *Brain and Language, 70,* 187–204.

Sava, F. A. (2000). Is attention-deficit hyperactivity disorder an exonerating construct? Strategies for school inclusion. *European Journal of Special Needs Education, 15*(2), 149–157.

Seikel, J. A., King, D. W., & Drumright, D. G. (2008). *Anatomy and physiology for speech, language, and learning* (2nd ed.). San Diego, CA: Singular.

Shulman, B. B. (1998). Child development. In W. O. Haynes & B. B. Shulman (Eds.), *Communication development: Foundations, processes, and clinical applications* (pp. 59–72). Baltimore: Williams & Wilkins.

Simos, P. G., Breier, J. I., Fletcher, J. M., Bergman, E., & Papanicolaou, A. C. (2000). Cerebral mechanisms involved in word reading in dyslexic children: A magnetic source imaging approach. *Cerebral Cortex, 10*, 809–816.

Singer, B. D., & Bashir, A. E. (1999). What are executive functions and self-regulation and what do they have to do with language-learning disorders? *Language, Speech, and Hearing Services in Schools, 30*, 265–273.

Sousa, D. A. (2006). *How the brain learns* (3rd ed.). Thousand Oaks, CA: Corwin.

Springer, S. P., & Deutsch, G. (1985). *Left brain right brain*. New York: W. H. Freeman.

Werker, J. F., & Tees, R. C. (1984). Cross-language speech perception: Evidence for perceptual reorganization during the first year of life. *Infant behavior and development, 7*, 49–63.

Westmoreland, B. F. (1994). *Medical neurosciences: An approach to anatomy, pathology, and physiology by systems and levels*. Baltimore: Williams & Wilkins.

Zera, D. A., & Lucian, D. (2001). Self-organization and learning disabilities: A theoretical perspective for the interpretation and understanding of dysfunction. *Learning Disability Quarterly, 24* (2), 107–118.

Zimmerman, B. J. (1989). A social cognitive view of self-regulated academic learning. *Journal of Educational Psychology, 81*, 329–339.

CHAPTER 7

American Speech-Language-Hearing Association. (2009). *What should my child be able to do?* Retrieved from http://www.asha.org/public/speech/development/23.htm

Bates, E., Benigni, L., Bretherton, I., Camaioni, L., & Volterra, V. (1979). In E. Bates, L. Benigni, I. Bretherton, L. Camaioni, & V. Volterra (Eds.), *The emergence of symbols: Cognition and communication in infancy* (pp. 69–140). New York: Academic Press.

Bates, E., Bretherton, I., & Snyder, L. (1988). *From first words to grammar*. New York: Academic Press.

Bernstein, D. K., & Levey, S. (2009). Language development: A review. In D. K. Bernstein & E. Tiegerman-Farber (Eds.), *Language and communication disorders in children* (pp. 28–100). Boston: Pearson.

Brown, R. (1975). *A first language: The early stages*. Cambridge, MA: Harvard University Press.

Capone, N. (2007). Tapping toddlers' evolving semantic representation via gesture. *Journal of Speech, Language, and Hearing Research, 50*, 732–745.

De Hirsch, K., Jansky, J. J., & Langford, W. S. (1966). *Predicting reading failure*. New York: Harper & Row.

Delpit, L. (2006). *Other people's children: Cultural conflict in the classroom* (Rev. ed.). New York: New Press.

Eimas, P., Siqueland, E., Jusczyk, P., & Vigorito, J. (1971). Speech perception in infants. *Science, 171*, 303–306.

Eisenberg, A. R. (1985). Learning to describe past experiences in conversation. *Discourse Processes, 8*, 177–204.

Goldstein, B. (2000). *Cultural and linguistic diversity resource guide for speech-language pathologists*. San Diego, CA: Singular.

Halliday, M. (1975). *Learning how to mean: Explorations in the development of language*. New York: Edward Arnold.

Hirsh-Pasek, K., & Golinkoff, R. M. (1997). *The origins of grammar: Evidence from early language comprehension*. Cambridge: MIT Press.

Hirsh-Pasek, K., Golinkoff, R. M., & Eyer, D. (2003). *Einstein never used flash cards: How our children really learn—and why they need to play more and memorize less*. Emmaus, PA: Rodale.

Horton-Ikard, R., & Weismer, S. E. (2007). A preliminary examination of vocabulary and word learning in African American toddlers from middle and low socioeconomic status homes. *American Journal of Speech-Language Pathology, 16*, 381–392.

James, S. L. (1990). *Normal language acquisition*. Boston: Allyn & Bacon.

Johnston, J. R., & Wong, M.-Y. A. (2002). Cultural differences in beliefs and practices concerning talk to children. *Journal of Speech, Language, and Hearing Research, 45*, 916–926.

Jusczyk, P. W. (1992). Developing phonological categories from the speech signal. In C. A. Ferguson, L. Menn, & C. Stoehl-Gammon (Eds.), *Phonological development: Models, research, implications* (pp. 17–64). Timonium, MD: York Press.

Kamhi, A., & Masterson, J. (1989). Language and cognition in mentally handicapped people: Last rites for the difference delay controversy. In M. Beveridge,

G. Conti-Ramsden, & I. Leudar (Eds.), *Language and communication in mentally handicapped people* (pp. 83–111). London: Chapman & Hall.

Karmiloff-Smith, A. (1995). *Beyond modularity: A developmental perspective on cognitive science.* Cambridge: MIT Press.

Lahey, M., Liebergott, J., Chesnick, M., Menyuk, P., & Adams, J. (1992). Variability in children's use of grammatical morphemes: Implications for understanding language impairment. *Applied Psycholinguistics, 13,* 373–398.

Levey, S., & Schwartz, R. G. (2002). Syllable omission by two-year-old children. *Communication Disorders Quarterly, 23*(4), 169–177.

Mandel, D. R., Jusczyk, P. W., & Pisoni, D. B. (1995). Infants' recognition of the sound patterns of their own names. *Psychological Science, 6,* 314–317.

McCabe, A., & Rosenthal Rollins, P. (1994). Assessment of preschool narrative skills. *American Journal of Speech-Language Pathology, 3,* 45–56.

McLaughlin, S. (1998). *Introduction to language development.* San Diego, CA: Singular.

McShane, J. (1980). *Learning to talk.* New York: Cambridge University Press.

Miller, P., & Sperry, L. (1988). Early talk about the past: The origins of conversational stories of personal experience. *Journal of Child Language, 15,* 293–315.

Owens, R. E. (2008). *Language development: An introduction* (7th ed.). Boston: Pearson.

Patterson, J. L., & Westby, C. E. (1998). The development of play. In W. O. Haynes & B. B. Shulman (Eds.), *Communication development: Foundations, processes, and clinical applications* (pp. 135–163). Baltimore: Williams & Wilkins.

Paul, R., & Alforde, S. (1993). Grammatical morpheme acquisition in 4-year-olds with normal, impaired, and late-developing language. *Journal of Speech and Hearing Research, 36,* 1271–1275.

Pearson, B., Fernandez, S., & Oller, D. K. (1993). Lexical development and word combinations of Spanish-English bilingual toddlers: Comparison to monolingual norms. *Language Learning, 43,* 93–120.

Peccei, J. S. (1999). *Child language* (2nd ed.). London: Routledge.

Piaget, J. (1954). *The construction of reality in the child.* New York: Basic.

Piaget, J. (1962). *Play, dreams, and imitation in childhood.* New York: Norton.

Platt, J., & Coggins, T. E. (1990). Comprehension of social-action games in prelinguistic children: Levels of participation and effect of adult structure. *Journal of Speech and Hearing Disorders, 55,* 315–326.

Rescorla, L. (1989). The language development survey: A screening tool for delayed language in toddlers. *Journal of Speech and Hearing Disorders, 54,* 587–599.

Rescorla, L., Roberts, J., & Dahlsgaard, K. (1997). Latetalkers at 2: Outcomes at age 3. *Journal of Speech, Language, and Hearing Research, 40,* 556–566.

Rescorla, L., & Schwartz, E. (1990). Outcome of toddlers with specific expressive language delay. *Applied Psycholinguistics, 11,* 393–407.

Roth, F. P., & Clark, D. M. (1987). Symbolic play and social participation abilities of language-impaired and normally developing children. *Journal of Speech and Hearing Disorders, 52,* 17–29.

Scarborough, H., & Dobrich, W. (1990). Development of children with early language delay. *Journal of Speech and Hearing Research, 33,* 70–83.

Searle, J. (1983). *Intentionality: An essay in the philosophy of mind.* New York: Cambridge University Press.

Seymour, H., Bland-Stewart, L., & Green, L. (1998). Difference versus deficit in child African American English. *Language, Speech, and Hearing Services in the Schools, 29,* 96–108.

Smitherman, G. (2000). *Talkin that talk: Language culture and education in African America.* London: Routledge.

Sokolov, J. L., & Snow, C. E. (1994). The changing role of negative evidence in theories of language development. In C. Gallaway & B. J. Richards (Eds.), *Input and interaction in language acquisition* (pp. 38–55). Cambridge, UK: Cambridge University Press.

Stambak, M., & Sinclair, H. (Eds.). (1993). *Pretend play among 3-year-olds* (H. Sinclair & M. Sinclair, Trans.). Hillsdale, NJ: Erlbaum. (Original work published 1990)

Stark, R. (1986). Presspeech segmental feature development. In P. Fletcher & M. Garman (Eds.), *Language acquisition* (pp. 149–173). New York: Cambridge University Press.

Thal, D., Tobias, S., & Morrison, D. (1991). Language and gesture in late talkers: A 1-year follow-up. *Journal of Speech and Hearing Research, 34,* 604–612.

Thelen, E., & Bates, E. (2003). Connectionism and dynamic systems: Are they really different? *Developmental Science, 6,* 378–391.

Tomasello, M. (2001). *The cultural origins of human cognition.* Cambridge, MA: Harvard University Press.

Tomasello, M., & Farrar, M. J. (1986). Joint attention and early language. *Child Development, 57,* 1454–1463.

Watt, N., Wetherby, A., & Shumway, S. (2006). Prelinguistic predictors of language outcome at 3 years of age. *Journal of Speech, Language, and Hearing Research, 49,* 1224–1237.

Werker, J., & Tees, R. (1984). Cross-language speech perception: Evidence for perceptual reorganization during the first year of life. *Infant Behavior and Development, 7,* 49–64.

CHAPTER 8

Adams, M. J. (1990). *Beginning to read.* Cambridge: MIT Press.

Battle, D. (2009). Assessment and intervention for culturally and linguistically diverse children. In D. K. Bernstein & E. Tiegerman-Farber (Eds.), *Language and communication disorders in children* (pp. 28–100). Boston: Pearson.

Baumann, J. F., & Kameenui, E. J. (1991). Research on vocabulary instruction: Ode to Voltaire. In J. Flood, J. M. Jensen, D. Lapp, & J. R. Squire (Eds.), *Handbook of teaching the English language arts* (pp. 602–632). New York: Macmillan.

Bernstein, D. K., & Levey, S. (2009). Language development: A review. In D. K. Bernstein & E. Tiegerman-Farber (Eds.), *Language and communication disorders in children* (pp. 28–100). Boston: Pearson.

Bernstein, D. K., & Seiger-Gardner, L. (2008). Chapter 5: Promoting communication development. In S. A. Raver (Ed.), *Early childhood special education (0–8 years): Strategies for positive outcomes* (pp. 113–148). Boston: Pearson.

Brown, R. (1973). *A first language: The early stages.* Cambridge, MA: Harvard University Press.

Catts, H. W., & Kamhi, A. G. (Eds.). (1999). *Language and reading disabilities.* Boston: Allyn & Bacon.

Cooper, D. H., Roth, F. P., Speece, D. L., & Schnatschnedier, C. (2002). The contribution of oral language skills to the development of phonological awareness. *Applied Psycholinguistics, 23,* 399–416.

Dickenson, D. K. (2001). Book reading in preschool classrooms: Is recommended practice common? In D. K. Dickenson & P. Tabors (Eds.), *Beginning literacy with language* (pp. 201–203). Baltimore: Paul Brookes.

Gallagher, A., Frith, U., & Snowling, M. (2000). Precursors of literacy delay among children at genetic risk of dyslexia. *Journal of Child Psychology and Psychiatry, 41,* 202–213.

Hirsch, E.D. (2001). *Overcoming the language gap: Make better use of the literacy time block.* Retrieved June 10, 2010, from http://archive.aft .org/pubs-reports/american_educator/summer 2001/lang_gap_hirsch.html

Justice, L. (2008). Evidence-based terminology. *American Journal of Speech-Language Pathology, 17,* 324–325.

Justice, L. M., Invernizzi, M. A., & Meier, J. D. (2002). Designing and implementing an early literacy screening protocol: Suggestions for the speech-language pathologist. *Language, Speech, and Hearing Services in Schools, 33,* 84–101.

Logan, K. J. (2003). The effect of syntactic structure upon speech initiation times of stuttering and nonstuttering speakers. *Journal of Fluency Disorders, 28,* 17–36.

Nelson, N. W. (1986). Individual processing in classroom settings. *Topics in Language Disorders, 6,* 13–27.

Nelson, N. W. (1993). *Childhood language disorders in context: Infancy through adolescence.* New York: Macmillan.

Nelson, N. W. (1998). *Childhood language disorders in context: Infancy through adolescence* (2nd ed.). Boston: Allyn & Bacon.

Nelson, N. (2010). *Language and literacy disorders: Infancy through adolescence.* Boston: Allyn & Bacon.

Owens, R. E. (2008). *Language development: An introduction* (7th ed.). Boston: Pearson.

Paradis, J. (2005). Grammatical morphology in children learning English as a second language: Implications of similarities with specific language impairment. *Language, Speech, and Hearing Services in Schools, 36*(3), 172–187.

Patterson, J. L., & Westby, C. E. (1998). The development of play. In W. O. Haynes & B. B. Shulman

(Eds.), *Communication development: Foundations, processes, and clinical applications* (pp. 135–163). Baltimore: Williams & Wilkins.

Paul, R., & Jennings, P. (1992). Phonological behavior in toddlers with slow expressive language development. *Journal of Speech and Hearing Research, 35,* 99–107.

Paul, R., & Smith, R. L. (1993). Narrative skills in 4-year-olds with normal, impaired, and late-developing language. *Journal of Speech and Hearing Research, 36,* 592–598.

Pellegrini, A. D., & Perlmutter, J. C. (1989). Classroom contextual effects on children's play. *Developmental Psychology, 25*(2), 289–296.

Peterson, C., Jesso, B., & McCabe, A. (1999). Encouraging narratives in preschoolers: An intervention study. *Journal of Child Language, 26,* 49–67.

Roth, F. P., Speece, D. L., & Cooper, D. H. (2002). A longitudinal analysis of the connection between oral language and early reading. *Journal of Educational Research, 95,* 259–272.

Sachs, J. (1984). Children's play and communication development. In R. Scheifelbusch & J. Pickar

(Eds.), *The acquisition of communicative competence.* Baltimore: University Pack Press.

Sander, E. K. (1972). When are speech sounds learned? *Journal of Speech and Hearing Disorders, 37,* 55–63.

Schwartz, R., Leonard, L., Folger, M., & Wilcox, M. (1980). Again and again: Reduplication in child phonology. *Journal of Child Language, 7,* 75–89.

Stewart-Bland, L. M. (2003). Phonetic inventories and phonological patterns of African American two-year-olds: A preliminary investigation. *Communication Disorders Quarterly, 24,* 1–15.

Tough, J. (1979). *Talk for teaching and learning.* Portsmouth, NH: Heinemann.

Valdez-Menchaca, M.C., & Whitehurst, G. J. (1992). Accelerating language development through picture book reading: A systematic extension to day care. *Developmental Psychology, 28,* 1106–1114.

Zevenbergen, A. A., & Whitehurst, G. J. (2003). Dialogic reading: A shared picture book reading intervention for preschoolers. In A. van Kleeck, S. A. Stahl, & E. B. Bauer (Eds.), *On reading books to children: Parents and teachers* (pp. 177–200). Mahwah: NJ: Erlbaum.

CHAPTER 9

Abrami, P. C., Bernard, R. M., Borokhovski, E., Wade, A., Surkes, M. A., Tamin, R., et al. (2008). Instructional interventions affecting critical thinking skills and dispositions: A stage 1 meta-analysis. *Review of Educational Research, 78,* 1102–1134.

Anderson, R. C., & Freebody, P. (1981). Vocabulary knowledge. In H. Singer & R. B. Ruddell (Eds.), *Theoretical models and processes of reading* (3rd ed., pp. 343–371). Newark, DE: International Reading Association.

Beck, I. L., & McKeown, M. G. (1991). Conditions of vocabulary acquisition. In R. Barr, M. L. Kamil, P. Mosenthal, & P. D. Pearson (Eds.), *Handbook of reading research* (Vol. II, pp. 789–814). White Plains, NY: Longman.

Beck, I. L., Perfetti, C., & McKeown, M. G. (1982). Effects of long-term vocabulary instruction on lexical access and reading comprehension. *Journal of Educational Psychology, 74,* 506–521.

Bernstein, D. K., & Levey, S. (2009). Language development: A review. In D. K. Bernstein & E. Tiegerman-Farber (Eds.), *Language and communication disorders in children* (pp. 27–94). Boston: Allyn & Bacon.

Cain, K., & Oakhill, J. (2007). Reading comprehension difficulties: Correlates, causes, and consequences. In K. Cain & J. Oakhill (Eds.), *Children's comprehension problems in oral and written language: A cognitive perspective* (pp. 41–75). New York: Guilford.

Carey, S., & Bartlett, E. (1978). Acquiring a single new word. *Papers and Reports on Child Language Development, 15,* 17–29.

Carlisle, J. (1987). The use of morphological knowledge in spelling derived forms by learning disabled and normal students. *Annals of Dyslexia, 37,* 90–108.

Carlisle, J. (1988). Knowledge of derivational morphology and spelling ability in fourth, sixth, and eighth graders. *Applied Psycholinguistics, 9,* 247–266.

Carlisle, J. (2000). Awareness of the structure and meaning of morphologically complex words: Impact on reading. *Reading and Writing: An Interdisciplinary Journal, 12,* 169–190.

Cavell, T. A. (1990). Social adjustment, social performance, and social skills: A tri-component model of social competence. *Journal of Clinical Child Psychology, 19,* 111–122.

Chall, J. S., Jacobs, V. A., & Baldwin, L. E. (1990). *The reading crisis: Why poor children fall behind.* Cambridge, MA: Harvard University Press.

Chan, Y. L., & Marinellie, S. A. (2008). Definitions of idioms in preadolescents, adolescents, and adults. *Journal of Psycholinguistic Research, 37,* 1–20.

Cometa, M. S., & Eson, M. E. (1978). Logical operations and metaphor interpretation: A Piagetian model. *Child Development, 49,* 649–659.

Cunningham, A. E., & Stanovich, K. E. (1997). Early reading acquisition and its relation to reading experience and ability 10 years later. *Developmental Psychology, 33,* 934–945.

Douglas, J. D., & Peel, B. (1979). The development of metaphor and proverb translation in children grades 1 through 7. *Journal of Educational Research, 73,* 116–119.

Henry, M. (1988). Beyond phonics: Integrated decoding and spelling instruction based on word origin and structure. *Annals of Dyslexia, 38,* 258–275.

Henry, M. (1993). Morphological structure: Latin and Greek roots and affixes as upper grade code strategies. *Reading and Writing: An Interdisciplinary Journal, 5,* 227–241.

Henry, M. (2008). *Unlocking literacy: Effective decoding and spelling instruction.* Baltimore: Paul Brookes.

Hirsch, E. D., Kett, J. F., & Trefil, J. (1988). *The dictionary of cultural literacy.* Boston: Houghton Mifflin.

Hoff-Ginsberg, E. (1985). Some contributions of mothers' speech to their children's syntax growth. *Journal of Child Language, 12,* 367–385.

Hoff-Ginsberg, E. (1986). Function and structure in maternal speech: Their relation to the child's development of syntax. *Developmental Psychology, 22,* 155–163.

Hoff-Ginsberg, E. (1990). Maternal speech and the child's development of syntax: A further look. *Journal of Child Language, 17,* 337–346.

Hoff-Ginsberg, E., & Shatz, M. (1982). Linguistic input and the child's acquisition of language. *Psychological Bulletin, 92,* 3–26.

Hunt, K. W. (1970). Syntactic maturity in school children and adults. *Monographs of the Society for Research in Child Development, 35*(1), Serial No. 134.

Huttenlocher, J., Haight, W., Bryk, A., Seltzer, M., & Lyons, T. (1991). Early vocabulary growth: Relation to language input and gender. *Developmental Psychology, 27,* 236–248.

Inhelder, B., & Piaget, J. (1958). *The growth of logical thinking: From childhood to adolescence.* New York: Basic.

Klecan-Aker, J. S., & Hedrick, D. L. (1985). A study of the syntactic language skills of normal school-age children. *Language, Speech, and Hearing Services in Schools, 16,* 187–198.

Lazar, R. T., Warr-Leeper, G. A., Nicholson, C. B., & Johnson, S. (1989). Elementary school teachers' use of multiple meaning expressions. *Language, Speech, and Hearing Services in Schools, 20,* 420–430.

Leung, D.Y. P., & Kember, D. (2003). The relationship between approaches to learning and reflection upon practice. *Educational Psychology, 23,* 61–71.

Loban, W. (1976). *Language development: Kindergarten through grade twelve.* Urbana, IL: National Council of Teachers of English.

Mahoney, D. L. (1994). Using sensitivity to word structure to explain variance in high school and college reading ability. *Reading and Writing: An Interdisciplinary Journal, 6,* 19–44.

Massachusetts Department of Education. (2006). *Earth and space science learning standards, Massachusetts science and technology/engineering curriculum framework.* Retrieved from http://www.doe.mass .edu/frameworks/scitech/1006.pdf

Medo, M. A., & Ryder, R. J. (1993). The effects of vocabulary instruction on readers' ability to make causal connections. *Reading Research and Instruction, 33,* 119–134.

Moats, L. C., & Smith, C. (1992). Derivational morphology: Why it should be included in language assessment and instruction. *Language, Speech, and Hearing Services in Schools, 23,* 312–319.

Nagy, W. E., Herman, P. A., & Anderson, R. C. (1985). Learning words from context. *Reading Research Quarterly, 20,* 233–253.

Nippold, M. A. (1991). Evaluating and enhancing idiom comprehension in language-disordered students. *Language, Speech, and Hearing Services in Schools, 22,* 100–106.

Nippold, M. A. (1993). Adolescent language developmental markers in adolescent language: Syntax, semantics, and pragmatics. *Language, Speech, and Hearing Services in Schools, 24,* 21–28.

Nippold, M. A. (2007). *Later language development: School-age children, adolescents, and young adults* (3rd ed.). Austin, TX: Pro-Ed.

Nippold, M. A., Allen, M. A., & Kirsch, D. I. (2001). Proverb comprehension as a function of reading proficiency in preadolescents. *Language, Speech, and Hearing Services in Schools, 32*, 90–100.

Nippold, M. A., & Duthie, J. K. (2003). Mental imagery and idiom comprehension: A comparison of school-age children and adults. *Journal of Speech, Language, and Hearing Research, 46*, 788–799.

Nippold, M. A., & Fey, S. H. (1983). Metaphoric understanding in preadolescents having a history of language acquisition difficulties. *Language, Speech, and Hearing Services in Schools, 14*, 171–180.

Nippold, M. A., & Haq, F. S. (1996). Proverb comprehension in youth: The role of concreteness and familiarity. *Journal of Speech and Hearing Research, 39*, 166–176.

Nippold, M. A., & Martin, S. T. (1989). Idiom interpretation in isolation versus context: A developmental study with adolescents. *Journal of Speech and Hearing Research, 32*, 59–66.

Nippold, M. A., & Rudzinski, M. (1993). Familiarity and transparency in idiom explanation: A developmental study of children and adolescents. *Journal of Speech and Hearing Research, 36*, 728–737.

Norris, J. A. (1998). Early sentence transformations and the development of complex syntactic structures. In W. O. Haynes & B. B. Shulman (Eds.), *Communication development: Foundations, processes, and clinical applications* (pp. 263–310). Baltimore: Williams & Wilkins.

Oakhill, K., & Cain, K. (2007). Introduction to comprehension development. In K. Cain & J. Oakhill (Eds.), *Children's comprehension problems in oral and written language: A cognitive perspective* (pp. 3–40). New York: Guilford.

Perfetti, C. A. (1994). Psycholinguistics and reading ability. In M. A. Gernsbacher (Ed.), *Handbook of psycholinguistics* (pp. 849–894). San Diego, CA: Academic Press.

Peth-Pierce, R. (2000). *A good beginning: Sending America's children to school with the social and emotional competence they need to succeed.* Bethesda, MD: Child Mental Health Foundations and Agencies Network, National Institute of Mental Health.

Piaget, J. (1959). *The language and thought of the child.* New York: Humanities Press.

Prutting, C. A., & Kirchner, D. M. (1987). A clinical appraisal of the pragmatic aspects of language. *Journal of Speech and Hearing Disorders, 52*, 105–119.

Roseberry-McKibbin, C. (2007). *Language disorders in children: A multicultural and case perspective.* Boston: Pearson.

Rydell, A. M., Hagekull, B., & Bohlin, G. (1997). Measurement of two social competence aspects in middle childhood. *Developmental Psychology, 33*, 824–833.

Scott, C. M. (1988). Spoken and written syntax. In M. Nippold (Ed.), *Later language development: Ages 9 through 19* (pp. 49–65). Austin, TX: Pro-Ed.

Scott, C. M., & Stokes, S. L. (1995). Measures of syntax in school-age children and adolescents. *Language, Speech, and Hearing Services in Schools, 26*, 309–319.

Selman, R. L., Beardslee, W., Schultz, L. H., Krupa, M., & Podorefsky, D. (1986). Assessing adolescent interpersonal negotiation strategies: Toward the integration of structural and functional models. *Developmental Psychology, 22*, 450–459.

Stahl, S. A., & Nagy, W. E. (2006). *Teaching word meanings.* Mahwah, NJ: Erlbaum.

Stanovich, K. E., & Cunningham, A. E. (1992). Studying the consequences of literacy within a literate society: The cognitive correlates of print exposure. *Memory & Cognition, 20*, 51–68.

Stanovich, K. E., & Cunningham, A. E. (1993). Where does knowledge come from? Specific associations between print exposure and information acquisition. *Journal of Educational Psychology, 85*, 211–229.

Turkstra, L., Ciccia, A., & Seaton, C. (2003). Interactive behaviors in adolescent conversation dyads. *Language, Speech, and Hearing Services in Schools, 34*, 117–127.

Wellman Owre, D., & Kennedy Brennan, M. (2002). *Literacy and communication: Expectations from kindergarten through fifth grade.* Retrieved from http://www.asha.org/uploadedFiles/slp/schools/profconsult/LiteracyK5Teachers.pdf#search = %22first%22

Wentzel, K. (1991). Social competence at school: Relation between social responsibility and academic achievement. *Review of Educational Research, 61*, 1–24.

Westby, C. E. (1998). Communicative refinement in school age and adolescence. In W. O. Haynes & B. B. Shulman (Eds.), *Communication development: Foundations, processes, and clinical applications* (pp. 311–360). Baltimore: Williams & Wilkins.

Winner, E., Rosenstiel, A. K., & Gardner, H. (1976). The development of metaphoric understanding. *Developmental Psychology, 12*, 289–297.

CHAPTER 10

Adams, M. (1990). *Beginning to read.* Cambridge: MIT Press.

Beck, I. L., McKeown, M. G., & Kucan, L. (2002). *Bringing words to life.* New York: Guilford.

Biancarosa, G., & Snow, C. E. (2004). *Reading next: A vision for action and research in middle and high school literacy: A report to Carnegie Corporation of New York.* Washington, DC: Alliance for Excellent Education.

Blachman, B. (1994). Early literacy acquisition: The role of phonological awareness. In G. Wallach & K. Butler (Eds.), *Language learning disabilities in school-age children and adolescents* (pp. 253–274). New York: Macmillan.

Bloodgood, J. (1999). What's in a name? Children's name writing and literacy acquisition. *Reading Research Quarterly, 34,* 342–367.

Burns, P. C., Roe, B. D., & Ross, E. P. (1992). *Teaching reading in today's elementary schools.* Princeton, NJ: Houghton Mifflin.

Bus, A. G., van Ijzendoorn, M. H., & Pellegrini, A. (1995). Joint book reading makes for success in learning to read: A meta-analysis on intergenerational transmission of literacy. *Review of Educational Research, 65,* 1–21.

Carlisle, J. F. (1988). Knowledge of derivational morphology and spelling ability in fourth, sixth, and eighth graders. *Applied Psycholinguistics, 9,* 247–266.

Carlisle, J. F., & Katz, L. A. (2005). Word learning and vocabulary instruction. In J. Birsch (Eds.), *Multisensory teaching of basic language skills* (2nd ed.). Baltimore: Paul Brookes.

Catts, H. W., & Kamhi, A. G. (Eds.). (1999). *Language and reading disabilities.* Boston: Allyn & Bacon.

Chall, J. S. (1996). *Stages of reading development.* New York: McGraw-Hill.

Cousins, L. (2001). *Maisy goes shopping.* Cambridge, MA: Candlewick.

Cunningham, A. E., & Stanovich, K. E. (1997). Early reading acquisition and its relation to reading experience and ability 10 years later. *Developmental Psychology, 33*(6), 934–945.

Dickinson, D., & Neuman, S. B. (Eds.). (2006). *Handbook of early literacy research* (Vol. 2). New York: Guilford.

Diehl, S., & Silliman, E. (2009). Making sense of language learning disability: Assessment and support for academic success. In D. K. Bernstein &

E. Tiegerman-Farber (Eds.), *Language and communication disorders in children* (6th ed., pp. 496–535). Boston: Allyn & Bacon.

Dole, J. A., Brown, K. J., & Trathen, W. (1996). The effects of strategy instruction on the comprehension performance of at-risk students. *Reading Research Quarterly, 31,* 62–88.

Dyson, A. (2000). Writing and the sea of voices: Oral language in, around, and about writing. In R. Indrisano & J. Squire (Eds.), *Perspectives on writing* (pp. 45–65). Newark, DE: International Reading Association.

Dyson, A. H., & Freedman, S. W. (1991). Writing. In J. Flood, J. M. Jensen, D. Lapp, & J. R. Squire (Eds.), *Handbook of research on teaching English language arts* (pp.129–148). New York: Macmillan.

Ehren, B., Lenz, B., & Deshler, D. (2004). Enhancing literacy proficiency with adolescents and young adults. In C. A. Stone & E. R. Silliman (Eds.), *Handbook of language and literacy* (pp. 681–702). New York: Guilford.

Ehren, B. J. (2005). Looking for evidence-based practice in reading comprehension instruction. *Topics in Language Disorders, 25*(4), 310–321.

Ehri, L. (2000). Learning to read and learning to spell: Two sides of a coin. *Topics in Language Disorders, 20*(3), 19–49.

Graham, S., & Perin, D. (2007). A meta-analysis of writing instruction for adolescent students. *Journal of Educational Psychology, 99*(3), 445–476.

Harste, J. C., Woodward, V. A., & Burke, C. L. (1984). *Language stories and literacy lessons.* Portsmouth, NH: Heinemann.

Harris, K. R., Santangelo, T., & Graham, S. (2008). Self-regulated strategy development in writing: Going beyond NLEs to a more balanced approach. *Instructional Science: An International Journal of the Learning Sciences, 36*(6), 395–408.

Hart, B., & Risley, T. (1995). *Meaningful differences in everyday parenting and intellectual development in young American children.* Baltimore: Paul Brookes.

Hedberg, N. L., & Westby, C. E. (1993). *Analyzing storytelling skills: Theory to practice.* Tucson, AZ: Communication Skill Builders.

Hill, M. (2003). *Signs in the store.* New York: Scholastic Children's Press.

Huebner, C. E. (2000). Promoting toddlers' language development through community-based intervention. *Journal of Applied Developmental Psychology, 21*(5), 513–535.

Lipson, M., Valencia, S., Wixson, K., & Peters, C. (1993). Integration and thematic teaching: Integration to improve teaching and learning. *Language Arts, 70*(4), 252–263.

Malone, L. D., & Mastropieri, M. A. (1992). Reading comprehension instruction: Summarization and self-monitoring training for students with learning disabilities. *Exceptional Children, 58*(3), 270–279.

Mastropieri, M. A., Leinart, A. W., & Scruggs, T. E. (1999). Strategies to increase reading fluency. *Intervention in School and Clinic, 34*(5), 278–283, 292.

Meltzer, J., Smith, N. C., & Clark, H. (2001). *Adolescent literacy resources: Linking research and practice.* Providence, RI: Brown University, Northeast and Islands Regional Educational Laboratory.

Moats, L., & Tolman, C. (2009). *Language essentials for teachers of reading and spelling (LETRS): The speech sounds of English: Phonetics, phonology, and phoneme awareness.* Boston: Sopris West.

Nagy, W. E., & Herman, P. A. (1985). Incidental vs. instructional approaches to increasing reading vocabulary. *Educational Perspectives, 23*(1), 16–21.

National Reading Panel. (2000). *A report of the national reading panel: Teaching children to read.* Washington, DC: National Institute of Child Health and Human Development.

Neuman, S. B., & Celano, D. (2001). Access to print in low-income and middle-income communities. *Reading Research Quarterly, 36*(1), 8–27.

Neuman, S. B., & Dwyer, J. (2009). Missing in action: Vocabulary instruction in pre-K. *Reading Teacher, 62*(5), 384–392.

Neuman, S. B., & Roskos, K. A. (1990). Play, print, and purpose: Enriching play environments for literacy development. *Reading Teacher, 44,* 214–221.

Neuman, S. B., & Roskos, K. (1992). Literacy objects as cultural tools: Effects on children's literacy behaviors in play. *Reading Research Quarterly, 27,* 202–225.

Ogle, D. (1986). K-W-L: A teaching model that develops active reading of expository text. *Reading Teacher, 39,* 564–570.

Pearson, P., & Camperell, K. (1994). Comprehension of text structures. In R. B. Ruddell, M. R. Ruddell, & H. Singer (Eds.), *Theoretical models and processes of reading* (pp. 448–467). Newark, DE: International Reading Association.

Perks, K. (2006). Reconnecting to the power of reading. *Principal Leadership, 7*(1), 16–20.

Persky, H. R., Daane, M. C., & Jin, Y. (2003). *The nation's report card: Writing 2002.* Washington, DC: Government Printing Office.

Phillips, B. M., Clancy-Menchetti, J., & Lonigan, C. J. (2008). Successful phonological awareness instruction with preschool children: Lessons from the classroom. *Topics in Early Childhood Special Education, 28*(1), 3–17.

Reutzel, D. R. (1997). Integrating literacy learning for young children. In C. H. Hart, D. C. Burts, & R. Charlesworth (Eds.), *Integrated curriculum and developmentally appropriate practice* (pp. 225–254). Albany: State University of New York Press.

Reutzel, D. R., & Wolfersberger, M. (1996). An environmental impact statement: Designing supportive literacy classrooms for young children. *Reading Horizons, 36*(3), 266–282.

Roskos, K., & Neuman, S. (2001). Environment and its influences for early literacy teaching and learning. In S. B. Neuman & D. K. Dickinson (Eds.), *Handbook of early literacy research* (Vol. 1, pp. 281–294). New York: Guilford.

Schubert, B. (1993). Literacy—What makes it real: Integrated, thematic teaching. *Social Studies Review, 32*(2), 7–16.

Shipley, K. G., & McAfee, J. G. (2009). *Assessment in speech-language pathology: A resource manual.* Florence, KY: Cengage.

Snow, C., & Biancarosa, G. (2004). *Reading next: Adolescent literacy development among English language learners.* New York: Alliance for Education, Carnegie.

Snow, C. E., Porche, M. V., Tabors, P. O., & Harris, S. R. (2007). *Is literacy enough? Pathways to academic success for adolescents.* Baltimore: Paul Brookes.

Stadler, M. A., & Ward, G. C. (2005). Supporting the narrative development of young children. *Early Childhood Education Journal, 33*(2), 73–80.

Stahl, S. A., & Kuhn, M. R. (2002). Making it sound like language: Developing fluency. *Reading Teacher, 55*(6), 582–584.

Storch, S. A., & Whitehurst, G. J. (2001). The role of family and home in the literacy development of children from low-income backgrounds. *New Directions for Child and Adolescent Development, 92,* 53–71.

Strickland, D., Snow, C., Griffin, P., Burns, M., & McNamara, P. (2002). *Preparing our teachers: Opportunities for better reading instruction.* Washington, DC: Joseph Henry Press.

Teale, W., & Sulzby, E. (1986). *Emergent literacy: Writing and reading.* Norwood, NJ: Ablex.

Tompkins, G. (2003). *Literacy for the 21st century.* Upper Saddle River, NJ: Pearson.

Torgesen, J. K., Houston, D. D., Rissman, L. M., Decker, S. M., Roberts, G., Vaughn, S., et al. (2007). *Academic literacy instruction for adolescents: A guidance document from the Center on Instruction.* Retrieved September 29, 2007, from http://www.centeroninstruction.org

Tunnell, M. O., & Ammon, R. (1993). *The story of ourselves: Teaching history through children's literature.* Portsmouth, NH: Heinemann.

Van Kleeck, A. (2006). Fostering inferential language during book sharing with prereaders: A foundation for later text comprehension strategies. In A. van Kleeck (Ed.), *Sharing books and stories to promote language and literacy* (pp. 269–317). San Diego, CA: Plural.

Van Kleeck, A. (2008). Providing preschool foundations for later reading comprehension: The importance of and ideas for targeting inferencing in storybook-sharing interventions. *Psychology in the Schools, 45*(7), 627–643.

Van Kleeck, A., & Vander Woude, J. (2003). Book sharing with preschoolers with language delays. In A. van Kleeck, S. A. Stahl, & E. Bauer (Eds.), *On reading to children: Parents and teachers* (pp. 58–92). Mahwah, NJ: Erlbaum.

Wagner, R. K., & Torgesen, J. K. (1987). The nature of phonological processing and its causal role in the acquisition of reading skills. *Psychological Bulletin, 101*, 192–212.

Walker, J., & Hauerwas, L. B. (2006). Development of phonological, morphological, and orthographic knowledge in young spellers: The case of inflected verbs. *Reading and Writing, 19*, 819–843.

Walker-Dalhouse, D., & Risko, V. J. (2009). Crossing boundaries and initiating conversations about RTI: Understanding and applying differentiated classroom instruction. *Reading Teacher, 63*(1), 84–87.

Weaver, C. (1994). *Reading process and practice: From socio-psycholinguistics to whole language* (2nd ed.). Portsmouth, NH: Heinemann.

Whitehurst, G. J., Epstein, J. N., Angell, A. L., Payne, A. C., Crone, D. A., & Fischel, J. E. (1994). Outcomes of an emergent literacy intervention in Head Start. *Journal of Educational Psychology, 86*(4), 542–555.

Whitehurst, G. J., & Lonigan, C. J. (1998). Child development and emergent literacy. *Child Development, 69*(3), 848–872.

Wilford, S. (2000). *From play to literacy: Implications for the classroom* (Occasional paper No. 2). Bronxville, NY: Child Development Institute, Sarah Lawrence College. (ERIC Document Reproduction Service No. ED443583)

Wolfersberger, M. E., Reutzel, D. R., Sudweeks, R., & Fawson, P. C. (2004). Developing and validating the classroom literacy environmental profile (CLEP): A tool for examining the "print richness" of early childhood and elementary classrooms. *Journal of Literacy Research, 36*(2), 211–272.

Wright, D., & Ehri, L. C. (2007). Beginners remember orthography when they learn to read words: The case of doubled letters. *Applied Psycholinguistics, 28*, 115–133.

Yopp, H. K., & Yopp, H. (2009). Phonological awareness is child's play! *Young Children, 64*(1), 12–21.

Zevenbergen, A. A., & Whitehurst, G. J. (2003). Dialogic reading: A shared picture book reading intervention for preschoolers. In A. van Kleeck, S. A. Stahl, & E. B. Bauer (Eds.), *On reading books to children: Parents and teachers* (pp. 16–36). Mahwah, NJ: Erlbaum.

CHAPTER 11

Barry, A. K. (1991). Narrative style and witness testimony. *Journal of Narrative and Life History, 1*(4), 281–294.

Bishop, D. V. M., & Edmundson, A. (1987). Language-impaired four year olds: Distinguishing transient from persistent impairment. *Journal of Speech and Hearing Disorders, 52*, 155–173.

Bliss, L. S., & McCabe, A. (2008). Personal narratives: Cultural differences and clinical implications. *Topics in Language Disorders, 28*(2), 162–177.

Calkins, L. M. (1994). The art of teaching writing (New ed.). Portsmouth, NH: Heinemann.

Cazden, C. (1985). Classroom discourse. In M. C. Wittrock (Ed.), *Research on teaching* (3rd ed., pp. 432–463). New York: Macmillan.

Champion, T. B. (2003). *Understanding storytelling among African American children*. Mahwah, NJ: Erlbaum.

Charon, R. (1993). Medical interpretation: Implications of literary theory of narrative for clinical work. *Journal of Narrative and Life History, 3*, 79–97.

Damico, J., & Oller, J. W. (1980). Pragmatic versus morphological/syntactic criteria for language referrals. *Language Speech and Hearing Services in Schools, 11*, 85–94.

De Hirsch, K., Jansky, J. J., & Langford, W. J. (1966). *Predicting reading failure*. New York: Harper & Row.

Heath, S. B. (1983). *Ways with words: Language, life, and work in communities and classrooms*. Cambridge, UK: Cambridge University Press.

Hyon, S., & Sulzby, E. (1994). African American kindergartners' spoken narratives: Topic-associating and topic-centered styles. *Linguistics and Education, 6*, 121–152.

James, P. (1974). *James language dominance test*. Austin, TX: Learning Concepts.

Mayer, M. (1969). *Frog, where are you?* Hong Kong: South China Printing.

Mayer, M. (1970). *One frog too many*. Hong Kong: South China Printing.

McCabe, A. (1996). *Chameleon readers: Teaching children to appreciate all kinds of good stories*. New York: McGraw Hill.

McCabe, A., Bailey, A., & Melzi, G. (in press). *Spanish-language narration and literacy: Culture, cognition, and emotion*. Cambridge, UK: Cambridge University Press.

McCabe, A., & Bliss, L. S. (2003). Patterns of narrative discourse. Boston: Allyn & Bacon.

McCabe, A., & Rollins, P. R. (1994). Assessment of preschool narrative skills. *American Journal of Speech-Language Pathology, 3*(1), 45–56.

Michaels, S. (1991). The dismantling of narrative. In A. McCabe & C. Peterson (Eds.), *Developing narrative structure* (pp. 303–352). Hillsdale, NJ: Erlbaum.

Minami, M., & McCabe, A. (1991). Haiku as a discourse regulation device: A stanza analysis of Japanese children's personal narratives. *Language in Society, 20*, 577–600.

Minami, M., & McCabe, A. (1996). Compressed collections of experiences: Some Asian American traditions. In A. McCabe (Ed.), *Chameleon readers: Teaching children to appreciate all kinds of good stories* (pp. 72–97). New York: McGraw-Hill.

Miranda, A. E., McCabe, A., & Bliss, L. S. (1998). Jumping around and leaving things out: Dependency analysis applied to the narratives of children with specific language impairment. *Applied Psycholinguistics, 19*, 657–668.

Peregoy, S. F., & Boyle, O. F. (2005). *Reading, writing, and learning in ESL*. Boston: Allyn & Bacon.

Peterson, C. A., & McCabe, A. (1983). *Developmental psycholinguistics: Three ways of looking at a child's narrative*. New York: Plenum.

Peterson, C., & McCabe, A. (1994). A social interactionist account of developing decontextualized narrative skill. *Developmental Psychology, 30*(6), 937–948.

Roth, F. P., & Spekman, N. J. (1986). Narrative discourse: Spontaneously generated stories of learning-disabled and typically achieving students. *Journal of Speech and Hearing Disorders, 51*, 8–23.

Rubin, E., & Lennon, L. (2004). Challenges in social communication in Asperger syndrome and high-functioning autism. *Topics in Language Disorders, 24*(2), 286–297.

Safran, S. P., Safran, J. A., & Ellis, K. (2003). Intervention ABCs for children with Asperger syndrome. *Topics in Language Disorders, 23*(2), 154–165.

Silva, M. J., & McCabe, A. (1996). Vignettes of the continuous family ties: Some Latino American traditions. In A. McCabe (Ed.), *Chameleon readers: Teaching children to appreciate all kinds of good stories* (pp. 116–136). New York: McGraw-Hill.

Snow, C. E., Porche, M. V., Tabors, P. O., & Harris, S. R. (2007). *Is literacy enough?* Baltimore: Paul Brookes.

Tabors, P. O., Snow, C. E., & Dickinson, D. K. (2001). Homes and schools together: Supporting language and early literacy development. In D. K. Dickinson & P. O. Tabors (Eds.), *Beginning literacy with language* (pp. 313–334). Baltimore: Paul Brookes.

Tsatsanis, K. D. (2004). Heterogeneity in learning style in Asperger syndrome and high-functioning autism. *Topics in Language Disorder, 24*(4), 260–270.

Westby, C. E. (1994). The effects of culture on genre, structure, and style of oral and written texts. In G. P. Wallach & K. G. Butler (Eds.), *Language learning disabilities in school-age children and adolescents* (pp. 180–218). New York: Merrill.

Westby, C. E., & Cutler, S. K. (1994). Language and ADHD: Understanding the bases and treatment of self-regulatory deficits. *Topics in Language Disorders, 14*(4), 58–76.

Westby, C., & Watson, S. (2004). Perspectives on attention-deficit hyperactivity disorder: Executive functions, working memory, and language disabilities. *Seminars in Speech and Language, 25*(3), 241–254.

Wright, H. H., & Newhoff, M. (2003). Narration abilities of children with language-learning disabilities in response to oral and written stimuli. *American Journal of Speech-Language Pathology, 10*, 308–319.

CHAPTER 12

Auer, P. (1999). Bilingual conversation revisited. In P. Auer (Ed.), *Code-switching in conversation: Language, interaction, and identity* (pp. 1–24). London: Routledge.

Baber, C. (1992). Ethnic identity development and literacy education. *Reading Psychology, 13,* 91–98.

Baker, C. (2002). Bilingual education. In R. Kaplan (Ed.), *The Oxford handbook of applied linguistics* (pp. 229–242). Oxford, UK: Oxford University Press.

Banks-Wallace, J. (1998). Emancipatory potentional of storytelling in a group. *Image Journal of Nursing School, 30*(1), 17–21.

Banks-Wallace, J. (1999). Storytelling as a tool for providing holistic care to women. *American Journal of Maternal Child Nursing, 24*(1), 20–24.

Banks-Wallace, J. (2002). Talk that talk: Storytelling and analysis rooted in African American oral tradition. *Qualitative Health Research, 12*(3), 410–426.

Baratz, J., & Shuy, R. (1969). *Teaching black children to read.* Washington, DC: Center for Applied Linguistics.

Bereiter, C., & Engelmann, S. (1966). *Teaching disadvantaged children to read.* Englewood Cliffs, NJ: Prentice Hall.

Cecil, N. L. (1988). Black dialect and academic success: A study of teacher expectations. *Reading Improvement, 25*(1), 34–38.

Champion, T. (1998). "Tell me somethin' good": A description of narrative structures among African American children. *Linguistics and Education, 9*(3), 251–286.

Champion, T., Katz, L., Muldrow, R., & Dail, R. (1999). Storytelling and storymaking in an urban preschool classroom: Building bridges from home to school culture. *Topics in Language Disorders, 19*(3), 52–67.

Champion, T., Seymour, H., & Camarata, S. (1995). Narrative discourse of African American children. *Journal of Narrative and Life History, 5*(4), 333–352.

Charity, A. H., Scarborough, H. S., & Griffin, D. M. (2004). Familiarity with school English in African American children and its relation to early reading achievement. *Child Development, 75*(5), 1340–1356.

Collins, J. (1985). Some problems and purposes in narrative analysis in educational research. *Journal of Education, 167*(1), 57–70.

Connor, C. M., & Craig, H. K. (2006). African American preschoolers' use of African American English and their emergent literacy development: A complex relation. *Journal of Speech, Language, and Hearing Research, 49*(4), 771–792.

Cooper, J. A., & Schleser, R. (2006). Closing the achievement gap: Examining the role of cognitive developmental level in academic achievement. *Early Childhood Education Journal, 33*(5), 301–306.

Craig, H. K., & Washington, J. A. (1994). The complex syntax skills of poor, urban, African American preschoolers at school entry. *Language, Speech, and Hearing Services in Schools, 25*(3), 171–180.

Craig, H. K., & Washington, J. A. (2006). *Malik goes to school: Examining the language skills of African American students from preschool–5th grade.* Mahwah, NJ: Erlbaum.

Craig, H. K., Washington, J. A., Thompson, C. A., & Potter, S. L. (2004). Performances of elementary grade African American students on the gray oral reading tests. *Language, Speech, and Hearing Services in Schools, 35*(2), 141–154.

Dandy, E. B. (1991). *Black communications: Breaking down the barriers.* Chicago: African American Images.

De Villiers, P., & Burns, F. (2003, November). *Assessing narrative skills in children*. Presentation at the annual meeting of the American Speech-Language-Hearing Association, Chicago.

Delpit, L. (2001). The politics of teaching literate discourse. In E. Cushman, E. R. Kintgen, B. M. Kroll, & M. Rose (Eds.), *Literacy: A critical sourcebook* (pp. 545–554). Boston: Bedford/St. Martin's.

Delpit, L. (2002). No kinda sense. In L. Delpit & J. K. Dowdy (Eds.), *The skin that we speak: Thoughts on language and culture in the classroom* (pp. 31–48). New York: New Press.

Delpit, L. (2006). *Other people's children: Cultural conflict in the classroom* (Rev. ed.). New York: New Press.

Delpit, L. D. (1996). *Other people's children: Cultural conflict in the classroom*. New York: New Press, Norton.

Dyson, A. H. (1993). *Social worlds of children learning to write in an urban primary school*. New York: Teachers College Press.

Engel, S. (1994). *The stories children tell: Making sense of the narratives of childhood*. New York: W. H. Freeman.

Fazio, B., Naremore, R. C., & Connell, P. J. (1996). Tracking children from poverty at risk for specific language impairment: A 3-year longitudinal study. *Journal of Speech, Language, and Hearing Research, 39*(3), 611–624.

Fogel, H., & Ehri, L. (2000). Teaching elementary students who speak Black English vernacular to write in Standard English: Effects of dialect transformation practice. *Contemporary Educational Psychology, 25*, 212–235.

Fogel, H., & Ehri, L. (2006). Teaching African American English forms to standard American English-speaking teachers: Effects on acquisition, attitudes, and responses to student use. *Journal of Teacher Education, 57*(5), 1–17.

Foster, M. (1987). *"It's cookin' now": An ethnographic study of the teaching style of a successful Black teacher in an urban community college*. Unpublished doctoral dissertation, Harvard University, Cambridge, MA.

Foster, M. (1995). "Are you with me?": Power and solidarity in the discourse of African American women. In K. Hall & M. Bucholtz (Eds.), *Gender articulated: Language and the socially constructed self* (pp. 329–350). New York: Routledge.

Foster, W. A., & Miller, M. (2007). Development of the literacy achievement gap: A longitudinal study of kindergarten through third grade. *Language, Speech, and Hearing Services in Schools, 38*(3), 173–181.

Green, L. (2002). A descriptive study of African American English: Research in linguistics and education. *International Journal of Qualitative Studies in Education, 15*(6), 673–690.

Hardin, B. J., Roach-Scott, M., & Peisner-Feinberg, E. S. (2007). Special education referral, evaluation, and placement practices for preschool English learners. *Journal of Research in Childhood Education, 22*(1), 39–54.

Hart, B., & Risley, T. R. (1995). *Meaningful differences in the everyday experience of young American children*. Baltimore: Paul Brookes.

Heath, S. B. (1983). *Ways with words: Language, life, and work in communities and classrooms*. Cambridge, UK: Cambridge University Press.

Hester, E. (1996). Narratives of young African American children. In A. Kamhi, K. Pollock, & J. Harris (Eds.), *Communication development and disorders in African American children: Research, assessment, and intervention* (pp. 227–246). Baltimore: Paul Brookes.

Hilliard, A. (2002). Language, culture, and the assessment of African American children. In L. Delpit & J. K. Dowdy (Eds.), *The skin that we speak: Thoughts on language and culture in the classroom* (pp. 87–105). New York: New Press.

Hymes, D. (1972). Introduction to Cazden, John, & Hymes. In C. B. Cazden, V. P. John, & D. Hymes (Eds.), *Functions of language in the classroom* (pp. vii–xi). New York: Teachers College Press.

Hyon, S., & Sulzby, E. (1994). African American kindergartners' spoken narratives: Topic-associating and topic-centered styles. *Linguistics and Education, 6*(2), 121–152.

Kamhi, A. G., & Catts, H. W. (2005). Language and reading: Convergences and divergences. In H. W. Catts & A. G. Kamhi (Eds.), *Language and reading disabilities* (2nd ed., pp. 1–25). Boston: Allyn & Bacon.

Kieffer, M. J. (2008). Catching up or falling behind? Initial English proficiency, concentrated poverty, and the reading growth of language minority learners in the United States. *Journal of Educational Psychology, 100*(4), 851–868.

Krashen, S. (2003). *Explorations in language acquisition and use*. Portsmouth, NH: Heinemann.

Labov, W. (1972). *Language in the inner city: Studies in the Black English vernacular.* Philadelphia: University of Pennsylvania Press.

Macaulay, R., & Trevelyan, G. (1973). *Language, education, and employment in Glasgow.* Paper presented at the Report to SSRC, Mimeo.

Mattison, E., & Aber, M. S. (2007). Closing the achievement gap: The association of racial climate with achievement and behavioral outcomes. *American Journal of Community Psychology, 40*(1), 1–12.

McGregor, K. (2000). The development and enhancement of narrative skills in a preschool classroom: Towards a solution to clinician-client mismatch. *American Journal of Speech-Language Pathology, 9,* 55–71.

Michaels, S. (1981). "Sharing time": Children's narrative styles and differential access to literacy. *Language in Society, 10,* 423–442.

Michaels, S. (1984). Listening and responding: Hearing the logic in children's classroom narratives. *Theory Into Practice, 23*(3), 218.

Michaels, S., & Cazden, C. B. (1986). Teacher/child collaboration as oral preparation for literacy. In B. B. Schieffelin & P. Gilmore (Eds.), *The acquisition of literacy: Ethnographic perspectives* (pp. 132–154). Norwood, NJ: Ablex.

Milroy, J., & Milroy, A. L. (1974). *A sociolinguistic project in Belfast.* Belfast, UK: Queen's University Belfast.

Neuman, S. B., & Celano, D. (2006). The knowledge gap: Implications of leveling the playing field for low-income and middle-income children. *Reading Research Quarterly, 41*(2), 176–201.

Ochs, E., & Capps, L. (2001). *Living narrative: Creating lives in everyday storytelling.* Cambridge, MA: Harvard University Press.

Planty, M., Hussar, W., Snyder, T., Kena, G., KewalRamani, A., Kemp, J., et al. (2009). *The condition of education 2009 (NCES 2009-081).* Washington, DC: National Center for Education Statistics, Institute of Education Sciences, U.S. Department of Education.

Purcell-Gates, V. (2002). " . . . As soon as she opened her mouth!": Issues of language, literacy, and power. In L. Delpit & J. K. Dowdy (Eds.), *The skin that we speak* (pp. 121–144). New York: New Press.

Restrepo, M. A., & Dubasik, V. (2008). Language and literacy practices for English language learners in the preschool setting. In L. M. Justice & C. Vukelich (Eds.), *Achieving excellence in preschool literacy instruction* (pp. 242–260). New York: Guilford.

Saiegh-Haddad, E. (2003). Linguistic distance and initial reading acquisition: The case of arabic diglossia. *Applied Psycholinguistics, 24,* 431–451.

Smitherman, G. (2000). *Talkin that talk: Language, culture, and education in African America.* London: Routledge.

Snow, C. E., & Griffin, P. (Eds.). (1998). *Preventing reading difficulties in young children.* Washington, DC: National Academy Press.

Stubbs, M. (2002). Some basic sociolinguistic concepts. In L. Delpit & J. K. Dowdy (Eds.), *The skin that we speak* (pp. 63–86). New York: New Press.

Taylor, M. A. (1982). *The use of figurative devices in aiding comprehension.* Unpublished doctoral dissertation, University of Illinois at Urbana-Champaign.

Thomas-Tate, S., Washington, J. A., & Edwards, J. (2004). Standardized assessment of phonological awareness skills in low-income African American first graders. *American Journal of Speech-Language Pathology, 13*(2), 182–190.

Van Keulen, J. E., DeBose, C. E., & Weddington, G. T. (1998). *Speech, language, learning, and the African American child.* Boston: Allyn & Bacon.

Washington, J. A., & Craig, H. K. (1994). Dialectal forms during discourse of urban, African American preschoolers living in poverty. *Journal of Speech and Hearing Research, 37,* 816–823.

Washington, J. A., & Craig, H. K. (1998). Socioeconomic status and gender influences on children's dialectal variations. *Journal of Speech and Hearing Research, 41*(3), 618–626.

Washington, J. A., & Craig, H. K. (2001). Reading performance and dialectal variation. In J. L. Harris, A. G. Kamhi, & K. G. Pollock (Eds.), *Literacy in African American communities* (pp. 147–168). Mahwah, NJ: Erlbaum.

Washington, J. A., & Thomas-Tate, S. (2009). How research informs cultural-linguistic differences in the classroom: The bi-dialectal African American child. In S. Rosenfield & V. W. Berninger (Eds.), *Implementing evidence-based academic interventions in school settings* (pp. 147–164). London: Oxford University Press.

Wheeler, R. S., Denham, K., & Lobeck, A. (2005). Contrastive analysis and codeswitching: How and why to use the vernacular to teach standard English. In K. Denham & A. Lobeck (Eds.), *Language in the schools: Integrating linguistic knowledge into K-12 teaching.* (pp. 171–179). Mahwah, NJ: Erlbaum.

Wolfram, W. (1971). Black-white speech differences revisited. In W. Wolfram & N. H. Clarke (Eds.), *Black-white speech relationships* (pp. 139–161). Washington, DC: Center for Applied Linguistics.

Wolfram, W., & Thomas, E. R. (2002). *The development of African American English* (Vol. 31). Oxford, UK: Blackwell.

Yeung, W.-J. J., & Pfeiffer, K. M. (2009). The Black-White test score gap and early home environment. *Social Science Research, 38*(2), 412–437.

Yu Cho, Y.-M. (2002). Diglossia in Korean language and literature: A historical perspective. *East Asia: An International Quarterly, 20*(1), 3–24.

CHAPTER 13

American Speech-Language-Hearing Association. (2009). *Responsiveness to Intervention (RTI).* Retrieved from http://www.asha.org/slp/schools/prof-consult/RtoI.htm

Anderson, R. (2004).First language loss in Spanish-speaking children: Patterns of loss and implications for clinical practice. In B. Goldstein (Ed.), *Bilingual language development and disorders in Spanish speakers* (pp.187–212). Baltimore: Paul Brookes.

Asher, J. J. (1966). The learning strategy of the total physical response: A review. *Modern Language Journal, 50*(2), 79–84.

Asher, J. J, (1969). The total physical response technique of learning. *Journal of Special Education, 3*(3), 253–262.

Asher, J. J. (1972). Children's first language as a model for second language learning. *Modern Language Journal, S6*(3), 133–139.

Asher, J. J. (2000). *The super school: Teaching on the right side of the brain.* Los Gatos, CA: Sky Oaks.

Baker, C. (2006). *Foundations of bilingualism and bilingual education.* Clevedon, UK: Multilingual Matters.

Baker, C., & Prys Jones, S. (1998). *Encyclopedia of bilingual education and bilingualism.* Clevedon, UK: Multilingual Matters.

Beaumont, C. (1992). Language intervention strategies for Hispanic LLD students. In H. Langdon with L. Cheng (Eds.), *Hispanic children and adults with communication disorders: Assessment and intervention* (pp. 201–272). Gaithersburg, MD: Aspen.

Bialystok, E. (2001). *Bilingualism in development: Language, literacy and cognition.* New York: Cambridge University Press.

Brisk, M. (2005). *Bilingual education: From compensatory to quality schooling* (2nd ed.). Mahwah, NJ: Erlbaum.

Calderón, M. (2001). Curricula and methodologies used to teach Spanish-speaking limited English proficient students to read English. In R. E. Slavin & M. Calderón (Eds.), *Effective programs for Latino students* (pp. 251–305). Mahwah, NJ: Erlbaum.

Carrasquillo, A. E., & Rodríguez, V. (2002). *Language minority students in the mainstream classroom* (2nd ed.). Philadelphia: Multilingual Matters.

Crockett, J. B. (2004). The science of schooling for students with learning disabilities: Recommendations for service delivery linking practice and research. In B. Wong (Ed.), *Learning about learning disabilities* (3rd ed., pp. 451–484). Boston: Elsevier.

Cummins, J. (1981). The role of primary language development in promoting educational success to language minority students. In Office of Bilingual Bicultural Education, California State Department of Education (Ed.), *Schooling and language minority students: A theoretical framework* (pp. 3–49). Los Angeles: Evaluation, Dissemination, and Assessment Center, California State University.

Cummins, J. (1984). *Bilingualism and special education.* Clevedon, UK: Multilingual Matters.

Cummins, J. (1989). *Empowering minority students.* San Francisco: California Association for Bilingual Educators.

Cummins, J. (2008). BICS and CALP: Empirical and theoretical status of the distinction. In B. Street & N. H. Hornberger (Eds.), *Encyclopedia of language and education* (2nd ed., Vol. 2, pp. 71–83). New York: Springer Science + Business Media.

Doherty, R. W., Hilberg, R. S., Pinal, A., & Tharp, R. G. (2003). Five standards and student achievement. *National Association for Bilingual Education: Journal of Research and Practice, 1*(1), 1–24.

Duffy, G. (2002). The case for direct explanation of strategies. In C. C. Block & M. Pressley (Eds.), *Comprehension instruction: Research-based best practices* (pp. 28–41). New York: Guilford.

Echevarría, J., Vogt, M., & Short, D. (2004). *Making content comprehensible for English learners: The SIOP model* (2nd ed.). Boston: Pearson.

Facella, M. A., Rampino, K. M., & Shea, E. K. (2005). Effective teaching strategies for English language learners. *Bilingual Research Journal, 29*(1), 209–221.

Farr, B., & Quintanar-Sarellana, R. (2005). Effective instructional strategies for students learning a second language or with other language differences. In E. Trumbull &. B. Farr (Eds.), *Language and learning: What teachers need to know* (pp. 215–267). Norwood, MA: Christopher Gordon.

Gordon, R. G. (Ed.). (2005). *Ethnologue: Languages of the world* (15th ed.). Dallas, TX: SIL International.

Gutiérrez-Clellen, V., & Kreiter, J. (2003). Understanding child bilingual acquisition using parent and teacher reports. *Applied Psycholinguistics, 24,* 267–298.

Herrera, S., & Murry, K. (2005). *Mainstreaming ESL and bilingual methods: Differentiated instruction for culturally and linguistically diverse (CLD) students.* Boston: Pearson.

Kagan, S. (1994). *Cooperative learning.* San Clemente, CA: Kagan Cooperative.

Kohnert, K. (2009, February). *Bilingual children and adults with language impairment: Intervention principles and procedures.* Paper presented at a conference at San Jose State University, San Jose, CA.

Krashen, S. (1981). Bilingual education and second language acquisition theory. In Office of Bilingual Bicultural Education, California State Department of Education (Ed.), *Schooling and language minority students: A theoretical framework* (pp. 51–79). Los Angeles: Evaluation, Dissemination, and Assessment Center, California State University.

Krashen, S., & Terrell, T. D. (1983). *The natural approach: Language acquisition in the classroom.* London: Prentice Hall.

Kuhlman, N. (2005). The language assessment conundrum: What tests claim to assess and what teachers need to know. *ELL Outlook, 4*(2). Retrieved from http://www.coursecrafters .com/ELL-Outlook/2005/mar_apr/ELLOutlook ITIArticle1.htm

Langdon, H. W. (1989). Language disorder or language difference? Assessing the language skills of Hispanic students. *Exceptional Children, 56,* 160–167.

Langdon, H. W. (2008). *Assessment and intervention for communication disorders in culturally and linguistically diverse populations.* Clifton Park, NY: Cengage.

Langdon, H. W., & Cheng, L. R. (2002). *Collaborating with interpreters and translators: A guide for communication disorders professionals.* Austin, TX: Pro-Ed.

National Association of School Psychologists. (2007). *Identification of students with specific learning disabilities* (Position statement). Bethesda, MD: Author.

Office of English Language Acquisition. (2002, October). *Survey of the states' limited English proficient students and available educational programs and services 2000–2001* (Summary report). Washington, DC: Author.

Oldin, T. (1989). *Language transfer: Cross-linguistic influence in language learning.* Cambridge, UK: Cambridge University Press.

Oldin, T. (2005). Cross-linguistic influence and conceptual transfer: What are the concepts? *Annual Review of Applied Linguistics, 25,* 3–25.

Reed, B., & Railsback, J. (2003). *Strategies and resources for mainstream teachers of English language learners.* Portland, OR: Northwest Regional Educational Laboratory.

Restrepo, A. (1998). Identifiers of predominantly Spanish-speaking children with language impairment. *Journal of Speech, Language, and Hearing Research, 41,* 1398–1411.

Roseberry-McKibbin, C. (2008). *Multicultural students with special language needs: Practical strategies for assessment and intervention.* Oceanside, CA: Academic Communication.

Ruíz, N. (1988). *Language for learning in a bilingual special education classroom.* Unpublished doctoral dissertation, Stanford University, Palo Alto, CA.

Savaria-Shore, M., & Garcia, E. (1995). Diverse teaching strategies for diverse learners. In R. W. Cole (Ed.), *Educating everybody's children: Diverse teaching strategies for diverse learners. What research and practice say about improving achievement* (pp. 47–74). Alexandria, VA: Association for Supervision and Curriculum Development.

Short, D. J. (1991). *How to integrate language and content instruction: A training manual* (2nd ed.). Washington, DC: Center for Applied Linguistics. (ERIC Document Reproduction Service No. ED359780)

Silver, J. (Ed.). (1995). *Profile of effective teaching in a multilingual classroom: Featuring Robin Liten-Tejado* [Video]. Santa Cruz, CA: National Center for Research on Cultural Diversity and Second Language Learning.

Slavin, R. (1995, Winter). A model of effective instruction. *Educational Forum, 59,* 166–176.

Vygotsky, L. (1962). *Thought and language.* Cambridge: MIT Press.

CHAPTER 14

Bernthal, J., & Bankson, N. (2004). *Articulation and phonological disorders* (4th ed.). Boston: Allyn & Bacon.

Brulard, I., & Carr, P. (2003). French-English bilingual acquisition of phonology: One production system or two? *International Journal of Bilingualism, 7,* 177–202.

De Groot, A., & Kroll, J. (1997). *Tutorials in bilingualism: Psycholinguistic perspectives.* Mahwah, NJ: Erlbaum.

De Houwer, A. (1990). *The acquisition of two languages from birth: A case study.* Cambridge, UK: Cambridge University Press.

Fabiano, L. (2006). *Phonological representation in bilingual Spanish-English speaking children.* Unpublished doctoral dissertation, Temple University, Philadelphia.

Fabiano, L., & Goldstein, B. (2004, May). *Phonological representation in simultaneous and sequential bilingual Spanish-English speaking children.* Seminar presented at the Child Phonology Conference, Tempe, AZ.

Fabiano, L., & Goldstein, B. (2005). Phonological cross-linguistic effects in bilingual Spanish-English-speaking children. *Journal of Multilingual Communication Disorders, 3*(1), 56–63.

Fabiano-Smith, L., & Barlow, J. (2009). Interaction in bilingual phonological acquisition: Evidence from phonetic inventories. *International Journal of Bilingual Education and Bilingualism, 31*(1), 1–17. Retrieved from http://dx.doi.org/10.1080/13670050902783528

Fabiano-Smith, L., & Goldstein, B. (2010). Phonological acquisition in bilingual Spanish-English speaking children. *Journal of Speech, Language, and Hearing Research, 53,* 160–178.

Gawlitzek-Maiwald, L., & Tracy, R. (1994). *Bilingual bootstrapping.* Unpublished manuscript, University of Tübingen, Germany.

Genesee, F., Paradis, J., & Crago, M. (2004). *Dual language development and disorders: A handbook on bilingualism and second language learning.* Baltimore: Paul Brookes.

Gildersleeve-Neumann, C., Kester, E., Davis, B., & Peña, E. (2008). English speech sound development in preschool-aged children from bilingual Spanish-English environments. *Language, Speech, and Hearing Services in Schools, 39,* 314–328.

Goldstein, B., Fabiano, L., Gildersleeve-Neumann, C., & Barlow, J. (2007). *Phonological characteristics of bilingual preschoolers.* Paper presented in seminar format at the annual convention of the American Speech-Language-Hearing Association, Boston.

Goldstein, B., Fabiano, L., & Iglesias, A. (2003, April). *Phonological representation in bilingual Spanish-English speaking children.* Poster presented at the Fourth International Symposium on Bilingualism (ISB4), Tempe, AZ.

Goldstein, B., Fabiano, L., & Washington, P. (2005). Phonological skills in predominantly English, predominantly Spanish, and Spanish-English bilingual children. *Language, Speech, and Hearing Services in Schools, 36,* 201–218.

Goldstein, B., & Washington, P. (2001). An initial investigation of phonological patterns in 4-year-olds typically developing Spanish-English bilingual children. *Language, Speech, & Hearing Services in Schools, 32,* 153–164.

Johnson, C., & Lancaster, P. (1998). The development of more than one phonology: A case study of a Norwegian-English bilingual child. *International Journal of Bilingualism, 2,* 265–300.

Kaiser, G. (1994). More about inflection and agreement: The acquisition of clitic pronouns in French. In J. Meisel (Ed.), *Bilingual first language acquisition: French and German grammatical development.* Hamburg, Germany: University of Hamburg.

Kehoe, M., Trujillo, C., & Lleó, C. (2001). Bilingual phonological acquisition: An analysis of syllable structure and VOT. In K. F. Cantone & M. O. Hinzelin (Eds.), *Proceedings of the colloquium on structure, acquisition, and change of grammars: Phonological and syntactic aspects* (pp. 38–54). Hamburg, Germany: University of Hamburg.

Keshavarz, M., & Ingram, D. (2002). The early phonological development of a Farsi English bilingual child. *International Journal of Bilingualism, 6,* 255–269.

Lleó, C., Kuchenbrandt, I., Kehoe, M., & Trujillo, C. (2003). Syllable final consonants in Spanish and German monolingual and bilingual acquisition. In N. Müller (Ed.), *(In)vulnerable domains in multilingualism* (pp. 191–220). Amsterdam: John Benjamins.

Meisel, J. M. (1989). Early differentiation of languages in bilingual children. In K. Hyltenstam & L. Obler (Eds.), *Bilingualism across the lifespan: Aspects of acquisition, maturity, and loss* (pp. 13–41). Cambridge, UK: Cambridge University Press.

National Center for English Language Acquisition and Language Instruction Education Programs. (2005). *The growing number of limited English proficient students.* Retrieved November 29, 2006, from http://www.ncela.gwu.edu/policy/states/reports/statedata/2004LEP/GrowingLEP_0405_Nov06.pdf

Nicoladis, E. (1994). *Code-switching in young bilingual children.* Unpublished doctoral dissertation, McGill University, Montreal.

Padilla, A., & Liebman, E. (1975). Language acquisition in the bilingual child. *Bilingual Review, 2,* 34–55.

Paradis, J. (2001). Do bilingual two-year-olds have separate phonological systems? *International Journal of Bilingualism, 5,* 19–38.

Paradis, J., & Genesee, F. (1996). Syntactic acquisition in bilinguals: Autonomous or interdependent? *Studies in Second Language Acquisition, 18,* 1–25.

Pearson, B., Fernandez, S., Lewedeg, V., & Oller, D. K. (1997). The relation of input factors to lexical learning by bilingual infants. *Applied Psycholinguistics, 18,* 41–58.

Schnitzer, M., & Krasinski, E. (1996). The development of segmental phonological production in a bilingual child: A contrasting second case. *Journal of Child Language, 23,* 547–571.

Swain, M. K. (1972). *Bilingualism as a first language.* Unpublished doctoral dissertation, University of California, Irvine.

Vihman, M. M. (1982). The acquisition of morphology by a bilingual child, a whole-word approach. *Applied Psycholinguistics, 3,* 141–160.

Wei, L. (2001). Dimensions of bilingualism. In L. Wei (Ed.), *The bilingualism reader* (pp. 3, 25). London: Routledge.

CHAPTER 15

Bandura, A. (1986). *Social foundations of thought and action: A social-cognitive theory.* Englewood Cliffs, NJ: Prentice Hall.

Bernstein, D. K., & Levey, S. (2009). Language development: A review. In D. K. Bernstein & E. Tiegerman-Farber (Eds.), *Language and communication disorders in children* (6th ed., pp. 28–100). Boston: Allyn & Bacon.

Bos, C. S., & Vaughn, S. (2002). *Strategies for teaching students with learning and behavior problems.* Boston: Allyn & Bacon.

Copple, C., & Bredekamp, S. (Eds.). (2009). *Developmentally appropriate practice in early childhood programs serving children from birth through age 8* (3rd ed.). Washington, DC: National Association for the Education of Young Children.

Friend, M., & Cook, L. (2003). *Interactions: Collaboration skills for school professionals.* Boston: Allyn & Bacon.

Heydon, L., & Reilly, J. (2007). Professional development for family learning programmes: A rationale and outline curriculum. *Literacy, 41*(3), 155–160.

Hurwitz, B., & Polirstok, S. (1985). Collaborative models for training parents of the handicapped. *Techniques: A Journal for Remedial Education and Counseling, 1*(4), 311–319.

International Reading Association. (2008). *Parent brochure series: What kids really want to read; Reading, writing, and technology: What is family literacy? Getting involved in your child's literacy learning.* Retrieved February 25, 2009, from http://www.reading.org/InformationForParents.aspx

Kauffman, J. (2004). *Characteristics of emotional and behavioral disorders of children and youth* (8th ed.). Upper Saddle River, NJ: Merrill/Prentice Hall.

Mandell Morrow, L. (2001). *Literacy development in the early years: Helping children read and write.* Boston: Allyn & Bacon.

Nippold, M. (2000). Language development during the adolescent years: Aspects of pragmatics, syntax, and semantics. *Topics in Language Disorders, 20,* 15–28.

Ordonez-Jasis, R., & Ortiz, R. (2006). Reading their worlds: Working with diverse families to enhance children's early literacy development. *Young Children, 61*(1), 42–48.

Polirstok, S. (1987). Ecological effects of home-based, school-based, and community-based training of parents of children with learning and behavior problems. *International Journal of Rehabilitation Research, 10*(3), 293–301.

Polirstok, S. (1989). *Training parents to utilize support strategies to maximize their children's school experiences and foster successful school completion* (Report No. UD027279). Washington, DC: Urban Education Clearinghouse. (ERIC Document Reproduction Service No. ED315496)

Prensky, M. (2001). Digital natives, digital immigrants. *On the Horizon, 9*(5). Retrieved from http://www.marcprensky.com/writing/Prensky%20-%20Digital%20Natives,%20Digital%20Immigrants%20-%20Part1.pdf

Strickland, D. (2004). The role of literacy in early childhood education: Working with families as partners in early literacy. *Reading Teacher, 58*(1), 86–88.

Tamis-LeMonda, C., & Rodriguez, E. (2008). Parents' role in fostering young children's learning and language development. In *Encyclopedia on early childhood development.* Retrieved from http://www.child-encyclopedia.com/en-ca/language-development-literacy/according-to-experts/tamislemonda-rodriguez.html

Vukelich, C., Christie, J., & Enz, B. (2002). *Helping young children learn language and literacy.* Boston: Allyn & Bacon.

Vygotsky, L. (1962). *Thought and language.* Cambridge: MIT Press.

White, C., & Coleman, M. (2000). *Early childhood education: Building a philosophy for teaching.* Upper Saddle River, NJ: Merrill/Prentice Hall.

Index

About the Editors

Sandra Levey, PhD, is an associate professor in the Department of Speech-Language-Hearing Sciences at Lehman College, where she is also the director of the Interdisciplinary Program in Linguistics. Dr. Levey has authored numerous articles that address the English-language acquisition of bilingual children and adults and has coauthored a chapter that offers a review of children's language development. She has been an invited reviewer for the journals *Language, Speech, and Hearing Services in Schools; Folia Phoniatrica et Logopaedica; Asian Pacific Speech and Hearing Review; Psychological Reports: Perceptual and Motor Skills;* and *Journal of Speech-Language-Hearing Sciences.* Dr. Levey was appointed to the Culturally and Linguistically Diverse Committee of the American Speech-Language-Hearing Association (ASHA, 2010) and received *Board Recognized Specialist in Child Language* from ASHA. She has also presented her work at numerous national and international conferences and has been awarded grants for research in bilingual language development, as well as grants for research in Kano, Nigeria, and Bratislava, Slovakia. Her background consists of working closely with classroom teachers and special-education teachers in assessment and intervention for infants and children with a variety of genetic and developmental speech and language disorders. Her current research focuses on the factors that affect English-learning children's reading abilities.

Susan Polirstok, EdD, is Dean of the College of Education and Professor of Special Education at Kean University and was Acting Dean of Education and professor of Special Education at Lehman College of the City University of New York for more than 2 decades. Over her career, she has worked with New York City school districts to provide professional development in special education, drawing on her background as a language arts and special education middle school teacher. She is author of articles and book chapters that address peer tutoring, parent advocacy and training, social skill development, strategies for teaching students with learning disabilities, attention-deficit hyperactivity disorder, self-monitoring, emotional intelligence, faculty development, and accreditation. Many of her articles on the application of the gentle teaching technique have been translated into Italian. She is a member of the Editorial Board of *Ciclo Evolutivo e Disabilita (Journal of Lifespan and Disability);* a member of the National Editorial Board of *Excelsior,* published by the New York Association of Colleges of Teacher Education; a contributing author to a text on faculty development at City University of New York, *Transformative Spaces;* and coedited a volume of *Topics in Language Disorders,* which focused on autism spectrum disorders. Dr. Polirstok is the principal investigator for several teacher training grants for modified alternate route programs for prospective teachers and is involved in a collaborative effort to implement a new science education model in school districts across New Jersey.

About the Contributors

Deena K. Bernstein is Professor and Chair of the Department of Speech-Language-Hearing Sciences at Lehman College of the City University of New York. Dr. Bernstein has numerous publications, has presented at national and international conferences, and has been a reviewer of several peer-reviewed journals. She is also a coeditor for the book *Language and Communication Disorders in Children*. She holds specialty recognition in children's language and has been a member of the American Speech-Language-Hearing Association and the Council for Exceptional Children.

Lynn S. Bliss is Professor Emerita of the Department of Communication Sciences and Disorders at the University of Houston. She holds the Certificate of Clinical Competency–Speech-Language Pathology. She has published extensively in the area of narrative discourse. She wrote *Discourse Impairments, Assessment, and Intervention Applications* and coauthored (with Allyssa McCabe) *Patterns of Narrative Discourse*. Her most recent work has been published in *The American Journal of Speech-Language Pathology* and *Topics of Language Disorders*.

Stephen A. Cavallo is Acting Associate Dean in the Division of Arts and Humanities and Associate Professor in the Department of Speech-Language-Hearing Sciences at Lehman College of the City University of New York. As Associate Director of New York Speech Consultants, he evaluates and treats adults and children with voice disorders. His research interests include normal and disordered speech and voice production.

Rochelle Cherry is Professor in the Department of Speech Communications Arts and Sciences at Brooklyn College of the City University of New York (CUNY); the AUD (clinical doctorate in audiology); and PhD program in Speech, Language, and Hearing Sciences at the Graduate Center, CUNY. She has more than 40 years of experience working with children and adults with hearing problems. She has published extensively in the areas of aural rehabilitation and auditory processing disorders and developed a screening test for early identification of auditory processing disorders.

Sylvia Diehl is a faculty member of the University of South Florida's Department of Communication Sciences and Disorders. Her publications have addressed successful school outcomes for children with autism spectrum disorders, and she has made major contributions to studies of literacy.

Leah Fabiano-Smith is an assistant professor in the Department of Communication Disorders at the State University of New York at New Paltz. Her research interests focus on phonological development and disorders in culturally and linguistically diverse populations.

Brian A. Goldstein, PhD, Certificate of Clinical Competency–Speech-Language Pathology, is an associate professor and chair in the Department of Communication Sciences and Disorders at

Temple University. He is the author of *Cultural and Linguistic Diversity Resource Guide for Speech-Language Pathologists,* the editor of *Bilingual Language Development and Disorders in Spanish-English Speakers,* was the editor of *Language, Speech, and Hearing Services in Schools* from 2004 to 2006, and is a Fellow in the American Speech-Language Hearing Association (ASHA). In 2007, he received the Certificate of Recognition for Special Contribution in Multicultural Affairs from ASHA.

Jo Hoffman, Associate Professor of Early Childhood Education, is currently the acting associate dean of the College of Education at Kean University. Since becoming a public school educator in 1991, she has taught teachers for kindergarten, multiage first and second grade, and preservice elementary and preschool. Her research interests are in the areas of developmentally appropriate practice and effective teaching and learning for the 21st century.

Henriette W. Langdon is a professor in the Communication Disorders and Sciences Department at San Jose State University in San Jose, California. She has more than 35 years of experience working with Hispanic children who have a variety of language and learning difficulties and their families. She has published and presented widely on this topic.

Allyssa McCabe, PhD, is Professor of Psychology at the University of Massachusetts Lowell. She founded and coedits a journal, *Narrative Inquiry,* and researches how narrative develops with age; how parents encourage narration; cultural differences in narration; and interrelationships among development of narrative, vocabulary, and phonological awareness.

Monique T. Mills, PhD, is an assistant professor of Speech and Hearing Science at Ohio State University. Her work centers on better understanding the role of language and social capital in the underidentification of African American students for talented and gifted education programs. She is particularly interested in the oral and written narrative abilities of gifted and nongifted children.

Cheryl Smith Gabig is an assistant professor in the Department of Speech-Language-Hearing Sciences at Lehman College, the City University of New York. Her research interests focus on the relationship between language and literacy in school-age children, adolescents, and special populations, including children with autism. She has been a reviewer for *Language-Speech-Hearing Services in Schools, Journal of Autism and Developmental Disorders,* and the e-journal *Journal of Speech-Language Pathology and Applied Behavioral Analysis* (slp-aba.net). She has more than 30 years of clinical experience working with children and adolescents with language disorders.

Julie A. Washington is a professor in the Language and Literacy Initiative at Georgia State University in Atlanta. Her research and publications address language and literacy development in diverse populations. Her work has focused on understanding cultural dialect use in young African American children, with a specific emphasis on language assessment, Specific Language Impairment, and academic performance. In addition, her work with preschoolers and kindergarteners has focused on understanding and improving the emergent literacy skills necessary to support later reading proficiency in high-risk groups.

Joyce F. West is a member of the Department of Speech-Language-Hearing Sciences at Lehman College of the City University of New York (CUNY) and the doctoral program at CUNY's Graduate Center. She is a fellow of the American Speech-Language-Hearing Association. The focus of her research and interests has been on the differences between right- and left-brain functions and the diagnosis and treatment of adult neurogenic disorders.